CORRUPTION AS POWER

Alfredo Schulte-Bockholt

CORRUPTION AS POWER

Criminal Governance in Peru during the Fujimori Era (1990–2000)

PETER LANG
Bern · Berlin · Bruxelles · Frankfurt am Main · New York · Oxford · Wien

Bibliographic information published by die Deutsche Nationalbibliothek
Die Deutsche Nationalbibliothek lists this publication in the Deutsche Nationalbibliografie; detailed bibliographic data is available on the Internet at ‹http://dnb.d-nb.de›.

British Library Cataloguing-in-Publication Data: A catalogue record for this book is available from The British Library, Great Britain

Library of Congress Cataloging-in-Publication Data

Schulte-Bockholt, Alfredo.
Criminal governance in Peru during the Fujimori era (1990-2000) /
Alfredo Schulte-Bockholt.
pages ; cm
Includes bibliographical references.
ISBN 978-3-0343-0616-4
1. Political corruption–Peru. 2. Peru–Politics and government
3. Fujimori, Alberto. I. Title.
JL3429.C6S38 2012
985.06'43–dc23

2012035368

Cover design: Didier Studer, Peter Lang AG

ISBN 978-3-0343-0616-4 pb. ISBN 978-3-0351-0496-7 eBook

Hochfeldstrasse 32, CH-3012 Bern, Switzerland
info@peterlang.com, www.peterlang.com

Table of Contents

Preface

Introduction

This work demonstrates the criminal nature of the Fujimori regime which held power in Peru between 1990 and 2000. I will show that corruption not only represented the most significant tool used by those in control, its consequences have also been far-reaching and long-lasting. In a previous work (Schulte-Bockholt 2006), I applied Max Horkheimer's concept of the protection racket to explain the links between criminal groups and societal elites. This book aims to show the workings of the protection racket in more detail by applying the concept to a specific regime.

Description of Chapters

Chapter 1 provides an introduction to Peru between 1990 and 2000. This part also includes a portrayal of the two characters who dominated Peru during this period: Alberto Kenji Fujimori and Vladimiro Illich Montesinos.

Chapter 2 gives an overview and critique of the definitions and theoretical perspectives to help illuminate the relationship between corruption and governance. This analysis is premised on insights provided by various sources. Included is the existing literature on corruption, from traditional to critical, produced in the English-speaking world. In addition, I am relying on perspectives provided by Peruvian scholars. Moreover, I have included material on corruption produced in the Federal Republic of Germany. Finally, I have included insights by Spanish scholars who have studied the Franco regime (1939–1975) as well as the subsequent democratic period.

Chapter 3 analyses the criminal governance practiced by the Fujimori regime by employing insights from the works of Max Horkheimer and Theodor Adorno, as well as Antonio Gramsci. Subsequent chapters explore the various national and international actors who contributed to the maintenance of an increasingly dictatorial regime.

Chapter 4 focuses on the activities of the *Servicio de Inteligencia Nacional* or SIN and of the armed forces in the organization of the criminal government of Alberto Fujimori. While one ought to be careful not to exaggerate Montesinos' personal part, there is little doubt that the corrupt and criminal activities of the SIN – and its ensuing control of important Peruvian institutions and organizations – provided the basis on which the regime operated; certainly by the latter half of the 1990s. Furthermore, although the military began as an independent partner in the Fujimori racket, it increasingly fell under the control of the SIN run by Montesinos.

Chapter 5 examines the development and subsequent decline of Peru's traditional political parties, a fact that greatly contributed to the rise of Fujimori. I will also look at the roles played by the country's Congress and Judiciary as well as other institutions in the running of a facade democracy, or a form of authoritarian government in disguise. Again, Montesinos played a key part manipulating these and other institutions to sustain the regime.

Chapter 6 analyses the role of the communications media, their opposition to, as well as their subversion by the regime, whereby corruption played a key role. This chapter will focus on the totalitarian-like methods used to smear the opposition, particularly the practices of the gutter press, the *prensa chicha.* The efforts to control the media once again involved SIN operatives controlled by Montesinos.

Chapter 7 analyses the relationship between the Catholic Church and the regime. While moderate or progressive elements of the church denounced corruption and human rights abuses, others, most notably members of the conservative *Opus Dei* sect such as the present archbishop of Lima, Cardinal Cipriani, openly supported Fujimori's government.

Chapter 8 will examine a clearly criminal dimension of the regime, namely the links between drug-trafficking organizations and members of the military directed by spy chief Vladimiro Montesinos. This section includes a discussion of the unofficial collaboration with criminals for the purpose of generating the funds needed to combat the *Sendero Luminoso* rebellion. These activities have continued after the defeat of the rebels and flourish to this day.

Chapter 9 studies the ambivalent roles played by international actors such as the United States (US) government and the Organization of American States (OAS). One important factor that needs to be considered when analyzing the Fujimori regime's foreign policies is the altered geopolitical and geo-economical situation since the end of the Cold war. Given his position Montesinos played a major role formulating Peruvian foreign policy vis-à-vis the United States.

Chapter 10 studies the role of multinational corporations, particularly mining companies. These often received large tax breaks, resulting in even greater profits generated by the exploitation of Peruvians and ecological destruction. In addition, the regime's Number Two was often involved in the privatization negotiations during the mid-1990s when the regime sold off many of the resource industries in the mining, energy, and petroleum sectors. This chapter's analysis goes beyond 2000 because of the many long-term consequences of policies introduced by the Fujimori regime during the 1990s.

Chapter 11, the conclusion, concentrates on the aftermath of the dictatorship. The concluding chapter of a book on corruption would be expected to contain a discussion of ways to overcome the problem. Instead I will focus on the justice (and impunity) which key members of the regime received to demonstrate that Peruvian society will require many more years to heal the wounds of the Fujimori-Montesinos dictatorship.

Acknowledgements

Generous thanks are due to Canada's Social Science and Humanities Research Council (SSHRC) for the major research grant, which I received between 2004 and 2007, that allowed me to investigate the Fujimori era in Peru. I am very grateful to the individuals who have provided me with feedback over the years (although they may not necessarily be aware of it any longer). These include Professor Jairo Bedoya from Medellín University, Colombia; Professor Rachel K. Brickner from Acadia University, Nova Scotia; Professor Max Cameron from the University of British Columbia and his partner Fabiola Bazo; Professors John Cameron and Julia Sagebien from Dalhousie University, Halifax, Nova Scotia; Professor Walter DeKeseredy from the University of Ontario – Institute of Technology (UOIT) in Oshawa, Ontario; Professors María Gomez and MacDonald Ighodaro from Saint Mary's University, Halifax; Professor Scott Kenney from Memorial University, Newfoundland; Professor Lada Kozlycky from Groningen University, Netherlands; Professor Harold Pepinski from Indiana University; Human rights lawyer Luis Augusto Sepulveda from Bogotá, Colombia; Professor Teivo Teivainen from Helsinki University, Finland, and Professor Matthew Yeager from the University of Western Ontario, Canada.

For my book I considered it to be important to wait with its completion until it after the trials of former Peruvian President Alberto Fujimori who had escaped justice in 2000 and whose sentencing was only concluded in 2010. As a result, I was able to rely on the scholarship of those whose works on the subject preceded my own. The most important contributors have been Sally Bowen, Jo-Marie Burt, Max Cameron, Julio F. Carrión, Catherine Conaghan, Manuel Dammert Ego Aguirre, Carlos Iván Degregori, Francisco Durand, Jane Holligan, Luis Jochamowitz, Steven Levitsky, Phillip Mauceri, Cynthia McClintock,

Pedro Planas, Alfonso W. Quiroz, Fernando Rospigliosо, Martin Tanaka, Coletta Youngers, Rául A. Wiener, and Oscar Ugarteche.

I also owe thanks to my research assistants in Canada who have contributed to this work over the years, notably Sande Ewart, Tameka Bowes, and Stephanie Poirier. I am especially indebted to Stephanie whose Master`s dissertation on corruption in Peru I supervised in 2010 in the Program of International Development Studies at Saint Mary`s University. Her thesis gave me the opportunity to contemplate important aspects of my own work.

Dr. Eduardo Toche from the *Centro de Estudios y Promoción del Desarollo* (DESCO) in Lima, Peru, also has my thanks for good advice and helping me to find my way around the documentation centre. This work would not have been possible had it not been for the access to the archive of the Lima newspaper *La República*, where I came across many important dailies and weekly magazines published during the Fujimori years. I am thankful for the personal intervention of *La República* owner Dr. Gustavo Mohme Seminario. I am very grateful to former *La República* journalist Francisco 'Paco' Mattos whose special connections saved my project. Simply put, his ability to find information has been amazing. Thanks are also due to *La República* journalist Miguel Gutiérrez who gave me lodging and many useful insights. I am indebted to his sister Rocío Gutiérrez from the non-governmental organization *Manuela Ramos* which struggles for women's rights in Peru.

My thanks are due to 'Chief', Craig, and Orville for contributing to my sanity during these years. Also, this book would have taken longer had I not received the generous offer to spend two months in seclusion in an apartment owned by my good friends Kevin Reid and Kay Hustwit in Guelph, Ontario, in the summer of 2011. I am grateful to Peter Meisenheimer for his excellent proof-reading job. In fact, he agreed to do so even though I still owe him several dinners from proof-reading my last book. Ursula Rettinghaus and Adrian Stähli, my contacts with the publisher Peter Lang AG, have my thanks for their patience and professionalism.

I owe a great debt to my comrade-in-life, Claire Hodge, who not only supported me every step of the way toward publishing this book but also helped with the type-setting and final proof-reading. This work is dedicated to my dear mother, Mrs. Angela Schulte-Bockholt, who unexpectedly passed away on December 2, 2008, and my daughter Maya who was born on December 24, 2011.

Chapter 1
Foreword on Peru

I don't trust him. We're friends.
(Bertolt Brecht)

1. Introduction

This book is about political corruption, its functions and consequences. It is not about petty corruption, the small bribe handed to the underpaid police officer to avoid being booked for a minor traffic violation, or the payoff that goes to a public functionary for being allowed to jump the queue. It is about the corruption of the powerful or grand corruption. The work is inspired by investigations on Peru during the presidency of Alberto Kenji Fujimori (1990–2000). Research began in 2003 with the original goal to explore the political corruption of the Fujimori regime. However, the project evolved into an inquiry of the criminal activities of a dictatorship posing as a democracy in which corruption played a key function.

This work focuses on two important dimensions of corruption which are rarely treated in the existing literature on the phenomenon:

First, corruption is a phenomenon which is likely present in some form in every society on the planet. However, in a dictatorship, such as Alberto Fujimori's Peru, the practice acquires an additional significance as it constitutes the cardinal facilitating mechanism or the primary tool of domination to control society. Corruption is an enabling tool which allows for the employment of various other instruments of control. Indeed, corruption in a non-representational political system, irrespective of whether it is an absolutist monarchy, a totalitarian dictatorship, or a military regime, is distinct from that in a democratic society. Most importantly, the practice is a crucial component in upholding the former, but hardly essential for the maintenance of the latter.

Second, the consequences of corruption can be far reaching and go well beyond the financial losses incurred when a corrupt bureaucrat or politician transfers stolen funds to a numbered bank account in the Cayman Islands or Switzerland. The results can be extremely negative not only for civil society and the democratic process, but also for economic development, the environment, or public health.

2. A Short History of Fujimori's Peru

When Alberto Fujimori became the president of Peru in 1990, he had not expected to win the election and lacked a plan for government action while the situation in his country was turning increasingly disastrous due to the rebellion of the Shining Path and the erratic economic policies of his predecessors (Jochamowitz, 1994; also see *Caretas-Dossier*, 2000; Taylor, 2000). Meanwhile, important members of the military, particularly within the army, had been pondering a coup and the formation of an authoritarian regime or a 'directed democracy', which was based on the so-called *Plan Verde* or Green Plan. What came about was the pairing between a president who lacked a plan and the leading faction within the military led by General Nicolás de Bari Hermoza, brought together through the courtesy of a shady former army officer and lawyer, Vladimiro Illich Montesinos Torres. During the 1970s, Montesinos had been dishonourably dismissed from the Peruvian military for spying on behalf of the Central Intelligence Agency (CIA). After earning a law degree while in prison, he turned lawyer, gaining notoriety for defending military officers accused of human rights violations, and drug traffickers (Taylor, 2000; also see Rospiglioso, 2000; *Caretas-Dossier*, 2000; Picasso and Martin, 2001).

Following the 1990 election Fujimori implemented a belt-tightening project, the so-called Fuji-shock, which was even more extreme than that proposed by his opponent, writer and Nobel-Prize-Laureate Mario Vargas Llosa during the presidential race. Fujimori had reversed his position, given that he was elected with the help of the left because he had promised a gentler approach than Vargas Llosa. The neoliberal program introduced in 1990 included a 3000 per cent hike in the price of gasoline while the costs of basic foods and public transportation increased between 200–300 per cent (Cockroft, 2001; also see *Oiga*, Apr. 16/90: 13–18; *Si*, Apr. 16/90a: 13–15; *Oiga*, Sept. 17/90a: 20).

Moreover, Fujimori essentially made the Plan Verde his own turning the military into a partner of the regime. After Peru's Congress had refused to implement several measures aimed at increasing the military's powers to fight the Shining Path rebellion, Fujimori, Montesinos and Hermoza put the Green Plan into motion. The *autogolpe* or self-coup of April 5, 1992 dissolved Congress, the constitution, and judiciary and resulted in the implementation of the most important components of the Plan Verde. The coup had the support of over 80 percent of the population because of the chaotic economic and political situation in the country. After the April 1992 autogolpe the regime intensified its anti-insurgency efforts and earned a number of successes. Following the capture of *Sendero Luminoso* leader Abimael Guzmán (actually netted by the police, not the military) in September of 1992, several thousand rebels surrendered by 1993. This resulted in a major decline in violence and greatly augmented Fujimori's popularity (Ibid; also see Tanaka, 2002; Conaghan, 2005).[1]

---

1 The analysis of a phenomenon like corruption requires different methods of proof than would be needed for a more conventional topic. It is for this reason that I often rely on multiple sources in the in-text references. When I subsequently use 'Ibid', it *always* refers to the first source cited in the previous in-text reference.

Without a significant power base of his own and confronted with a situation of economic chaos and internal strife, Fujimori made arrangements with Montesinos who presented the newly-elected president with such a political base, namely the military (Ibid, 550). In essence, Montesinos played the middleman between the president and the security apparatus over which he had established informal control through bribery, snooping, and the selection of officials loyal to him. Montesinos came to run the security apparatus, while Fujimori's rule was based on a fragile, populist mandate. The duo successfully ended the Sendero insurgency and reorganized the economy along neoliberal lines, but the two also relied on the extralegal methods introduced specifically to combat terrorism in order to keep themselves in power; particularly once the regime could no longer rely on the president's high approval ratings (Tanaka, 2002; also see Conaghan, 2005; Jara, 2007).

Corruption became the primary enabling tool used by the country's foremost secret service agency, the *Servicio de Inteligencia Nacional* (SIN) to monitor and suppress opposition activities, manipulate elections, and make use of its own propaganda machine in the gutter press to smear political opponents. Indeed, Dammert (2001: 11) called the Fujimori regime an "imagocratic" dictatorship because of its unique reliance on the yellow press to achieve political objectives, as opposed to the use of the repressive organs of the state which has historically been the norm for authoritarian governments in Latin America. The longer the regime lasted the more corrupt it became. By the year 2000 the internal contradictions of the dictatorship caused its downfall.

Peña Kolkenkautsky (2003) concluded:

> Never a Peruvian government managed to gain such absolute and ... unimaginable control as this duo had over the executive, the legislative, the judiciary, the electoral [institutions], the diplomatic corps, the armed forces, the universities, and ... [the] media of communications (2003: 66).

3. Fujimori and Montesinos: The Fearsome Twosome

No dictatorship endures entirely because of the role played by one individual. All the same, Vladimiro Montesinos stands out and merits further discussion. There are various perspectives on the power structures in Fujimori's Peru. Durand (2005) noted that the regime consisted of three distinct 'mafias'. Fujimori controlled the so-called "yellow mafia" comprised of descendants of Chinese and Japanese immigrants.[2] This group found its way into the ministry of the presidency, the non-governmental organizations (NGOs) *Aken* and *Apenkai* and the insurance company *Popular y Porvenir* (Ibid, 313). As noted by Quiroz (2008): "The Fujimoris' NGOs served to funnel an estimated $100 million worth of donations coming from Japan and local illegal sources into the family's coffers" (2008: 378).

Fujimori was directly involved and obtained illicit earnings from the activities of family members and close friends. Indeed, the president's family's activities were denounced by Fujimori's own wife, Susana Higuchi. On March 24, 1992, a few weeks before the autogolpe, Higuchi – who usually kept a low profile – gave a press conference and accused relatives of her husband of selling clothing which had been donated from Japan as a charity for orphaned children. She singled out Clorinda Ebisui, the wife of her brother-in-law Santiago, as well as Fujimori's older sister Rosa, the wife of Victor Aritomi, Peru's Ambassador to Japan (Jochamowitz, 1994; also see Wiener, 2001; Bowen and Holligan, 2003; *Si*, May 11/92a: 34). Higuchi's revelations severely embarrassed Fujimori who was about to embark on an official state visit to Japan. Indeed, a Japanese newspaper referred to the matter as 'Fujigate'. Eventually Fujimori himself ordered Higuchi's arrest in the government palace. Not only was she not allowed any visitors, including her own children, for weeks, while

---

2 The use of the term yellow by Durand should not be seen as derogative but is merely descriptive. Fujimori himself was popularly called 'El Chino' [The Chinese] even though he was of Japanese descent.

in custody she was allegedly beaten and subjected to electric shock treatment. The marriage between Higuchi and Fujimori was officially dissolved in 1998 (Wiener, 2001; also see *Oiga*, July 17/95b: 10–14; *Sí*, July 17/95: 13; Jochamowitz, 2002).

Jorge J. Camet, the Minister of Economy and Finance between 1993 and 1998, led the so-called "white mafia" which largely came from the private sector (Durand, 2005: 314). This group was involved in the co-optation of economic institutions, such as the tax and customs authorities, privatization committees, as well as negotiations with big business. The private sector wanted a government that reversed the nationalization of the economy and clamped down on labour, and it often actively participated in the regime's corrupt networks (Quiroz, 2008). The privatization process overseen by Camet was marred by corruption, as evidenced by the fact that in 2000 little was left from the funds brought in from the sale of public companies (Durand, 2005). Camet was also responsible for issuing Supreme Decree 120–94–EF.[3] The decree, which was unconstitutional because it had not been properly approved, allowed corporations to avoid paying income tax (Durand, 2004; also see *Gestión*, March 8/05: 18). Camet himself owned a construction company which became one of the largest in the country because of the numerous public works contracts secured by the minister (Quiroz, 2008).

Montesinos was in charge of the third 'mafia' which operated from the headquarters of the SIN, Peru's national intelligence agency. The spy chief controlled large finances such as the SIN's special operations fund and the military pension fund. The Waisman Commission, which was created after the collapse of the regime, demonstrated that some US$300 million had been siphoned out of the pension fund and subsequently 'invested' in bogus companies (Ibid). An additional source of illicit income for Montesinos was the narcotics trade as traffickers paid him protection money (Durand, 2005). Mon-

3 120–94–EF stands for Decree 120 issued in 1994 by the Ministry of Economics and Finances.

tesinos also received illegal earnings from the 'commissions' he obtained in arms deals he brokered (Quiroz, 2008).

According to another interpretation, the regime was largely run by Montesinos who oversaw a corrupt network that took control of the most important institutions. The spy chief used his powers to control key officials in the government and the bureaucracy to do his bidding (Conaghan, 2005). As observed by Grompone (2001), the president's security advisor has been the "sleepless guard" who "tortures, kills, intercepts telephone [calls], handles the opposition movements, makes the appointments in the armed forces, organizes the electoral campaign, [and] bribes congressional representatives" (2001: 110). Still, while Montesinos played a key role, the president was not merely a dupe who was taken in by his security advisor. It is my argument that the two have been mutually dependent partners in crime. Quiroz (2006) noted:

> In the case of Fujimori and Montesinos the network of corruption was one of divided tasks or specializations: Fujimori, his brothers, cousins and close friends controlled charitable organizations and illegal business dealings ... [involving] business leaders who benefited from official protection; Montesinos with his intimate circle of friends governed the dark secret intelligence service closely linked to key military and political figures (2006: 240).

According to Peña Kolkenkautsky (2003), the complicity between Fujimori and Montesinos was manifested by the fact that the former protected the latter – and himself – until the very end. The close relationship between the two was also confirmed in late 2000 when the former president – before fleeing Peru himself – unlawfully entered his spy chief's residence "to remove videos and documents" of a compromising nature (Ibid, 68). Peña Kolkenkautsky described the former president as follows:

> Fujimori showed ability ... but now we know much more, [namely that he displayed] a perverse relationship with power: excessive ambition, selfishness, authoritarianism, arrogance, duplicity, the tendency for deceit and ... permanent cynicism, denying everything negative and trying to appear beyond reproach, when he ... fully participated with his former advisor in all that occurred ...

[Thus,] in his capacity as President of the Republic Fujimori bears greater responsibility [than Montesinos] (Ibid, 65).

It is known today that Montesinos made thousands of tapes to document his corrupt dealings, the so-called Vladi-videos. In Vladi-video 943 of May 1998 Fujimori referred to the fact that he and Montesinos had "worked eight strong years as a team" (Jochamowitz, 2002a: 134). In video 1806 of December 1999 Montesinos observed that his relationship with Fujimori was of a symbiotic nature. Accordingly, the spy chief supplied important information while in turn receiving the president's trust and protection (Ibid, 135).

Elsewhere Jochamowitz (2002) described the close relations between Montesinos and the president's family. In 1993, Fujimori had moved his family (sans Susana Higuchi, his estranged wife) to the second floor of the SIN command centre in Chorrillos, Lima. Not only did the Fujimoris share the kitchen facilities with Montesinos and close members of his staff, the president's children Kenji and Keiko affectionately referred to the secret service boss as "Uncle Vladi" (2002: 160).[4] The family had moved into the SIN command centre, last not least, because of the worsening relations between Fujimori and his wife Susana Higuchi. As observed by Jochamowitz, the president, his children and mother moved to Chorrillos to avoid distasteful marital scenes. Thus the family lived elsewhere while the president's wife was confined in the presidential palace where she was allegedly victimized with an "unspecified medical treatment or torture" (Ibid, 70).

Quiroz (2006) pointed to various instances in Peruvian history dating back to the colonial era where corrupt networks were managed by a crooked twosome. Manuel Amat y Junyent, the Spanish Viceroy between 1761 and 1776 worked with lawyer Jose Perfecto Salas to cheat the royal treasury. After independence, military dictator Agustin Gamarra (1829–1833, 1839–1841) relied on fellow officer Antonio

5 Fujimori's son Kenji would apparently play pranks on Montesinos. For example, after the damaging revelations of Montesinos' dealings with the drug trafficker *Vaticano*, Kenji would yell the latter's name when he encountered the secret service chief on the premises of the SIN headquarters (Jochamowitz, 2002).

Gutierrez de la Fuente who was “responsible for the dirty work of collecting taxes and bribes” (2006: 242). General Jose Rufino Echenique who led the country between 1851 and 1855 worked with another military official, General Juan Chrisostomo Torrico, who was in charge of a corrupt network including a group of agents responsible for counterfeiting documents. In the early twentieth century President Augusto B. Leguia (1908–1912, 1919–1930) teamed up with lawyer Julio Ego Aguirre who became his key presidential advisor. After winning the 1919 elections Leguia “imposed a civil dictatorship with the aid of the military” (Ibid, 246). Leguia also inaugurated an era of corruption that was until then unmatched in Peruvian history involving Ego-Aguirre and close members of his associate’s family. These individuals had key positions in ministries such as public works or justice where the possibilities for illicit self-enrichment were considerable (Ibid). Quiroz concludes that Fujimori and Montesinos represent a tradition of “twosomes who in different ... historical junctures ... have participated in ... the appropriation of public resources for their own economic or political gain” (Ibid, 246–247).

Francisco ‘Paco’ Loayza Galván (1998) – who taught at Peru’s School of Naval Intelligence and who himself played a key role in Montesinos’ rise – wrote a book on the spy chief which was published in the late 1990s. In the work Loayza likened Montesinos to José López Rega who had turned himself into the right hand of Argentine dictator Juan D. Perón after his return from Spanish exile in 1973. Rega became a powerful figure mostly because he was an “individual located at the centre of information processing of the state” (1998: 8). Loayza also compared Montesinos to French Cardinal Richelieu (1585–1642), Napoleon I’s Minister of the Interior, Joseph Fouché (1759–1820), and the former American Secretary of State, Henry Kissinger. To these individuals

> the key to converting themselves into the real axis of power was their access to information, not only of the state ... but especially about the lives ... and vulnerabilities of the leaders of the government and the regime’s political-administrative elite, under whose shadow they act and whom they ... serve (1998: 10).

The initial contact between Fujimori and Montesinos was made through Loayza. In March of 1990, when according to the polls support for Fujimori had climbed to 4 per cent, Loayza got in touch with the former's campaign director, Victor Paredes. In a meeting shortly thereafter Loayza won Fujimori's trust and became part of his small electoral team (Bowen and Holligan, 2003; also see Arias Quincot, 1994). A month later Loayza introduced Montesinos to Fujimori who needed assistance dealing with a fraud accusation that threatened to derail his candidacy (Rospigliosi, 2001; also see Loayza, 1998). According to Cameron (2006), "Montesinos was not the sort of lawyer who won cases by arguing the merits; he was the kind who would walk out of a judge's office leaving behind a briefcase of cash" (2006: 273; also see *Oiga*, May 14/90a: 16; *Oiga*, May 28/90: 15–16). Jochamowitz (2002) observed that Montesinos resolved difficult cases by relying on bribery and the 'disappearing' of witnesses. Quiroz (2008) claimed that Montesinos planted a bomb near the house of the congressman who had launched the fraud accusation against Fujimori to silence him. Thus, the case was shelved allowing Fujimori to continue his candidacy.

Shortly after the 1990 election Montesinos further gained the confidence of the president-elect after showing him the military's Green Plan. Fearful of a coup against him, Fujimori began to depend on Montesinos who subsequently acquired a key role. He became the unofficial head of the national intelligence service, the SIN and the president's most trusted advisor, and concentrated power over various ministries in his hands. To describe the extent of his control, Montesinos once referred to Peru's "council of ministers ... [as] the reunion of the Muppets" (Arias Quincot, 1994: 72).

4. Montesinos and Fujimori: The Formative Years

According to Portocarrerero (2004), Vladimiro Montesinos is the oldest of five children by a father considered to be the black sheep of his family. Fernando Montesinos had defied his parents and married a woman from the so-called lower classes. In addition, he failed in various business ventures, began drinking, and was generally viewed as a "disgrace by the family" (Ibid, 100). By joining the military the son was to accomplish the social mobility the father had failed to achieve. In 1964, at nineteen years of age, Montesinos enrolled in the Military Academy at Chorrillos where he graduated with the title of second lieutenant in January 1966. During his second year at the academy Montesinos likely had his first contact with the world of espionage and intelligence, when he began a relationship with the CIA which was to last until his downfall in 2000. In February of 1965 Montesinos attended the School of the Americas (SOA), which was then located in Panama for a one-month training course. The school would eventually become the target of intense criticisms from human rights groups for teaching torture techniques to members of Latin American security forces (Ibid; also see Bowen and Holligan, 2003).

One role of the school that is less emphasized in its official curricula is the formation of Latin American officers who become assets for United States (US) intelligence agencies. Gill (2004) observed that the classes taken at the school are less significant than the personal relationships which are formed. According to one graduate, the "school permits the United States to have the future leaders of the (Latin American) armed forces in its hands" (2004: 111). As Jochamowitz (2002) observed, Montesinos was at the school approximately at the same time as Manuel Noriega who would also become a CIA asset as well as leader of Panama until 1989. Noriega ultimately ended up spending over two decades in a US prison for drug trafficking (Also see *Caretas-Dossier*, 2000).

While the initial contacts were likely made at the School of the Americas, Jochamowitz maintained that Montesinos did not work for the CIA until 1971 when he dealt with the agency's Lima operative Frank Ortiz. A good number of reports, including data and dispatches from the Lima Embassy, have since confirmed that Montesinos was of interest to US intelligence. As Bowen and Holligan (2003) observed:

> His special talents caught the attention of the American intelligence services, especially those of the CIA, from the beginning of the 70s. But Montesinos was a mercenary ... constantly searching for the most influential persons and for the most gratifying routes to financial benefits (2003: 14).

Montesinos allegedly played both sides and had links with Soviet intelligence. Accordingly, he delivered documents on the military capacities of Chile and Ecuador "to a Russian agent" (Ibid, 54–55).

Taking advantage of his links to top military officers he was able to provide US intelligence with secret information, for example, about the Soviet armaments bought by Peru in the 1970s (Zimmermann, 1997).[5] In 1976, Montesinos went on an unauthorized trip to Washington where he met with US officials, however, he was observed by a high-ranking member of Peru's military to whom he could not explain his presence in the US capital. He was subsequently charged with treachery and desertion and sentenced to a year in a military penitentiary (*Caretas-Dossier*, 2000). Montesinos was also sacked from the army and banned from Peruvian military establishments. The charges of treachery and desertion concealed the real reason why Montesinos had been purged, namely because he had worked for the CIA. The brass did not officially denounce him because this would have compromised top military officials (Zimmermann, 1997).

In October 1983 the military reopened the case; this time accusing Montesinos of treason as opposed to treachery. He escaped to Ecuador where he was arrested and allegedly tortured because he was deemed a Peruvian spy. Eventually, Montesinos was let go and he moved on to Argentina where he remained until 1985. The Peruvian military archived the accusation against Montesinos in 1984. How-

5 Montesinos himself compared the gathering of information to a drug addiction (Jochamowitz, 2002).

ever, the army's chief of staff ordered after Montesinos' return to Peru that his photograph be displayed at every army base in the country declaring him to be a persona-non-grata (Jochamowitz, 2002; also see Bowen and Holligan, 2003; Quiroz, 2008).

During his time in prison Montesinos had begun to study law and he apparently worked in a cousin's law office by February 1978. Montesinos made a 'name' for himself as a lawyer when he specialized in the defence of drug traffickers, and military officials accused of human rights violations (Ibid; also see *Caretas-Dossier*, 2000). According to Bowen and Holligan (2003) Montesinos did not only defend but join up with traffickers who supplied drugs to the Medellín Cartel. Roberto Escobar Gaviria (2000) claimed that Montesinos had dealings with his brother, the late Pablo Escobar, from the early 1980s until shortly before the trafficker's death in 1993. Thoumi (2009), a leading expert on the Colombian drug trade, likewise maintained that Montesinos had links to Escobar. In 2002, the drug trafficker Enrique Lucio Tijero Guzmán claimed before the Townsend Commission, which investigated corruption in Peru during the Fujimori years, that Evaristo Porras Ardila, a key supplier of the Medellín Cartel, had introduced him to Montesinos in the early 1980s (Gutiérrez, 2002). Moreover, Montesinos went beyond merely defending Porras Ardila after he had been captured in Peru. According to Jochamowitz (2002) Montesinos realized that the Colombian trafficker was too big a fish to merely rely on bribery in the court room. He therefore organized Porras Ardila's escape from prison.

Montesinos also defended military officials charged with human rights abuses. One of the most notable cases involved the successful defence of General José Valdivia who in 1988 stood accused of ordering the massacre of twenty-eight peasants in Cayara, Ayacucho (Bowen and Holligan, 2003). Montesinos won because "the five witnesses [for the prosecution] died under circumstances which were never clarified" while the prosecutor in charge of the case received threats until he sought refuge in a foreign embassy (Jochamowitz, 2002: 205). In a similar case Montesinos helped clear high-ranking police officers who had been linked to the drug trade. Meanwhile, the successful defence of police and military officials improved his status and "gained him renewed access to and praise from the officers who replaced his enemies after they retired from the army's high command. The military ban against Montesinos was lifted" (Quiroz, 2008: 364; also see Jochamowitz, 2002). As observed by Rospigliosi (2000), following the successful defence of General Valdivia, Montesinos had breakfast at the Lima headquarters of the Peruvian army which he had not been allowed to enter for years. In 1989, Montesinos was hired by the SIN as an intelligence analyst. A year later, he had turned himself into the trusted advisor of President-elect Alberto Fujimori and was the second most powerful man in the country.

Fujimori's early years differ greatly from those of his partner-in-crime-to-be. His father had arrived from Japan in the 1920s and worked as a tailor and tire repair person, while his mother had come to Peru in the early 1930s. Their son Alberto was born on July 28, 1938. The Japanese community in Peru was some 18,000 strong, and one of the largest in Latin America, a fact which would be of great import during the Second World War (Jochamowitz, 1994). The war years represented a time of insecurity for the Japanese in Peru because they were viewed with suspicion and subjected to discrimination and violence. On May 10, 1940, Japan's axis ally Nazi Germany unleashed the Blitzkrieg on Western Europe. Three days later rioting broke out in Lima during which ten Japanese-Peruvian citizen were lynched while hundreds of properties were damaged or destroyed. Police and military stood by idly and did nothing to stop the violence. The Fujimori's family business had been razed as well (Ibid; also see *Sí*, Apr. 10/90: 28–29, 80–B; *Oiga*, Apr. 23/90: 19–20).

After the December 1941 attack on Pearl Harbor Peruvians of Japanese ancestry were subjected to further discrimination. In 1943, approximately 1,800 Peruvian-Japanese were handed over to the United States where they lived in "relocation camps" (Ibid, 99). Some would take advantage of the misfortunes of the Japanese-Peruvians. For example, police and government bureaucrats extorted money in return for documents allowing the Japanese to avoid deportation. In May 1943, the Peruvian government ordered the confiscation of German and Japanese-owned properties. Following the loss of their possessions the Fujimori family was forced to move to La Victoria in the poor sector of Lima. La Victoria had a bad reputation and the Fujimori home was near a red light district. Fujimori's father found work in flower shop where he remained for some thirteen years. However, by the early 1950s the Fujimoris had sufficiently recovered from their losses which allowed them to move to San Isidro, one of Lima's most affluent districts (Ibid; also see *Si*, Apr. 10/90: 29).

The hostilities to which the Japanese in Peru were exposed during World War II must have been considerable. Jochamowitz (1994) noted that

> it is said that when the first letters arrived from relatives and friends [who] had been sent to the United States [they] told that nobody had been tortured, that they watched movies twice a week and were served chicken every Sunday ... [and] many felt that the fortune of the deported had been better (Ibid).

Fujimori himself admitted in a 1992 interview that he had suffered racism and described the hostility of the war years and thereafter. In the interview Fujimori talked about his father's loss of property during the Second World War and the treatment received during the Korean War (1950–1953) "when they regarded me as a Korean and not [like] a Peruvian ... ; [a behaviour which] I could not understand" (Ibid, 129). The experiences Fujimori had made during and after World War II, notably the discrimination suffered by his family and the Japanese community as a whole, very likely left their mark on the future president. Jochamowitz referred to the caution the Japanese-Peruvians had to practice during the war years because of their insecurity. This in turn produced an individual with a "taste for secrets" and who preferred to walk "in the shadows" (Ibid, 108). As observed by Fujimori, World War II "was a hard trial for the Japanese ... [They] found ... [themselves] in a country which had declared war against ... [their] own, and ... [their] attitude had to be one of reserve and utmost caution" (Ibid, 300).

Fujimori did well at school; he entered university, graduating in 1961 as the top of his class with an undergraduate degree in Agricultural Engineering from the *Universidad Nacional Agraria*, more commonly known as *La Molina*. Fujimori also studied at the University of Strasbourg, France, and at the University of Wisconsin in the United States where he obtained a Master's Degree in Mathematics in 1969. In addition, he received honorary doctorates from the universities of Gembloux, Belgium, and San Martin de Porres, Peru. Fujimori was subsequently made dean and then rector of La Molina. Finally, he became president of the *Asamblea Nacional de Rectores*, the National Assembly of [University] Rectors, a position that turned him into the foremost 'political' academic in Peru (Ibid; also see *Si*, Apr. 10/90: 29, 80–B).

Fujimori presented himself and was depicted as an independent and unknown outsider who came out of nowhere to become president. In reality he lacked neither political association nor experience, and he was not an unknown entity. Planas (2000) observed that Fujimori was elected president of the National Assembly of Rectors *because* of his links to the *Alianza Popular Revolucionaria Americana* (APRA) party and the government of Alan García. These ties have been cited by numerous sources. For example, Fujimori was offered – and declined – the position of minister of agriculture in the APRA government, which indicated his close proximity to the circles of power (Ibid).

Fujimori also received considerable aid from the García administration during the 1990 election campaign. Among other things, the pro-government media supported Fujimori and went after Vargas Llosa and his *Frente Democrático* (FREDEMO) party but remained silent when the former was accused of tax fraud (*Oiga*, May 14/90: 14). Levitsky and Cameron (2003) also maintained that the presidential candidate "Fujimori received behind-the-scenes-support from García" (2003: 7). Loayza (1998) observed that President García had instructed the then chief of the SIN, General Edwin Díaz, to provide assistance to Fujimori, including information on the vulnerabilities of Mario Vargas Llosa and other FREDEMO leaders. Fujimori received transcripts of telephone recordings taped by the SIN, as well as the opposition's plans for the second round, allegedly found in the trash bin at the Vargas Llosa campaign headquarters. These revealed, for example, that the noble laureate aimed to attack Fujimori during an upcoming televised presidential debate over his lack of a government program. According to Loayza, the SIN provided Fujimori with details on his opponent, such as that he had admitted to smoking marihuana in his youth, or that he had once supported the Velasco left wing military government. The information allowed Fujimori to turn the tables and it was Vargas Llosa who appeared weak during the debate (Also see Arias Quincot, 1994).

Daeschner (1993) also noted that Fujimori was not an unknown entity who came out of nowhere. Between 1987 and 1989 Fujimori had a program called *Concertando* on the state-owned television station Channel 7 (*Sí*, Apr. 10/90: 23). In Lima, where a good number of private television channels were available, Fujimori's program was hardly watched. However in the provinces where the state-owned channel was often the only one available, "many campesinos ... simply knew him as 'Señor Concertando'" (Daeschner, 1993: 89). Jochamowitz (1994) wrote:

> In Lima hardly anyone saw ... [the program]; at that time the screen is filled with Mexican and American [soap operas] ... The boring program on national issues, with the Japanese who never smiles, hardly speaks and always listens, was the last digit on the dial, only looked at briefly while passing from one channel to another. But outside of Lima it was different. In many parts of the country Channel 7 was the only signal that ... [could be received]. Week after week ... [Fujimori] was coming to a captive audience [in the provinces] ... [while in Lima] he was leaving a first trace in the memory, like a vaguely familiar face (1994: 260; also see Arias Quincot, 1994).

5. Conclusion

Portocarrero (2004) described the four dictums which guided the actions of Montesinos. It is the argument here that these mottos were, to considerable extent, shared by Fujimori. Portocarrero referred to the following rules:

First, “agreements should be respected [only] if they provide ... personal benefits” (Ibid, 61). Second, one “may accuse the other” of enjoying the very same illicit perquisites which oneself abuses (Ibid). Third, “being above the law ... is proof of [one’s] ... superiority” (Ibid). Fourth, “personal loyalty is the [most] fundamental value a subordinate can have” (Ibid; also see Jochamowitz, 2002a).

Chapter 2

Definitions and Theories of Corruption

A fondness for power is implanted in most men,
and it is natural to abuse it when acquired.
(Alexander Hamilton)

1. Introduction

Although scholarly works on the subject of corruption have been produced since the 1960s, if not earlier, the topic received little attention until the 1990s (Leff, 1989; also see Friedrich, 1966; Huntington, 1968; Myrdal, 1968; Oldenburg, 1987). Klitgaard (1988) observed that corruption in developing countries was still overlooked by scholars although it was "devouring the economies and politics of many ... nations" (1988: 7; also see Perry, 1997).

The recent emergence of corruption as a topic of scholarly investigation cannot be separated from the United Nations' (UN) program of good governance. The agenda stresses political accountability, judicial autonomy as well as anticorruption policies, participatory and transparent decision-making, civil society, the rule of law, as well as the protection of human rights and the environment (UNESCAP, 2006).

Weiss (2000) points to four reasons for the emergence of good governance:

(1) The manifest lack of "legitimacy" of repressive regimes whose transgressions were no longer ignored, and whose rulers no longer received support after the Cold War because their services were no longer in demand;

(2) The growing process of democratization in the global South, also styled the 'third wave' of democracy;
(3) The rising importance of non-state actors such as non-governmental organizations (NGOs) and transnational corporations (TNCs) as a result of which "economic and social policy is no longer" solely the realm of states;
(4) The increased emphasis on the protection of human rights and "responsibility as a necessary ... component of national sovereignty" which was combined with the traditional Weberian perspective that is based on "territory, people, and authority" (2000: 799–800).

Abrahamsen (2000) points to the failure of the structural adjustment programmes (SAPs) during the 1980s as the key factor which led to the incorporation of good governance into the development discourse. Notions such as political participation and accountability were deemed less significant when structural adjustment was implemented in the global South. Indeed, these were viewed as possibly harmful to the general purpose of "economic adjustment" (Ibid, 30). A strong system of checks and balances was equally viewed as a restraint on economic development (Philip, 1999).

Neoliberal economists had acclaimed that structural adjustment would be the engine of economic growth. When growth failed to materialize, institutions such as the World Bank attributed this outcome to the failure of governance (Abrahamsen, 2000). It was thus claimed that the desirable "political conditions" had to be in place for development to occur (Smith, 2007: 3). Democracy became an essential precondition for development, "not an outcome of it" (Leftwich, 1993: 605). However, while the UN stresses empowerment, freedom and democracy, the World Bank – whose outlook prevails over the former – views them as secondary to economic development (Weiss, 2000).

Critics charged therefore that the governance agenda was merely attached to provide "neoliberal economic policies" with a democratic makeover to revalidate the failed structural adjustment programmes (Abrahamsen, 2000: 42). The agenda has thus been denounced because it emphasized economic as opposed to human development, although the concept had been specifically introduced because of the lack of the latter (Ibid). An evident problem is therefore determining what conditions are required and how they are to be achieved, a fact complicated by the lack of consensus on how to define governance (Philip, 1999).

Abrahamsen (2000) also asserted that the good governance agenda was based on the "belief in the superiority of Western values" and was a return to the "colonial discourses and practices" of the past (2000: 36). She observed further that the agenda was inherently "linked to larger discursive practices through which global power and domination are exercised" (Ibid, 45).

Many countries lack the resources to implement the changes needed for good governance. Philip thus noted that the Bank's design was "too idealistic, insufficiently historically specific and overconfident" (1999: 226). He also contended that the Bank aimed for "perfect governance" rather than a goal which could be realistically achieved in a Latin American context (Ibid, 228). He noted that the "Bank's discussion of the issue ... [did] not do justice to real world dilemmas" (Ibid, 236). Philip concluded that the World Bank should focus on fighting "obvious abuses" rather than "telling the world how to govern itself" (Ibid, 242). Also, given Teivainen's (2002) observation that "institutions such as the World Bank" are themselves not run in accordance with democratic principles, policy-makers from said organization may not be in the best position to lecture others (2002: 621–622).

According to Leftwich (1993) World Bank decision-makers disregarded that good governance does not simply happen "but requires a particular kind of politics both to institute and to sustain it" (1993: 612). Hence, Grindle and Mason (2002) argue instead for 'good enough governance,' which does not impede "economic and political development" and allows for the introduction of "poverty reduction initiatives" (2002: 2).

Finally, based on his investigation of World Bank, International Monetary Fund (IMF), and Inter-American Development Bank

(IADB) policies implemented in Latin America, Adams (2003) noted that the restructuring projects had the purpose of advancing the neoliberal "economic agenda" of the above institutions (2003: 79). He also observed that such reforms were likely to worsen the existing social polarization while they furthered "the authoritarian and exclusionary nature of political systems" (Ibid, 29). Morten Bøås (1998: 119) thus points to "bad governance" which manifests itself in the concentration of political power, government neglect, and human rights abuse, as well as systemic corruption.

This chapter will provide a general, albeit not exhaustive, overview of various literatures which offer insights into the Fujimori government. The review aims to introduce concepts used in chapters 3 to 10 which discuss the regime's practices in detail.

2. Defining Corruption

As noted by Quiroz (2005), except for the general definition of corruption as 'the abuse of a public office for personal benefit', the social scientists involved in the study of this phenomenon agree on little. He indicates further that the lack of a "reliable data base" prevents the precise critique of "distinct and contradictory theoretical positions on corruption" (2005: 76).[1] McMullan (1961) had already observed decades earlier that it was not possible to support "arguments and statements about corruption" with the kind of proof which is

1 Curiously, Quiroz (2008) has partially reversed himself in his seminal work on corruption in Peru titled *Corrupt Circles* where he claims that "sundry historical sources for the study of corruption are generally abundant and, treated with necessary methodological caution, usually quite reliable in providing useful information" (2008: 4-5). Still, one ought to make a distinction between studying corruption as a historical phenomenon in a given setting or to examine corrupt practices in existing regimes. It was certainly more difficult, not to say dangerous, to study the Fujimori dictatorship's corruption while the regime was in power.

ordinarily made use of in the social sciences (1961: 183). This claim is confirmed from the police's perspective given that the investigation of transnational corruption is "highly technical, complex, and costly" (Harris, 2003: 137).

The above observations are similar to the cautionary notes provided by scholars on the amounts of *narcodollars* that enter a given Latin American country's financial system. The well-known Colombian researcher Franscisco Thoumi (1995), after an extensive investigation of the economic studies on the size of the cocaine economy in his native country, concluded these works demonstrated that the quantity of illegal funds which found its way into the Colombian economy had been considerable but that "neither the distribution of that capital ... nor the proportion that has been legitimized" could be determined (1995: 199). Even so, for the scholar who explores the impact these funds have on the economic and political landscape in a given location in Latin America, it is *not* essential to have precise calculations at hand. While it may be difficult to supply exact figures for the illicit funds which enter the various Andean economies, it is evident that this wealth has endowed criminal organizations with the resources to infiltrate their nations' power structures. A manifest example is the financing of paramilitary groups by Colombian traffickers. The same logic should apply to the study of corruption. While it is difficult to be precise on the extent of corrupt activities or on the sums of money transferred offshore, it is nevertheless possible to provide some conclusions about the impact of corruption on a given state, society and economy. This is possible in the case of Fujimori's Peru last not least because of the mountain of evidence left behind by the regime. By focussing on causes as well as consequences of corruption one may gain a better understanding of its extent.

Philp (1997) observed that it was unlikely that a "culture claimed to have the concept of bribery without believing that there was anything wrong with it" (1997: 26). Still, the search for a definition is complicated by a number of factors such as cultural differences whereby, let's say, a bribe is a bribe in one society and a gift in another. Likewise, the Colombian practice of *plata o plomo* [silver or lead], usually applied by the likes of the late Medellín drug lord Pablo Escobar in regards to judges, police, etc., falls into a grey zone given that the corruptor provides only the choice between the recruitment into a criminal network or the violent departure to the next world. What about the Nazi official who 'helped out' with the paper work which allowed German Jews or Communists to leave the country? Such individual, irrespective of whether he or she took a bribe, committed a 'wrongful' act according to the law of the land.

Heidenheimer, Johnston and Levine (1989) offer three types of definitions of corruption: Public-office-centred, market-centred, and public-interest-centred ones. Nye (1989) – who represents the first category – proposes that corruption is conduct that differs from the customary responsibilities of "a public official" who for services rendered receives financial or other benefits which are unlawful (1989: 966). Van Klaveren's (1989) observations describe the second category and depict a public official who treats his or her office as a "business, the income of which he [or she] will ... seek to maximize" (1989: 26).

Public-office and market-centred definitions focus on the greed of an individual and have been produced from the perspective of an observer who views the practice as the breaking of rules in a setting which is generally not dishonest. These two variants focus on the motivations of individual participants of corrupt acts, while they fail to consider the consequences for the general public. Indeed, Philp (1997) observes that Nye "explicitly excludes considerations of the public interest so as to avoid confusing the phenomenon with its effects" (1997: 24). In addition, the above definitions do not greatly differ between bureaucratic and political corruption although the impact of the latter is far more severe.

Such definitions are less useful in the context of a society, such as Peru, where the practice has historically been a manifestation of power with grave consequences for the general public. Vargas Haya (2005) observed that the corruption of the Fujimori years only differed in the methods used, while membership in Peru's political elite implied access to the public treasury for self-enrichment since the early days of independence from Spain.[2] Quiroz (2005) observed:

> The generalized and systemic corruption reached the most important institutions and personalities of the country: bureaucrats, judges, heads of national and international corporations, military officials, members of congress, ministers, and the highest echelons of the government (2005: 79).[3]

Technically speaking an act is only criminal if a law makes it so. In a developing country like Peru many activities may be unethical but not legally criminal because of lacking or flawed legislation (Robbins, 2000). The public-interest-centred definitions, however, are broader in scope and assume the existence of a societal concern that goes beyond the law itself (Gibbons, 1989).[4]

Public-interest-oriented definitions of corruption have their origins in the philosophers of Greek antiquity who viewed corrupt regimes as serving the interests of elites as opposed to those of the ruled. According to Amundsen (2006) the ancient Greeks deemed corruption a "perversion of sound government systems. Tyranny, for instance, was a corrupted monarchy" where the king or queen did not

---

2 Héctor Vargas Haya's 2005 book *184 años de corrupción e impunidad* is one of the best studies on historical corruption in Peru and in quality comparable to Alfonso W. Quiroz's *Corrupt Circles: A History of Unbound Graft in Peru.*Washington, D.C.: Woodrow Wilson Centre Press, 2008.

3 Such a situation may be described as "meta-corruption ... a stage beyond corruption ... when corrupt power no longer conceals its corruptness ..." (Timofeyev, 1992: 163-164).

4 One may also consider the moral lessons imparted by the tragedy *Antigone* written by Greek playwright Sophocles in antiquity. The female hero - who goes by the same name as the play - is placed into a position where she has to make a choice between the law of the King and that of the Gods. Put in modern terms, *Antigone* has to decide whether to follow the law of the State or the law of morality. This being a Greek tragedy she decides for the latter which ultimately not only leads to her own premature demise but also to the untimely death of many of the play's lead characters (*The Oedipus Plays of Sophocles*, 1958). The argument that the law goes beyond dictates of governments is neither new nor avant-garde.

govern for the welfare of the ruled but primarily looked after his or her own interests (2006: 5). Corruption was viewed as an impairment of society, a "general disease of the body politic"; a notion that strongly influenced the thinking of Machiavelli, Montesquieu and Rousseau (Friedrich, 1989: 18). To Machiavelli corruption was a threat to the fibre of society which undermined the virtuousness of citizens. Montesquieu viewed it as the means used whereby a sound "political order ... is perverted into an evil one" (Ibid, 18–19). Rousseau was troubled by the "moral corruption" he saw in eighteenth century France while he considered "political corruption" to be the natural result of the "struggle for power" (Ibid).

According to Friedrich (1966), corruption is in evidence when "a functionary or officeholder" receives unlawful financial or other types of benefits and engages in activities which profit those who supply the latter, and who "thereby does damage to the public and its interests" (1966: 74). Rogow and Lasswell (1970) also maintain that "violations of the common interest for special advantage are corrupt" (1970: 54).

German scholar Hans von Arnim (2001) asserted that "corruption and the common good are contrary concepts" because the practice negatively affects the third party, namely the general public (2001: 176–178). He contends, however, that the costs of corruption are distributed among many persons who are not individually identifiable and concludes that the practice is a "crime without victim" (Ibid, 178). Indeed this claim is not far removed from the assertions by the likes of Huntington (1968) or Nye (1989) who argued that corruption may be positive for economic and political modernization.

Huntington (1968) had maintained that corruption in developing societies was a by-product of modernization, while the practice supplied stability by preventing political violence. Corruption, he wrote,

> may thus be functional to the maintenance of a political system in the same way that reform is. Corruption itself may be a substitute for reform and both corruption and reform may be substitutes for revolution. Corruption serves to reduce class pressures for structural changes (Ibid, 64).

Nye (1989) claimed likewise that corruption may play a positive role in economic development by reducing red tape, generating capital, and bringing about "elite integration" to reduce discord which could cause a "destructive conflict" (1989: 968; also see Leff, 1989).[5] Theobald (1990) also maintained that corruption allowed a new regime "to weld contending factions together" (1990: 124).

Charap and Harml (1999) refer to this earlier literature as "apologetic" among other things because it defended corruption on the grounds that "it increased economic efficiency" (1999: 3). Meanwhile, Friedrich (1989) argued that "there is typically gain for corrupter and corrupted, and loss for others" (1989: 17). Warren (2006) observes similarly that the direct participants benefit from corruption while the "excluded" lose out (2006: 804). In sum, "corruption is ... more likely to preserve existing advantages" (Ward, 1989: 18). Ward also noted:

> While many of us still recognize the opportunities that corruption, illegality, and informality may offer to less advantaged groups, we are also acutely aware that such practices do little to address the underlying structural inequalities within society that lead to poverty ... While offering some relief, corruption may intensify and extend existing relations of exploitation, dependency, and stunted - life chances for the majority of the population (Ibid, 1).

Von Arnim's (2001) notion of victimless crime betrays his Eurocentric outlook because the impact of corrupt practices in the global South has been enormous. When a developing country loses up to 4 per cent of its annual GDP to high-level corruption, it is not possible to track down the names of those who suffered as a result, as von Arnim correctly observed. Still, the victims are likely those who would have received an education or health care infrastructure had

5 Girling's (1997) differentiation between "functional" and "dysfunctional" corruption is also descriptive of this category (1997: VIII, 24). Thus, corruption may be viewed as useful if it helps to surmount the "rigidities of an over-regulated economy" and remains "wealth-producing", but it becomes "wealth-consuming" when it wastes resources (Ibid). According to Mauro (1995), corruption is likely to cause a decrease in foreign investment which in turn reduces economic growth.

these funds been properly invested. Or the casualties may be the dead and injured of a public housing project that collapsed during an earthquake because of shoddy construction materials used as a result of corrupt practices. When international mining companies get away with contaminating rivers and lakes by bribing government officials, or by influencing environmental legislation, the injured parties are those who suffer adverse health effects or whose livestock dies off. It is often difficult to agree on the common good or what is in the public interest. All the same, the cases presented in this work, such as ecological destruction or electoral fraud, would be widely accepted to represent neither.

One important step toward a revised perspective is to build on definitions that include an emphasis on the public interest. Corruption so perceived would also incorporate a focus on the damage done to society irrespective of who perpetrates the act as long as those involved perform functions that officially serve the general public. This view implies that an act will be deemed criminal although it has been made legal by law, for example, through legislation created by the corrupt in power. The extrajudicial killings by the Peruvian death squad *Grupo Colina* during the Fujimori years and the laws of impunity implemented thereafter are representative of such practices (See Chapter 5).

By allowing for a definition that also focuses on the public interest one may be charged with overloading the term corruption. Yet corruption cannot be identified as such without a moral guide post.[6] Noonan (1984) points to the evident reality that corrupt practices are condemned across the world, which he claims, implies the "moral

---

6 Heidenheimer (1970) offers a fourth type of definition which he based on public opinion or public perception of corruption. He introduces the notion to make up for the difficulty of defining the normative dimension of the public interest, especially in those situations when an act may be considered corrupt but the law is silent on the matter. Public perception, however, may not necessarily be the most reliable when it comes to determining what is corruption. Moreover, especially in Latin America, the absence of the law is as much of a problem as the failure to apply it.

nature of the matter" (1984: 702–703). As noted earlier, Philp (1997) observed that in a society that has an understanding of the concept of corruption it is generally believed that the practice is unethical. The consequences of a corrupt act, such as electoral fraud, merely amplify its scope. It should thus be manifest that the effects of an act of corruption ought not to be separated from the activity which generated this outcome. This is especially true when the corrupt transaction does not only involve the exchange of a favour for financial gain but negatively affects the general public. Conversely, those who are in disagreement may consider that a definition which lacks such a guide post is technically also applicable in Nazi Germany whereby the law of the land determines what is or is not corrupt.

Without considering the effects of corruption one cannot provide working solutions, including sanctioning the guilty. The focus on corrupt acts and those who participate in them – as opposed to the consequences suffered by the general public – is reflected by the commonly legalistic treatment of corruption as a minor transgression. In Peru those found guilty of the offence not only receive light sentences, but they often serve no prison time at all. Those condemned to four years of prison or less have their sentences reduced to house arrest which is generally spent in comfortable surroundings at home. Conversely, in a criminal justice system that uses a definition of corruption that includes an emphasis on the public interest the practice may be viewed as treasonous, which would result in harsher punishments (Salas López, 2005). Friedrich (1989) observed that earlier law codes of various European nations viewed the attempt to bribe a government official as "comparable to treason" (1989: 21).

Theobald (1990) refers to the claim that the idea of "public office ... is essentially a western concept" (1990: 3). Van Klaveren (2002) asserted that in some regime types, such as patrimonial or autocratic ones, the rulers were technically not committing acts of corruption because the distinction between private and public depended on the 'discretion' of the governing. This assessment may apply in an environment dominated by a quick-tempered warlord, however, today most regimes, repressive or not, maintain some sort of a code of conduct (or social contract) that guides their relationship with the governed, if only for the purpose of appearances. Also, codes of conduct covering corruption have been in existence in practically all civilizations since the days of Hammurabi (c. 1810 BC–1750 BC), although the overwhelming majority of these societies did not know participatory practices. As noted by Quiroz (2008), "acts of corruption and their punishment have been ... legislated since ancient ... times" (2008: 6). Von Arnim (2001) pointed to the practices during the Roman republic which in theory were guided by the motto of *Salus publica suprema lex*, that the public good was the highest law. Hence, to those serving in a public function – whether appointed or elected, it was a constitutional obligation to attend to the public interest.

Von Arnim also discussed more recent historical regimes that gave significance to the public interest independently of the will of the people. He compared the enlightened absolutism of Prussian King Frederick II who referred to himself as the 'first servant of the state' to the absolutist ruler of France, Louis XIV, who considered himself to be 'the state' (Ibid). Theobald (1990) mentions the "Prussian Legal Code of 1794" which placed "the monarch ... under the law ... (1990: 34).

The use or abuse of discretional powers by elites in non-representational regimes has historically been decided by the personal conduct of those in power. Impunity from the law due to one's social position has certainly been the norm for Latin American elites. As observed by O'Donnell (1999):

> Latin America has a long tradition of ignoring the law or ... twisting it in favour of the powerful or for the repression ... of the vulnerable. When a shady businessman recently said in Argentina, "To be powerful is to have [legal] impunity", he expressed a presumably widespread feeling that, first to ... follow the law is something that only idiots do and, second, that to be subject to the law is ... a sure signal of social weakness. This is [evidenced by] ... the stubborn refusal of the privileged to submit themselves to regular administrative procedures ... [and] the scandalous criminal impunity that they often obtain (1999: 313).

In addition, Maingot (1995) maintains that corruption is often understood as something involving only the members of government and state whereas this practice is not covered in "private, non-governmental areas" (1995: 1). Durand (2005: 287) noted that "many analysts and international organizations" ignored this dimension of corruption. Conversely, Klitgaard (1996) pointed out that "the private sector ... [was] involved in every kind of government corruption" (1996: 58; also see Nef, 2001). The 2006 Global Corruption Report by Transparency International (TI) defines the practice as "the abuse of entrusted power" which takes into consideration the privatization of public services such as health care (TI, 2006: xvii; also see TI, Aug. 3/11).

The belief that corruption is limited to government officials and bureaucrats should be re-evaluated in the light of the present-day privatization of many services originally associated with the state. Is the president of a private consulting agency who receives a bribe from a transnational mining company to write an environmental impact study which downplays the likely contamination done to rivers, lakes and drinking water not as corrupt as the official who does the same in an agency run at public expense? Moreover, what if corruption is not necessary because the president of the consulting agency knows he or she will only receive said contract because it is assumed on the part of the management of the mining corporation that the desired assessment would be provided? Or the practice Hellman, Jones, and Kaufmann (2000: 2) term the "capture of the state", namely when private economic interests have infiltrated the political process to such an extent that they can dictate the laws that legalize their unethical practices. The concept has been used to depict the penetration of modern states by business interests in very different parts of the globe. Daniel Smith (2007) described "the Nigerian state ... [as] a price to be captured" (2007: 13). Adamek and Otto (2008) have similarly referred to the Federal Republic of Germany as a 'bought state' given that German corporations have representatives in the country's ministries where they 'help' write the law of the land. The negative consequences of the above-described practices for the general welfare of society can be considerable. In order to account for a situation where the corporate interests have legalized illicit practices Talwar (2006) defines corruption as the "privatization of public policy" (2006: 146–147). While

Talwar's approach is of utility his definition nevertheless fails to consider the negative effects of corruption on society. I argue therefore that corruption may not merely represent the privatization of public policy but of the public interest.

3. A Digression on Political Corruption

This work focuses on political corruption which makes it necessary to define the term in detail. It is important to distinguish between political and bureaucratic corruption because the main difference between the two is one of severity of impact. Klitgaard (1996) had observed that a small bribe paid to a public official does little damage to society. Political corruption, however, is a means to an end with potentially grave consequences for the general public. Goodman (1989) noted that

> political corruption ... usually has the end of building party cadres and political machines which will, in turn, support ambitious politicians in their search for power ... Bureaucratic corruption ... does not have a political purpose at all, but is for the enrichment of the corruptor and the corrupted, usually, at the expense of the public. While political corruption may actively involve the public in voting and other activities, bureaucratic corruption tries to exclude the general public to the greatest degree possible (1989: 655, Endnote 5).

As observed by Amundsen (2006), political corruption transpires

> at the highest levels of the political system, and can thus be distinguished from administrative or bureaucratic corruption. Bureaucratic corruption takes place at the implementation end of politics, for instance in government services ... Political corruption takes place at the formulation end of politics, where decisions on the distribution of the nation's wealth and the rules of the game are made (2006: 4).

Amundsen noted furthermore that the practice has two dimensions, namely that it "can be for private and group enrichment, and for power preservation purposes" (Ibid, 3). The first dimension refers to the methods employed by corrupt rulers to obtain funds to "enrich themselves" (Ibid, 5). A further dimension refers to the illicit use of funds by elites to maintain existing power structures (Ibid).

A corrupt leadership will aim to take over resources "through bribes, embezzlement, and fraud" (Ibid, 6). Access to economic resources can similarly be attained through privatization and land deals, the allocation of public contracts, government loans, and by catering to the commercial interests of elite members (Ibid). Corrupt political elites can extort the private sector by requesting "bribes, 'commissions', and fees" as well as through the receipt of illicit payments for awarding and providing services, permits, guarantees and loans, public building projects, etc.,. Moreover, those in power request bribes for providing "relief from ... tax ..., environmental protection, and labour laws" (Ibid). Elites also accumulate illicit wealth by providing preferential treatment to enterprises which they partly or wholly own themselves. Ruling groups may likewise steal from privatisation sales or from the earnings of extractive industries such as mining or oil (Ibid). Such practices can impact negatively by hindering economic activities, restricting foreign investment, and adding to "economic inequality and inefficiency" (Ibid; also see Mauro, 1995; Hellman, Jones, and Kaufmann, 2000). The negative fallout is also political because such practices "erode trust ... in the government ... and can foster authoritarian tendencies" (Ibid, 7).

The second dimension of political corruption is the use of the illegally acquired resources for the purpose of maintaining elite rule. Here corruption takes the shape of "favouritism, clientelism, cooptation, patronage politics and vote buying" (Ibid). Financial and material incentives are used to generate loyalty. This can be achieved in a number of ways ranging from direct bribery in cash or the possibility thereof to offering important assignments or posts in government or publically owned corporations.

In addition, corrupt elites will aim to subdue those public institutions responsible for the checks and balances. Congressional majorities can be manufactured through subornment. The same illegal enticements can also bring about desirable decision-making and the lax handling of regulations by control and oversight agencies (human rights, fiscal, or environmental), electoral commissions, and the courts which in turn furthers impunity. This dimension likewise includes the use of public resources by a corrupt leadership to manipulate the electoral process (Ibid).

Finally, Gibbons (1976: 12–13) specifically refers to "criminal political corruption" which describes a situation when elites engage with members of criminal organizations. A well-known example is the campaign financing of Colombian presidential candidates by drug cartels during the 1990s. The typology used by German scholar Britta Bannenberg (2003) also includes such a category. She is concerned with the danger posed by the merger between organized crimes groups and societal institutions. This dimension has been observed in Peru, such as the ties between drug traffickers and the military during the 1990s. The consequences of this type of political corruption for the general public in Peru have been grave (See Chapter 8).

For the purpose of this analysis, political corruption refers to the privatization of the public interest through the abuse of public office, or of a similar authority which serves the public, by groups of elected or appointed officials in senior positions in state and government, who also collaborate with the private sector, whereby their activities serve the purpose of gaining and maintaining economic and/or political advantage (and power) for themselves and their associates while often causing harm to the general public.

4. On Theories of Corruption

Three primary approaches are used to explain corruption. The first identifies economic causes such as "excessive or badly designed regulation" (Aroche, 2005: 233; also see Maingot, 1994). Zegarra (2002) argues that state interventionism, such as price controls, tariff duties, and subsidies, is the primary cause of corruption. Such measures cause "distortions in the economy" and create the motivation to take part in illicit transactions (Ibid, 57). Canadian scholar Bruce Welling (1991) observed that an individual may partake in illegal acts as long as the expected gains are more likely than discovery and punishment.

Zegarra (2002) distinguishes various costs on the parts of both private individuals (who bribe) and public officials (who get bribed). The first cost is the amount paid by the person doing the bribing to receive "an exclusive good or service" (Ibid, 37). The second cost is "the expected ... punishment" in case of being found out (Ibid). The third refers to the "moral costs" caused by the "personal unhappiness" of the corruptor whose conscience is tortured by guilt over his or her conduct (Ibid). Conversely, Zegarra identifies the costs of the public agent who was corrupted as the punishment as well as the loss of salary in case of discovery, and once again the moral plight suffered over the accepted payment (Ibid, 38). The utility of the approach is restricted by its limited focus on individual participants, its lack of distinction between political and bureaucratic corruption, and its failure to consider the impact on society.[7] Another version of the perspective is modelled after the so-called Enterprise theory of organized crime. Maingot (1994) writes that

> the very forces of supply and demand make it easy for even law-abiding individuals who have access to the desired commodities (or who can make the desired decisions), to stray into the illegal part of the supply chain. The very concept of an 'enterprise' indicates that we are ... talking about ... a whole gamut ranging from the legal to the illegal (1994: 49).

Earlier historical or cultural approaches that 'explained' corruption in modern Latin America with a Eurocentric perspective were viewed as "condescending and racist" by scholars from the developing world (Ortiz de Zevallos and Calderón, 2005: 129). Quiroz (2008) likewise dismissed works by "[h]istorical and anthropological relativists" who

---

7 One exception is Mauro (1995) who argues that corruption is likely to result in a decrease of foreign investment which in turn reduces economic growth.

"assume that particular cultural constants make corruption an ... accepted fact" in the global South (2008: 7). Examples of such works include Kalman H. Silvert (1966: 176) who maintained that of all the nations of Latin America he was familiar with "only [in] Costa Rica and Chile" did he not encounter corruption. Similarly, Needler (1968) argued that the practice was more prevalent in the "mulatto" countries (e.g. Brazil or Venezuela) of Latin America than the "mestizo" ones (e.g. Ecuador or Peru) (1968: 15–16; also see Burkholder and Chandler, 1978; Lapalombara, 1978).

Recent scholarship has been more insightful. The studies by Portocarrero (2004) or O'Phelan (2005) on corruption in colonial Spanish America demonstrate that the present cannot be divorced from the past. Rico's (1998) analysis not only includes the colonial period, but also the pre-Columbian societies. The Aztec, Inca, Maya and Chibcha civilizations shared a number of common features: They were theocratic, authoritarian military societies which practiced a rigid sexual code, human sacrifice and slavery, while maintaining a system founded on social class, societal segmentation and intense oppression. Terrible punishments awaited those caught violating any one of the many laws, although in some societies the penalty given for an offence depended on the social position of the accused. The higher the person's position in society, the harsher the punishment.

Much of the colonial era in Peru was marked by uprisings against the Spanish which were violently repressed. The most important was the rebellion of Tupac Amaru II which almost succeeded in overthrowing colonial rule in the 1780s (Means, 1919). Colonialism remade societal structures based on class and racial make-up with Spanish from the peninsula on top, followed by those born in the Americas. Further down the social ladder came mestizos, blacks and natives. The Spanish introduced their own repressive sexual and religious moral codes and established the Inquisition in Lima (and Mexico City) in 1571 (Rico, 1998).

According to Quiroz (2008) "corruption was central to the colonial system ..." (2008: 83). Bribery and patronage were used to assure political stability in the viceroyalty of Peru. The promise of easy wealth had attracted many newcomers who found the spoils of conquest were already divided. A system of patronage was set up to satisfy their interests. Moreover, patronage was used by the Spanish viceroy who brought in individuals of his trust to ensure loyalty. The most important kinds of corruption during colonial times involved the sale of public offices, the contraband trade, and the administration of the gold and silver mines. Galeano (1982) had observed that large amounts of gold and silver were smuggled out of the Spanish Americas and never entered the official statistics. Still, while banditry became the form of lawbreaking predominant in the rural regions, from the beginnings of the colonial period

> the development of the cities and of the bureaucracy ... [produced] innumerable ... [illicit practices]: corruption of public officials, nepotism, systematic [judicial] arbitrariness, violation of private communications, embezzlement of public funds, concealment of royal decrees, the existence of brothels, [and] gambling ... (Rico, 1998: 193–194).

Portocarrero (2004) also traces the presently existing corruption to practices under colonialism. Colonial administrations, composed of peninsular Spanish, viewed the Americas as a place where unlawful earnings could be made by exploiting the natives and cheating the royal treasury. Independence did not end these practices because self-rule implied that Spanish (and Europeans) born in the Americas replaced those born in Spain as the dominant group, while the mestizo, black and native populations remained excluded. After independence the bad example set by the Spanish slowly spread to all of society.

Still, the cultural-historical perspectives shed light on a specific setting in which corrupt practices occur while they fail to sufficiently explain the very existence of these acts. Corruption is a global phenomenon which manifests itself irrespective of time and place, although it will do so in accordance with time and place. Kahn and Formosa (2002) argue that corruption is neither a manifestation of pre-modernity or of incomplete development, nor is it limited to non-western cultures. Rather, corruption is part and parcel of capitalist practices because "there is no such thing as 'pure' ... economic relations disembedded from particular relations of power" (Ibid, 61).

Institutional perspectives examine the "political, economic and social institutions" which generate corrupt practices, but fail to "implement mechanisms of detection and sanction" (Aroche, 2005: 232). Corrupt behaviour is generated by the barriers to rightful "social ... advancement" when existing "social structures" make it necessary to resort "to deviant means ... to achieve socially approved goals" (Maingot, 1994: 4).

Nieto (2004) specified some of the institutional factors which contribute to corruption. These include "administrative" chaos, "impunity" from the law, the lack of a "fiscal culture," the general "institutional weakness," and the "absence of democracy, transparency" and accountability (Ibid, 59–60). The judicial system is generally viewed unfavourably. A poll taken in Central American countries in 1997 revealed that 40 per cent of those questioned felt that the justice system was "good for nothing," and over 50 per cent expressed their complete lack of confidence in it, while three-quarters of respondents felt it favoured the affluent (Rico and Chinchilla, 2002; also see Bou, 2004). Similar attitudes can be found across Latin America.[8]

Presently existing conditions also represent important factors in the generation of political corruption. Accordingly, social unrest, the absence of significant sectors of the population from the political process, foreign meddling, or the games played by political parties, are key features of "Latin American ... reality with evident criminogenic" effects (Rico, 1998: 194).

Njaim (1996) discussed changes in the nature of corruption that occurred over various decades. In the oligarchies of the nineteenth and early twentieth century clientelism was associated with the traditional local overlord or patron, usually a landholder. With the emergence of 'democracy' arose the patron linked to political parties, still the pattern of clientelist corruption did not change. As a result, Latin Ame-

8 For Latin Americans' views on democracy, political parties, or the justice system see <www.latinobarometro.org>.

rican party systems, like that of Venezuela, were in severe crisis by the 1990s (Also see Jones, 2007).

While the above noted theories provide useful insights, their greatest defect lies in their limited focus when analyzing corruption. These perspectives generally consider the individual participants of an act of corruption or within a corrupt network, the links between corruptors and corruptees, as well as the transactions and their causes. But little distinction is made between political and bureaucratic corruption, while the impact on the general public is also less of a concern.

During the 1990s the traditional duplicity of Peru's elites merged with that generated by transnational corporations creating a new combination of corrupt practices that has deeply affected society and continues to do so (Ugarteche, 2005). Quiroz (2005) described the regime as one of the worst in the country's history since independence in the 1820s. He calculated that the losses to development during the 1990s amounted to an annual average of 4 per cent of the country's Gross Domestic Product (GDP) or US$1.4 billion. The above perspectives thus do not indicate that self-enrichment in public office has been a traditional privilege of elite membership and a reflection of power relations in Peru (Vargas Haya, 2005). The corrupt practices of the Fujimori dictatorship cannot be analysed with such theories.[9]

An additional perspective based on Marxist thinking has been applied by a minority of scholars. Karl Marx viewed political corruption as an integral part of the capitalist system; he wrote on the phenomenon as a journalist and political observer. For example, in an article published in *The New York Daily Tribune* of September 4, 1852 which analysed the parliamentary elections in Britain, Marx depicted scenes of police and hooligans who were employed by the party in power to threaten opposition voters (Marx, 1852). However, Marx did

---

9 Indeed, the following observation made by Phillips (1987) on the utility of theories of criminology of North American origin for the study of crime in Latin America is also useful here. Phillips concluded "that the theories are [not] illogical, or even ... inapplicable ...; rather, they make so much sense that they are common. We would not feel that we had gained any greater insight as ... than if we had simply left the answer to informed intuition" (Ibid, 185).

not include corruption as a theme in his critique of capitalism. He was concerned with working class leaders whose corruption or "embourgeoisment" would cause confusion and demoralization among the workers (Mayer, 1993: 640). Still, neither Marx nor Engels viewed corruption even of the working class as an overly serious issue. As Mayer noted, corruption presented a hurdle merely insofar as it delayed the evolution of history (Ibid).

The Marxist scholar who worked most with the concept of corruption is Antonio Gramsci who also viewed the practice as part and parcel of the existing social order. However to Gramsci corruption had a far more sinister meaning. He wrote:

> The demagogy, the trickery, the untruth, the corruption of capitalist society are not accidental by-products of its structure; they are inherent in the disorder, in the unleashing of brutal passions, in the ferocious competition in which and by which capitalist society lives ... (Gramsci, *Ordine Nuovo*; by Eugenio Garin in *Studi Gramsciani*, 407; as quoted in Williams, 1960: 593).

Gramsci's perspective was influenced by the corruption of Italian politics which he viewed as extremely harmful to society (Buttigieg, 1995). Politics in Italy worked in accordance with the notion of *trasformismo*, the co-optation of competing elites into the power structure through various incentives including corruption. This practice guaranteed domination for a small group of business leaders from the country's north and prevented any serious public debate about the nation's problems (Adamson, 1990). I will further discuss Gramsci's view on corruption in Chapter 3.

5. Observations on the Dark Side of Politics

As noted by Friedrich (1989: 16) "the degree of corruption varies inversely to the degree that power is consensual" which implies that authoritarian regimes are more likely to be afflicted with the phenomenon than democratic ones. The following section explores some of the literature on non-participatory government in Latin America and elsewhere written mostly by political scientists. In addition, I have included a general discussion on the practices by unsavoury regimes, which was largely produced by scholars from criminology. While the works and concepts presented do not address corruption per se and lack the capacity to account for the totality of the Peruvian experience between 1990 and 2000, they nevertheless explain important aspects of the regime which will be discussed in detail in the later chapters.

Scholars have explored the dictatorial nature of the Fujimori government which is not surprising given the region's experiences with authoritarian rule. Nonetheless, while the Pinochet dictatorship in Chile was somewhat of a model for the coup plotters of April 5, 1992, what came into being in Peru differed considerably from the military regimes of the southern cone (Wiener, 2001; also see Rospigliosi, 2001; Teivainen, 2002).

In the more advanced countries of Latin America, such as Argentina or Chile, the development achieved had not fulfilled the expectations of parts of the middle and lower classes. Political parties and labour unions pushed for structural reforms and the redistribution of societal goods; goals for which they managed to mobilize large segments of the population. In this conflict situation the military intervened on behalf of traditional societal elites during the 1970s and 80s, suppressed the unions and political parties, persecuted perceived and true opponents, and reduced the level of mobilization. The military claimed to rule without political preferences based on pragmatism and reliance on technocrats, while in fact furthering the interests of traditional elites. The military also increased spending through weapons purchases and by granting privileges to its officials (Nef, 1974; also see Nohlen and Thibault, 1992). The regimes established in the southern cone, referred to as bureaucratic-military, neither possessed the necessary institutions nor vehicles like a mobilizing political party to recruit new blood and to generate participation from below (Linz, 1991). This aspect is shared to some extent with the regime set up in Peru after 1992 where Fujimori created political parties for the elections only to dismantle them thereafter. And like in Peru the legitimacy of the dictatorships in the southern cone was based on the argument that the military's intervention was precipitated by the inability of political parties to create stable government (Ibid; also see Nohlen, 1989; for an in-depth discussion of bureaucratic-military regimes see O'Donnell, 1979; Mackinnon and Petrone, 1999; Linz, 2000).

Given their respective backgrounds, which were discussed in the previous chapter, Fujimori and Montesinos considered "concealment" to be an important component of the strategy to end the Sendero rebellion (Poole and Rénique, 2003: 162; also see Jochamowitz, 1994). By doing so, however, the state imitated "the tactics" of the Shining Path (Ibid). Nevertheless, given the paradoxical nature of the Fujimori government – an authoritarian regime pretending to be a democracy – the repression of those opposed not only had to be kept at a low profile but generally differed from the more direct and brutal approach practised by the military dictatorships of either Argentina or Chile. Still, according to the Peruvian human rights organization *Coordinadora Nacional de Derechos Humanos*, some 12,000 people were detained and accused of membership in terrorist organizations during the first six months of 1993 (LAWR, July 15/93: 322).

According to McClintock (1999) observers north of the Río Grande applied "variants of the concept of populism" to avoid calling the regime dictatorial (1999: 69). Even if her claim is rather sweeping, the argument that the Fujimori government has been populist as opposed to authoritarian is contradictory. This is the case given the authoritarian tendencies displayed by populist regimes in Latin America. Populism is based on a political culture that relies more on personal leadership than the foundations of the democratic state. It is attractive to many Latin Americans who regularly experience fraudulent elections which produce governments that neither meet societal needs nor demands for more inclusive political participation. Populism thus reflects the view that democracy has failed to deliver the goods. The democratic institutions deemed responsible for this state of affairs are usually the congress or parliament, the political parties which represent the establishment, and the justice system (Roberts, 1996a;

also see Schmidt, 1996; Mainwaring, 2006). According to Gratius (2007) the phenomenon of populism is characterized by the following:

(1) The lack of a political orientation and/or political programme;
(2) The direct bond between the leader and the citizenry in a structure of vertical power relations;
(3) The coming to power of newcomers opposed to the traditional power structure;
(4) High degrees of popular backing, and inclusion of lower class groups;
(5) The reduction of democratic institutions, notably the "systems of checks and balances" (2007: 2; also see Roberts, 1996a; Levitsky and Cameron, 2003).

It is not possible to define the phenomenon in terms of a precise ideology. Rather, populism is based on an alliance that encompasses the lower and middle classes, and possibly the armed forces; it can be left or right wing (Mainwaring, 2006; also see Mires, 2006). The second factor, namely the direct link between the leader and people without involving political parties, represents populism's principal contradiction to democracy. A leader who personifies the will of the people (and who arbitrarily determines it) and in whom the citizens have confidence is a manifest feature of populism. Populism requires charismatic leadership in order to survive which, however, may cause it to develop authoritarian tendencies (Stokes, 1997; also see Ávila Molero, 2003; Mires, 2006).

Populist leaders, because of their backgrounds and personal histories, are able to differentiate themselves from the traditional societal elites (Ibid; also see Olano Alor, 2000; Mainwaring, 2006). In the unique case of Fujimori his Japanese origin certainly made him stand out in Peru. While Fujimori suffered discrimination during the 1940s and 50s, he subsequently morphed into the "Japanese Inca" (Jochamowitz, 1994: 314). It is apparently believed by many Quechua-speaking inhabitants of the Andean regions of Peru that Manco Capac, the mythical founder of the Inca Empire, was of Japanese origin. Accordingly, a Japanese fishing boat was carried by the ocean current to the coast of

South America. Upon arrival its occupant turned into Manco Capac who brought progress and civilization to the barbarian tribes of Peru. While no historical evidence exists to substantiate these beliefs, Fujimori was nevertheless able to seize on the image and cast himself in the role of modernizer who brought his people out of the dark (*Oiga*, Apr. 2/90: 35). Fujimori may have been the outsider who was not a member of the traditional political class but by turning himself into a reincarnation of the 'Japanese Inca' he attained the very legitimacy denied to the outsider. Moreover, the allusion to the Inca of olden days – who was after all an all-powerful monarch – helped legitimize Fujimori's authoritarian rule, particularly among Peru's Andean population. Jochamowitz (1994) writes:

> The son of the tailor Naoichi Fujimori who became president of Peru is almost as surprising as the Japanese fisherman who became Manco Capac ... The Neo-Inca has spoken of a new solar day when we will become moderns ... The ... self-coup [and] the re-election are the first signposts of a conduit from the edge of time. The Neo-Inca conjures the past and precipitates the future (1994: 329).

Also, populist regimes are generally democratically elected and require high levels of public support. Populist leaders lose their hold on power once they can no longer rely on the backing of the multitudes. Democracy is part of the discourse because the regime's rise and fall depends on public opinion. In accordance with the identification of the leader with the governed a populist regime endorses the political incorporation of the excluded (or parts thereof) which may in fact strengthen democracy. Conversely, the leader sets up his or her personal power structure which bypasses the institutions of democracy (Ferrero Costa, 1993; also see Kay, 1996; Cameron, 1998; Laclau, 2005; Mainwaring, 2006).

What's more, populism tends to replace democratic practices with strong leadership, assuring speedy answers without making recourse to formal structures. Populist leaders claim to put into practice a so-called direct democracy. The antiparty stance is usually reflected by the struggle between government and parliament. Populist regimes in general disdain political parties and rule by undermining parliament either through outright dissolution or through reliance on presidential edicts. The relationship with the justice system is also often contentious as populist leaders generally put 'their people' into important positions (Roberts, 1996a; also see Cameron, 1998; Tanaka, 2000). The late Peruvian specialist Ivan Degregori (2001) argued that traditional populism, such as Peronism in Argentina, was an "open political pact" which involved the inclusion of previously excluded sectors of society (2001: 375). Meanwhile, Fujimori "gained the complicity of a majority" in society to downgrade democracy and human rights (Ibid, 376).

Latin American scholar Fernando Mires (2006) concluded that populism not only resulted from political corruption but represented one of "the greatest dangers" to democracy (2006: 14). Burt (2006) observed that the term failed to take into account "the coercive dimensions of power" (2006: 43). It is noteworthy that by 1998, the great majority of Lima citizens characterized their country as "undemocratic", "authoritarian" and even "dictatorial" (McClintock, 1999: 78).

One of the English-speaking academics as well as foremost experts on Peru who early on pointed to the authoritarian nature of the regime – in a work published only two years after the *autogolpe* – was Canadian scholar Max Cameron (1994). He noted that Fujimori "preferred to rule by decree ... in an authoritarian style [and] to rely on the armed forces" (1994: 12). In a later work, Cameron (1997) drew on *The Eighteenth Brumaire of Louis Bonaparte*, Karl Marx's analysis of the coup of December 2, 1852, in France, which brought about the second empire of Napoleon III, clearly a dictatorship, to explain Fujimori's April 1992 self-coup. Peruvian scholar Arias Quincot (1994) also referred to Marx's work in his examination of Fujimori's autogolpe. In sum, Fujimori's Peru was populist and authoritarian.

Important insights can also be gleaned from the field of parapolitics which emerged as a result of the failure of the dominant paradigms in politics and international relations to explain the grey zone where crime and politics meet and become indistinguishable from one another (Cribb, 2009). "Para-politics ... is the study of criminal sovereignty" which refers to

> a form of authority ... [that] is criminal both in its subversion of the formal political process and its dependence on illegal trade, but which has important attributes of sovereignty by virtue of veto power within established parties and its control of territory which is then used for criminal purposes (Ibid, 8).

A key conception of para-politics is the heterogeneous nature of the state which is not a coherent monolithic whole but rather a set of contending groups or "sub-statist entities" operating in accordance with the dictums of place and time (Wilson, 2009: 29). Para-politics implies the existence of "a tripartite relationship" involving the armed forces and secret services, global crime groups, and "quasi-states" (Cribb, 2009: 8). Such arrangements may be seen as "as *positive* phenomena" because they supply "security/protection or effective dispute resolution" when the agencies of the state are, for whatever reason, incapable of the task (Wilson, 2009: 42).

In Peru, what Cribb (2009: 8) calls a "tripartite relationship", was indeed in existence. The first and most influential factor of the three has been the control of the SIN by Montesinos and of the military by General Hermoza; both allies of the president. Second, the criminal partner of the arrangement was represented by several dozen or so drug-trafficking organizations; however, these were the weakest component of the Peruvian triumvirate and could be discarded once the relationship proved of no further benefit. In the world of international narcotics Peruvian trafficking groups have historically been minor players acting mainly as suppliers for large Colombian (1970s–1990s) and Mexican drug cartels (1990s–present). These Peruvian crime syndicates nevertheless played a significant role in the early 1990s during the conflict with the Shining Path by contributing to the military's war effort. Still, once *Sendero* was defeated many of the drug traffickers who had been protected by the military were put behind bars. The affiliation can be described as a form of "criminal political corruption" as defined by Gibson (1976: 12–13). I have discussed this relationship in Schulte-Bockholt (2006). In this work I provide an updated analysis of the links between Peruvian drug traffickers and military (See Chapter 8). Third, the equivalent of what Cribb (2009) perceives as the 'quasi-state' would be Peru's ministries of the presidency, defence, and economics and finances, which after 1992, together with the military and intelligence agencies, formed a 'shadow government' within the government.

Other useful concepts for understanding the Fujimori era are the following:

McSherry (1998) describes the notion of the "guardian democracy" (1998: 16). In such a setting the military maintains a counterweight to democracy whereby the possibilities for opposition politics are limited (Ibid). This kind of regime has several features:

(1) The increased presence of the military "in civilian institutions";
(2) The reliance on undemocratic "practices by civilian governments";
(3) Reliance on "political intelligence" to control the opposition;
(4) Activities "by paramilitary groups" or death squads linked to the state;
(5) Evident "impunity" for human rights abusers (Ibid, 18).

Jeffrey Haynes' (2001: 6) discussion of the concept of the "facade democracy" also helps explain the reality of Fujimori's Peru. Such a setting is characterized by the following attributes:

(1) Elites have little interest in true democracy;
(2) Rulers stage regular elections with predictable outcomes;
(3) Elites in such regimes are closely linked to the military;
(4) "In sum, the democratic characteristics ... are minimal, quantitatively and qualitatively less than countries identified as electoral democracies" (Ibid).

Briscoe (2008) discusses the notion of the "parallel state" (2008: 6). Its main feature is the merger of official political structures and institutions with an unofficial camarilla that is closely joined with the state, yet which tends to its own interests and works in partnership with crime groups or paramilitaries. Korner, Maass, Siebold, and Tetzlaff (1986) explore the concept of a kleptocracy which refers to a regime where a corrupt and repressive leadership wastes such amounts of wealth on self-enrichment that it might cause an economic crisis. This is possible because those in power control institutions which provide them with direct access to illegitimate wealth.

Criminologists have also written on unsavoury regimes, albeit from a distinct angle given the difference in discipline. Academics dealing with state crime constitute a relatively small group of critical scholars who are not part of the mainstream of the discipline. Most criminologists focus on conventional deviance such as street or youth crime and ignore state crime altogether.

Some of the first studies of state crime are associated with US scholar William J. Chambliss (1988; 1989). Chambliss (1989) referred to activities of intelligence agencies, such as drug trafficking, as "state-organized crime" because state officials were ordered "to engage in criminal acts" (1989: 185–186; also see Barak, 1990). Kauzlarich, Matthews and Miller (2001) have produced a useful model for a 'Victimology of State Crime'. The victimized are those "who have experienced economic, cultural, or physical harm, pain, exclusion, or exploitation" at the hand of the agencies of the state (Ibid, 176). Victims generally fall into two categories. They are either casualties of (1) domestic or (2) international state crime. The former occurs when a state violates "the social, economic, or political rights of its own citizens" while the latter harms individuals in foreign nations (Ibid, 177). This results in a fourfold typology:

(1) "Domestic-international governmental crime" occurs when a state breaks international law at home;
(2) "International-international governmental crime" transpires beyond "a state's geographic" boundaries and breaches international accords;
(3) "Domestic-domestic governmental crime" refers to violations of a country's law which takes place on its own territory;
(4) "International-domestic governmental crime" occurs "outside a state's" territory in violation of its domestic laws (Ibid, 177– 183).

Jamieson and McEvoy (2005) discuss a reality that is manifest in the global South, namely the victimization in the name of the state but which is committed by proxy agency such as paramilitaries and private security companies.

The concept of institutional violence has been applied by Latin American criminologists (Birkbeck, 1994). Del Olmo (1975) referred to four types of violence which were prevalent south of the Río Grande, namely individual or criminal violence; structural violence (poverty and exploitation); the violent acts committed by state agencies, such as the police and military, and the aggressions perpetrated by the various guerrilla groups. Moreover, she argued that the above-mentioned types of violence were interrelated (Ibid). The topic was also studied by political scientists in the region after many of the countries south of the Río Grande had turned into dictatorships. For example, Colombian scholar Palacio Castañeda (1991) coined the phrase 'para-institutional violence' when referring to the activities of death squads (Also see Jones, 2004).[10] State repression is generally justified as a response to the violence generated by left wing rebels or other so-called subversives. Latin America has a long history of rebellion dating back to the colonial period (Means, 1919; also see Gott, 1970; Strong, 1992; Van Engeland, 2008). Rico (1998) summarizes as follows:

> The majority of Latin American countries are characterized by forms of illegitimate authority, which stay in power thanks to illegal detentions, human rights violations, from torture to murder ... And if we try to answer the question 'What is a crime?' or 'Who is the criminal?' we observe that in Latin America those guilty of murder, torture, or illegal detention are not considered criminals by the justice [system] (1998: 103–104).

The above literature is not exhaustive nor does it focus on corruption per se. However keeping in mind Friedrich's (1989) dictum it is not

---

10 Rico (1998) did not use the term death squad; even so he described the same phenomenon when he pointed to the selective murder of some "2800 intellectuals, students, union leaders, and peasants" by right wing terrorist organizations in Guatemala in 1968 (1998: 117). For useful insights on institutional violence in Latin America, see Huggins (1991) or Campbell and Brenner (2000).

unreasonable to argue that many of the described activities can only transpire in a setting that is corrupt and less than democratic. In chapter 3 I will discuss Jeffrey Ian Ross' (2003) model of state crime which incorporates a category for political corruption.

6. A Digression on State-Corporate Crime (and Criminology)

Chapter 10 of this work focuses on the unethical practices of multinational mining corporations in Peru. Corporate deviance, however, is not a topic that is generally addressed by political scientists. This makes it essential to provide insights from the disciplines of criminology and economics. Like the scholars examining state crime those engaged in the study of state-corporate crime also do not necessarily belong to the mainstream of their respective disciplines.

Ross and Trachte (1990: 2) argue that global corporations are engaged in an "economic war of each against all" thereby creating a potentially criminogenic environment. In such surroundings the prospects for lawful financial gains may be limited which induces corporate managers to pursue illegal means which are assessed "as superior" to existing lawful options (Box, 1983: 35). According to Bakan (2004) the harms caused by corporate practices are viewed as "inevitable and acceptable consequences" or "externalities" (2004: 60). The late Milton Friedman described "an externality" as "the effect of a transaction ... on a third party who has not consented to or played any role in ... the transaction" (Ibid, 61; also see OECD, 2003). An externality can be positive like a well-paying job; or negative, for example, ecological damage (Ibid).

As noted earlier, Amundsen's (2006) understanding of political corruption includes an important economic dimension. Criminologist Jeffrey Ian Ross (2003) argues that close links are made between state and corporate officials who have shared objectives, such as income maximization and market stability. Moreover, the state generally claims the role of "investigator ..., prosecutor, and fact-finder/adjudicator (judge)" even though its own agents are responsible for violating the law (Ibid, 153).

As determined by various commissions which were formed after the fall of Fujimori the regime was involved in numerous illicit deals with partners from the private sector (See Chapter 10). The concept of state-corporate crime is therefore of utility when exploring the ties between Fujimori's circle of power and foreign and domestic business interests. Michalowski and Kramer (2006) defined the phenomenon as

> illegal or socially injurious social actions that result from a mutually reinforcing interaction between (1) policies and/or practices in pursuit of the goals of one or more institutions of political governance and (2) policies and/or practices in pursuit of the goals of one or more institutions of economic production and distribution (2006: 20).

Even though state-corporate crime is related to the field of state crime the study of the phenomenon has developed separately from the latter. The original examinations on the subject are attributed to criminologist Richard Quinney who during the 1960s and 1970s laid the foundations for the study of state-corporate crime (Kramer, Michalowski and Kauzlarich, 2002). The practice manifests itself twofold: a) state-initiated corporate crime, which consists of deviance that is either approved or commanded by the state; and b) state-facilitated corporate crime, whereby state agencies neglect to control unlawful business activities because of mutually shared interests (Matthews and Kauzlarich, 2000). Michalowski and Kramer (2006) contend that some activities may not violate a country's criminal code but will breach international law and human rights conventions and should hence be reckoned criminal. It is informative here to point to the 1985 UN Declaration of Basic Principles of Justice for Victims of Crime and Abuse of Power. It obligates governments to protect their citizens from abuse by state and corporations alike and to compensate victims if such abuse has occurred (UN, 1985).

Case studies of state-corporate crime have mainly focused on industrialized countries. While a comprehensive study of the extent and impact of corporate crime on developing societies has not yet been written, it is possible to extrapolate from existing works which usually focus on specific events. One of the best studied cases is the December 1984 explosion at the Union Carbide plant in Bhopal, India, which killed thousands and maimed tens of thousands. Pearce and Tombs (1998) concluded that the disaster's "causes were all too common" because many developing nations, to attract foreign investment and technological and scientific knowhow, created business climates with few regulations for the treatment of harmful materials or plant emissions (1998: 217; also see McMullan, 1993).

Green and Ward (2004) have provided a more recent work on state-corporate crime in the global South "to explore the theoretical and empirical parameters" of the concept (2004: 30). In two case studies, Green and Ward demonstrate how the present global economic setting places such burdens on developing nations that state officials frequently collude with corporations that promise capital growth. This often involves the loosening of environmental and other regulations. Moreover, governments engage in political corruption and authoritarian rule which in turn provide a fertile ground for an array of state crimes (Ibid).

The first case involves the shrimp aquaculture industry in Ecuador, Guatemala, Honduras, and Mexico. Since the early 1980s corporations have set up large-scale shrimp farms in the coastal mangrove forests of these nations with negative results for the environment and the local populations. According to Green and Ward the case represented a form of state-facilitated corporate deviance. The state played an important role through the uncontrolled distribution of land concessions to aquaculture corporations, the failure to implement environmental laws for the protection of the mangrove forests, while turning a blind eye when private security forces working for said corporations repressed local dissent (Ibid).

Similarly, in Nigeria large corporations have exploited petroleum reserves while destroying flora and fauna and repressing the opposition. The Nigerian situation qualifies as state-initiated crime given the state's direct involvement in the brutal oppression of "local dissent" to avoid harm to oil industry interests (Ibid, 34). Ward and Green point out that the 'arrangements' between the state and corporations in both cases resulted in the forced removal of communities, ecological destruction as well as violence at the hands of private or state security forces against dissident groups (Ibid). Ward and Green thus confirm Klitgaard's (1996) observation that corruption which results in ecological destruction may have an impact that is "socially corrosive" (1996: 57). In Peru's mining sector, state agents, corporate officials, and private security companies have collaborated to the detriment of local populations and the environment from the Fujimori era to the present (See Chapter 10).[11] In sum, as put by Braithwaite (1979), the political corruption practised by multinational corporations in the global South has negative consequences because it brings to power politicians and officials who place personal interests before those of the public and the benefit of transnational corporations before that of the country they serve.

7. Some Comments on Method

The above observations demonstrate that the lack of reliable data and the complexity of the phenomenon under investigation represent serious challenges to the scholars researching corruption (and to the police officials investigating it) (Quiroz, 2005; also see McMullan, 1961; Harris, 2003). This state of affairs in turn has consequences for

11 Francisco Ramirez Cuellar (2005), President of the Colombian Mine Workers Union (SINTRAMINERCOL), the union representing workers in the Colombian state-owned mining company MINERCOL, argues that US corporations obtained access to his country's resources, such as oil, coal, or gold, by relying on paramilitary violence, forced displacement, mass murders, and disappearances as tactics to move out populations and protect their investments.

building theory. If the information is flawed, then the theories stemming from it would necessarily suffer from the same predicament. Even if premised on valid information, most theoretical perspectives can at best be impermanent descriptions fixed by time and place. A theoretical perspective of utility for explaining, let's say, certain aspects of corruption in the United States during the 1960s will not likely be applicable to illustrate Peruvian practices of the 1990s. However, it may be possible to modify perspectives created in one context for use in another.

The exploration of corruption demands a multi-paradigmatic understanding because no single perspective is adequate to explain it. Any paradigm, assuming it is based on reliable information, can only shed light on a particular section of the phenomenon's reality whereby the insights acquired are limited by time and place. Reality can generally be explained with distinct and often incompatible theories (Hein and Simonis, 1973). Yet, it is also interrelated (Albert, Cagan, Chomsky, Hahnel, King, Sargent, and Sklar 1986; also see Young, 1994). The application of any given perspective does not contradict the recognition of the complexity of the processes at work. It should be manifest however that the insights gained will help illuminate some aspects of the phenomenon's reality but not others. I nevertheless do claim that this work will address aspects of corruption which thus far received little attention and were obscured by the way scholars analysed the problem.

The late Paul Feyerabend (1993) likely would have judged corruption to be a phenomenon that is more complex "than even the best historian and the best methodologist can imagine" (1993: 9). For such eventuality he advocated a methodological "anarchism" that would allow the scholar to employ "whatever procedure seems to fit the occasion" (1993: 10). In Feyerabend's words, "anything goes" (Ibid, 18–19). This work is based, at least in part, on a reconstruction of occurrences which may not be precise in every particular. My analysis is nevertheless in accordance with the observation of a famous fictional detective who argued that "once one has eliminated the impossible, then whatever remains, however improbable, must be the truth" (Doyle, 1987: 185).

The construction of any perspective that aims to explain a phenomenon of complexity is also stymied by the manifest quantity of knowledge available. Most social scientists are primarily specialists and therefore likely to analyse a phenomenon with the instruments available in their respective academic fields; a predicament already strongly deplored by Ortega y Gasset (1960) who observed that "the specialist knows very well his own tiny corner of the universe" (1960: 111). The incalculable increase in knowledge not only resulted in divisions between different disciplines but even created boundaries within them. The study of political corruption should nevertheless be an interdisciplinary exercise. Criminology or political science should be seen as integrative social sciences that amalgamate the research results of a diverse set of disciplines. Scholars ought to increase their efforts to understand social processes in their totality by taking into account existing linkages (See for example, Bellers and Woyke, 1989).

This investigation into the machinations of a crooked regime is therefore a work of political criminology, the study of criminal governance and of criminals in government. Peru is particularly fitting for such an inquiry given the well-documented practices of the Fujimori era. The video collection, the so-called Vladi-videos created by the informal head of intelligence, Vladimiro Montesinos, demonstrates systemic political corruption involving hundreds of individuals from the highest echelons of society.[12]

---

12 During my various research stays in Peru I came across various scholars who expressed their appreciation for Montesinos' contributions to the social sciences. The evidence left behind, such as his video collection, has generated important research which has greatly added to the scholarly knowledge on corruption. Unfortunately, most of the works produced by leading academics, such as Francisco Durand, Luis Jochamowitz, Felipe Portocarrero, Alfonso Quiroz, Óscar Ugarteche or Héctor Vargas Haya, only exist in Spanish and are generally not available in the book stores and university libraries of Europe and North America. My book is also an effort to introduce readers to the works of prominent scholars from Peru.

The analysis that follows is the result of research done between 2003 and 2007. In addition to interviews and personal experiences I rely on a large selection of academic and journalistic literature produced in English, German, or Spanish, as well as daily or weekly news reports from the Canadian, Colombian, German, Peruvian, Spanish, and US press. Aside from works on Peru I am utilizing publications on corruption in Colombia, Germany, Nigeria, Russia or Spain, authored by experts in their fields and published largely in English, German, or Spanish.

Furthermore, to overcome the limitations imposed by the complexity of the issues, it is a central prerequisite to learn about the specifics of a given society where corruption takes place. To gain some understanding of Peruvian society one needs to be acquainted with the country's history, culture, and politics. I have relied on works produced in English, German, or Spanish, by scholars from various disciplines such as anthropology, criminology, history, international relations and development studies, political economy, or sociology.

For much of the work I utilized news published during the Fujimori era by the main Lima dailies. I also extensively used internet sources from Latin American news agencies as well as web sites maintained by the Peruvian government, press, and non-governmental organizations. All sites were visited or revisited between July 2010 and April 2012 unless indicated otherwise.

I have incorporated excerpts from my previous work (Schulte-Bockholt, 2006) in original or modified form in this book; particularly from the chapters dealing with theory and Latin American organized crime respectively. As in my earlier work I did 'borrow' from Stirk's (1992) translations of some of Max Horkheimer's and Theodor Adorno's observations on the racket. I have included material and direct quotations, translated into English by myself from works produced in either German or Spanish, some of which have also been published in English elsewhere. All mistakes are my own, and any resemblance with existing translations is unintended and accidental.

This book is a work of critical research. The Frankfurt School's Max Horkheimer (1937) distinguished between so-called critical and traditional scholars. Canadian International Relations scholar Robert Cox (1981) similarly referred to the academic engaged in so-called problem-solving-theory who accepts the reality he or she comes across "as the given framework for action" (1981: 128). Conversely, the critical scholar "does not take institutions and social and power relations for granted" (Ibid). Rather, he or she looks at the tension between reality and possibility, between what is and what could be, which is viewed as a historical relationship that can be undone by human practice. Philosophy and theory of society become one in as far as the critique of existing conditions engenders the possibilities for change and exposes the forces and tendencies impeding the realization of human emancipation (Hülst, 1989).

Critical social science can only be rightly critical if it contributes to a decrease of repression and the emancipation of the excluded. Critical social science proves itself in practice (Hein and Simonis, 1973). At present, however, the solutions offered by critical academics are mostly ignored while those advocated by traditional scholars are implemented although they rarely address fundamental problems, and may even perpetuate them.[13] Still, as handicapping as this situation may be, it does not free the critical scholar from pointing to the quandaries produced by the social reality one lives in. Critical International Relations scholar Mark Hoffmann (1994) observed that even if ready answers to global problems cannot be produced one "should [not] abandon the attempt to clarify our understanding of dilemmas in the effort to develop practical guidelines for action" (1994: 39). Hein and Simonis (1973) had argued decades earlier that critical scholars should

---

13 A case in point is the US Drug war which has been declared in 1973. Critical academics have pointed to the many short-comings of the strategy since the 1980s and 90s and have referred to proven alternatives (See, for example, Wisotsky, 1986, 1990; Elias 1991). Even the conservative RAND Institute has described the strategy as a massive failure because it increased the US prison population, turned inner city slums into war zones while doing little to reduce domestic drug consumption. The institute suggested that the money used in the drug war should be spent on treatment instead (See, for example, Rydell and Everingham, 1994).

offer alternative readings of reality to confront the false impression that only the dominant paradigms can provide valid explanations.

Chapter 3

Criminal Governance, Corruption and Power

Corruption is authority plus monopoly minus transparency.
(Unknown)

1. Introduction

In the 1990s the United Nations (UN) introduced the concept of good governance as a guiding principle "to ensure sustainable human development" (UNESCAP, 2006). The good governance agenda, as noted earlier, emphasizes political accountability, the independence of the courts, anticorruption programs, participatory as well as transparent decision-making processes. The agenda also stresses civil society, the rule of law, and the safeguarding of human rights and of the environment, etc., (Ibid).

Good governance was brought in by the World Bank hand in hand with neoliberal reforms because it was deemed that the latter would only be successfully implemented by clean government. For that reason the agenda was turned into "a political and economic conditionality ... for developing and formerly socialist bloc countries" (Weiss, 2000: 801; also see Smith, 2007). However, the World Bank's understanding of good governance – which differs from the UN's and which prevails over the latter's – puts considerably more weight on practical matters and favors the economic component of said agenda (Weiss, 2000). As previously noted, Morten Bøås (1998) concluded therefore that World Bank practices effectively furthered the concentration of political power, human rights violations, systemic corruption, as well as non-representational and unresponsive government; all of which amounted to "bad governance" (1998: 119).

Good governance is often a distant ideal in many countries of the global South. Indeed, the present conditions are more aptly described as bad governance, as claimed by Bøås. However, it is my argument that in some cases, such as Fujimori's Peru, governance is not merely bad but can be criminal – and criminogenic – because the lack of accountability, transparency, and rule of law go hand in hand with corruption, human rights abuse, or ecocide. The label is also valid because members of the regime had links with the criminal underworld in a manner that Gibbons (1976) would define as "criminal political corruption" (1976: 12–13).

2. Observations on Criminal Governance

The following assertion by the well-known Canadian Political Science and International Relations scholar Robert Cox (1981) should also hold true for the theoretical approaches of other disciplines in the social sciences:

> Theory is always for someone and for some purpose. All theories have a perspective. Perspectives derive from a position in time and space. The world is seen from a standpoint definable in terms of nation or social class, of dominance or subordination, of rising or declining power, of a sense of immobility or of present crisis, of past experience, and of hopes and expectations for the future (1981: 128).

Most social scientists in the global North, including critical ones, view the state if not as a competent, then at least as a potentially benevolent, technically impartial and improvable entity. They may differ on how to organize the presence of the state within society, but it remains a basic component of their respective paradigms. It follows that the theoretical perspectives used by political scientists or criminologists from the North are less useful when confronted with a reality, such as in Latin America, where the state and its agents are either absent, or worse, perpetrators of crimes against the very population they are sworn to protect.

Policing as well as the judging and imprisoning of criminals are functions commonly associated with the state and go to the core of what Max Weber understands as the "monopoly of legitimate use of physical force within a given territory" (Gerth and Mills, 1958: 78–79). Yet, when states fail to impose their monopolies, other actors fill in the vacuum and take over functions generally associated with the former. Such parties may not possess the legitimacy of state agencies in the Weberian sense nor are they likely to govern by what Antonio Gramsci called a hegemonic process. Thus it is more realistic to refer to a *monopoly of violence* which an organization imposes in a territory it controls (Ibid). Indeed different actors may impose multiple, even overlapping monopolies or *oligopolies of violence*. Aside from government agencies, a country's territory or parts thereof may be controlled by national and international private security companies, criminal organizations, paramilitaries, rebel forces, local self-protection groups, or combinations of the above.[1]

Political violence, Campbell and Dillon (1993) point out, is the "the basic subject of what politics is ultimately about" (1993: 1). And as observed by North (1981), the actor with the most violence poten-

1 As observed by Max Weber, "a state is a human community that (successfully) claims the monopoly of the legitimate use of physical force within a given territory" (Gerth and Mills, 1958: 78–79). Giddens (1985) refers to the state "as a political organization whose rule is territorially ordered and which is able to mobilize the means of violence to sustain that rule" (1985: 20). This definition acknowledges the possible lack of legitimacy of state agencies (Ibid). The definition by political geographer Joe Painter (1995) is even further removed from the Weberian original. He defines states as "spatialized social practices which are to a greater or lesser extent institutionalized (in a 'state apparatus') and which involve claims to authority which are general in social scope and which secure at least partial compliance through either consent, or coercion, or both" (1995: 34).

tial may have a "comparative advantage" (1981: 21; also see Bedoya, 2010). Hence, it is not only important who controls the state, but also who replaces it when it is not in control. The kind of control practiced depends on the nature of the organizations imposing their respective monopolies, or oligopolies of violence. A private security firm operates differently from a left wing rebel group, or a right wing paramilitary unit funded by organized crime. The following groups and organizations may potentially replace or share power with the security agencies of the state:

Para-police Forces

In large Latin American cities the well-off pay additional taxes to provide funding for a municipal para-police service for increased security, such as the *Serenazgo* in Lima, Peru. Created initially during the 1980s in the upper-middle class Lima district of San Isidro to improve the safety of citizens while police were preoccupied with fighting the Shining Path rebels, the force had grown to some 5,000 Serenazgo agents in Lima and its port city of Callao by 2005. Its agents, who are equipped with a cell phone and a baton, patrol in cars or on motorcycles. Depending on the affluence of the district agents receive between US$ 250–400 in monthly pay, though they usually lack health insurance or any other coverage. The district of Villa Salvador can afford ten agents while the middleclass neighborhood of Jesús María pays for twenty-five. Agents from the well off neighborhood of San Isidro have four months of training, while their colleagues from the badly off district of Rimac will receive one. Serenazgo agents have been criticized for their poor training, excessive use of force, and lack of co-ordination with police and the municipal para-police units of other districts. According to Peru's 2005 national victimization survey 66 per cent of Lima and Callao residents had little trust in their municipal para-police (*El Comercio*, Aug. 6/06: A16; also see Rico and Chinchilla, 2002).

Informal Urban Policing

Informal security guards usually work in urban areas; generally for a low pay. A person employed as a body guard by a private security company in Peru can expect to garner between US$ 800–900 per month, while his or her company will earn US$ 4000 from the work. An informal body guard may earn up to US$ 350, while an informal night watch hired by the inhabitants of a given neighborhood or apartment building will earn less than US$ 200. Those working in the latter capacity often do so to add to the meager incomes from their day jobs. Many informal night watches are high school teachers, a grossly underpaid profession in Peru (*La Razón*, Dec. 29/06: 11; also see El *Comercio*, Sept. 3/06: A11; *El Comercio* (*Dia_1*), Dec.11/06: 17).

Urban Policing by Criminal Gangs

In the squatter communities of large Latin American and Caribbean cities security is often supplied by local criminal groups. According to Neuwirth (2002) the favelas of Rio de Janeiro, Brazil, were among the city's safest neighborhoods as street crime was violently suppressed by local drug gangs practicing vigilante justice. The gangs initially moved into these communities because the lacking police presence greatly facilitated the drug trade. Rio gangs provided 'policing' to keep out law enforcement to avoid interruptions to the trade. A similar phenomenon has been observed in Kingston, Jamaica (Rapley, 2003).

Informal Policing in Rural Regions

The rural poor often organize their own security which, however, may be based on a rough brand of justice. Diez Canseco (2003) observed that in Peru the so-called *rondas campesinas* – or peasant militias – were initially formed in the 1970s to combat local crime. After apprehending a criminal, they would hand him or her to the police where the person was often released because of lack of proof, payment of a bribe, or a benign criminal legislation. The members of the rondas or *ronderos* therefore took matters into their own hands and implemented an alternative system of sanction that included physical punishment, community work, or repair of the damage caused by the offence. Ronderos are also involved in resolving family or land disputes and other conflicts that typically transpire in a rural community. As a result, the rondas have obtained considerable social legitimacy. Bolivia's *Ponchos Rojos* or Red Ponchos, indigenous local militias set up by Aymara natives, play a similar role in that country. Not only have they effectively replaced the state in parts of Bolivia, they merged and turned into a powerful political force in support of President Evo Morales (*El País*, Feb. 19/07). All the same, community justice easily turns into vigilantism. Presumed criminals may be lynched unless the police arrive in time. Rico and Chinchilla (2002) observe that this practice is most notable in Guatemala; though some 50 per cent of those killed likely have been innocent (Also see Han Chen, 1998).

Private Security Companies

Recent years have seen the emergence of a global private security industry. While political and social turmoil increase in many parts of the world as states lose their monopoly on legitimate armed force, private companies provide military services and protection to governments, NGOs, and businesses (Davis, 2002; also see Rigakos, 2002). As rates of political and criminal violence shot up during the 1980s Peru experienced a large increase in the number of private security companies; from a few dozen in 1980 to over a thousand in 1992, although their number has declined since. After the millennium, some 350 security companies had been registered in Peru generating about US$ 375 million annually and employing some 50,000 people (*La Razón*, Dec. 29/06: 11; also see *El Comercio*, Sept. 3/06: A11; *El Comercio* (*Dia_1*), Dec. 11/06: 17). One such company is Forza, which, among other things, is responsible for guarding the operational sites of international mining corporations. Forza employees have also been involved in the suppression of legal opposition to mining. In 2006, Forza hired the services of a private detective company to snoop on the environmental NGO GRUFIDES in order to find evidence of indiscretion in the private life of the Catholic priest in charge of the organization (*La República* (Sunday Supplement), Dec. 3/06: 1–8). A more extreme example involves the Coca-Cola Company, and its Colombian subsidiary and business affiliates. The company was charged with employing death squads to slay, torture, kidnap, and intimidate union leaders at its Colombian bottling plants. The case was taken to a US court where the law suit was partially successful. The court decided that Coca-Cola's Colombian associates were indeed responsible but not the mother company itself (Gill, 2007; also see *The Guardian*, July 21/01).

Paramilitary Policing and Social Cleansing

Local business men hire off-duty police officers or ex-military personnel for the purpose of social cleansing (Rico and Chinchilla, 2002). The phenomenon first appeared in Latin America in the early 1980s and quickly grew into an organized method of doing away with so-called undesirables in the region's large cities. The forty or so local death squads active in Colombia during the 1980s targeted "petty criminals, prostitutes and homosexuals", members or supporters of the rebel groups, as well as "artists, intellectuals, journalists, and lawyers" (Pearce, 1990: 20).[2]

2 While I did come across examples of paramilitary policing in the literature (e.g., Huggins, 1991) I can also provide some personal observations. In November of 1992, during travels in Colombia, I attended an aboriginal music festival in the Andes. As it turned out, the area where the event took place was controlled by an alliance of local police, military and drug lords. The following transpired after midnight when many people were intoxicated from consuming wine and hard liquor at the festival. A Colombian soldier, recognizable by his uniform with rank and insignia, patrolled the streets of the city accompanied by a member

> has become a permanent aspect of urban living ... A rising crime rate, weak judicial system, corrupt police and a tendency towards zero-tolerance policies together create a fertile breeding ground for social cleansing groups to carry out their grisly business (Moloney, 2005).

Rebel Forces

Antigovernment guerrillas administer and police territory 'liberated' from state control. However, rebel forces generally do not share authority with other organizations but replace them entirely. For example, the town of San Vincente was part of the territory ceded to the rebels from Colombia's *Fuerzas Armadas Revolucionarios de Colombia* (FARC) as a safe area during the peace talks with the Pastrana government during the late 1990s. Prior to the arrival of the FARC inhabitants regarded San Vincente as "a lawless frontier town" (*The Globe and Mail*, July 19/99: A11). The FARC ran out the official judges, substituting their own. The high murder rate the community experienced while occupied by the military dropped to almost zero once the rebels patrolled the streets. While the FARC was in town, most criminal cases brought before the rebel courts involved domestic violence and spousal abuse (Ibid).[3]

---

of the local paramilitary outfit. The paramilitary was as heavily armed and wore camouflage clothing. However, his uniform resembled the fantasy mercenary apparel one would see in a Rambo movie. Their job at the time was to keep the peace, although their primary task was the maintenance of the social order, namely, to keep out Marxist guerrillas. The mere appearance of the two significantly calmed the high spirits of party revellers. Still, they also sent people home, checked identification cards, and stopped fights using the butts of their M-16 rifles on those who had been too drunk to notice their arrival.

3 Conversely, the revolutionary law prescribed by Peru's Shining Path rebel movement included the death penalty for many offences. Gonzáles (1994) observed that *Sendero* laws "were enforced with iron-handed discipline: There were no second chances, with offenses punishable by either exile or summary execution" (1994: 128). The the now largely defunct Peruvian Maoist rebel

3. Toward Understanding State Crime

The above observations should amply demonstrate that one ought to be careful when transferring theories produced in one context and applying them in another. The Venezuelan scholars Encinoza Riera and Del Olmo (1981) already noted some thirty years past:

> Experience shows that the passive acceptance of analyses and interpretations developed in the framework of theoretical and ideological concerns derived from another reality leads us down the path of error and not the path of success (1981: 63).[4]

The model of state crime by Jeffrey Ian Ross (2003) is useful for delineating in more detail how criminal governance may manifest itself. It is however based on a Eurocentric understanding because the analysis is largely limited to developed societies like the United States (US) or the United Kingdom (UK).

Ross (2000) has called for additional studies on state crime in the global South, even though he himself almost exclusively analyzed the phenomenon in highly developed industrialized countries. He argued that the study of state crime is made easier when comparing cases which transpire in similar political systems. Besides, it is more difficult to obtain information about countries in the global South, which is complicated further by the motley of agencies involved in state crime (Ibid). Still, Ross' typology – with some modifications – provides very important insights for understanding the various criminal dimensions of the Fujimori regime. The practices described in the

---

movement not only earned a reputation for excessive cruelty, it also practiced social cleansing by persecuting homosexuals and prostitutes (Pearce, 1990: 22; also see Isbell, 1994; Theidon, 2000).

4 While I could also be accused of employing 'foreign' theory, I would like to emphasize the following: First, I am applying theoretical perspectives which Latin Americans have themselves used to analyze their reality, such as the scholarship produced by the Frankfurt School of Critical Theory. Second, I am making an effort to adapt the imported theory to a developmental context.

model have indeed been committed by states in the developed world. Yet unlike in many parts of the global South the activities of the security apparatus generally do not leave deep permanent scars on the political landscapes of these nations.[5]

Regardless, Ross' (2003) model includes the following categories:

The first is "political or grand corruption" which involves elected or appointed government officials, judges, and so on (2003: 96). Ross' use of the term is unclear though because he includes both political and bureaucratic corruption in this category.

To continue, Ross (2003) identifies "illegal information-gathering activities," namely when government agents listen in on telephone conversations, or intercept mail, etc., without proper approval (2003: 106–120). In Peru, the collection of thousands of so-called Vladi-Videos put together by spy chief Vladimiro Montesinos speaks for itself. These videos are secret recordings of the corrupt interactions between Peru's Number Two and members of the country's elite.

Moreover, Ross refers to the categories "human rights violations", such as torture and extrajudicial killings, as well as "state violence" which includes deaths in custody or police use of deadly force (Ibid, 121–147). Evidently, the two overlap and the difference between them is one of perspective. While human rights abuse implies victimization, state violence points to the perpetrator. Other scholars, such as state crime researcher Gregg Barak (1990), do indeed merge the two. The selective murders committed by the death squad *Grupo Colina* or the illegal sterilizations of hundreds of thousands of

---

5 The very constructive assessments made by Kauzlarich, Mullins and Matthews (2003) are also more fitting for a developed society. When discussing the role of elites in controlling the state and its agencies, they claim that it is not "useful" to regard the state exclusively as being controlled by elites because it must also answer to the needs of the citizenry "in order to preserve larger state goals and to avoid undermining the state itself" (2003: 252). This statement is certainly true, however, everything is relative. It may be broadly pertinent within the context of a developed society in Europe or North America but it is less applicable in the global South where the elites in many countries often disregard the needs of the population (Stepan, 1978; also see Sumner, 1982; Stanley, 1996).

Peruvian native women during the 1990s fall into either category (Tamayo, 1999; also see Burt, 2006; Vasquez del Aguila, 2006).

The last type identified by Ross (2003) is "state-corporate crime" which occurs when "organizations ... in both the private and public sectors ... pursue goals" that result in "injury, disease, death, and ecosystem destruction" (2003: 148). Multinational mining corporations, many of which entered Peru as a result of the Fujimori government's privatization, have not only caused great damage to the country's flora and fauna but exercise an undue influence over government policy to this day.

I would add another dimension which is of significance in a Latin American context, namely collusion with criminal groups on the part of state actors. This collaboration forms part of the tripartite arrangement described by Wilson (2009) as para-politics. In an earlier work I have demonstrated that under certain conditions, notably when threatened by the same adversary, state and economic elites may join forces with criminal organizations to maintain their dominance (Schulte-Bockholt, 2006). As shown then, the Peruvian military collaborated with drug trafficking organizations, particularly in the early 1990s, in order to finance the civil war against the Shining Path rebels who themselves relied on the proceeds of the drug trade to fund their side of the conflict (Ibid). Finally, while Ross includes political corruption as one of various manifestations of state crime, I argue that it represents the essence and primary resource of a non-representational regime (e. g., authoritarian). Political corruption prepares the ground for the commission of an array of state crimes such as those described in the model.

As previously observed, Friedrich (1989) argued that "the degree of corruption varies inversely to the degree that power is consensual" (1989: 16). The Chilean scholar Fernando Mires (2006) also maintained:

> In no case does the corruption of a democracy exceed that of dictatorships. Dictatorships are corrupt by definition because they usurp or rob power which is not theirs ... The [corruption] of a dictatorship becomes known after the dictators have left (2006: 13).

Based on the experiences made during the Franco regime (1939–1975) Spanish scholar Francisco Laporta (1997) argues that "in dictatorships corruption tends to be more intense than in democracies" (1997: 29). Laporta does not deny that corruption is a phenomenon also produced in democratic societies, however, the conditions for its emergence and continued existence are better provided for in an authoritarian one. A developed democratic society that makes efforts to socially integrate its citizens, maintains a well-organized bureaucracy, has a fair legal system, practices pluralism, and where those in power are controlled by the law, will not only generate less corruption, but also possesses the means to deal with it when the problem arises. Other important characteristics of such a democracy are an "institutional system of information" which allows for investigating and exposing alleged corrupt practices, and a well-working news media (Ibid, 32). These features, writes Laporta, "are perfectly contradictory to an authoritarian mind set" (Ibid, 31). It is noteworthy that corruption has traditionally been lowest in the Scandinavian countries, which has been attributed to the high degree of access to public information (Bannenberg and Schaupensteiner, 2004).

Jiménez de Parga (1997) observed that corruption was not simply another trait of a dictatorship, but that such a regime could not do without. He wrote on the Franco era in Spain that

> neither the defenders of the ... regime nor its detractors paid special attention to the irregular practices ... [regarding] administrative procedures, the collection of commissions, the arbitrariness in the use of decision-making powers, the clientelism, the [use of] connections or the innumerable ways of employing illicit and unseen pressures to obtain results which the regular channels did not provide (Ibid, 135–136).

As noted by Charap and Harml (1999), in an authoritarian setting corruption is a comprehensive tool that allows those in power to obtain wealth while simultaneously assuring allegiance to guard against rebellion (1999: 14). Corruption thus also represents a privatization of power. Spain's General Franco considered corruption like the drop of oil indispensable for the upkeep of his regime, with the advantage that it tied to the dictatorship those whom it compromised (Payne, 1987; also see Lamo de Espinosa, 1997).

Charap and Harml (1999) maintain furthermore that corruption must be examined in the milieu in which it transpires because the practice "is endogenous to the political process" (1999: 3). US criminologist William J. Chambliss (1988) argued similarly that one needs to be familiar with the nature of "the social structure that creates the institutionalization of criminality" (1988: 208).

While authoritarian and other non-representational regimes may share important features, they are nevertheless unique in regard to the constellation of groups which form their respective ruling structures. In his analysis of the Franco dictatorship historian Sánchez Jiménez (1991) referred to three distinct but overlapping political elites who formed the backbone of the regime while the *Caudillo* maintained the balance of power between them: the Fascist party or *Falange*, the military, and various ultra-conservative Catholic Church groups, notably the *Opus Dei* sect. These elites were allied to private business, the aristocracy and the emerging middle class, all of whom supported and "with their compromise" upheld the regime (1991: 280–285).

Durand's (2004) analysis is somewhat remindful of the tripartite arrangements of para-politics (sans the criminal element) as he describes a "triangle of power" consisting of the "presidency ..., the intelligence service and the repressive police-military apparatus" as well as the ministry of economics and finances (2004: 122). This triangle was supported by domestic private business, foreign corporate and political interests, and the ultra-conservative Catholic Church organization Opus Dei, as in the Spanish case (Ibid).

Conversely, the Fujimori regime differed from the Iberian dictatorship because arrangements were more informal than those under Franco. As noted by Grompone (2001), the regime did not "constitute a power block or a relatively articulated group of the dominant elites" (2001: 109). Peru's "social actors," such as the traditional political parties, were ineffective which in turn not only made unnecessary the creation of a "power block" in the Gramscian sense, but also obviated the need to go beyond "selective repression" (Ibid, 108). Fujimori "was a paradoxical guarantee of continuity" at a time when the country's elites were glum about their future but had few designs of their own to improve the situation (Ibid, 113). Rather than "a pact of domination" set up by the elites, the Fujimori regime was based on "informal links" which were "constantly redefined" (Ibid, 109). Grompone describes the regime as a cabal that took advantage of the "weakness of the state" (Ibid, 108). This cabal

> ... is affirmed from the inside by the use of threat and blackmail, and from the outside because the departure from [this group] results in the exposure of illicit acts from which one cannot extricate [himself or herself] because one no longer has a rearguard of protection (Ibid, 109).

4. The Protection Racket: Toward a Model of Political Repression

McCamant (1984) observes that Marxism has been primarily concerned with exploitation, namely that of the working class. It is "not a theory of repression" of the "political opposition" (Ibid, 25). Indeed, Marx and Engels viewed the state as the instrument of the ruling class and saw no need to differ "between those who own the means of production and those who control the means of coercion" (Ibid). However, in *The Eighteenth Brumaire of Louis Bonaparte* Marx did differ between the two. In his analysis of the coup of December 2, 1852, in France, which brought about the Second Empire of Napoleon III, Marx argued that French elites were in fear of the left and in consequence allied themselves to the Bonapartist party and the military. By doing so, they handed over political power to maintain social power. Ironically, after the Bonapartist regime had suppressed the left, French elites themselves were subjected to a similar fate (Marx, 1971). Thus Marx recognized a state actor that was evidently not controlled by the ruling class, but he neglected to further examine his own insights and make the necessary changes to his theory of the state, namely

> to allow for [the] consideration of political repression. The state must be seen as potentially autonomous and the means of coercion should be seen to be equal in importance, if not superior, to the means of production (McCamant, 1984: 27–28).

Indeed, the closest to such a perspective on political repression has been the underdeveloped theory of the protection racket created by Frankfurt School scholars Max Horkheimer, and to a lesser degree, Theodor Adorno. During his US exile in the 1930s and 40s Horkheimer wrote various essays equating Nazism to American-style organized crime. Horkheimer aimed to revise the Marxist notion of classes to include the interests and loyalties of the sub-groups which are part of such formations (Stirk, 1992: 140). While seeking to formulate an account of capitalist society that emphasized "power" over "market allocation," and explained the "privatization of power" as well as violence of Fascist regimes, he arrived at the concept of the society of rackets (Ibid).[6]

In Horkheimer's view the notion of rackets encompassed the groups, cliques, councils, decision-making bodies, or committees of different epochs, cultures and subcultures, whose social function was guided by the imperative to preserve and increase their own power.

---

6 In 1941 the German playwright Bertolt Brecht (1965; 1987) wrote *Der aufhaltsame Aufstieg des Arturo Ui* [The Resistible Rise of Arturo Ui] while in exile. In this play the author shifts the Nazi seizure of power in Germany to a criminal milieu in the United States. Key stages of Adolf Hitler's political career between 1932 and 1938 – from the backroom dealings in 1933 that resulted in his becoming chancellor to the annexation of Austria in 1938 – take place in a Chicago underworld setting. Brecht had in mind to make the Nazis look absurd and divest them of their demonic attributes by associating them with common gangsters who fight over control of the city's cabbage trade. Still, Brecht simultaneously illustrated that Fascism and organized crime had in common features such as violence and tyrannical decision-making. This analogy was commonly reflected in the writings of other intellectuals who had fled Germany, such as Horkheimer and Adorno who wrote several essays on this subject in the 1930s and 1940s.

The dominant class is a structure of rackets rooted in a specific mode of production which "holds down and protects the lower orders" (Horkheimer, 1985: 288). He defined rackets as groups that push for their "collective interests against the interests of the whole" (Horkheimer, 1988a: 334). Although engaged in constant bickering and infighting rackets nevertheless maintain internal class links to preserve shared basic interests that unite them against common foes. The Frankfurt School scholar describes rackets as "pragmatic totalities" which are neither universal nor individual but particularistic in character, while such organizations also symbolize the rise of the group over individual and society (Horkheimer, 1985a: 290; also see Stirk, 1992). Similar to Grompone's (2001) observations on the cabal which ran Peru between 1990 and 2000, Horkheimer (1988b) wrote that "those allowed to join [a racket] are secure, however, they now are obligated to it. Towards [those on] the outside the racket member has no conscience and no responsibility" (1988b: 340).

Horkheimer went beyond Marx when he compared the means of production to the weapon of a criminal. While Marx found capitalism to be lacking, he accepted that it functioned following some tenets of justice and impartiality. Horkheimer (1985) came to view coercion and injustice as its key attributes. He emphasized rackets instead of classes to include the notion of coercion – explicit or implicit – as the common denominator of history (Horkheimer, 1997a). "In the beginning of the history of the modern racket stand the inquisitioners, at its end the leaders of the Fascist racket" (Ibid, 334). To Horkheimer "history was a history of domination" (Stirk, 1992: 143). Likewise, Adorno (1990) referred to "a history of group struggles, gangs and rackets" (1990: 381).

Horkheimer's (1985a) examination focused on important facets shared between organized crime and Fascism, in particular their criminal nature, the "parasitical" extraction of payment, "the conspiratorial distortion of language" or propaganda, and the "monopolization of socially necessary functions" (1985a: 288–290; also see Stirk, 1992). The Frankfurt School scholar argued further that rackets incorporate a criminal dimension because the "boundaries between respectable and illegal rackets are unclear" (Horkheimer, 1997: 258). The dual nature of the phenomenon is evidenced by the fact that a racket means protection from victimization as well as the extraction of tribute under the threat of violence. Hence, "the racketeer is both protector and exploiter" (Stirk, 1992: 141). Still, the racketeer is also an agent of corruption engaged in the privatization of the public interest.

In short, rackets are regimes of exclusion or forms of organized social, economic, and political activity which make use of corruption, disinformation, and, if necessary, repression, that elites employ to further their own interests and those of their associates at the expense of others. Horkheimer viewed the racket as the principal manifestation of power in history. Thus, the powerful "have always protected and at the same time exploited their clients. Protection is the archetype of domination" (Horkheimer, 1982: 35).

Rackets are similar to the elites which constitute Antonio Gramsci's hegemonic bloc. The key difference between the two concepts lies in the emphasis put on distinct aspects of social control. While Horkheimer stressed the strife and violence of elites, Gramsci focused on the manner those in power stay in control without coercion. Gramsci discerned three forms of hegemony. Integral hegemony described an environment where the regime and citizens live in general agreement. Such conditions only exist when "well-organized, wide-spread opposition is absent ... and when the ruling class performs a progressive function" (Femia, 1981: 46). Decadent hegemony depicts a state of affairs where the "dominant group has exhausted its function" and "the ideological bloc tends to decay" (Ibid). Thus social conflicts can break out at anytime. In the context of what Gramsci calls minimal hegemony he refers to a situation where elites stay on top through *trasformismo*, the practice of "incorporating the leaders ... of potentially hostile groups" into the power structure which brings about the construction of a larger ruling alliance (Ibid). As part of this process Gramsci (1971) recognized the role of corruption in the preservation of elite rule.

Accordingly,

> hegemony ... is characterized by the combination of force and consent ... Between consent and force stands corruption/fraud (which is characteristic of certain situations when it is hard to exercise the hegemonic function, and when the use of force is too risky) (1971: 80; also see Merrington, 1968).

Bellamy and Schecter (1993) noted that the Italian state "was hopelessly compromised by the politics of trasformismo" (1993: 12; also see Howson, 2008). Influenced by Gramsci's writings, Arrighi (1993) argued that corruption and fraud represented "surrogates of power" and "tactical weapons" because ruling elites provided incentives to motivate the leaders of emerging counter-hegemonic groups to join with the alliance in power (1993: 149; also see Graziano, 1977; Etzioni-Halevy, 1989). Ward (1989) referred to "counter-elites" in the global South who could play a role in mobilizing opposition to corruption, or who alternatively join with "the network of corruption themselves" (1989: 36).[7]

Still, as observed by Anderson (1976/77), while Gramsci was cognizant of the role of corruption, he did not integrate the notion into his main concept of hegemony. Still, the claim that corruption and fraud were tools of domination is manifestly true for the Fujimori era. As a result of the international pressure following the April 1992 *autogolpe*, the Fujimori government could not continue as an openly authoritarian regime comparable to the military dictatorships of the southern cone and thus turned into a facade democracy maintained largely by Montesinos and the SIN.

To summarize, Gramsci claimed that as long as the dominant groups fulfilled a progressive function, the hegemonic bloc was able to rule without coercion (Buci-Glucksmann, 1980; also Femia, 1981; Fontana, 1993). Meanwhile Horkheimer (1982: 35) contended that coercion (i.e., protection) was the "archetype of domination" and viewed the racket as a principle that was evident irrespective of time

---

7 It is noteworthy that Gramsci's view of corruption represents the mirror image of Huntington's (1968) or Nye's (1989) views (See Chapter 2).

and place, but which would manifest itself in accordance with the stipulations of a given time and place.

While the notion of the racket can be applied to the power structures of developed nations, it is just as useful in the context of developing ones. Proposing a merger between Frankfurt School and Gramscian concepts, I contend that these operate as a continuum such that specific regimes incorporate varying proportions of hegemonic (Gramscian) and coercive (Horkheimerian) ingredients. Rackets in developed nations display relatively more hegemonic elements, while those in the global South, including Latin America, manifest more of the coercive components. The latter emerge when elites suffer a crisis of hegemony, causing social fragmentation and disruption in society. A regime turns into a repressive racket when it introduces coercion and rules by dominance rather than hegemony. In Peru the 1992 autogolpe transformed a regime with relatively more hegemonic components to one based on more coercive ones. All the same, rackets remain the prime feature of most societies, developed or not.

Protection racket regimes of the Horkheimerian variety may survive for many years and implicitly use violence – or the threat thereof – to extract surplus regardless of the opposition generated. Stepan (1978) discusses "corporatist regimes" which during times of crisis rely on violence to such an extent that they generate ongoing resistance and fail to secure "ideological hegemony in the Gramscian sense" (1978: 86). Sumner (1982) refers to a state that "is likely to rely less on an integrated dominant class hegemony than on ... the terrorism of its secret police" (1982: 28). Midlarsky and Roberts (1985) observed Nicaraguan and Salvadoran elites had for generations disregarded rule by means of a hegemonic process to defend "the perpetually threatened economic interests of the elite" (1985: 188). While Tilly (1985) stressed that the protection rackets of the elites in the European states in the sixteenth or seventeenth century served to thwart external threats, Stanley (1996) noted that in Latin America elites utilized the equivalent to guard against domestic foes. In his study of El Salvador he claimed that

> the ... military state was essentially a protection racket: the military earned the concession to govern the country (and pillage the state) in exchange for its willingness to use violence against class enemies of the country's ... small but powerful economic elite. To put it another way, state violence was a currency of relations between state and non-state elites (Ibid, 6–7).

Such a regime was also well described by George Orwell (1960) who wrote that "[t]he war is waged by each ruling group against its own subjects, and the object of the war is not to make or prevent conquests of territory, but to keep the structure intact" (1960: 164).

Horkheimer's observations on the society of rackets represent not only an attack on Fascist corporatism but also on the pluralist, corporatist and neo-corporatist models of the state. To Horkheimer these as well as Soviet-style Socialism merely represented different versions of racket rule produced by twentieth century societies (See, for example, Horkheimer, 1988: 132). Horkheimer passed away in the early 1970s. If alive today he would likely view neoliberal governments and multinational corporations as the most advanced manifestations of racket rule. Still, he had the following to say about the relationship between the global North and South:

> There is also the rift ... between the people in the privileged nations and those, who in this shrinking world are not only ruled by their own traditional elites, but also by the leading groups in the industrially developed countries. The principle [of the racket] has not changed (Horkheimer, 1985: 89).

Canadian scholar Robert Cox (1993) was one of the first to apply Gramsci's concept of hegemony to the international arena. More recently, US scholar William I. Robinson (2005) used that concept in his analysis of the globalization process. The global power bloc or transnational capitalist class (TCC) is made up

> of various economic and political forces whose politics and policies are conditioned by the new global structure of accumulation. At the centre of the globalist bloc would be the TCC, comprised of the owners and managers of the transnational corporations and private financial institutions ... The bloc would also include [those] who administer ... agencies ... such as the IMF, the World Bank and the WTO, other transnational forums, and the states of the North and the South (2005: 7).

According to Robinson, the hegemony of the global power bloc, just like the national one, requires the consensus of the governed. However, this hegemonic project has been in crisis since the late 1990s. Robinson observes that the activities of the global power bloc appear "to have contributed to a new 'politics of exclusion' ... [whereby] coercion plays an increasingly salient role over consent" (Ibid, 12). Robinson also discusses the concept of trasformismo, yet he does not mention corruption and fraud although it should be manifest that they are "tactical weapons" in the global arena as well as the national one (Arrighi, 1993: 149; also see Arrighi, 1994).

The concepts of 'soft', 'economic' and 'hard power' respectively, as discussed by US scholar Joseph S. Nye, may be of utility when identifying 'corruption' and 'fraud' in the international arena. Nye (2004) defined soft power as the ability to affect the behavior of others by influencing their preferences. He added that soft power is "attractive power" and "the ability to attract ... often leads to acquiescence" (2004: 6). Hard power implies reliance on "coercive diplomacy" and coalitions, while Nye's category of economic power refers to "aid, bribery and sanctions" (2004a: 31). Nye (2008) admits that "soft power is not good per se", nevertheless its application increases the options which are available. Nye's inclusion of bribery as a tool of a state's economic power arsenal appears odd because his understanding of the concept of soft power can far better accommodate the practice. It is noteworthy that Nye's (1989) earlier work has been in the field of corruption where his definition is still widely used by scholars. Regardless, the category of soft power is rather fuzzy and may very well include unethical practices. Vibert (2008) expresses his unease about soft power when he points out that it involves activities which are murky. He claimed further that soft power allowed for the subjective use of authority while it was an exclusive practice. Murkiness and the essentially covert use of power may easily produce as well as hide from view corrupt activities.

Roslycky (2011) comes to a similar conclusion. She differs between "Kantian", "Lockean" and "Hobbesian" approaches to soft power and notes that the last "may not only be illegitimate, it may be criminal" (2011: 63). Roslycky also points to the twilight zone occupied by "state intelligence services" which rely on "less kosher" methods (Ibid, 42). Activities such as the manipulation of cultural organizations by western intelligence agencies during the Cold War evidently fall into the "less kosher" category (Ibid). The attempt by the government of one country to display its soft power by secretly funding the electoral campaign of a preferred candidate in another represents a violation of "the economic, political or social rights of citizens" in the latter (Kauzlarich, Matthew and Miller, 2001: 177).

Likewise, the US maneuvers to garner support for the 2003 invasion of Iraq could be viewed as the use of fraud and corruption in international politics, even if technically speaking no laws were broken. Newnham (2008) analyzed the incentives provided to the nations who joined the US led coalition which had been dubbed the alliance of the 'bribed and bullied'. He concluded that

> the various economic levers examined ... [here] clearly seem to have played a role in influencing the cost / benefit calculations of many states, inducing them to ... [play a part] ... It is difficult ... to think of a non-economic motivation for ... Palau or the Dominican Republic to join the coalition" (Ibid, 197).

Roslycky (2011) work on the conflict-ridden relations between Russia and the Ukraine not only points to the dark dimension of soft power, but she also demonstrates the involvement of criminal actors. Her analysis confirm Gibbons' (1976: 12–13) observations on "criminal political corruption" albeit internationalized (Also see Roslycky, 2009). In sum, it is my argument that fraud and corruption represent the dark side of what Nye calls soft power; they are tools which can be relied upon in the international as well as domestic arena "when coercion is too dangerous and consent is too ineffectual" (Arrighi, 1994: 365). Corruption and bribery are, after all, relatively inexpensive if compared to the resources required to make use of the tools available in a state's economic and hard power arsenals.[8]

---

8 The US diplomatic documents released by Wikileaks in 2010 also revealed 'less kosher' aspects of soft power. Consider the following: An individual who was

5. The Cardinal Players of the Fujimori Racket

The Servicio de Inteligencia Nacional (SIN) and the Military

One key to political domination in Fujimori's Peru, certainly by the late 1990s, was the "instrumentalization of fear" attained through the control of the military and of society by the SIN directed by Vladimiro Montesinos (Burt, 2006: 33). While the military began the alliance as an independent institution, it gradually fell under the influence of the intelligence services controlled by Montesinos.[9] As noted earlier, the spy chief has been the "sleepless guard" whose machinations greatly contributed to the upkeep of the regime (Grompone, 2001: 110). Still, the number of victims was relatively small when compared with the more infamous Latin American dictatorships of the 1970s and 80s.

The Private Sector

Another important factor was the endorsement the regime received from foreign and domestic business groups. Durand (2005) observed that Peru's entrepreneurs broadly supported the "new course of commercial opening, privatization, the clamp down on labor ..., and

---

the secretary to the leader of Germany's Liberal Party – without bribery or coercion – took the very minutes of the coalition discussions with the Christian Democrats after the 2004 elections to the US ambassador in Berlin. Thus, Washington knew about the compromises made, and about the make-up of the future cabinet before Germans did. The individual involved merely lost his employment (Weiland, *Der Spiegel*, Dec. 2, 2010; also see Friedmann et al, *Der Spiegel*, Nov. 30/10; *Der Spiegel Spezial* 1, Dec. 10/10: 32–33). In the criminal codes of many countries, likely including that of the United States, this person's activity would amount to a form of treason which asks for a harsher punishment than dismissal from one's job.

9 While several intelligence agencies maintained by the various branches of the armed forces and police existed in Peru, all of these reported directly to Montesinos and the SIN.

government deregulation" (2005: 311). Corruption entered the game with Jorge J. Camet who was the minister of economics and finance between 1993 and 1998. Camet became linked to a "privileged" group which "benefitted from ... privatization [deals], public works, [and] tax reductions" (Ibid, 311–312; also see Zapata, 2005). Durand (2004) noted that a faction of entrepreneurs sided openly with the regime "while the majority ... was a key support [group] ... until the end" (2004: 120).

The Media

A crucial component of the network of corruption often ignored or underestimated in the literature on the regime, but which provided Fujimori and Company with the most effective means to combat their political opponents, was the mass media. Jochamowitz (2002) argued that Fujimori and Montesinos used television "as an instrument of crime" (2002: 226–227). Montesinos had hired the services of the so-called *prensa chicha* or yellow press and the bulk of Lima's tabloids were working in favor of the government. Similarly, most of the proprietors of Peru's television channels had been bribed (Conaghan, 1999; also see Lynch, 2000; Bowen and Holligan, 2003; Youngers, 2003; Durand, 2004; 2005). The extent of media control achieved explains Dammert's (2001: 11) description of the regime as the "new imagocratic totalitarianism", a form of Orwellian domination that is based on the power of the image rather than open repression.

The Catholic Church and Opus Dei

Orthodox Catholic Church groups strongly aided the regime. Most notably, members of the ultraconservative Catholic sect Opus Dei entered important positions and not only provided crucial technical support, they also had a role in playing down accusations of human rights abuse and corruption. One of the most influential supporters of the regime has been Monsignor Juan Luis Cipriani Thorne, formerly Bishop of Ayacucho, and presently the Archbishop of Lima and Cardinal of Peru. Cipriani, a controversial figure in the eyes of many, openly defended the regime's abuses (Sosa, 2000; also see *Liberación*, March 5/01: 3). Peruvian researcher César Arias Quincot (1994) concluded that "the persons linked to traditional Catholicism played a role [that was] little less than decisive" (1994: 91; also see Rochabrun, 1996; Durand, 2004).

Criminal Organizations

The Peruvian military, particularly during the early 1990s, because of budgetary problems, collaborated with drug trafficking organizations to gain funds to acquire armaments and supplies in order to fight the conflict against *Sendero*. The military was ill-equipped, underpaid, and lacked basic supplies, and consequently relied "to a significant extent, on local resources (i.e., drug money) to finance ... operations" (Palmer, 1996: 183–184). The collaboration was facilitated by the fact that the regime's No. 2, spy chief Vladimiro Montesinos, enjoyed good relations with drug traffickers whom he had defended in court as a lawyer during the 1980s (See Chapters 1 and 8 in this book).

6. Conclusion

The merger of the perspectives of Adorno, Gramsci, and Horkheimer allows for the argument that specific types of racket regimes are home to distinct balances of hegemonic and coercive elements to maintain control. Racket regimes either rely mostly on hegemonic or Gramscian components, or they may evolve into the repressive Horkheimerian variant. In general, those in developed nations tend to incorporate relatively more hegemonic components of rule, while their counterparts in developing nations rely more on the coercive ones.

From independence in the 1820s to the present Peru and other Latin American nations have been dominated by rackets, largely comprising of the descendants of Spanish and other Europeans, who generally put their "collective interests against the interests of the whole" (Horkheimer, 1988a: 334). Meanwhile, political and socio-economic reforms neither produced basic changes in societal power structures nor created demonstrable improvements for the majority of these nations' excluded populations. Racket regimes preserve elite domination through the use of corruption, disinformation, propaganda, and, if necessary, violence against large excluded groups in societies that experience conditions of substantial social inequality. Regardless, while the grounds of exclusion or marginalization differ (e.g., class, gender, ethnicity, political opinion or association, etc.,), this condition is likely to manifest itself in economic disadvantage, if not exploitation and political repression.[10]

Inclusion in turn often implicitly entails the power to exploit, repress, and corrupt. The practice of corruption is an essential component of power relations of racket regimes, certainly those of the authoritarian variety, and cannot be separated from power. Indeed, in such a setting power is the precondition for corruption, and corruption is the precondition for power. Power cannot be exercised unless it is corrupt. The following observation by Horkheimer (1982) thus describes the Fujimori regime, namely that "government ... was not usurped by gangsters who forced an entry from without; rather social domination led to gangster rule by virtue of its own economic principle" (1982: 34).

10 According to Elbert (2004) "marginalization has a disciplinary role to play, so that those fortunate enough who still have a job, consent to keep it under whatever condition imposed. Economically excluded people are left to fend for themselves, and are forced to rely on their own resourcefulness in the middle of indifference, anomie, pessimism, and the fragmentation of common values and grounds" (2004: 389).

Chapter 4

Controlling Society: The SIN and the Military

The test for whether one is living in a police state is that those who are charged with enforcing the law are allowed to break the laws with impunity.
(Jon Roland)

1. Introduction

Peru's armed forces have historically been involved in their country's politics. Of the seventy-six presidents who governed Peru between independence in 1821 and the 1968 revolution, fifty came from the military. This fact helps explain the historical weakness of political parties in that country (Philip, 1978; also see Cleaves and Pease García, 1983; Skidmore and Smith, 1984; Durand, 1997). Between 1992 and 2000 Peru was not officially run by a military government, nevertheless the armed forces played a powerful role in society. As described by Kay (1996), the military was the political party that Fujimori lacked. Degregori (2001) observed similarly that "the intelligence services and the armed forces replaced" the need for a "government party" (2001: 78). Levitsky and Cameron (2003) noted that Fujimori's reliance on the military establishment as opposed to a political party only added to his partiality "for illegal and covert campaign activities" (2003: 21). Given the president's inexperience "with the give and take of democratic politics ..., [he] opted for an authoritarian strategy for political survival ..." (Ibid, 7). Moreover, while Peru's military was a relatively independent partner in the early years of the government, it increasingly fell under the sway of Montesinos and the *Servicio de Inteligencia Nacional* (SIN), notably after the 1998 dismissal of General Hermoza, the armed forces' commander in chief. This chapter will analyze the role of the security forces in maintaining the Fujimori regime.

2. Foreign Influences

A fundamental factor that should be considered in the context of Peru's military is the doctrine with which it has been imbued. Rospiglioso (2001) observed that the Peruvian armed forces were strongly influenced by German and French military thinking. The first is represented by the thought of General Erich von Ludendorff, Imperial Germany's chief of staff during the second half of World War I; notably his 1935 book titled *Total War*. In the work Ludendorff argued that modern conflict was not only determined by military factors but also economic and psychological ones. In addition, the civilian population as a whole participated in the war effort because of the necessity to muster all of the nation's resources. Ludendorff proposed that absolute power in matters of military and political decision-making should be handed to a high ranking general, while the politics of the state ought to be subjected to the requirements of the military to conduct the war. Ludendorff thus went against von Clausewitz's famous dictum 'that war is the continuation of politics by other means' which implies that the conflict is ultimately decided by politicians, not military officials. Ludendorff's book was known in Peru and his ideas were incorporated into the works of that country's military intellectuals during the 1940s (Rospigliosi, 2001; also see Arias Quincot, 1994). Moreover, as observed by Rodríguez (1983), "the total war doctrine, despite its militarist and Fascist background, was re-legitimated by the Pentagon in the context of the Cold War" (1983: 84). In Peru, the doctrine of total war merged with the concept of antirevolutionary warfare developed by the French who also had a strong impact on the development of that country's military institutions. The French had been called upon in 1896 to reorganize the military after Peru's disastrous defeat by Chile in the Pacific War (1879–1883). Thus, after Chile had asked Germany to provide military training for its army, Peru turned to that country's arch rival in Europe, notably France, to drill its troops. In 1898, the French army sent a military mission and helped set up a Peruvian military college. While the mission left in 1940 military links between Peru and France continued through the exchange of officials. The doctrine of antirevolutionary warfare was based on the French experience with colonial rebellions in Indochina and Algeria in which Peruvian officers participated as observers (Toche, 2005).

According to Rospigliosi (2001), the French influence was manifested in the military's 1963 manual which focused on "civic action", namely "population control and the need to rely on military and non-military approaches", such as "projects of social welfare and public works" taken on by the military (2001: 68; also see *Oiga*, Aug. 26/91: 8–9). Indeed, Peruvian doctrine gives the military a strong role supervising the country's development (Obando, 1996). While the armed forces were increasingly exposed to US doctrine, the French influence remained strong. Toche (2005) even observed that the "Peruvian military officials ... [who came to the United States for military training in the 1950s had little] to learn from the Americans" (2005: 28). One of the most manifest consequences of French-German military thinking for Peruvian doctrine during the conflict against Sendero was the fact that once an area had been declared an emergency zone the appointed military commander was also the highest political authority. As such he (or she) was in control of the civilian government agencies, including the police. In September 1993, half of Peru's twenty-four departments had been declared emergency zones (LAWR, Sept. 23/93: 437; also see Toche, 2008). Arias Quincot (1994) noted further that the doctrine was based on the notion that the state's security forces should spread "more fear" than the rebels. The justice system prevents the reliance on "counter-terror [which makes] "it is necessary to ... [use]

illegal repression: death squads, massacres, [and the] massive use of torture" (1994: 99; also see McCoy, 2006).

Arias Quincot observed further that the French "doctrine ... in Indochina ... [was based on] 'illegal repression', that is to say the use of kidnapping, torture, and extrajudicial executions" (Ibid). Following World War II, the French had attempted to re-establish their colonial authority in Indochina where they faced a militant resistance movement, the Communist *Vietminh* under Ho Chi-minh. This fact greatly contributed to the financial dilemma the French experienced as they tried to recover from the defeat, devastation, and humiliation of World War II. In turn, the military in Indochina took over the administration of the opium trade, which was illegal under French law. Through drug trafficking, which was managed by the French Secret Service, the *Service de Documentation Extérieure et du Contre-Espionage* (SDECE), France helped fund the conflict against the Vietminh in the late 1940s and 1950s (McCoy, 1991; also see Porch, 1995). In the process, the SDECE allied itself with a regional Mafia group, the *Binh Xuyen*. The French would buy the raw opium from *Hmong* tribal people. It was then processed into smoking opium by their partner-in-crime to whom the French had ceded the administration of the red-light districts of Saigon, today Ho Chi-minh City. In turn, the gangsters shared the profits with French intelligence to finance clandestine military operations. Opium which could not be sold locally was either shipped to the British crown colony of Hong Kong, or acquired by French gangsters from the *Union Corse*, who exported it to Marseilles, France, where it was converted into heroin and subsequently re-exported into the United States. Meanwhile, Washington provided almost 80 per cent of the costs to keep the French army in the field in Indochina (Ibid; also see Morton, 1999).

The German journalist Peter Scholl-Latour had spent time in Vietnam in 1946 as a French Foreign legionary and returned many times afterwards. Scholl-Latour (1979) described the alliance between the French and the Binh Xuyen as follows:

> These cutthroats were not only given policing powers over Saigon, but also the colossal profits of the red light districts of Cholon. The Binh Xuyen were feared and hated by the population. They were of gruesome efficiency, and there were ghastly rumours about their interrogation methods (1979: 87–88).

The Binh Xuyen profited from the opium trade, prostitution, and extortion. Meanwhile, the French relied on the gangsters to crack down on the Vietnamese Communists. The Binh Xuyen's leader, General Le Van Vien, had been given 'carte blanche' and his "heavily armed gangsters" were feared more than the "Communist partisans and ... succeeded in eliminating the active Communist resistance in the Saigon region" (Ibid, 47). McCoy (1991) maintained that the collaboration between the French SDECE and organized crime represented an informal counter-insurgency model. He noted:

> By exploiting the rackets for the French, the Binh Xuyen had developed the only effective method ever devised to countering urban guerrilla warfare in Saigon. Their formula was a combination of crime and counterinsurgency; control over the municipal police allowed systematic exploitation of the vice trade; the rackets generated large sums of ready cash; and money bought an extensive network of spies, informants and assassins (1991: 161).

Even so, colonialism in Indochina ended following the disastrous French military defeat at the hands of the Vietminh at Dien Bien Phu in 1954. After the French withdrawal from Indochina, the United States became embroiled in the Vietnam War. Like the SDECE the US Central Intelligence Agency (CIA) turned to the trafficking of heroin to finance its secret operations while turning a blind eye even when the mother country was the final destination of the drug (Ibid, 193–261). By the 1980s, the CIA found itself in a similar relationship with the Nicaraguan right wing rebels known as *Contras* and Colombian drug traffickers. This particular collaboration is so well-known that it has made its way into an actual text book on organized crime (Lyman and Potter, 2000). As determined after a three-year investigation in 1989 by the US Senate Subcommittee on Terrorism, Narcotics, and International Operations, also known as the Kerry committee, the Contras had been deeply involved in cocaine smuggling.

The committee report further determined that the CIA, and the National Security Council (NSC), in an operation directed by Lieutenant Colonel Oliver North, had relied on the same pilots, planes and military infrastructure to maintain the covert Contra operations against the left wing *Sandinistas* in Nicaragua, which drug traffickers with direct links to the highest echelons of the Colombian cartels used to smuggle narcotics into the United States (Ibid; also see US Senate Committee, 1989; Scott and Marshall, 1991). Inquiries by several Costa Rican commissions confirmed the findings of the Kerry committee and concluded that the part of the Contra supply network which was run from Costa Rica, and administered by North was connected to drug traffickers (Avirgan and Honey, 1989; also see Lee and Solomon, 1992; Weir, 1996).

Regardless, following the example set by French (and US) doctrine the military entered into a "tacit alliance" with Peruvian drug trafficking organizations to defeat the Shining Path (Zapata, 2005: 257). While this collaboration contributed to the rebels' defeat, it also resulted in the corruption of many military officials (Ibid). Montesinos – who already had close links to Colombian and Peruvian drug traffickers since the 1980s – played a leading role in the organization of this relationship (Thoumi, 2009). According to Rospigliosi (2001), many of those involved were not investigated or put on trial. If they were dealt with, the military command had approved. This state of affairs increased Montesinos' control because officers who had been corrupted could be easily blackmailed and "had to obey him if they did not want to be put on trial" (2001: 33; also see Rospigliosi, 1993; *Caretas*, March 4/99; CVRa, 2003).[1]

1 This observation brings to mind Grompone's (2001) claim that a corrupt circle "is affirmed from the inside by the use of threat and blackmail, and from the outside because the departure from [this group] results in the exposure of illicit acts from which one cannot extricate [himself/herself] because one no longer has a rearguard of protection" (2001: 108–109).

3. The Green Plan

The military's design for a coup against the government of Alan García, which later became known as *Plan Verde* or Green Plan, had been developed in 1988–1989 amid growing economic chaos and Sendero violence (Rospigliosi, 2001). According to an interview given to the journal *Oiga* in November 1990 Peruvian military officials visiting Washington had informed the CIA of the plot to remove García (*Oiga*, Nov. 25/90: 11). Fujimori himself was made aware of the existence of the project shortly after his election (Cameron, 1998). In December 1989, the now extinct weekly *Oiga* had published a report titled "Green Plan" which revealed the existence of a military project to take over the government. The plan, apparently developed by high ranking officials, endorsed the following:

(1) The creation of an authoritarian regime similar to the one set up by Augusto Pinochet in Chile in order to confront subversion;
(2) The new government would be opposed to any socialist tendencies. It would support the neoliberal model and start the process of privatization of national industries (Wiener, 2001; also see Rospigliosi, 2001; Zapata, 2005).

The coup was not carried out at that time for various reasons, but the existing plan was later used by the military (Rospigliosi, 2001). On the 5th of April, 1992, Fujimori and Montesinos, with the support of the commander in chief of the Peruvian military, General Hermoza, engineered the *autogolpe* with the intent to govern the country for decades to come. Accordingly, Fujimori, Hermoza, and Montesinos planned a project that "would have as its main objective the institutional reform of the country" and the creation of an "authentic democracy" with the strong involvement of the armed forces (De Bari Hermoza, 1996: 303). The objective of the government in its fight against Sendero was based on the following framework:

(1) Conduct of the conflict with an "integral strategy";
(2) Strengthening and integrating the branches of intelligence;
(3) Creation of the necessary legal framework;
(4) Organization of the population for the purpose of self-defence (Ibid, 265).

Rospigliosi (2001) observed that the initial Green Plan had not been updated since 1989. Fujimori's coup did target APRA politicians and party offices, although that party had been out of power since 1990. In addition, the military moved to occupy the premises of left wing media outlets which no longer existed in 1992, while it was late closing down a TV station which was not on the list because it had not been established in 1989 (Ibid).

4. Analysis of a Coup

In his seminal work on the coup d'état D. J. Goodspeed (1967) pointed to three factors that needed to be considered, namely "the sympathies of the nation's armed forces, the state of public opinion, and the international situation" (1967: 227). Regarding the first condition for a successful coup, Peru's armed forces were in support of a military take-over since 1989 (*Si*, Nov. 19/90: 8–12; also see *Oiga*, Nov. 25/90: 8–13). Most members of Peru's officer corps approved of the coup because they shared Fujimori's contempt for political parties while favouring his free-market policies (Obando, 1996).

Montesinos played a key role in the preparatory phase of the coup. In July 1990, he persuaded President-elect Fujimori that an assassination plot against him had been uncovered. It was recommended that for his own security he should stay under the protection of the armed forces. Fujimori believed the unfounded claim and took refuge in the rather luxurious Lima Military club, where he met up with the country's highest-ranking military officials whom he credited with saving his life (Salvatteci, 1995; also see *Oiga*, July 16/90: 16–17).

In November 1991, the government introduced a number of key legislative decrees in order to be granted the necessary extraordinary powers which would establish the legal framework for the conflict against Sendero. The opposition in Congress subsequently annulled or modified some of them (Cotler, 2001). Grompone (2001) observed that the government's maneuver gave rise to the autogolpe of April 5, 1992 because the reaction by the "Congress had been anticipated as a pretext for the coup" (2001: 98). After April 1992, most of the decrees rejected by the opposition in Congress were re-issued as presidential directives. The following are the most significant:

(1) Legislative decree 726 permitted the presence of police and military units on the country's university campuses (which were viewed as hotbeds of Sendero activism);
(2) Legislative decree 734 allowed the military to enter the prisons (where Sendero prisoners had often taken effective control);
(3) Legislative decree 740 made possible the use of fire arms by the *rondas campesinas* or peasant militias;
(4) Legislative decree 746 or the law on the system of national intelligence gave broad powers to the SIN. The country's other intelligence services, e.g. the army's *Servicio de Inteligencia del Ejército* (SIE), were put under the control of the SIN.
(5) Legislative decree 749 expanded the powers of the military commanders in the conflict areas. In short, local and regional political authorities were put under military control in support of a unified war effort. The decree also permitted the use of local "economic and financial resources, [and] goods and services" in the emergency zones for the purpose of stamping out Sendero Luminoso (Rospiglioso, 2001: 113–118; also see *Congreso de la República*, Nov. 12/91; *Oiga*, Nov. 18/91: 30–36; *Sí*, Jan. 20/92: 8–9; Alvarez Pedroza, 1996; Wiener, 2001; Burt, 2006).

As observed by Mauceri (1991) decree 740 and subsequent laws passed after April 5, 1992, turned the rondas campesinas "into frontline troops" in the war against Sendero (1991: 25). The *ronderos* provided some two hundred thousand additional combatants to the counterinsurgency effort and their presence freed the army for more urgent tasks (LAWR, March 5/92: 1; also see Bauer, 1995; Dammert, 2001; Grompone, 2001; Youngers, 2003).

According to Abad Yupanqui (2001), the SIN became a bloated apparatus with increased powers and a budget which was kept secret. The personnel swelled greatly to some 10,000 individuals who were either directly or indirectly employed. McClintock and Vallas (2005) maintained that in the late 1990s the SIN had some 1,500 individuals on its pay-roll, while another 13,500 agents worked for the other branches of the military (Also see Degregori, 2001). The widening powers of the SIN via decree 746 not only served the purpose of controlling the military. Montesinos used the SIN to manipulate the legislative and judiciary (See Chapter 5), the media (See Chapter 6), or foreign governments (See Chapters 8 and 9).

Moreover, Legislative decree 749 brought about the creation of so-called "political-military commands" in the areas of conflict "where constitutional guarantees were suspended and civilian authorities sidelined by military officials" (Burt, 2006: 47). This concept is a direct inheritance of the French-German influence on Peruvian military doctrine. Another important legislation passed was Legislative decree 752 which made it possible for the president to "prolong ... the appointment of the commander in chief" of the armed forces (Rospigliosi, 2001: 116). Previously, the military itself had selected its own commander in chief every year, usually the highest ranked officer. The law was portrayed as essential to win the war against Sendero, but in truth it was Fujimori who gained the most because the measure allowed him to secure his own position. Legislative decree 762 was viewed as a major threat against the media because it made punishable by long prison terms the disclosure, duplication, public display, or dissemination of material that discussed the operations of the SIN (Ibid).

Thus, Montesinos was able to implement important modifications in the military and police command structures between the time of

Fujimori's election in 1990 and the coup of April 1992, mostly by putting in place loyal officers (Burt, 1992; also see Obando, 1996; Rospigliosi, 2001). As pointed out by Youngers (2003), the authority of the president strongly depended on the ability to control the security forces, notably the SIN, as an "instrument of repression" (2003: 310). An important step was the appointment of a military official to head the ministry of the interior in 1991 (*Oiga*, Apr. 8/91: 24; also see *Oiga*, Nov. 11/91: 14). One of Montesinos' first acts was the removal of some one-hundred and fifty high ranking police officials. In short, the military came to be in charge of the police, a situation that had not existed since the days of the military government (1968–1980) (Rospigliosi, 2001). In December 1991, Montesinos orchestrated the appointment of General Hermoza to head the military because he was deemed sufficiently slow-witted and easily controllable. After Legislative decree 752 had been approved in Congress in November 1991 the president could appoint officers of his own choosing while he was also no longer required to replace them annually (Ibid; also see Obando, 1993; *Oiga*, Jan. 6/92: 8–12; *La República* (Sunday Supplement), Aug. 25/96: 5).

Rospigliosi (2001) noted that Hermoza turned out cleverer than anticipated. The general built up his own powerbase within the army and it was not possible for Montesinos to do away with him until 1998. "Thus emerged the triumvirate Montesinos, Fujimori, [and] Hermoza" (2001: 38; also see *Si*, Aug. 5/90: 16–19, *Si*, Aug. 5/90a: 20–23; LAWR, Jan. 20/94: 23). Cotler (2001) observed that Montesinos cleansed the military of Hermoza appointees after the general's removal from power. In the year 2000, twelve of the seventeen division generals in Peru had belonged to Montesinos' 1966 graduation class at the military academy (McClintock and Vallas, 2005; also see *Caretas*, Apr. 8/98: 36–43; *Caretas*, Jan. 14/99: 19). The extent of military corruption also becomes apparent when one considers that a dozen high ranking military officers, including Hermoza, were arraigned on charges of corruption after the fall of the regime.[2] It is likewise revealing that by late 2001 close to 500 military officials, including 200 brigade generals, had been removed from the military (Ibid). The scope of military corruption should not be surprising. As noted by Rospigliosi (2001), Peru's Congress had exercised some control over the military prior to April 5, 1992, a fact which had already generated great unhappiness among the officer corps. After the autogolpe the legislative practiced little to no oversight.

In addition, for a coup attempt to go well public opinion is of some significance. According to Goodspeed (1967), the public's backing for the coup "may be passive – mere acquiescence is enough to maintain a government in power" (1967: 228–229). One of the key differences between the Fujimori regime in Peru and the earlier military dictatorships of the southern cone has been the support the various coups received from their respective populations. This divergence can at least partially be explained with the situation experienced by Peruvians as opposed to Chileans or Argentines. While militant left wing organizations were active in both Argentina and Chile, the violence perpetrated by these groups was negligible compared to what was being experienced in Peru.

The brutality of the Shining Path not only contributed to the increase in the violence used by the security forces but strongly affected those caught in the middle, the peasantry. The savagery employed by Sendero "exceeded anything the villagers could imagine" (Theidon, 2000: 542). Following Sendero incursions "villagers would go out with large burlap bags and collect the body parts of their dead loved ones ..." (Ibid). According to the insurgents every village was to pay its "quota of blood" and a million lives would be the cost of the Sendero revolution (Ibid). For Sendero leader Abimael Guzmán violence was "not the midwife" but the "mother of history" (Degregori, 1997: 67). Therefore, the public's support for the 1992 coup was over-

2 Hermoza was forced to return US$ 14 million which he had acquired illegally during corrupt arms deals (Zapata, 2005).

whelming. Degregori (2001) observed that some 80 per cent approved of the actions taken by Fujimori.

Fear of Sendero created a climate in which the majority of the population not only came out in support of the autogolpe but was willing to ignore human rights violations as collateral damage, a situation which persisted at least until after the 1995 elections (Cameron, 1998a; also see Burt, 2006). To use Wilson's (2009: 42) analysis, the "para-political structures" established after the 1992 autogolpe "were understood as *positive* phenomena" because they were perceived as "providing security/protection" against the violence of the Shining Path from which the previous democratic governments were seemingly unable to deliver society. The country did experience a decline in political violence after 1992. While 1,634 terrorist attacks were recorded in that year, the number declined to 1,306 in 1993, and 394 by 1994 (*Oiga*, May 29/95: 7). Most attacks by *Sendero Luminoso* and the smaller *Movimiento Revolucionario Tupac Amaru* (MRTA) took place in 1989 (2117), 1990 (2049), and 1991 (1656) (Ibid). The government also claimed that over 4,000 Sendero and MRTA members had surrendered between mid-1992 and mid-1994 (LAWR, June 16/94: 257). The decline in violence greatly augmented Fujimori's popularity and allowed him to win the 1995 presidential elections – without the major fraudulent manipulations that would mar the 2000 campaign.[3]

Undoubtedly, the domestic support which Fujimori received greatly impacted on the third factor, namely the reaction in the rest of the world because it helped to mute international criticism of the coup. Still, while it may have been the intent of the Peruvian coup organizers of 1992 to install a military dictatorship along the lines of the

3 The regime already committed many offences during the 1995 campaign and the outcome may have been different had the election been clean. Nevertheless, the 1995 election was declared to be a clean one by the Organization of the American States (OAS) despite the irregularities. As observed by Schmidt (1999) the SIN monitored the opposition candidates during the 1995 election campaign and tapped their phones, while it also exchanged ballot boxes (For additional information on the 1995 election see Chapter 9).

Chilean model, this goal became unattainable given the international climate which had fundamentally changed since the 1970s. This made necessary the creation of a facade democracy. Most important was the stance taken by Washington which officially opposed the coup and used its influence in the international financial world threatening to cut the flow of badly needed funds to Peru. Still, without the strong domestic support in favour of the coup it would have been more difficult to avoid sanctions (*Sí*, Apr. 20/92: 12–16, 88; also see *Sí*, Apr. 27/92: 20–21; *Sí*, May 11/92:19).

5. Montesinos' Death Squad: El Grupo Colina

Ames and Rotta Castilla (2005) observed that "the regime only infrequently practiced the selective repression" of the opposition (2005: 288). Still, the studies done by the 2003 Peruvian Truth and Reconciliation Commission indicate that these activities were widespread, at least between 1991 and 1993. Montesinos, the unofficial head of the SIN, was also in charge of the military death squad *Grupo Colina* which had been linked to a series of killings. The group consisted of some two dozen members from the army's intelligence service, the SIE, as well as from the Army Intelligence Directorate, the *Dirección de Inteligencia del Ejército* (DINTE). The unit had its origin in a similar organization, the *Grupo Escorpio*, which was active during the late 1980s when its members had been involved in the extrajudicial executions of peasants in the Alto Huallaga region. The Grupo Escorpio was led by then Captain Martín Rivas who later came to be in charge of the Grupo Colina under the direct command of Montesinos and Hermoza (Conaghan, 2005; also see Cordero, *El País*,

Oct. 2/10; *Diario La Primera*, July 18/10; *Observadorglobal.com*, Oct. 2/10).[4]

The members of the Grupo Colina have been condemned and sentenced for a series of crimes. The most important ones include:

The *Barrios Altos* massacre involved the summary execution of sixteen individuals on November 3rd, 1991. The victims, including an eight-year old boy, were suspected of being Sendero activists. The official in charge of the operation was Captain Rivas who was later promoted to major. Initially, the massacre was attributed to Sendero Luminoso, but it was already speculated at the time that a paramilitary unit controlled by the government had been responsible (*Oiga*, Nov. 11/91a: 18–22; also see U.S. Embassy (Lima) Cable, Sept. 22/93; U.S. Embassy (Lima) Cable, March 15/94; Long, *Los Angeles Times*, June 30/95; Levitsky, 1999; Schmidt, 2000; *Caretas*, Nov. 21/02: 12–14; Youngers, 2003; *Caretas*; July 10/03: 12–14; CVRc, 2003).

The *Santa* massacre was the mass murder of nine peasants by members of the Grupo Colina in Santa Province in the Department of Ancash on May 2nd, 1992. The death squad had allegedly been hired

4 According to a Peruvian officer stationed in the Alto Huallaga valley during the early 1990s the SIE used various torture techniques. In his testimony to a Lima human rights NGO in 1994, he described the following methods:
"The 'grill': the detainee is tied onto a metal bed frame to which electric cables have been connected. The victim is then doused with water while electric current is applied.
The 'submarine': the detainee is introduced head-first into a tank of water, with his hands and feet tied.
The 'rag': the detainee is made to lie on his back with his hands and feet tied. His head is covered with a wet towel and water is poured on top of his head, half-drowning him.
The 'stick': a stick is introduced into the anus, or in the case of women, the anus and vagina.
The 'brawl': the detainee is tied up and forced to lie on the floor while being beaten by at least ten soldiers until he or she loses consciousness.
'Hanging': the detainee is hung by his forearms or wrists, after towels have been tied around them to avoid leaving marks.
The 'magneto:' electricity is applied to the testicles" (HRW, Dec. 1/97; also see *Coordinadora Nacional de Derechos Humanos*, 1994: 21–22).

out to a local business man who paid each member a commission of US$ 15.000 for 'resolving his troubles' with the nine peasants who he claimed were linked to Sendero. These individuals were taken from their homes and subsequently executed. After the kidnapping members of Grupo Colina left behind Sendero slogans and propaganda material to create the impression that the Maoist rebels had been responsible. The execution squad had the collaboration of local law enforcement which looked the other way and whose commander was in charge of the subsequent police investigation into the massacre (CVRd, 2003; also see *La República*, Jan. 5/03).

On July 16th, 1992, Sendero Luminoso exploded a car bomb on Calle Tarata in the Lima middle-class district of Miraflores, killing some two dozen people and injuring hundreds more. In response, President Fujimori authorized the Grupo Colina to engage in the extralegal executions of alleged Sendero sympathizers (*Perú 21*, Jan. 26/09; also see CVRg, 2003). Two days after the bombing, Professor Hugo Muñoz Sánchez and nine students from *La Cantuta* University were 'disappeared' and put to death. By 1993, plausible and detailed allegations surfaced that this crime as well as the Barrios Altos massacre had been carried out by a military death squad formed in 1991 to combat Sendero in Lima. In early May 1993, General Rodolfo Robles publicly accused Montesinos of running a military death squad. According to Robles, the army's commander in chief, General Hermoza, had also approved (Nash, *The New York Times*, May 12/93: A10; also see LAWR, May 30/93: 220; LAWR, Aug. 26/93: 395; CVR, 2003). Hermoza himself maintained during his 2003 trial that the president had not only given "the green light" to the La Cantuta operation but afterwards "congratulated ... Rivas and other members of the Grupo Colina for an intelligence job well-done" (*Caretas*, July 10/03: 12–13).

Pedro Yauri Bustamante was in charge of the program called *Punto Final* on Radio Universal in the city of Huacho in the Department of Lima. On his radio program he accused the authorities of abuses against the local population, notably arbitrary detentions by the military. In the early morning hours of June 24th, 1992, half a dozen uniformed men entered Yauri's dwelling where they tied up and blindfolded the journalist. He was then put onto a truck which left for an unknown destination. Pedro Yauri's body was never recovered. An official judicial inquiry was not made until after the collapse of the Fujimori regime. It was later revealed that members of the Grupo Colina were responsible for the crime (*Oiga*, April 3/95a: 28; also see CVRf, 2003; *Huacho.info*, Oct. 3/10).

Investigations by human rights groups and journalists also linked the Grupo Colina to the disappearances and murders of several dozen students from the *Universidad Nacional del Centro* in Huancayo in the Department of San Martin. According to the 'Final Report on the Presidency of Alberto Fujimori' by Peru's Congress which was issued in June 2002, fifty-three students were 'disappeared' between January 1992 and November 1993. Of these five resurfaced. The bodies of some were found; most remained *desaparecidos* and were presumably victims of extrajudicial executions (Youngers, 2003; also see Speck, *The Miami Herald*, March 18/94: 18A; *Congreso del Peru*, June 15/02: 11; CVRb, 2003; McClintock and Vallas, 2005).

On December 18, 1992 trade union leader Pedro Huillca Tecse, the secretary general of Peru's labour federation, the *Confederacíon General de Trabajadores del Perú* (CGTP), was murdered by unknown assailants. Huillca rejected Fujimori's neoliberal economic program and as leader of Peru's most powerful labour union he was in a strong position to organize opposition to the government's plans. The killing was initially attributed to a commando of Shining Path rebels. However, subsequent investigations determined that Huillca was a victim of the Grupo Colina (Tanaka, 2002; also see CVRe, 2003; CIDH, 2004; Burt, 2006; Sandoval, 2008).

The suspicious April 2000 death of Gustavo Mohme Llona, opposition politician, owner of the daily *La República*, and one of the strongest critics of Fujimori and Montesinos, has been attributed to the SIN. Mohme had already been the target of the yellow press (See Chapter 6). According to independent investigations the left wing politician as well as Cardinal Augusto Alzamora, both of whom had assailed the government over its human rights record, were allegedly assassinated with the aid of Chilean intelligence (Molina Sanhueza, 2002).

6. A Short Digression on Population Politics

One of the worst human rights violations committed during the Fujimori years has been the forced sterilization of Peruvian women. Officially, some 300.000 sterilizations were realized between 1996 and 2000. During this time the regime institute a 'voluntary' surgical contraception programme (tubal ligation) which had the goal of introducing far-reaching reductions in the country's birth rate.[5] Peruvian human rights lawyer Giulia Tamayo (1998) wrote a study which demonstrated that rather than relying on voluntary methods the women were either coerced into – or misled about – the procedure to induce them to participate. Tamayo also noted that the sterilizations were aimed largely at poor, indigenous, and rural women. In May 2009, Peru's public prosecutor Jaime Schwartz – who headed the inquiry into the activities of various health ministers and other implicated officials between 1996 and 2000 – archived the case claiming that the statute of limitations had expired. The prosecutor maintained as well that there was no proof human rights violations had actually taken place because forced sterilisation did not constitute an indictable offence (Ibid; also see Tamayo, 1999; Vasquez del Aguila, 2006; *La República*, May 29/09: 11; *La República*, Apr. 26/11: 10; *La República*, June 3/11: 11). While this particular crime cannot be directly attributed to the security forces, it was nevertheless a part of state policy that was formulated in the original Plan Verde. The project referred to the "sterilization of culturally backwards and

5 Tubal ligation is a surgical method for sterilization in which a woman's fallopian tubes are blocked or severed to stop eggs from getting to the uterus for fertilization.

economically impoverished groups" because they represented unnecessary burdens on Peru's path to modernity (Rospigliosi, 2001: 78–79; also see Oiga, Aug. 4/95: 10–12). The Peruvian state's role in population control has also been enshrined in Article 6 of the 1993 Constitution (Arias Quincot, 1994).

7. The Military Opposition

On November 13th, 1992, a number of high ranking military officials led by General Jaime Salinas Sedó launched an unsuccessful insurrection. The plotters claimed they wanted to arrest the president, reinstate the 1979 Constitution, and bring back the Congress that existed before April 5th, 1992. It was also the goal to prevent the upcoming election for the Constituent Democratic Congress that was to work out the new constitution. According to the coup leaders, the election was going to be a fraud organized by the regime. In addition, the officers in revolt were unhappy about the manner in which military appointments were being made. It was also the intent to arrest Montesinos because of his connections to the drug trade. Following the bungled coup attempt many officers linked to the plotters or otherwise deemed unreliable were replaced with loyal ones (*El Mundo*, Nov. 14/92: 9; also see *Sí*, Nov. 16/92: 5–11; *Sí*, Nov. 30/92: 22–23).

The events of November 13, 1992, nevertheless demonstrated the existence of groups of officers, mostly in the middle ranks, who opposed the regime. Within the military two secret organizations named – *Leon Dormido* [Sleeping Lion] and *COMACA*, an acronym which stands for Commanders, Majors, and Captains – had emerged which provided information to the public and the opposition media about the unsavoury activities of the SIN and the corruption within the armed forces. Many officials were genuinely unhappy about the increasingly dictatorial nature of the regime as well as deeply ashamed of the corrupt Montesinos-appointed officials who came to lead them. Others likely were discontented because expected promotions did not come through due to the changes made to the military appointments procedure (*Oiga*, March 21/94: 23; also see Obando, 1996; Rospigliosi, 2001). As Grompone (2001) observed the military "resistance reached certain levels of effectiveness ... [as] demonstrated by the fact" that its members identified the officers responsible for the La Cantuta and Barrios Altos murders which forced the regime to put some perpetrators on trial (2001: 100).

The best known Peruvian military official representative of the opposition in the armed forces has been General Rodolfo Robles who publically revealed the existence of the Grupo Colina and the participation of military officials in extralegal executions of alleged rebel supporters. Robles had to flee to Argentina after receiving threats to his life. For his revelations he was officially branded a "criminal, coward and traitor" in a declaration signed by over fifty generals (LAWR, May 27/93: 236; also see *Oiga*, May 30/94b: 22). In the fall of 1996, after his return from exile, Robles was openly kidnapped by government agents but released after national and international protests (*Caretas*, Nov. 28/96: 12–13). Robles' wife also received death threats (*La República*, July 27/94: 2).[6]

Another officer in the military opposition has been Major Evaristo Castillo Aste. In October 1992, Castillo denounced military corruption and involvement with drug traffickers to the commander in chief, General Hermoza. However, instead of an investigation into these allegations, his claims resulted in a visit by SIE intelligence

6 During an interview in August 1996 retired General Rodolfo Robles denied that Peru's military had been involved in any drug dealing. Yet, in an article written a few years earlier from exile in Argentina, to where Robles had fled after having exposed human rights abuses of the Grupo Colina, he expressed a different view. Among other, Robles pointed to a group of politicians and military officials who were seriously compromised by corruption and drug trafficking (*LAWR*, May 30/93: 220; also see *Oiga*, May 30/94b: 22; Robles, 1996). However, Robles' initial 'disinformation' was likely based on his apprehension of recriminations against his family and himself on the part of the country's secret service, the SIN.

officers who confiscated his documentation (*La República*, June 27/94:17–19; also see *La República*, Sept. 22/96: 2; *La República*, Aug. 12/97: 8). In February 1993, he was kicked out of the army and fled to Spain from where he continued to denounce the regime (*Oiga*, Feb. 14/94: 35; also see *La República*, Sept. 22/96b: 20-22). Castillo Aste (2001) also authored a book on military corruption and drug trafficking during the 1990s titled *La conjura de los corruptos*.

A further example of resistance within the armed forces was the so-called *Chanamé* report of 1994. A member of the army's intelligence service, the SIE, who only identified himself as Chanamé, leaked a report to the media which confirmed the links between traffickers and the military. The document claimed that several drug-trafficking organizations were operating in the vicinity of Campanilla in the Upper Huallaga valley, the most important of which was controlled by Demetrio Chávez Peñaherrera, better known as *Vaticano*. The report's author asserted that the officers in charge of the army unit stationed at Campanilla, Anti-subversive Battalion No. 30 (BCS–30), fully collaborated with Vaticano and protected his organization. Chanamé claimed that the base commander received US$3,000 - 4,000 for every drug flight. He also noted that the whole population of Campanilla was openly working in the drug economy, without fear from the army (*La República*, Feb. 29/92: 14-15; also see *Oiga*, Jan. 24/94: 18-22).[7]

A similar leak had less fortunate consequences. Mariella Barreto Riofano and Leonor La Rosa Bustamante had both been agents of the SIE. Barreto was the one-time girlfriend of Martín Rivas, the commander of the Grupo Colina. Barreto and Rivas also had a daughter. In

---

7 The Chanamé report has been translated into English and reprinted in a US publication (See Chanamé, 1998). The drug trade may have created even stranger bedfellows. According to a report by the Peruvian daily *La República*, MRTA rebels maintained a temporary local alliance in the Upper Huallaga valley with army and police units. Their collaboration served the purpose of ensuring that the proceeds from the sale of coca leaves and paste would not fall into the hands of advancing Sendero rebels. Allegedly, MRTA and police jointly administered secret air strips and patrolled jungle towns (*La República*, Jan. 31/92: 13-14).

late 1996, the SIN put into motion various schemes (*Plan Narval*, *Plan Bermuda*) to harass, intimidate, and discredit the opposition media. The plans for these activities were smuggled to the opposition daily *La República* and published in December of that year. Barreto and La Rosa were accused of having supplied the information to the press and both were tortured. In early 1997, Barreto's decapitated and mutilated body was found at the road side in the outskirts of Lima. La Rosa was saved because human rights activists and US ambassador Dennis Jett intervened in her case. Still, she was paralyzed as a result of torture (Conaghan, 2005; also see *Caretas*, Apr. 10/97: 10–16; *Caretas*, June 19/97: 18–21; *Caretas*, June 2/00; McClintock and Vallas, 2005).[8]

8. On Impunity

The regime lasted because of impunity produced by legalized corruption. Those who committed or ordered the described acts had little to worry about because they received protection. In 1994, the government was under considerable pressure to put the members of the Grupo Colina on trial because of the La Cantuta murders. However, in breach of the constitution, Congress voted to transfer the case from civilian to military jurisdiction. The trial that transpired was a mockery of justice. Ten members of the Grupo Colina were sentenced to anywhere between one and twenty years in prison. The convicted spent their time in military barracks where they

> enjoyed the comforts of tennis courts, cellular phones, color televisions, a bar, and regular visits from family members and the army paymaster who cashed

8 It has been alleged that Rivas himself killed his former girlfriend Mariela Barreto, a charge which he denied. However, he did admit to "his responsibility in the massacres of La Cantuta and Barrios Altos" claiming these acts had been ordered from above (*Caretas*, Nov. 21/02: 13).

their monthly checks, augmented by occasional bonuses in dollars (Obando, 1996: 35).

The 1995 amnesty law was representative of this impunity but it was also important because by passing the legislation the regime institutionalized criminal behaviour. On June 14th, 1995, Peru's Congress passed Law 26479, a blanket amnesty that pardoned the members of the security forces who had been accused, investigated, put on trial and sentenced, or who were already serving their sentences for crimes committed during the civil conflict in Peru. The amnesty law provided pardons to officials who had participated in human rights violations as well as officers – like General Robles – who had been charged with treason for exposing the very same crimes (*Oiga*, May 30/94b: 22–23; also see *La República*, June 17/95: 9; *La República*, June 18/95: 15; *La República*, June 19/95: 3).

The amnesty law confirms O'Donnell's (1999) observation that to "be powerful" means to "have impunity" (1999: 313). Judge Antonia Saquicuray had opted not to recognize the law in the case of the Barrios Altos massacre which she was investigating because doing so would have violated the constitution and the international legislation signed by Peru. In mid-July 1995, the Eleventh Division of the Superior Court of Justice of Lima archived the case claiming that the law violated neither the constitution nor the international human rights treaties signed by Peru. The court also ordered an inquiry into Judge Saquicuray's actions alleging she had applied the law improperly. Moreover, Congress passed an additional decree forcing judges to comply with the amnesty law (*Oiga*, Apr. 24/95: 13; also see *Oiga*, July 10/95: 21–22; *Oiga*, July 24/95a: 16–19; Burt, 1998).

Impunity only came to an end when Montesinos lost his own protection. On August 21, 2000, Fujimori and Montesinos appeared at a press conference to announce the exposure of a case of arms trafficking to the *Fuerzas Armadas Revolucionarias de Colombia* [The Revolutionary Armed Forces of Colombia], Colombia's most powerful rebel movement which is better known under the acronym FARC. Montesinos claimed the credit for uncovering the arms contraband which included the sale of tens of thousands of AK-47 assault rifles. Shortly thereafter facts came to light which demonstrated that Montesinos himself had devised the gunrunning scheme rather than bring it to an end. The arms were airlifted from Jordan – via Peru – to the guerrillas in southern Colombia. One of the individuals involved in the operation revealed that he had been hired by Montesinos to bring 'electronics equipment' from the Middle East. The operation turned out to be the cause of Montesinos' ultimate decline. In September 2000, while visiting the United States, Fujimori met with the US Secretary of State, Madeleine Albright, and the head of the National Security Council (NSC), Samuel Berger, and was informed that he should terminate his relationship with Montesinos (*Caretas-Dossier*, 2000; also see Loayza, 2003; Bowen and Holligan, 2003).

9. Conclusion

The activities of Montesinos, the SIN and the Grupo Colina are examples of what Cribb (2009) called "para-politics" which refers to the "study of criminal sovereignty, of criminals behaving like sovereigns and sovereigns behaving like criminals in a systematic way" (2009: 8). Peruvians were willing to accept this state of affairs as long as they perceived the threat of terrorism. However, when the violence declined they began to question the state repression on which the regime continued to rely (Arias Quincot, 1994). This was evidenced by the fact that Peruvians in overwhelming numbers rejected the 1995 amnesty law that freed the members of the Grupo Colina (*La República*, June 19/95: 3).

Chapter 5

Peru's Institutions: The Stables of Augias

An honest politician is one who, when he is bought, will stay bought.
(Simon Cameron)

1. Introduction

When Fujimori first came to power in 1990, his party lacked a majority in Congress and thus he had to compromise and find allies among other parties to get important laws approved (De Eiden, 2006). Following the *autogolpe*, Fujimori's *Nueva-Mayoria-Cambio 90* (NM90) party gained 71 out of 120 seats in the new Constituent Assembly elected in November 1992. Most traditional political parties had boycotted the election thereby handing a majority to the pro-Fujimori forces who in turn would put their imprint on the new constitution (Cockroft, 2001). In July 1993, the assembly elected the previous year presented a draft for a constitution which included stipulations that would permit the president to suspend parliament without reason, to turn down legislation, to give out an unlimited number of emergency decrees and to be able to run for immediate re-election (LAWR, July 15/93). The Peruvian politician Henry Pease from the left wing *Moviemiento Democrático de Izquierda* party described the spirit of the document as dictatorial, "... neoconservative and centralizing" (Ibid). The 1993 Constitution restricted the autonomy of the Congress, concentrated power and "militarize[d] the justice system for cases vaguely defined as terrorism" (*Americas Update*, Jan.–Feb. 1994: 4).

Bernales Ballesteros (1993) claimed that the new constitution allowed for the

> minimize[d role of] parliament and the political parties ... Everything which was done objectively turned the Congress [into an institution] without power [and] without ... the [ability] to make its own decisions; that is to say ... [it lacked] ... independence and autonomy (1993: 70).

Burt (2006) observed that the post-1993 Congress failed to keep an eye on the activities of the military which had achieved complete control over the conduct of the conflict, "and became a virtual rubber-stamp of executive initiatives" (2006: 47).

This chapter will focus on Peru's legislative (Congress and political parties) and judiciary during the Fujimori era. Democratic political structures generally function under a system of checks and balances to control the three branches of government, namely the executive, the legislative, and the judiciary. According to the 1993 Constitution, such system also exists in Peru "so that each branch controls and is, at the same time, controlled by the others" (De Eiden, 2006: 67). During the Fujimori years, however, this system was intentionally made ineffective in favour of strengthening the executive.

In order to gain a better understanding of the developments between 1990 and 2000 I will provide a discussion of the evolution of Peru's political landscape as well as short descriptions of the most relevant political groupings.

2. A Short History of Political Parties in Peru

The country's political parties have not been strong, self-perpetuating institutions, except for the left-of-centre *Alianza Popular Revolucionaria Americana* (APRA) which was founded in 1924. Neira (1973) observed that unlike other countries in Latin America there was no continuous evolution of political parties in Peru. According to González (1999), the history of Peruvian political parties has undergone two cycles beginning in the late nineteenth century. First, he refers to the cycle of "elitist parties" such as the *Partido Civil*, founded by Manuel Pardo in 1871 (1999: 308). While this political grouping did gain some importance shortly after its foundation it was eclipsed by the militarism that ensued with the War of the Pacific (1879–1883); however, the party re-emerged thereafter as a strong force. In 1895, the Democratic Party established by Nicolás de Pierola was elected inaugurating what has been referred to as the era of the 'aristocratic republic' which lasted until 1919. The existing political system allowed only males with wealth and/or education to vote and to be voted for. In Peru, a country which was mainly inhabited by poor illiterate indigenous and mestizo populations the 'aristocratic republic' represented the consolidation of a small elite. Peru's traditional oligarchy included bankers, large coastal plantation owners, and the landholders of the middle and high Sierra in the Andes. González called it an "oligarchic pact" which provided the domestic base that made possible the country's entry into the global economy (Ibid, 308–309; also see Arias Quincot, 1994).

The second cycle describes the period between 1919 and 1989, the era of the "mass parties", which put an end to the days of the 'aristocratic republic' (Ibid, 310). The 1920s saw the foundation of the Peruvian Communist Party and APRA, and the first appearance of middle class and public intellectuals. The oligarchy was no longer able to rule on its own but its various factions were forced to seek accommodations with these new societal forces, notably APRA (Ibid, 310–311). During the 1930s, Peru also modernized its electoral system by introducing proportional representation and the secret and obligatory vote using government issued documentation. However, the vote was limited to males above the age of twenty-three years. Universal suffrage was only introduced in 1980. These reforms, however, amounted to little in practice as the country was ruled by a succession of military and authoritarian regimes between 1933 and 1963. APRA, for example, was only allowed to enter the Peruvian Congress in 1963 (Revesc, 1996; also see Gerassi, 1973; Levitsky and Cameron, 2003).

The consolidation of the party system following the return to democracy in 1963 was short-lived because it was interrupted by the 1968 military coup. The left wing military regime set up by General Juan Velasco Alvarado did not defend the oligarchic order but put an end to it. As noted by González (1999), the Velasco coup "accomplished what neither APRA nor the Marxist parties had managed to do: liquidate the oligarchic system" (1999: 315; also see Revesc, 1996). The military introduced important changes, such as agrarian reforms and the nationalization of industries like mining. During this time, political parties were largely irrelevant if not illegal, although some party leaders remained as advisors to the government (Ibid; also see Neira, 1973). The growing divide between radical and moderate officers resulted in Velasco's removal and replacement by the more conservative General Francisco Morales Bermúdez (Revesc, 1996).

The political parties were weakened during the period of military rule. The years of inactivity caused a growing distance between political parties and the electorate and party machineries crumbled. While the parties stayed static, society changed (González, 1999). Although the 1968 coup initially had popular support, it became evident by the late 1970s that military rule could only be maintained by force. The government therefore initiated a process leading up to the creation of a new constitution and the reintroduction of democracy by 1980. In the 1978 elections for a Constituent Assembly to work out the new constitution APRA had received 35 per cent of the vote (Revesz, 1996). It was therefore expected that APRA leader Haya de la Torre was the most likely person to win the election of 1980. But he died while his inheritors squabbled among each other. In consequence, *Accíon Popular* (AP) party leader Fernando Belaúnde Terry won the presidency. During the 1980 election also occurred the burning of the ballot boxes in Chuschi, Ayacucho; the symbolic action that marked the beginning of the Shining Path insurgency (Ibid).

Following the return to civilian rule in 1980, Peru's political landscape was split up "into three roughly equal blocs" (Taylor, 2007: 3). On the political right was Acción Popular founded in 1956 (Neira, 1973). The party had won the 1980 general election, receiving some

40 per cent of valid votes cast for the Senate and 39 per cent for the House of Deputies. Meanwhile, AP's small coalition partner, the *Partido Popular Cristiano* (PPC), received 10 per cent of the overall vote (Taylor, 2007). APRA emerged left of centre; Peru's oldest and best organized party scored over 28 per cent of the vote and sent a respecttable number of representatives to Congress. To the left of APRA, five Marxist parties had contended during the 1980 election and received few votes. These parties formed the Izquierda Unida (IU) which was considerably more attractive to the electorate. In 1983, Peru's political landscape was dominated by a seemingly stable party system whereby each electoral bloc roughly received one third of the vote. According to Taylor, "the combined AP–PPC vote reached 31 per cent nationally, with APRA at 33 per cent and IU attaining 29 per cent" (Ibid, 3).

In the 1985 elections the voters punished AP which had been unable to address the country's problems. Thus AP support declined to 7 per cent. Meanwhile, APRA and IU received 53 and 25 per cent respectively, giving a majority to APRA leader Alan García for his first presidency (Revesz, 1996). While the APRA government initially improved conditions in the country, by the late 1980s Peru was seemingly turning chaotic. In addition, the country's democratic left offered little hope. The IU which had made gains during the early 1980s split again resulting in the creation of another party on the left, the *Izquierda Socialista* (IS) (Tanaka, 2002).

The country was increasingly thrown into crisis by growing unemployment, out-of-control inflation as well as a worsening of *Sendero* violence. Between 1980 and 1990 the country's debts rose from US$ 9.6 to 17.6 billion which represented the equivalent of 63 per cent of Peru's Gross Domestic Product (GDP); an amount five times larger than its 1990 exports. The country also suffered hyperinflation which had climbed to over 7,000 per cent in 1990 causing large reductions in income. Between 1985 and 1990 the minimum monthly pay diminished to the equivalent of US$ 36. While official employment had increased from 34 to 60 per cent between 1985 and 1987, it rapidly declined to 5.3 per cent (!) in 1990, the year Fujimori was elected president. In the capital Lima, underemployment figures climbed correspondingly from 34.9 per cent in 1987 to 86.4 per cent in 1990. These developments greatly contributed to the growth of the informal economy (*The New Internationalist*, July 1989: 24–25; also see Fuhr and Hörmann, 1992). Finally, the civil war had victimized tens of thousands since 1980 (Costa Ferrero, 1993; also McClintock and Vallas, 2005).

While most Latin American political parties were in crisis during the 1990s, the Peruvian experience was one of the most dramatic ones (González, 1999). Tanaka (2000) noted that Peru's party system "collapsed" (2000: 102). While the tally for the traditional parties in 1980 came to 96.7 per cent, it fell to 63 per cent in 1990, and 8 per cent in 1995 (González, 1999). In April 2000, the presidential candidates for APRA and AP received less than 3 percent of the vote (Tanaka, 2000). Levitsky and Cameron (2003) observed that the "political party system decomposed to a degree that surpassed even the most notoriously fragmented systems in Latin America ..." (2003: 1–2).

In other countries which experienced similar developments "there was more of an evolution" (Tanaka, 2000: 102). In Argentina, Bolivia, or Mexico, "new actors appeared" to challenge the supremacy of traditional parties which nevertheless remained significant actors on the political scene. The Peruvian situation can only be compared to Venezuela where the traditional parties' collapse was even more impressive (Ibid, 102–03; also see Degregori, 2001). The inability of established political parties to address the problems of the country not only led to their decline, it also made possible the emergence of the political outsider Alberto Fujimori. Moreover, while the Fujimori regime differed from the bureaucratic-authoritarian military governments of the 1970s and 80s, the president shared their dislikes for political parties (Burt, 2006).

Fujimori claimed that his heavy-handed approach was the only option given the country's many problems. Meanwhile, he incessantly assailed politicians, labour unions, and human rights organizations. Fujimori renamed democracy "as 'party-cracy' to imply it had been corrupted to its core by party elites and special interests" (Ibid, 43; also see Planas, 1991; Arias Quincot, 1994; Roberts, 1996; Teivainen,

2002). Fujimori maintained that he did not need a party because he represented the interests of the majority of Peruvians (Oliart, 1996). According to Mires (2006), the populist ruler presumes to act "in accordance with a general will which only he [she] represents because he [she] is the personified synthesis of this will ..." (2006: 17). The violence perpetrated by Sendero "directly contributed to a reordering of political and social meanings", causing general disenchantment with democratic practices and providing support for the "authoritarian political project" set up after April 1992 (Burt, 2006: 43).

Fujimori only relied on the vehicle of a political party during elections. As observed by Levitsky (1999),

> Fujimori ... has made no attempt to establish an institutionalized relationship to his mass base, relying instead on personalistic appeals and periodic spending projects. Rather than building a political party, he has created 'disposable parties' – minimalist organizations that are ... [relied on] for a single election and then discarded. Thus far, Fujimori has created three such parties (Change '90 in 1990, New Majority in 1995, and Let's Go Neighbours in 1998), and he is reportedly preparing at least one more for the 2000 elections (1999: 82).

The party vehicle created for the 2000 election was *Perú 2000*. According to Tanaka (2000), such movements were connected to the government and did "not exist on their own, [and did] not have an organic life and organization of their own" (2000: 114). Salas López (2005) observed similarly that aside from a few exceptions such parties generally have no "real organization" but are mere facades (2005: 61). Likewise, the 'disposable parties' lack ideological identification. As a result of the vagueness of these organizations' political outlooks such parties are labelled after their respective leader, e.g., Fujimorista or Toledista (Ibid). Durand (1996) observed that the conservative parliamentary group *Renovación* was the only one of various new organizations "that openly expresse[d] an ideology" (1996: 108).[1]

1 One of the most important members of the party Renovación and of Peru's Congress is Rafael Rey who has been linked to *Opus Dei* (Durand, 1996).

3. The Congress as a Rubber Stamp

Dammert (2001) argued that the 1993 Constitution and the congressional rules set up in 1995 were designed to allow for the establishment of an authoritarian regime by reducing the representative role of Peru's Congress in a number of ways. The most significant development has been the institution's reduction from a bicameral body to a unicameral one which considerably diminished its ability to represent, the more so because it was also reduced in size from two hundred and forty deputies to half that number (Ibid; also see Mauceri, 1997; 2006).

Usually, the second chamber or senate serves the purpose of reaffirming, rejecting, or overhauling legislation approved by the first chamber. Other nations also have unicameral systems but proposed legislation has to pass additional debates before being turned into law (Damnert, 2001). Conversely, the Fujimori regime used the unicameral Congress to restrict the time in which a proposed bill would become law. According to Cameron (1998a), the "Congress ... [could] literally pass legislation into law within twenty-four hours" (1998a: 235). The government relied on various practices to speed up legislation and cut down on public and congressional debate. Aside from limiting debating time for a proposed bill, the Fujimori majority would use what Dammert (2001: 61) called "ambush tactics" whereby debate would begin on one project which was unexpectedly changed for another. Indeed, the infamous 1995 'amnesty law' which freed the members of the death squad *Grupo Colina* was introduced in this way (Ibid). According to De Eiden (2006), those in the Fujimori camp were given beepers to receive instructions on how to vote.

The Fujimori majority in the Congress regularly dispensed with the creation of commissions to discuss proposed bills. Under the old constitution, it was necessary to have a 2/3 majority to do so. In the post-1993 Congress the approval for waiving this procedure required a majority of half of the representatives *present* – plus one – during a given congressional session (Ibid). The NM–90 majority in Congress also managed to prevent investigations into allegations of corruption or human right abuse potentially harmful to the regime (Conaghan, 2005). The opposition parties in Peru's Congress put forward two-hundred and sixty motions between 1995 and 2000 calling for the formation of working groups to investigate corruption or human rights abuse. Of these motions, only six resulted in the formation of commissions. Almost half (48 per cent) were thrown out, while the rest was withdrawn again or shelved (Dammert, 2001). Cameron (1998) noted that Peru's Congress not only failed in its supervisory role, but also generated few laws. While most bills before the autogolpe were initiated in Congress, the bulk of the legislation after 1992 was introduced by the regime.

Similarly, the post-autogolpe Congress enjoyed less authority vis-à-vis the executive under the 1993 Constitution. For example, the president no longer needed the blessings of Congress before signing treaties with foreign governments, or the naming of ambassadors and of high level military officials (Mauceri, 1997). More importantly, under the 1979 Constitution the president needed to request "decree powers from the Congress" (Ibid, 906). The 1993 Constitution made it possible to use such powers without having to ask for them. As Mauceri observed, "decrees which are declared 'urgent' by the executive cannot even be revised or changed ..." (Ibid).

According to Dammert (2001), "1003 decrees of urgency" were issued between 1993 and 2000, many of which turned out to be unconstitutional (2001: 74). Also, secret decrees were never brought before Congress. For example, the funds for the controversial purchase of MIG-29 and SU-25 planes bought from Belorussia between 1996 and 1998 were acquired by a decree that remained secret. Accordingly, urgency decrees also authorized the use of public funds, including assets attained from the privatization of state-owned industries, which were distributed like "gifts" from the president (Ibid, 75). Dammert noted that by relinquishing its fiscal responsibility, the Congress gave license "to the abuse of public funds while promoting a clientelist culture" (Ibid; also see Salas López, 2005). According to

Rospigliosi (2001), Peru's Congress exercised some limited control over the military prior to the April 1992 coup, but not thereafter.

The 1993 Constitution itself contributes to impunity. Salas López (2005) observes that in accordance with Article 38 Peruvians are obligated to defend the constitution and hold duties toward the nation and society. However, the constitution makes no mention of any penalties for those who fail to conform. Salas López concluded therefore that "when there are no specific sanctions for those guilty of breaching the constitution, this leads to impunity" (Ibid, 98). Fujimori's control of the legislature certainly meant that he could act with impunity. Quiroz (2008) observed:

> The pro-Fujimori majority in Congress, especially during the legislature of 1995–2000, had systematically surrendered congressional and oversight rights ... The degree of servile behaviour observed among many members of Congress can only be explained by taking into account the massive distribution of bribe money in their midst (2008: 385).

4. Transfuguismo

The decline of political parties can also be attributed to the actions and characteristics of the individuals elected to Congress which in turn has contributed to the low opinion that most Peruvians have of their representatives. Salas López (2005) noted that most members of Congress were unqualified for their positions. Their previous backgrounds generally have not prepared them for legislative work, while their morals and ethics are doubtful. Thus, people are elected "who embarrass themselves because of the ridiculous things they say and do ... [while] others are true criminals" (2005: 48). Aside from a few exceptions, the representatives in Peru's Congress primarily want to reap the economic benefits and the perquisites that come with their positions while "they fail to comply with the constitution, and protect each other when accused of evident failures" (Ibid, 49).

Salas López claims furthermore that the existing practices regarding the selection and election of candidates make it difficult for honest individuals to find their way into congress. Candidates as a rule have shelled out money to be on the electoral lists, and if elected they will want to regain their investment.[2] The above observations were echoed by Levitsky and Cameron (2003) who noted that the members of Peru's Congress

> were essentially free agents; ... Many legislators viewed elections as a commercial venture, involving an up-front investment to get onto the winning list. Once in power, they would recover their investment through perquisites of office and the opportunities for illicit enrichment it would present (2003: 20).

These observations are evidenced by the practice of *transfuguismo*, the defection from one's party to another. 'Crossing the floor' whether to join the government party, the opposition, or the ranks of the independents – while often frowned upon – is not automatically illegal. A representative who switches to another party for reasons of conscience, or who believes that such a change is in the best interest of his or her constituents, and who does so with their approval, may not ruffle many feathers. Even the once Liberal Member of the British Parliament, Winston Churchill – after an ideological conversion – subsequently switched to the Conservatives. After all, individuals have the right to join – or leave – political organizations as they please. The practice is not legal if it is the result of "bribery, pressure, promises of economic advancement, or any other cause that is not political or

2 In early 1994, a member of Peru's Congress earned over 16.000 *Nuevos Soles* plus additional bonuses which is an amount that allowed the former a very comfortable existence (*Oiga*, March 21/94a: 44–45). The income of Peru's members of Congress has increased greatly since. In 2005, a member of Congress could expect to earn 56.000 *Nuevos Soles* or over US $17.000 monthly while receiving additional bonuses for Christmas, the national holidays, and schooling purposes respectively (Salas López, 2005). In comparison, a Canadian Member of Parliament earned about US$ 11,000 a month in 2010 (See Indemnities, Salaries and Allowances Members of the House of Commons, Ottawa, Canada, 2010).

ideological" (Landa Arroyo, 2001: 223). Then the illegal defector violates "the popular will by affecting the plurality of parliamentary representation" (Ibid).

The Fujimori regime relied on transfuguismo through bribery to illegally change the make-up of the political parties in the Peruvian Congress, notably after the 2000 election (Ibid). The president's party had only received 42 per cent at the polls. Through bribery this outcome was converted to 58 per cent which assured the president of the necessary support for his government (Olano Alor, 2001). According to Landa Arroyo (2001), thirty-one members of Congress from various opposition parties either officially switched to Fujimori's party or turned 'independent' after the 2000 election. Those who converted to the government's side usually declared that they wanted to be active "for the country" rather than for a political party (Levitsky and Cameron, 2003: 19). Those *transfugas* who had joined the ranks of the 'independents' regularly voted "with the government" (Ibid). Other members of Congress were bribed as well but were asked to "remain in their ... political parties to act as informants" (McMillan and Zoido, 2004: 86–87; also see Jochamowitz, 2002a). The individual responsible for the operation which converted several dozen opposition party parliamentarians into supporters of the regime was Vladimiro Montesinos Torres, the informal head of Peruvian intelligence. As observed by Dargent (2005), "corruption did the political work of the regime: it brought about alliances and loyalties of officials ..., it bought opposition members, it rented the press" (2005: 398; also see Olano Alor, 2001; Jochamowitz, 2002a; Levitsky and Cameron, 2003; Salas López, 2005).

These practices served the purpose of weakening the opposition by reducing its ability to challenge the government or probe its activities. For example, in June 1995, Congress passed the amnesty law which allowed the perpetrators of the *La Cantuta* crime to go free (Obando, 1996; also see Burt, 1998). In August 1996, the Fujimori majority in the Congress approved the so-called Law of Authentic Interpretation. The law permitted the president to run for office for a third time even though the manoeuvre was illegal according to the

1993 Constitution. Subsequently, in May 1997, Congress sacked the three members of the Constitutional Tribunal who had maintained that the legislation was unlawful. The justification offered by Congress was that the panel had violated the constitution by issuing a ruling against the re-election law enacted in 1996. Thereafter, the Constitutional Tribunal's President, Ricardo Nugent, resigned in protest and the court was left in limbo because those who had departed or had been ejected were never replaced (Cameron, 1998; also see Burt, 1998; Teivainen, 2002). The law which made possible the second re-election bid of the president was also deemed unconstitutional by "a broad spectrum of independent political commentators and legal experts" (Schmidt, 2000: 120). When a coalition of citizen groups – in accordance with the 1993 Constitution – organized a petition with some 1.5 million signatures in 1998 calling for a referendum on the question of the president's second re-election bid, the official majority in "Congress voted the attempt down" (McSherry, 1998: 19). According to Jochamowitz (2002a), Montesinos bribed various members of Congress for their votes to prevent the referendum.

Also, the disclosure in late 1999 that up to a million fake signatures had been produced to register Fujimori's new party Perú 2000 for the upcoming election should have resulted in a serious inquiry. After all, it had been revealed that José Portillo, the person in charge of the *Oficina Nacional de Procesos Electorales* (ONPE), the electoral processing office, participated in the scheme with various pro-Fujimori members of Congress (Quiroz, 2008). However, the congressional investigation chaired by a member of Fujimori's party found no evidence of wrong-doing (Levitsky and Cameron, 2003). The institution in charge of organizing elections in Peru, the *Jurado Nacional de Elecciones* (JNE) was also controlled by pro-Fujimori forces and regularly came to the aid of the president defending him against accusations of electoral illegalities (Quiroz, 2008).[3]

3 The Oficina Nacional de Procesos Electorales (ONPE), the electoral processing office is the institution in charge of conducting and counting the vote. The Jurado Nacional de Elecciones (JNE) or National Election Board is the

In sum, the reduced ability of Congress to provide a check on presidential power proved to be detrimental to the democratic process during the Fujimori's years. Rather than hold the government accountable and to legislate, the Congress made it possible for the regime to govern "in an autocratic and discretionary manner, often disregarding constitutional norms" (Cameron, 2006: 279).

5. The Judiciary

The pre-1993 judicial system had evidently been corrupt and inept, largely caused by poor working conditions and low wages. This was used as a rationalization for reforming the judicial apparatus. Although the reorganization increased the efficiency of the justice system in some respects, it did not deal with fundamental issues such as judicial independence. The lack of autonomy on the part of judges due to "the interference of the executive branch in" selecting them continued to be a serious problem after the 1993 reorganization (De Eiden, 2006: 75).

After 1992 the government sacked many judges but rehired them in interim positions in order to better control the judicial apparatus. In turn, judges found themselves in insecure positions and were more likely to decide in favour of the regime. McClintock (1999) observed that in mid-1998 "some 40 per cent of judges including those on the Supreme Court were provisional" (1999: 85). Mauceri (1997) observed that "judges ... [were forced] to end their investigations or to offer inconclusive findings" in "cases of corruption" implicating the government (1997: 907). Montesinos placed his chums in positions in the court system to make certain that legal decisions would be "pronounced in his – and Fujimori's – personal interest" (García Calderon,

organization that oversees the overall fairness of elections and the conduct of those participating.

2001: 49; also see Levitsky, 1999; Levitsky and Cameron, 2003). This was evidenced in August 1996 when Peruvian drug trafficker *Vaticano* revealed his links to spy chief Vladimiro Montesinos, however, State Attorney Blanca Nélida Colán refused to allow further questionning and concealed the facts (*Caretas*, Aug. 22/96: 16–19; also see *Caretas*, Nov. 9/00: 18–20).

A system was created in which the corrupt received bonuses while those following the law were disciplined and accused of crimes they did not commit. For example, in early 1995, Judge Carmen Rojassi Pella vigorously investigated the links between a criminal organization called *Los Norteños* and high ranking members of the Peruvian military and police. In turn, Rojassi was herself accused of collusion with drug traffickers by the country's state attorney and resigned her position (*Oiga*, Feb. 6/95: 20–21).

The 1993 Constitution had created the *Consejo Nacional de la Magistratura* [National Council of Magistrates] which was to control the appointments of new judges. The formation of the *Defensoría del Pueblo* or Office of the Ombudsman was another measure which aimed to protect the judiciary's autonomy. The Constitutional Tribunal was also given more powers than before (De Eiden, 2006). These steps, however, amounted to little in practice. To begin with, the Office of the Ombudsman was extremely limited in its ability to function; for example, it was prevented from questioning military officers, or denied information on national security matters (*Oiga*, July 17/95a: 8–9). Also, the members of the National Council of Magistrates were not only named by the government, four of the seven appointees were not even required to have worked in the justice system or in a law practice which greatly facilitated the appointment of individuals loyal to the regime (Fernández Segado, 1994).

Selections to the Constitutional Tribunal were made in Congress which could also remove the judges again from this court. As noted, in 1997, the Fujimori controlled Congress dismissed three judges from the tribunal for having voted against the president's second re-election bid (Planas, 1999; also see Dammert, 2001; Teivainen, 2002). Already in 1995 the government had introduced law 26430 which was unconstitutional. The law removed the requirement "to effectively control or sanction the infringements that occur in the electoral process" (even though the Constitutional Tribunal and the National Election Board had been created for this purpose) (*Oiga*, Feb. 6/95a: 29). This allowed Fujimori to avoid sanctions during the 1995 presidential campaign for the violations he permitted, such as the use of public officials including members of the military who openly drummed up support for his re-election (Ibid; also see *Oiga*, Apr. 3/95: 5–10; Kay, 1996).

The most infamous interferences into the country's judicial system took place in the area of human rights violations. When the mounting evidence pointed to the involvement of the Grupo Colina in the murders at La Cantuta University, the military put a dozen officials on trial who, however, received light sentences. Also, only lower ranking individuals had been investigated. Those sentenced were not discharged from the military, did not receive cuts in pay or benefits, but spent their time in military barracks (Obando, 1996). As noted earlier, Peru's Congress subsequently introduced an amnesty law for all military officers involved (*Oiga*, June 19/95: 4–11; also see *Oiga*, June 26/95: 6–8; *Oiga*, July 24/95: 16–19; *Caretas*, Nov. 21/02: 12–14). Burt (1998) referred to the case of Judge Antonia Saquicuray who investigated the Barrios Altos massacre. In response, Peru's Congress introduced an additional decree to force the judiciary to "obey the amnesty law" (1998: 38; also see *Oiga*, Apr. 24/95: 13).

What's more, trials for alleged Sendero members were transferred to military courts without any civilian oversight. During the procedures, the defence lawyers were neither provided with the evidence nor permitted to cross-examine witnesses. Most trials were concluded within a few minutes, while these courts had a conviction rate of 97 percent (Gamarra, 1995; also see *Oiga*, May 1/95: 24–27).

According to Human Rights Watch (HRW) Fujimori acknowledged himself that many of those incarcerated were innocent. In 2002, some 2,500 individuals were still behind bars in Peru who had been sentenced under the antiterrorist laws (HRW, March 20/02; also see *Oiga*, July 24/95a: 27).

Another check on government usually comes from civil society. Peruvian civil society organizations had greatly increased during the 1970s and 1980s both in numbers and political participation, but these were often reduced if not dismantled during the Fujimori era (Roberts, 1996; also see Mauceri, 2006). Civil society generally influences public opinion, whether through news media or public dissent. During the 1990s, however, its organizations were "either repressed or co-opted into new governmental agencies" (Ibid, 58). Fujimori and Company worked to restrict civil society through various measures including bribery, "surveillance and intimidation ... [as well as] outright repression" (Burt, 2007: 162). The regime effectively undercut attempts to rebuild Peruvian democracy because the most important societal "actors ... remained debilitated and fragmented" (Ibid).

A manifest example has been the way the regime emasculated the labour movement. President Fujimori's free market reforms "eased dismissals, limited the right to strike, facilitated temporary contract labour, and encouraged competing unions in the same workplace" (Roberts, 1996: 81). Simultaneously, the emergency laws introduced to deal with Sendero made it possible to associate opposition to neoliberal reforms (or membership in human rights organizations) with terrorist activities. As noted by Burt (2006), the laws introduced after 1992 had the effect that persons who participated in rightful dissent were taken into custody and imprisoned by the "hundreds, if not thousands ..." (2006: 49; also see *Si*, May 18/92: 32, 83; *Sí*, May 25/92: 20; *Sí*, June 1/92: 38–40). In 1992, the Grupo Colina assassinated Pedro Huillca, the President of the *Confederación General de Trabajadores del Perú* [General Confederation of Workers of Peru] or CGTP who strongly opposed Fujimori's neoliberal reform program (CVRe, 2003; also see Burt, 2006).

Fujimori also reversed the decentralization that had been initiated with the 1979 Constitution. The 1993 Constitution made it possible for the president to pick the governors of Peru's provinces whose input was reduced "to supervising the implementation of the central government's programs" (Mauceri, 1997: 907). In late 1994, Peru's Congress approved a new tax law which reorganized municipal funding. The decree greatly diminished the access of municipal administrations to local taxes making them reliant on handouts from Lima. In turn, municipal administrators had to maintain good relations with the regime. The funding from Lima was largely channelled into those regions where support for Fujimori had been weak during the 1993 referendum in order to shore up support for the upcoming 1995 presidential election (Conaghan, 2005; also see *Oiga*, July 17/95: 8; *Oiga*, Aug. 4/95a: 16–17; Rotta Castillo, 2005).

Kay (1996) identified the use of "social development agencies, controlled by the executive branch, which bypass pre-existing institutions" such as Congress as one of the key factors contributing to the maintenance of the regime (1996: 74). The ministry of the presidency played a great role in this regard and its budget had "increased nine-fold between 1990 and 1995" (Mauceri, 1997: 906). Funding for social and infrastructure projects came directly from this ministry (Ibid). According to Rospigliosi (2001), spending by the presidential palace increased seventeen times from 1991 to 1992. Expenses were not only geared toward infrastructure projects but also intelligence-gathering and a growing personal staff. McClintock (1999) observed that in 1992 the ministry of the president controlled 3 per cent of the annual budget. This figure rose to 10 per cent in 1995 and 23 per cent in 1996. After the 1993 referendum on the constitution, the government – through the ministry – greatly boosted spending on the rural and urban poor by constructing schools and improving the transportation and public service infrastructure. According to Schmidt (2000), spending increased "by nearly 60 per cent in 1994 and another 90 per cent in 1995" (2000: 104). These projects were realized by sidestepping the usual channels, notably the institutions of regional and local government. In this manner, the president personally met with the poor on his excursions but he did not set up "institutionalized channels for representation or demand aggregation" (Ibid, 105). The government was thus in the position to provide funding directly to local and regional politicians who were loyal, or turn them down if they were not (McClintock, 1999; also see *Oiga*, May 29/95a: 11; Burt, 2006).[4]

6. Conclusion

In sum, the increased centralization of power in the hands of the executive as well as the elimination of most checks on that power created an opportunity structure whereby those at the top could carry out illegal activities without fear of being caught and punished. Based on the new 1993 Constitution, the regime contained all the trappings of an ostensibly functioning democracy such as political parties, parliament, or judiciary. Nevertheless, the constitution which was created under foreign pressure (and is still in force today) allowed for the creation of a facade democracy by providing all the outward appearances of a functioning democracy, while it simultaneously furthered and legitimized abuses of power. Tanaka (2002: 51–52) concluded that the "constitution was not exactly an instrument" of the regime, however, "one cannot deny that the constitution expressed the interests of the Fujimori majority" in Congress.

4 See Arias Quincot (1994) for a discussion of the changes Fujimori and Montesinos made to Peru's diplomatic corps.

Chapter 6

Consent by Corruption: The Imagocratic Dictatorship

How strangely will the tools of a tyrant pervert the plain meaning of words!
(John Adams)

1. Introduction

The scholarship on the relationship between the media and politics is extensive. According to Degregori (2001) this literature can roughly be divided into two categories. One perspective argues that the media has a negative impact on democracy and humanity in general. Protagonists of this view include the Frankfurt School's Herbert Marcuse, Neil Postman, and Giovanni Sartori.[1] Conversely, the likes of Mar-

1 Herbert Marcuse (1964) claimed that the mass media determined how individuals perceived the world. In short, the never-ending production of the mass media generates a false consciousness which is impervious to different interpretations of reality. This in turn negatively impacts people's willingness to bring about social change. Neil Postman (1985) has argued that the mass media is not able to convey essential concepts. Television has diminished the importance of the printed word where problematical issues can be communicated without condensing matters. Postman maintained that television jumbled important issues by degrading and impairing political discourse and twisting valid, multi-faceted problems into a form of entertainment. Giovanni Sartori (1998) contends that television is changing the essence of politics and democracy by personalizing political affairs, portraying politics as events, and influencing emotions. The Italian scholar denies that television is capable of conveying any real public opinion because the various media outlets themselves are responsible for creating the different currents of

shall McLuhan and Alvin Toffler argue for the positive or unifying aspects of the media. Both groups have been criticized; for example, the former for elitism and the latter for its underestimation of the unequal distribution of power (Ibid).

If there is one factor which makes Fujimori's authoritarian rule unique, it is the use and abuse of information and of the media in favour of the regime's interests. As observed earlier, Damnert (2001) maintained that the Fujimori regime was based on "imagocratic totalitarianism" (2001: 11). Jochamowitz (2002) described Fujimori's and Montesinos' use of television (TV) "as an instrument of crime" (2002: 226–227). Peruvian sociologist Arturo Manrique depicted the use of the media by the regime as "the administration of scandal" and as "a mechanism of social control" (as quoted in Arias Martinez, 2001). The manipulation of information not only enabled the regime to justify the introduction of various laws of a clearly dictatorial nature. Moreover, it allowed those in power to govern in a corrupt environment and to enjoy complete impunity. This was made possible on one hand by the repression and on the other by the silence and active collusion of the media.

According to López (2001) forms of corruption in the media include:

(1) The artificial creation of news to confuse or distract public opinion and evade important topics which merit to be brought to the attention of the public;
(2) Baseless campaigns to smear the image of an individual or a group associated with the opposition;
(3) The biased promotion of favoured candidates;
(4) The neglect of topics which would upset the sponsors (advertisers);

---

opinion which are then represented as the views of society. Television takes a certain reality and reduces it to the utmost. Messages are either trimmed down or they represent fabrications which have been manipulated in accordance with the beliefs of those in power and what they want to communicate.

(5) Activities that lead to monopolized control of the means of communication;
(6) The activities of journalists who do public relations work for the government;
(7) Government regulations and practices which compromise journalistic independence (Ibid).

The mechanisms employed by Fujimori and his advisor Montesinos to manipulate information and the media were numerous:

(1) Threats and violence against opposition media and journalists, as well as attacks against technical installations;
(2) Extensive Machiavellian campaigns of blackmail and defamation (ranging from the political to the sexual), orchestrated against the opposition press from within the government, the *Servicio de Inteligencia Nacional* (SIN) and ad agencies linked to the regime;
(3) Bribing most owners of Peruvian TV networks, such as *América Television* (Channel 4), *Panamericana Television* (Channel 5), *Andina de Radiodifusion* (Channel 9) and *Red Global* (Channel 13), in exchange for coverage favouring the regime;
(4) The use of state-funded political advertising in favour of the regime, especially the so-called *prensa chicha* or yellow press, which targeted opposition politicians with devastating effect;
(5) The confiscation of *Frecuencia Latina* (Channel 2), taken from owner Baruch Ivcher – because he had allowed critical reporting – and given to the minority share-holders who placed the network at the disposal of the government;
(6) The imposition of arbitrary and unfair taxes against the opposition media and its owners;
(7) The denial of free access to public information for media critical of the government, which, for example, was excluded from official state ceremonies;
(8) The exclusive use of the state-owned media, such as the daily *El Peruano*, which belong to all Peruvians in favour of the governing party (Conaghan, 1999; also see *Oiga*, Apr. 3/95a: 27–

30; Gargurevich, 2000; Tanaka, 2000; *Caretas*, May 26/00: 12–13; Lynch, 2002).

McClintock and Vallas (2005) observed that the military repressed the media during the actual coup on April 5th, 1992, by taking over most major dailies, weekly magazines as well as TV and radio stations while some two dozen journalists were taken into custody. However, the troops vacated the premises of media outlets after a few days and released those arrested. Still, during the 1995 Reunion of the *Sociedad Interamericana de Prensa*, the Interamerican Press Society, a report was issued on the situation of press freedoms in Peru which noted threats and violence against members of the press, and illegal detention and incarceration of journalists (Ibid). Fujimori often maintained the existence of the freedom of the press in Peru. However, other branches of the government, notably the military, behaved openly hostile toward the media "without receiving presidential disapproval" (Ibid, 259).

2. Media Control and Propaganda

As observed earlier, Grompone (2001) argued that the Fujimori regime did not constitute a hegemonic "pact of domination" in the Gramscian sense, rather it was based on "informal links" which were "constantly redefined" (2001: 109). This is reflected by the fact that Fujimori did not rely on the media for the presentation of "a hegemonic discourse which did not exist, but ... [for] the reproduction of his charisma and political survival" (Degregori, 2001: 113). Press freedom is generally viewed as an indicator of democracy, an impression the regime needed to advertise abroad (Fonseca, 2004). Thus the government found itself in a situation which was extremely conflicted as far as its media policy was concerned. To begin with, the media had the task of providing the president and the members of his government with a positive image despite activities like those of the Grupo Colina which contradicted this picture. In addition, the regime had to manage what was circulated to the public, without relying on open censorship and without creating the appearance that the media was being controlled (Burgos, 1997).

Boas (2005) dismisses "theories of political communication [which] suggest that television will benefit neo-populists", however, he identifies "biased coverage" as a key factor resulting in the 2000 electoral win by Fujimori (2005: 45). Indeed, the use of the media as a political weapon is one dimension that is shared with the propaganda machine of a totalitarian regime such as National Socialist Germany (1933–1945). According to Qualter (1962), both totalitarian and democratic societies make use of propaganda. The two differ because in a totalitarian society one encounters only the propaganda of the regime while democracies are characterized by "rival propagandas" of government and opposition parties (Ibid, 153). The author warns that "without the stimulating effects" of opposing types of propaganda, one may find oneself in a "closed society in which despotism flourishes" (Ibid).

One key distinction between the two regime types consists in the fact that the media of a totalitarian society is generally completely controlled by the government. Still, through corruption and intimidation the Fujimori regime achieved a degree of media control that was far-reaching, albeit not complete. More importantly, the methods used by Montesinos and the SIN to silence the opposition were reminiscent of the practices of Nazi propagandists who relied on a few simple rules:

(1) Simplification and focus on one enemy;
(2) Exaggeration and disfiguration;
(3) Orchestration;
(4) Transfusion;
(5) Unanimity and transmission (Domenach, 2005: 52–74).

The rule of simplification and the concentration on single enemies implies that attacks are to be undertaken not against specific social groups, but individuals or organizations within them. For example, Hitler did not attack the German working class but the Communists who formed part thereof (Ibid). Similarly, the propaganda apparatus of the Fujimori regime zoomed in on a number of key individuals or groups, for example, the traditional political parties associated with chaotic 1980s or the candidates running against the president in the 2000 election (Durand, 2005).

The rule of exaggeration and disfiguration refers to the methods employed when targeting the political enemy, namely the use of defamatory language and personal insults (Domenach, 2005). The Peruvian yellow press engaged in such practices by targeting opposition political candidates, particularly during the 2000 election campaign (Dammert, 2001).

The rule of orchestration pertains to the fact that in a totalitarian society all of the media would be engaged in certain themes as directed by those in charge of the regime's propaganda. Not only daily newspapers or weeklies but the radio stations and films would spout the same propaganda lines (Domenach, 2005). The control of the media in Peru was never as complete as in Nazi Germany because the opposition media, albeit persecuted, was able to play a role. Still, those parts of the media which were controlled by the state, or had been subverted, namely the government-owned *El Peruano*, the right-wing daily *Expreso*, the bulk of yellow press publications such *El Tío* or *La Yucca*, or 'converted' weekly journals like *Sí* or *Oiga*, and the majority of the Peruvian television stations were used in an orchestrated manner remindful of practices in Germany after 1933. The SIN used the Internet by creating a web page for an organization called APRODEV, the *Asociación Pro Defensa de la Verdad* [Association for the Defence of Truth]. The web page contained a black list of journalists and politicians who were denounced as "traitors, spies, and sexual deviants" (Bowen and Holligan, 2003: 367). APRODEV also copied the falsehoods produced by the yellow press. The themes of the anti-opposition press in Peru were created and directed by the propaganda unit of the SIN (Degregori, 20001).

The rule of transfusion refers to the ability of the propagandist to operate within a context with which the target audience can identify (Domenach, 2005). For example, in Nazi Germany the rulers would point to the perceived injustices of the Versailles treaty of 1919 which had brought hardships to the country. Likewise, the pro-regime media would often remind Peruvians of the economic misrule during the APRA government (1985–1990), or of the *Sendero* terrorism from which Fujimori had delivered the nation. Meanwhile, opposition leaders were depicted as if they desired a return to these conditions (Degregori, 2001).

The rule of unanimity and transmission refers to the intent of propaganda to artificially amplify the size of support given to a party or movement in order to convince an undecided individual to assume the same political views of these many others who allegedly have already been persuaded to support the regime. Included here is the use of known sports or film personalities (Domenach, 2005). In Peru, Héctor Chumpitaz, a former captain of the national soccer team, ran for the regime as a candidate in municipal elections – in return for a US$ 30.000 bribe (Quiroz, 2008). Talk show host Laura Bozzo openly supported the regime on her programs (Dammert, 2001). In addition, the government would arrange for protests against opposition politicians. Those participating, such as groups organizing social programs, were depicted as being representative of ideals with which all Peruvians could identify (Protzel, 1999; also see Degregori, 2001; Fowks, 2001).

3. Television

According to Boas (2005), television is not primarily a tool for an individual to get elected although it may help; rather it is more useful for the purpose of maintaining power. Still, Fujimori himself became a frontrunner in 1990 because of television. As previously observed,

Fujimori had directed a national TV show called *Concertando* on the state-owned Channel 8 (Daeschner, 1993). Moreover, Fujimori had initially intended to run for a seat in the Senate and he only declared himself to be a presidential candidate because by doing so his campaign would automatically receive free TV coverage. (Jochamowitz, 1994; also see Taylor, 2000). Boas (2005) observed:

> In particular television may be essential to neo-populists' style of governance once in office, even if it does not necessarily help them get there. The ability to communicate effectively and mobilize support for policies via television rather than intermediary organizations is a potentially important factor ... In contrast to traditional forms of intermediation, television is principally a one-way forum for communication – candidates can effectively present themselves to voters, but a disaggregated mass of voters cannot articulate demands to politicians via the television set (2005: 46).

The most effective ways the Fujimori regime combated its opponents was through the use of its own mass media apparatus. Luis Jaime Cisneros Hamann (1993) maintained that in the early 1970s the print media in Peru had been "politically more important than the [political] parties" (1993: 124). However, as observed by Dammert (2001), the number of households with televisions in Peru almost doubled to 3.5 million between 1985 and 1995. Conversely, the readership of the Lima dailies strongly declined (Ibid). During the 1990s the most important Peruvian daily, *El Comercio*, was read by "some 600,000 and the sensationalist *Ojo* ... [by] some 300,000" compared to a television audience of millions (McMillan and Zoido, 2004: 86). Conaghan (1999) observed similarly that the comparatively low circulation of reputable dailies and weeklies, such as *El Comercio*, *La República*, or *Caretas*, restricted their impact on public opinion. By the 1990s, the great majority of Peruvians, over 90 per cent, had access to a TV set at home. Television is the medium relied on by most to learn about political events (Ibid; also see Taylor, 2000; Boas, 2005).

Once elected Fujimori generally excluded critical journalists. As observed by Bowen and Holligan (2003), he assured his positive coverage by working with a number of reporters referred to as "geishas" who enjoyed special connections "to the government palace" and whose harmless queries aimed to boost the president's image while simultaneously shielding him from the more hostile members of the media (2003: 343).

Moreover, while the pro-government media received preferential treatment such as access to state publicity, the opposition media was subjected to higher taxes and other financial pressures. For example, the General Sales Tax for newspapers, which was either low or from which the press was exempted altogether in most of Latin America, had been increased to 18 per cent in Fujimori's Peru. The government also used fiscal audits to pressure newspaper and TV station owners (Marcus-Delgado and Tanaka, 2001; also see *Oiga*, Apr. 3/95: 27–30). Meanwhile, those media of communication loyal to the regime could count on tax forgiveness or additional income through advertising. Accordingly, spending on advertising rose by 52 per cent between 1997 and 1999. The government became the main disburser of TV ads replacing beer and soft drink companies. In return for positive news coverage for Fujimori the owners of TV channels also received favours from Montesinos to resolve judicial or debt problems (McMillan and Zoido, 2004; also see Lynch, 2002).

Moreover, the SIN under Montesinos came to control the majority of the Peruvian TV stations; largely as a result of corruption. The owners of Channel 2 or Frecuencia Latina, the brothers Samuel and Mendel Winter, in return for US$ 500.000, signed a contract in November 1999 which denied the opposition access to the station programs and commercials. The Winter brothers also agreed to join the daily meetings of the SIN to co-ordinate the coverage. Channel 4 was owned by José Francisco Crousillat, who was already close to the government, and received a payment of US$ 1.5 million. Ernesto Schutz, owner of Channel 5, obtained US$ 10 million. Schutz, although in favour of the regime, apparently convinced Montesinos that it would be advantageous if his channel would have some room for movement. He therefore invited opposition candidates onto his programs. Julio Vera Abad, proprietor of Channel 9, received US$ 50,000 to cancel the critical news program *Sin Censura*. The program's director, Cecilia Valenzuela, had caused problems for Montesinos with her dogged investigations. Similarly, critical journalist César Hildebrandt was taken off the air at Channel 13 after a deal between Montesinos and the owner Genaro Delgado Parker. Channel 10 had been bought outright by Montesinos in early 1999, while Channel 7 was already government-owned (Dammert, 2001; also see Bowen and Holligan, 2003; Quiroz, 2008).

The size of the bribes paid reveals the importance which Montesinos attached to the control of the television media. McMillan and Zoido (2004) observed that the combined bribes paid to the members of Congress came to "less than US$300,000 per month" while the monthly payments to judges amounted to a quarter of a million US dollars (Ibid, 82). However, the monthly price tag for buying off the television media "was more than US$ 3 million" (Ibid).

The importance of television as a medium of control becomes manifest in the Baruch Ivcher case. Ivcher, originally from Israel, was the majority owner of the TV net work Frecuencia Latina or Channel 2 and a supporter of the Fujimori government. Frecuencia Latina's coverage strongly favoured the armed forces. However, the character of the coverage began to change. In August 1996, the program *Contrapunto* showed explosive stories which pointed to links between Montesinos and the drug trade (Conaghan, 1999). On April 6th, 1997, Contrapunto brought an interview with Leonor La Rosa, the *Servicio de Inteligencia del Ejército* (SIE) agent who had been tortured by her own colleagues for allegedly revealing information to the press. A week later, on April 13th, Contrapunto reported on Montesinos' tax declaration. That day's program showed that the spy chief's income by far exceeded the remuneration a regular employee of the state would ordinarily receive. Worried about his personal safety Ivcher left Peru in mid-May 1997 for the United States, while the staff of Contrapunto aired a few more reports critical of the government. In July 1997, Contrapunto reported on the telephone surveillance conducted against opposition politicians and journalists by the regime during the presidential elections two years earlier. The program was finally shut down in September 1997 after the government had revoked Ivcher's

Peruvian citizenship which in turn deprived him of the right to own a TV station in that country. Channel 2 was taken over by the previously mentioned minority share holders Samuel and Mendel Winter who fully collaborated with the SIN. While Montesinos rejoiced at the time, he underestimated Ivcher's ability to do damage to the regime. From exile in Miami Ivcher continued his fight. He not only gained support from the international media, important politicians as well as the Jewish community in the United States, the case ended up before the Interamerican Court of Human Rights considerably damaging the regime's reputation. In December 2000, shortly after the downfall of the dictatorship, Ivcher regained control of Frecuencia Latina (Ibid; also see Conaghan, 2005; Dammert, 2001; Wiener, 2001; Bowen and Holligan, 2003; Vargas Haya, 2005).

César Hildebrandt, who worked for the television network Red Global, provides an additional example. Hildebrandt had already been one of Peru's leading television journalists during the 1980s (Rodrich, 1993). He had fled the country after the 1992 coup but returned to Peru and launched a critical news program called *La Clave* and subsequently ended up on Montesinos' hit list. In 1999, Hildebrandt was fired from Channel 13 by the network's owner Genaro Delgado Parker in return for Montesinos' assistance in his business dealings (Conaghan, 2005). Thereafter, Hildebrandt became the director of an outspoken daily newspaper, *Liberación*, until it was closed down in May 2000 due to financial pressures (Fowks, 2000). It re-appeared again for a few years after the fall of the regime.

The control of television did not merely involve shutting down news programs. According to Bowen and Holligan (2003) Montesinos also took into service "comedians" and "talk show hosts" (2003: 362). "Political satire" disappeared off the air waves only to be replaced "by asinine programs filled with sexual jokes" (Ibid).

In this context it is worthwhile to refer to the talk show *Laura en América* moderated by one Laura Bozzo, apparently an admirer of Montesinos. Laura en América was modelled after the *Jerry Springer Show* in the United States. Bozzo presented herself as a feminist and defender of women's rights. During the late 1990s her show had top ratings in Peru despite its generally vulgar themes. Dammert (2001) maintained that those in charge of the show did not have qualms about using falsified information or concoct stories and exhibit alleged victims who had been enticed with financial rewards. The show was taken off the air in neighbouring Chile in 2001 because "program participants ... [were] harmed in their dignity through humiliation ..." (Acevedo, 2001: 6; also see Vargas Gutiérrez, 1998).[2]

In addition, one of the Vladi-videos featured a conversation between Montesinos and the owner of channel 4, América Televisión, José Francisco Crousillat where the two were seen and heard discussing how Laura en América could contribute to Fujimori's re-election in 2000. Montesinos utilized Bozzo's show during the campaign in his attempt to dismantle the opposition candidates, while favouring Fujimori. In one of her shows Bozzo displayed the illegitimate daughter of opposition candidate Alejandro Toledo "urging people not to vote for a coward who did not recognize his own daughter" (Bowen and Holligan, 2003: 364). On another occasion, she presented an individual who claimed that Toledo had illicit financial dealings. Later investigations revealed that this person had been coerced to incriminate Toledo. In July 1999, Bozzo aired a show that gave the regime's account of the detention of a leading member of the Shining Path and praised Fujimori's and Montesinos' efforts to defeat terrorism (Ibid). Charged and sentenced to three years of house arrest after the collapse of the dictatorship, Bozzo claimed she never was a member of the regime although she admitted to being fully supportive of Fujimori's war on the Shining Path and to a certain infatuation with Montesinos (*Caretas*, Apr. 28/05: 30; also see *Caretas*, Apr. 19/07: 59). Still, according to a leading authority on Peruvian television, Fernando Vivas, Bozzo's program was "demagogic" while he observed a "symbiotic relationship between the populist discourse in Laura en

2 For example, one of Bozzo's shows which had the theme 'What would you do for money?' showed a woman from the audience lick the sweat of a man's armpit for ten US dollars (Bowen and Holligan, 2003).

América and the Fujimori regime" (Acevedo, 2001: 3; also see Protzel, 2001).

The relationship between the opposition press and the government worsened once the *La Cantuta* case was being investigated. The disappearance of nine students and a university professor in July of 1992 had aroused little attention until it was revealed a year later that these individuals had been 'disappeared' by the death squad Grupo Colina (Conaghan, 1999). The journalists involved in the investigation received death threats while the newspapers they worked for were subjected to "commercial pressures" (Ibid, 261). In the fall of 1996 a television station belonging to Red Global which aired *La Clave*, a program directed by César Hildebrandt, was bombed. The individuals arrested by police were identified by General Robles as members of the Grupo Colina death squad (Ibid; also see *Caretas*, Nov. 28/96: 12–16). Also, as noted previously, members of the SIN murdered one agent of the SIE, Mariela Barreto, and tortured another, Leonor La Rosa, for allegedly revealing various schemes (*Plan Bermuda*, *Plan Narval*) for the repression of the media to the opposition press. In April 1997, the two investigative reporters working for *La República* who covered the case of the SIE agents were assaulted. Blanca Rosales, *La República's* news director, was kidnapped for a short time in July of 1997 (Conaghan, 1999). The above-mentioned schemes served the purpose of harassing and silencing the left wing congressman and *La República* director Gustavo Mohme Llona as well as members of the daily's investigative unit, notably Edmundo Cruz, Miguel Gutiérrez, Francisco ('Paco') Mattos, and Angel Páez (Conaghan, 2005).[3]

3 'Paco' Mattos, whom I have known for many years, is generally not mentioned in this context. Mattos was a member of *La República's* investigative unit for most of the time that Fujimori was in power, and he paid dearly for his dedication. He was unable to maintain a daily routine. Mattos would not own a car out of fear that the SIN might install a bomb. He would only travel by taxi, but he would not get into a cab at the same spot twice. Travelling home from work Mattos would never choose a taxi near his office at *La República* in downtown Lima but walk around a few minutes before randomly selecting one. Mattos was

4. The Prensa Chicha

The word *chicha* derives from the Quechua word for maize. The term is identified with Peruvian mass culture and the growing presence of indigenous Andean people in the capital of Lima since the 1950s who have created their own subculture. The term chicha is also used in a derogative fashion to refer to something of bad taste or low quality (Cappellini, 2004). In contrast to the information media, the prensa chicha is generally sensationalist and "characterized especially by its vulgar exploitation of the female gender, hurtful ... attacks on public persons, the elderly, the handicapped ..." (Ibid, 34; also see Palomino, 2001).

The origins of the prensa chicha can be traced back to the 1950s, however, this brand of journalism did not become popular until the 1980s. Degregori (2001) noted that various prensa chicha publications had existed in Peru prior to the arrival of Alberto Fujimori, while a good many others were created only after 1992. Most of the publications whose owners had signed up with Montesinos for the 2000 election had been established between 1998 and 1999 (2001). For the election Montesinos had 'rented' the services of the prensa chicha in the sense that fifteen of the seventeen Lima tabloids were writing in favour of the government (Bowen and Holligan, 2003). Tabloid chain owner Augusto Bresani admitted in court during his trial years later that he had "arrived at a lucrative contract with Montesinos to put his ... [dailies] at the service" of Fujimori's 2000 re-election campaign (Ibid, 365–366). Apparently, the headlines were faxed directly from the SIN offices to the various dailies who would receive up to US$ 3000 for each (Ibid; also see Macassi Lavander, 2002; Youngers, 2003). Or as described by Degregori (2001), the prensa chicha was

arrested by the SIN in the early 1990s and 'interrogated'. Mattos' family received numerous death threats, a fact that contributed to the breakdown of his marriage and to his bad health.

used for the purpose of obliterating the "democratic competition" (2001: 141).

One important characteristic of prensa chicha publications is their low purchasing price. Dailies like *El Chino*, *El Tío*, *La Chuchi*, *La Yucca*, or *Referendúm*, sold for fifty Peruvian centavos or roughly six US cents. Meanwhile, the country's more reputable dailies like *El Comercio* cost two Nuevos Soles which is over fifty US cents (Gargurevich, 2000). New technologies have made production considerably cheaper. Not only can the actual plant area be reduced significantly, the handling of the technologies does not require the best trained personnel. Newspapers can hire very young people just out of the universities who are willing to work for less and who want to gain job experience (Ibid). This kind of press serves a double function; it is to be bought and read while its headlines, often displayed at a kiosk, are to be viewed by those passing by. Indeed, during the 2000 election campaign many of the headlines on the cover pages of prensa chicha publications had no corresponding articles (Macassi Lavander, 2002).

According to Poole and Rénique (2003) Montesinos had set up a division for "psychological operations" within the SIN which were closely linked to the activities of the prensa chicha (2003: 158). SIN agents working in the division were referred to as

> psychosocial operatives [who] ... spread rumours ... through such tactics as fabricating stories ... Oppositional figures, public celebrities, popular leaders, business men, and even high officials in the armed forces were blackmailed into supporting the government through rigged tapes and recordings (Ibid).[4]

Some of the most vicious attacks by the prensa chicha were directed against Gustavo Mohme Llona, a congressional representative from

---

4 The SIN agents not only published slanderous accounts about opposition politicians but also planted preposterous reports such as stories about the image of Virgin Mary which shed genuine tears, or about the alleged materialization of Jesus Christ, or about a horrific beast which terrorized people in lower class neighbourhoods (Bowen and Holligan, 2003).

the opposition party UPP, the *Union por el Perú*, and director of the daily *La República*, as well as the journalists from that newspaper's unit of investigation. Mohme was described as a traitor and a Communist who received funds from North Korea. The attacks on his person by far exceeded what can be described as good taste. The articles were full of references to Mohme's alleged homosexuality and detailed descriptions of his amorous relations to leaders of the left (Fowks, 2000; also see Degregori, 2001). Existing circumstantial evidence also suggests that Mohme was in fact murdered by the regime in April 2000 (Molina Sanhueza, 2002).

Publications like *El Chino* or *El Tío* published slanderous articles characterizing journalists associated with the opposition as alcoholics, traitors, or terrorists. For example, a member of *La República* special investigation unit, Angel Páez, was "accused of treason for reporting on arms purchases" by the regime (Conaghan, 1999: 269). The nature of the operation against Páez made manifest the participation of the military and the SIN, which was denied by prensa chicha directors. However, a member of the *El Tío* staff supplied documentation to *La República* which revealed that a military official authored the yarns on Páez (Ibid). Regardless, Páez regularly received death threats and became accustomed to a life without identifiable routines, often spending the night at different locations (Bowen and Holligan, 2003). It was a common belief among opposition journalists that the SIN was spying on them (Conaghan, 1999). As noted by Bowen and Holligan, "SIN agents ... convert themselves into journalists and journalists turn SIN agents" (Ibid, 342).

What made the allegations of the prensa chicha more credible was the orchestration of falsified news involving some of Peru's respectable media which would spout similar headlines, such as the right wing daily *Expreso* which has a largely middle-class readership. *Expreso* owner Eduardo Calmell Del Solar regularly defended the regime against critics who claimed that Peru's media was not free (Conaghan, 2005). Jaime de Althaus (1993), the paper's editorial chief not only came out in favour of the April 5 *autogolpe*, he argued that activities such as General Rodolfo Robles' denunciation of the murders of the Grupo Colina were indicative of the anti-civilian attitude of a small minority of officers who were unhappy with the military's reduced role in society. He wrote:

> A sector [of the military] ... is not resigned to lose power which [in the past] gave it total control over the political [domain] ... The fact that today the designation of the commander in chief ... is the responsibility of the President of the Republic and not of the ... armed forces is the pit that some cannot ... swallow (1993: 30).[5]

The means used by the regime were not limited to slander in the prensa chicha. McMillan and Zoido (2004) also observed that Montesinos relied on blackmail, for example, by obtaining video footage of individuals engaged in "sexual indiscretions" and utilized the evidence for his purposes (2004: 84). Those targeted were generally unable to protect their reputations, among other, because the courts did little to defend them (Degregori, 2001).

5. The Media during the 2000 Election Campaign

The regime had already relied on the prensa chicha during the election of 1995. Schmidt (2000) noted that presidential contender Alejandro Toledo was smeared after he had reached double digits in the polls. Accordingly, stories were "allegedly planted by the SIN" in the yellow press claiming that Toledo was linked to a notorious financial swindler, and that he had embellished his university education (2000: 108). Although these claims were questionable Toledo's support declined again (Ibid, 109). Regarding the 2000 presidential election, Degregori (2001) observed that opposition candidates were tarnished in various ways. For example, they were depicted as

5 Jaime de Althaus and fellow journalist Manuel D'Ornellas eventually departed from *Expreso* in protest of Fujimori's 2000 re-election project (Conaghan, 2005).

(1) Associates of former President Alan García, architect of the country's collapse in the late 1980s;
(2) Incompetent and dishonest;
(3) Insensitive to the needs of poor;
(4) Favouring political violence and terrorism (Ibid).

Degregori also points to the "feminization of ... [opposition politicians]" (Ibid, 161). Thus, opposition leaders were "given ... characteristics which the traditional ... [Latin American male] attributes to females" (Ibid). The opposition's presidential candidates were invariably depicted as fragile, spineless, lacking confidence, nervous, unstable, childish, and emotionally disturbed.

The television coverage of the 2000 election campaign strongly favoured the president. Thus, most of the coverage was on Fujimori who received between some 80–90 per cent of air time. If an opposition candidate's air time increased than often because he received negative coverage (Boas, 2005). According to a study comparing the coverage of the four leading candidates by América Television (Channel 4) during the last 90 days of the 2000 campaign "100 per cent of the air time for each of the opposition candidates was labelled negative coverage, while 97 per cent of the coverage of Fujimori was positive and 3 per cent was neutral" (Ibid, 36). The study came to similar conclusions about the other three leading Peruvian television networks (Ibid). According to the final report of the National Democratic Institute (NDI)/Carter Centre on the 2000 elections the candidates of the opposition were either prevented from buying ads altogether or were asked to pay exorbitant "rates ... for access ... on Peru's most widely watched ... television channels" (NDI, 2000:16). The report also pointed out that the coverage of opposition candidates was "openly biased and hostile", while the articles in the "prensa chicha ... escalated to the level of character assassination" (Ibid, 17; also see Tanaka, 2000; Cappellini, 2004).

The use of the press as a weapon was clearly effective during the first phase of the election campaign when the regime managed to demolish Luis Castañeda Lossio and Alberto Manuel Andrade Carmona. In December 1998, Fujimori was in third place with 12.8 per cent in the polls, behind Andrade and Castañeda. Had the election taken place in April 1999, Andrade would have received over 55 per cent of the vote compared to just 28 per cent for Fujimori. Fujimori would also have lost to Castañeda. Due to the malicious attacks the support for Andrade had fallen to 9 per cent by March 2000. Meanwhile Castañeda, who in September 1999 still had an approval rating of 26 per cent, was down to 5 per cent by March of the following year. On the day of the presidential vote, April 9, 2000, Andrade and Castañeda received 2.8 and 1.7 per cent respectively (Peñaflor, 1999; also see Tanaka, 2000; Marcus-Delgado and Tanaka, 2001; Bowen and Holligan, 2003).

The non-governmental organization (NGO) *Civil Transparencia* analysed the headlines of six prensa chicha dailies (*El Chato*, *El Chino*, *El Mañana*, *El Diario Más*, *El Men*, *El Tío*) and the depictions of the opposition candidates Andrade, Castañeda, and Toledo, as well President Fujimori for the period between January 11 and March 10, 2000. Andrade, the initial front-runner against Fujimori, was portrayed as being emotionally disturbed, a violent agitator and pro-Sendero, and a bourgeois who was unaware of the needs of the poor. He was also made fun of because of his overweight. Meanwhile, the name of his political party *Somos Peru* which translates as 'We are Peru', was referred to in the prensa chicha with names like *Somos Desastre* [We are a disaster] or *Somos Historia* [We are History], or *Somos Basura* [We are Garbage]. Castañeda was likewise accused of insensitivity toward the less fortunate and depicted as emotionally disturbed, having dubious sources of income, maintaining links to Alan García, and being gay (Gargurevich, 2000; also see Arias Martínez, 2001; Carrión, 2001).

According to a poll taken in March 2000, over 50 per cent of those questioned felt that Andrade stood for the rich and was disrespectful of others. Likewise, some 35 per cent of respondents had come to believe that Castañeda had been involved in some illicit financial scheme and was soft on terrorism (Degregori, 2001). Conversely, President Fujimori was seen as somebody who gave to the needy, initiated important public works, and strongly opposed terrorism. During the early phase of the 2000 campaign Toledo profited from the fact that Montesinos' press machine was directed against the front runners Andrade and Castañeda both of whom were dismantled by the vicious attacks. His rating increased from 6 per cent in October 1999 to 37 per cent in April 2000 (Ibid; also see Tanaka, 2001). However, once Toledo had emerged as a serious contender he became the main target of the prensa chicha and other media controlled by the government (Garguevich, 2000). The key themes in the attacks on him included:

(1) Participation in a pyramid scheme set up by the *Centro Latino-Americano Empresarial* (CLAE) where the then presidential contender was able to rescue a large part of his investments, while many ordinary Peruvians lost all of theirs;
(2) Unfounded claims that Toledo maintained a friendly relationship with Alan García, who was deemed responsible for the economic misery of the late 1980s and early 90s;
(3) Toledo's denial of his illegitimate daughter;
(4) Allegations that Toledo wanted to cut popular government-assisted social programs such as public kitchens for the poor (*Comedores Populares*) or the Glass-of Milk (*Vaso de Leche*) project for children;
(5) Claims which linked Toledo to terrorist movements such as Sendero Luminoso (Degregori, 2001; also see Cappellini, 2004).

The accusations made against Alejandro Toledo in the prensa chicha grew more preposterous after the first round of presidential elections once he had emerged as Fujimori's main challenger. What added to their effectiveness was the fact that some of the allegations were indeed true, while others were simply lies or complete distortions. For example, Toledo did have potentially dubious dealings with CLAE, as well as an illegitimate daughter whom he had not recognized at that time. Conversely, accusations that he received orders from former President García, wanted to end popular social programs, or maintained links to terrorism, were absurd. Toledo was damaged less because of a certain wear-off effect given the similarities with the attacks on Andrade and Castañeda. For example, the latter was discredited in November 1999 by claims that he had links to terrorists and members of APRA and engaged in dubious financial dealings. In May 2000, before the second round of the presidential poll, the prensa chicha made identical claims about Toledo (Degregori, 2001).

6. Conclusion

Montesinos and the SIN controlled the majority of Peru's media, but not all of it. Ultimately, it was the media which delivered the blow that would topple the regime when *Canal N* – owned by the daily *El Comercio* – aired the video that showed the SIN chief bribe a member of Congress, Alex Kouri, for switching to Fujimori's faction. Ironically, Montesinos had dismissed the significance of Canal N which was only available to a few thousand individuals with access to cable television (Jochamowitz, 2002a). Still, as noted by Durand (2004), of the Peruvian business elites who collaborated with the regime, the owners of the media were the most tainted by corruption.

Chapter 7

Conservative Catholicism, Human Rights and Democracy: Sad Tales from Peru

The surest way to corrupt a youth is to instruct him [or her] to hold in higher esteem those who think alike than those who think differently.
(Friedrich Nietzsche)

1. Introduction

One of the least explored chapters of the Fujimori dictatorship is the support the regime received from the Catholic Church. It is the argument here that conservative sectors of the Church, notably from the order *Opus Dei* (OD), provided the regime with much needed backing and legitimacy. However, the influence of such conservative Catholic orders is not limited to Peru but has been growing in much of Latin America and Europe. Similar groups are the *Legionarios de Christo* [Legionnaires of Christ] in Mexico, *Sodalitium Christianae Vitae* [Company of Christian Life] from Peru, *Ciudad de Dios* [City of God] in Nicaragua, or *Comunione e Liberazione* [Communion and Liberation] which stems from Italy. This development is a direct outcome of policy shifts effectively resulting in a rollback of the reform process initiated by the Second Vatican Council (1963–1965). These turnabouts, introduced since 1978 by the late Pope John Paul II and continued by his successor Benedict XVI, have resulted in a loss of influence by the moderate and progressive forces within the Vatican, notably the Jesuit order and other organizations who identified with concepts such as Liberation theology or the decentralization of the

Church. Opus Dei – often described as secretive – was the object of unwanted media attention generated by the 2006 Hollywood film *The Da Vinci Code*. In the movie, which merged fact and fiction, the order was depicted as a menacing lot whose leadership formed a camarilla within the Church, and whose most fanatical members used flagellation and were willing to commit murder for their superiors. Before addressing the role played by proponents of Opus Dei during the Fujimori years, it is important to shed some light on the history of this particular organization as well as its adverse relationship with the progressive forces in the Church (Della Cava, 1993; also see Sosa, 2000; Houtart, 2005; Straßner, 2007).

2. The Origins and Organization of Opus Dei

Opus Dei is Latin for the 'work of God.' It is an ultraconservative Catholic order established in 1928 by Spanish priest José María Escrivá de Balaguer (1902–1975) (Moyano, 2002). It was the founder's original goal to combine the spiritual and professional dimensions of religious men. Instead of becoming monks who joined a monastery Escrivá de Balaguer believed that individuals with a secular as well as a religious calling ought to be allowed to practice both. His answer was Opus Dei, an order whose members gave vows of poverty, sexual abstinence and obedience, while working in society and handing their earnings over to the organization. A female division was set up in 1930 (*Time Magazine*, March 18/57; also see De Blaye, 1976; Lernoux, 1990; Walsh, 1989).

Opus Dei remained largely a Spanish affair until the end of the Second World War. Today, the order is present in over 50 countries, and has an estimated membership of about 80,000 worldwide. Some 35,000 of these reside in Spain, although the order is also strongly represented in Latin America. The book by OD founder Escrivá de Balaguer, titled *El Camino* [The Way or The Road], originally published in 1939, has been translated into thirty-eight languages (Walsh, 1989; also see Escrivá de Balaguer, 1963; Allen, 2005; Bauernfeind, 2006). The order's rise to power within the Catholic Church began after the 1978 election of Pope John Paul II who elevated Opus Dei to the category of a personal prelature, which in Vatican terms gives it special status. The organization is directly responsible to the pope and its operations are not under the jurisdiction of local bishops, and like any other religious order of the Church it can ordain its own priests (Ibid; also see Patriau, *Liberación*, Sept. 13/00: 13).

Opus Dei is organized as follows: On top one finds the Prelate or President General who resides in Rome. According to Dehan (1994), there are several categories within Opus Dei: Numeraries, Supernumeraries, Associates, Co-operators and Candidates. The Numeraries form the core of the organization and represent about 20 per cent of the total membership. They usually live in group residences run by Opus Dei and have taken vows of "chastity, poverty, and obedience" (Ibid; also see De Blaye, 1976; Sosa, 2000; Allen, 2005). The Numeraries are themselves divided into five sub-groups: Electors, Inscribes, Ordinaries, Servants, and Oblates. The first two are involved in running the organization, while the other three are engaged in more menial tasks. Allegedly they have written last wills which make the order the recipient of their earthly belongings after death (Ibid). According to the Opus Dei Awareness Network (ODAN), Numeraries not only take a vow of celibacy and generally live in residences run by Opus Dei, but also hand over most of their earnings to the order, render incoming and outgoing mail to their superiors, and carry out various kinds of physical mortification. This implies among other the use of the *cilice*, a spiked string attached around the thigh, and of the *discipline*, which is a belt with knots designed for strapping oneself (ODAN, 2002).[1]

Numerary priests become members of the order as lay people, but are later selected by Opus Dei higher-ups to become ordained. These

1 Physical mortification is practised by only a minority of some 30 per cent of OD members; mostly the Numeraries who have pledged celibacy (Allen, 2005).

priests hold the top administrative positions not only within Opus Dei, but increasingly within the Vatican itself given the rising prominence of the order since the late 1970s. Each OD residence is allotted such a Numerary priest. His duties include the holding of religious services, doing confessionals and giving religious guidance to the members. Numerary assistants are women who pledge chastity and are in charge of upkeep and cleaning at the order's residences. According to Rich and de los Reyes (2005), the general employment of female OD members for "lowly domestic duties ... [has] become controversial" (2005: 95).

The Supernumeraries may get married and live with their kin but must comply with the teachings of the Church on matters such as faithfulness in marriage or sexual intercourse. They observe the same rules as the Numeraries and also contribute large parts of their income to the order (ODAN, 2002; also see Allen, 2005). OD Associates likewise make a vow of celibacy, however in general they do not live in the order's residences. Associates often do not have the same middle or upper class upbringing and education as the Numeraries. They include those who must remain with their families for personal reasons. OD Co-operators render financial support to the order, but are not reckoned full members. The Co-operators take no vows, but participate in the activities of the order, and are not even required to be Catholic (Sosa, 2000; also see *Time Magazine*, March 18/57; ODAN, 2002; Allen, 2005).

The last are the Candidates, usually young people of both sexes who come from middle or upper middle class families. Recruitment often takes place on university and college campuses, or social clubs frequented by the young. Those attracted are invited for activities like "seminars, excursions, spiritual retreats ... [depending on] age and gender" (Ibid, 68–69). According to Lernoux's (1990) investigations, the order itself claims to have a presence at over four-hundred universities and higher educational institutes on five continents, although predominantly in Spain and Latin America. In addition, in many countries OD members engage in pedagogical and social work for the young in primary and secondary, technical, and trade schools (Ibid; also see Walsh, 1989; Bauernfeind, 2006).

Those who initially participate in events co-ordinated by Opus Dei are often unaware that the activities are organized and take place in locations owned by the order. In some countries, Opus Dei has been officially or unofficially included in the list of dangerous cults and sects because of its focus on the young and its methods of recruitment and indoctrination (Sosa, 2000). In 1997, the Belgian Parliament had voted to include the order among a list of organizations considered dangerous sects. Opus Dei's actual inclusion was prevented, however, by protests from Belgian bishops. In the United States various groups have been formed to warn the young about Opus Dei. One of these is the previously mentioned Opus Dei Awareness Network or ODAN. It was established in 1991 by a former member with the goal to inform about the danger the order poses to adolescents. ODAN publishes a newsletter on OD activities. In Catalonia, Spain, the non-governmental organization (NGO) AIS likewise provides information to parents. According to an AIS spokesperson, the organization received "daily requests for help against Opus Dei's indoctrination of minors" (Ibid, 69–70; also see Moyano, 2002). Lernoux (1990) observed that in 1981 the English Cardinal Basil Hume had decreed that it was not legal for Opus Dei to recruit youngsters "under the age of eighteen or without consultation with his or her parents" (1990: 304; also see Sosa, 2000). Officially, internal guidelines prescribed a minimum recruiting age of fifteen years which was raised to seventeen in 1982. However, according to a former member, Opus Dei allegedly has tried to enlist children as young as eight or ten (Ibid).

3. Opus Dei, Secrecy, and Affinity to Authoritarian Regimes

Those aspiring to join Opus Dei have to give a declaration of loyalty. According to Rich and de los Reyes (1997; 2005), would-be members provide an oath of obedience which apparently does not merely include the requirement to be discreet but the obligation to maintain the utmost confidentiality about the order's affairs (1997; 2005: 97). Lernoux (1990) noted that OD founder Escrivá de Balaguer had a "mania for secrecy" which he considered essential for operating in Spanish society because it was strongly anticlerical" (1990: 304). Finding converts would be better left to "lay people who did not identify themselves with ... a religious organization" (Ibid). However, what started out as a useful practice in Spain turned into a project of concealment. As observed by Rich and de los Reyes (1997), Opus Dei's failure to disclose its ties "with a number of organizations which were entirely controlled by it" contributed to its bad reputation in some quarters.

This tendency has also invited comparisons with the Freemasons and other secret societies (Lernoux, 1990; also see Allen, 2005; Rich and de los Reyes, 2005). Tefft (1992) defines a secret society as an organization with "a set of well-defined norms, secret rituals and oaths ... [etc.,] that are intended to subjectively bind members to the secrecy required by the group's affairs" (1992: 1). Such associations can be revolutionary, nationalistic, religious, occult, criminal, etc., and should be considered a universal phenomenon, which will, however, manifest itself differently depending on time and place. Historically, secret societies use forms of communications, membership rules, initiation rites and/or other ceremonies which serve to distinguish members from the rest of society as well as to conceal their activities (Heckethorn, 1966; also see Daraul, 1969; MacKenzie, 1971). These traits are also observed in Opus Dei.

Serious scholars have largely ignored secret societies as an area of research, leaving the field to conspiracy theorists. As Roberts (1972) indicates:

> [T]he charlatan, the axe-grinder and the paranoiac long had the field to themselves ... The result has been the mountain of rubbish ... which explains everything from the collapse of the Roman Empire to the Russian Revolution in terms of secret societies (1972: 10–11).

Still, it is important to analyse the degree to which such groups are indeed involved in political decision-making behind the scenes in order to assess their true impact.[2] As noted by Mann (1986), secret societies share a number of traits with the state. These groups may protect the interests of elites or counter elites. Moreover,

> [they] employ the same power strategies ... to neutralize opposition, guard against repression or destruction, and to maintain internal discipline. State power strategies are merely centralized versions of power found in secret society organizations or other social structures (1986: 172).

Mann's observation is significant in light of the fact that Opus Dei emerged in Spain during the Franco dictatorship where it came to play a prominent role in government. Moreover, the order has been identified as a frequent ally of right wing authoritarian and/or military regimes in Latin America. In Franco's Spain, aside from the Fascist *Falange* party and the military, a conservative Catholic Church hierarchy, represented to a large extent by members of Opus Dei, was the third pillar of the regime. Generalissimo Franco put most trust into those of his own kind while his reliance on the other two fluctuated with time and international events. For example, between 1938 and 1951, the military received key posts in government, generally a third of ministerial positions available, including defence and interior. Conversely, while military officers had also been strongly present in administrative positions in industry and commerce, their influence was reduced by the late 1940s, although never completely relinquished. Initially members of the Falange played a more prominent role in the regime following the Nationalists' victory in the Spanish Civil war in 1939. However, their influence waned after the 1945 defeat of Franco's Axis allies Nazi Germany and Fascist Italy, while that of the Church and Opus Dei in particular rose. Between 1938 and 1945 Falange members had held over 30 per cent of ministerial posts, a figure which declined to some 23 per cent by 1951. Conversely, Opus Dei went up from 11 per cent of

2 After all, according to sociologist Georg Simmel (1906), "the folly which treats the unknown as the non-existent, and the anxious imaginativeness which inflates the unknown at once into gigantic dangers and horrors, are wont to take turns in guiding human actions" (1906: 497).

ministerial positions in 1938 to 17.2 per cent by 1951. By 1969, twelve of the nineteen ministers of the regime were supplied by Opus Dei (Sánchez Jiménez, 1991; also see *Time Magazine*, March 18/57; Payne, 1987; Walsh, 1989; Patriau, *Liberación*, Sept. 13/00: 13; Fusi, 2001).

The large OD presence in the Spanish government caused some unease in the US State Department which resulted in a study prepared for President Nixon in 1969 (Martín de Pozuelo, 2007). While Opus Dei professed to simply apply Christian values in daily life, the Catholic order in fact co-operated with the dictatorship. Moreover, the US investigators found a strong OD presence within Spanish power circles. Not only did Opus Dei have control over the Banco Popular, one of the most important banks of the country, the report also concluded that the order likely had "strong interests in, if not actual control over two other prominent banks" (Ibid). The report also claimed that an estimated "40 per cent of faculty positions at Spanish universities were occupied by members of Opus Dei" (Ibid). Moreover, with the blessing of the regime, Opus Dei established its own university in the city of Navarre (*Time Magazine*, March 18/57). Fusi (2001) observed that during the 1950s conservative Catholicism in Spain "achieved an intellectual hegemony" which had not been in existence for a century (2001: 139).

OD members as well as those from similar Catholic organizations in Franco's Spain shared a common view, namely an "elitist vision of politics and politicians" based on a "new aristocracy of knowledge" instead of birthright (Sánchez Jiménez, 1991: 284). This group generally had a university background in "philosophy, military studies, political science and journalism" and was strongly represented in the regime's bureaucracy, particularly in the civil administration occupying posts like "state attorneys, university professors, lawyers, notaries" and civil servants (Ibid, 284–285). Spanish researcher Martín de Pozuelo (2007) observed that OD members "were commonly known as 'the technocrats' ... whom Franco moved into [positions of] government" (2007: 252). Allegedly, the OD offices were for some time located in the building of Spain's interior ministry (Patriau, *Liberación*, Sept. 13/00: 12–13).[3]

The extent of Opus Dei's financial empire came to light following criminal investigations by the Spanish state after two major financial scandals in 1969 and 1983 respectively involving corporations and financial institutions owned or controlled by individuals linked to the order. It became clear that OD members had come to operate a "transnational network of ... financial institutes such as the Banco Popular" in Spain, but were also present in countries like Argentina, Peru, Hong Kong and Singapore (Walsh, 1989: 78; also see Fusi, 2001). The order allegedly also owns or controls newspapers, magazines, radio and television stations, news and ad agencies, as well as film production studios in Spain and abroad (Corbière, 2007; also see Lernoux, 1990; Bauernfeind, 2006). It would be misleading, however, to point to an active conspiracy. Rather, as noted by Walsh (1989), OD control implies that individuals who are known members own or run these companies or financial institutes. What is more, it is important to distinguish between the role of members who own or run banks or companies, and the power wielded by Opus Dei within the Vatican itself which according to some has been exaggerated, while others claim it to be considerable (Lernoux, 1990; also see Allen, 2005; Boberski, Bruckmoser, and Pfeifer, 2008).

Opus Dei has historically been involved with Latin American elites and the unsavoury regimes created and maintained by them. For example, the order arrived in Guatemala in 1953, where only a year later the Central Intelligence Agency (CIA) engineered a successful coup against President Arbenz who had planned agrarian reforms that would have taken away land from large estate owners and the US company United Fruit, now called Chiquita. Most OD members belonged "to the richest and most conservative families" of the country (Cardenal, 1990: 217). Levenson (2003) even alleged links between Guatemalan Fascists, death squads and Opus Dei. The order

3 Payne (1987) observed that the "ministers of economics ... [were] colloquially known as the Opus ministers" (1987: 475).

was also a strong supporter of the Pinochet military regime in Chile. Thus members of the Chilean branch had already begun organizing against the small-scale land reforms introduced by the conservative government of Eduardo Frei in the early 1960s. Following the 1970 election victory of Salvador Allende, the organization came to oppose the far more extensive agrarian reforms planned by the left wing government. Opus Dei supported the 1973 coup by General Augusto Pinochet and provided the regime with a number of important officials. OD members served in similar functions in the military governments of Argentina and Uruguay (Smith, 1982; also see Walsh, 1989; Lernoux, 1990; Moyano, 2007).[4] According to Corbière (2007), Opus Dei also played a role in the short-lived government of Pedro Carmona during the failed coup of 2002 against President Hugo Chavéz in Venezuela. Members of the order had worded the decree which abolished the 2000 Constitution that had been approved in a referendum by a large majority of the Venezuelan population.

Cavero-G. (1973) included Opus Dei in his list of so-called "neo-integrist movements" that emerged in response to the reforms of the Second Vatican Council. Indeed, the author wrote rather prophetically in an article published only weeks prior to the military coup in Chile of September 11, 1973 that such groups

> aim to present a pleasing image because their true face ... of elitism, of Fascism and Colonialism is too distorted to be attractive ... [Groups like Opus Dei are a form] of political camouflage and ... [gentle] oppression ... [They are] the new Mafias which operate under the ... [banner] of an integral Catholicism (1973: 10).

---

4 Shortly, after the 1973 coup, OD founder José María Escrivá Balaguer visited Chile. While he made no mention of the human rights violations committed by the military government in his homilies, he consistently denounced left wing priests accusing them of disloyalty to the Church (Sosa, 2000). Likewise, when Pope John Paul II visited Chile in 1987, he had nothing to say about the abuses of the regime. In contrast, the pope was publically critical about Castro's Socialism when visiting Cuba (Navarro, *Counterpunch*, Apr. 8/05). In Germany in 1985, Opus Dei successfully prevented the publication of a book which alleged that OD associates co-operated with death squads in Chile during the dictatorship (Walsh, 1989).

Integralism refers to a conservative movement within the Church of the late nineteenth century opposed to the 'heresies' of the modern age such as Darwinian evolutionary theory, Liberal Democracy, Socialism or trade unionism. Instead, integralists favoured a social order where State and Church were closely linked. The related concept of Integrism pertains to the "aim of bringing all aspects of a nation within a single political organization" (Hansen, 2006). Corbière (2007) uses these terms interchangeably and refers to a conservative Catholic movement that emerged in the late nineteenth and early twentieth century as the Church was attempting to deal with the challenges of modernity, industrialization and the like. So-called integral Catholics viewed their faith as the "response to all questions of private and public life" (2007: 23). Mallimaci (1995) observed that the integralist forces of the Church were opposed to Liberalism, Socialism, or trade unions, while being "highly tolerant of ... Fascism ..., Nationalism, anti-Semitism, or military dictatorships" (1995: 168). Adherents of Integralism were also opposed to liberal culture with its "secularism, laicism, permissiveness, hedonism, [and] consumerism" (Ibid, 171).[5] The following observations by Frankfurt School scholar Theodor Adorno (1964) are pertinent here:

> While religion has been deprived of the intrinsic claim of truth, it has been gradually transformed into 'social cement'. The more this cement is needed for the maintenance of the status quo and the more dubious its inherent truth becomes, the more obstinately is its authority upheld and the more its hostile, destructive and negative features come to the fore (1964: 730).

---

5 The renowned Swiss Church scholar Hans Urs von Baltasar (1905–1988), considered to be one of the leading theologians of the twentieth century, already warned of the dangers posed by Integralism and Opus Dei during the 1960s. In an article written for the *Neue Zürcher Zeitung* on November 23, 1963, he described Integralism as an unquestioning conformism which "constitutes the worst sort of perversion of the Gospel, for it leads to theocracy" (De Blaye, 1976: 438). Moreover, he considered Opus Dei to be "the most typical representative of modern integralism" (Ibid). Later on, he retracted his statements (Messori, 1997).

4. Opus Dei and Liberation Theology: The Cold War within the Catholic Church

The reforms of the Second Vatican Council (1963–1965) towards a more open Church had initially given credence to the ideas behind Liberation theology. In the aftermath of the council the Latin American bishops came to hold several reunions. The second one, held in 1968 at Medellín, Colombia, can be regarded as the official launch of Liberation theology as the majority of participants backed a 'preferential option for the poor' on behalf of Latin America's Catholic Church (Della Cava, 1993; also see McGovern, 1993; Daudelin and Hewitt, 1995; Comblin, 2003). Peru is also one of its birth places, among other things because several key works which defined the so-called Church of the Poor have been written by the priest and former theology professor at the Pontifical Catholic University of Lima, Father Gustavo Gutiérrez Merino. He is considered one of the co-founders of the movement. According to Gutiérrez (1973), Liberation theology is a position which has as its core the defence of the underprivileged. The priest meets God by interacting with those who have been exploited and abandoned by a society based on inequality (Ibid). The "Church and the Christian" should not merely have a "caritative paternalistic vision" but one that identifies the causes of the problems (Sosa, 2000: 86). While Liberation theology emerged in the 1960s, its origins date back further in the sense that the Second Vatican Council gave an official voice to groups within the Church that had already existed since the 1940s and 50s (McGovern, 1993; also see Pottenger, 1989).

Liberation theology, according to Leonardo and Clodovis Boff (1986), incorporates three levels of analysis: The "socio-analytical" one aims to investigate "why the oppressed are oppressed" (1986: 24). The second level, the "hermeneutical" analysis, includes among other things the reading of biblical texts (e.g., the book Exodus) which are more meaningful in the context of oppression as experienced in Latin America. This dimension, or what the Boff brothers style "liberative hermeneutics", aims to examine "what is God's plan for the poor"

(Ibid). The third level focuses on finding ways "to overcome oppression in accordance with God's plan" (Ibid; also see Petrella, 2004).

Liberation theology does contain elements of Marxist thought. According to Pottenger (1989), its adherents have borrowed from Antonio Gramsci as well as Erich Fromm and Herbert Marcuse (Also see Powers, 2003). Liberation theologians also accepted insights from Dependency as well as World System theory, most importantly the notion that developed nations fared well at the expense of underdeveloped ones (Petrella, 2004). To Gutiérrez Liberation theology implies

(1) "Socio-political-economic liberation from poverty, oppression and dependency;
(2) Liberation in history of all dimensions of human freedom, with humans becoming responsible for their own destiny and living in solidarity;
(3) Liberation from sin which is the ultimate root of injustice" (McGovern, 1993: 10).

According to the Boff brothers, the utilisation of Marxism is purely instrumental as it contributes to understanding why the poor are poor. Hence, "Marx (like any other Marxist) can be a companion on the way ... but he can never be the guide," because the Church has "only one teacher, the Christ" (Boff and Boff, 1986: 28). While Marxist influence cannot be discounted, Liberation theologians differentiate between theory and practice. In other words, while a Marxist-inspired analysis may be useful in describing social reality, it is not viewed as a practical solution to societal problems. To a Liberation theologian the notion of class struggle depicts an existing social reality in Latin America, not a program of action. According to McGovern (1993), "Liberation theology ... criticizes too many aspects of Marxism to consider it a guiding force of analysis" (1993: 230; also see Fleet, 1983).[6]

---

6 Even the most radical of Liberation theologians I came across in the literature did not openly advocate violence, even against repressive rule, except in self-defence against a dictatorship seen as sinful. Bonpane (1985), in recognition of the fact that the necessary "changes are not winnable at the ballot box" encouraged non-violent

Ayacucho journalist Magno Sosa, author of a book on Opus Dei in Peru, argues that the rise of the order in Latin America in general and Peru in particular was part of a campaign by an increasingly conservative Vatican to counteract the influence of progressive Church leaders and ideas associated with the 'Church of the Poor'. Indeed, the reforms at the Second Vatican Council were anathema to Opus Dei because of the order's links to "power ... [and] wealth" (Sosa, 2000: 72). Likewise, US scholar Coletta Youngers (2003) noted that the conservative leanings of the Church in Peru and elsewhere had increased during the papacy of John Paul II. While Opus Dei had been present in Peru since the 1950s, the order's breakthrough came about in the late 1980s. Youngers specifically identified the papal visit of May 1988 as the time when the shift occurred. During his stay Pope John Paul II came out strongly against Liberation theology. Following the papal visit conservative members of the clergy came to control Peru's Episcopal Commission, the Church's highest organ representing all of that country's Catholic bishops.

In Peru, as noted by Arias Quincot (1994), "many opinion leaders of conservative Catholicism" believed that the "real cause" for the existence of subversive groups like *Sendero Luminoso* or the *Movimiento Revolucionario Tupac Amaru* (MRTA) was not the social reality its inhabitants experienced, but "the penetration by Marxist mentality" of the country's "schools, universities, unions, the mass media, etc.," (1994: 90). In turn, "concepts like 'class struggle' or 'revolutionary violence' came to be viewed as normal" (Ibid). Thus, "to defeat armed subversion ... it was necessary to defeat ... the Marxist form of thinking" (Ibid).

These revisions were introduced since the papacy of John Paul II in 1979 and signalled the Vatican's intent to return to the traditional model of authority as well as the views and practices which had been

responses, including strikes, boycotts and civil disobedience (1985: 49, 111). It is noteworthy that one of most famous members of the Colombian left wing rebel group *Ejército de Liberación Nacional* (ELN) was the priest and professor of sociology Camillo Torres, killed in 1966. His decision to become a guerrilla has been – and remains – controversial (Gott, 1970; also see Meschkat, Rohde, and Töpper, 1983; Della Cava, 1993).

predominant prior to the Second Vatican Council. The rollback of reforms reflected the desire of conservative Church leaders who felt that the council had gone too far. Even so, it likewise implied a return to positions displayed during the 1930s and 40s for which the Church had been severely criticised, such as the rather ambiguous roles played by the official Churches of Nazi Germany and Fascist Italy (Lernoux, 1990; also see Klaiber, 1992; Lewy, 2000; Bauernfeind, 2006).

The Church's Congregation of the Doctrine of the Faith – formerly known as the Office of the Inquisition – which was headed by the then Cardinal Joseph Ratzinger who later became Pope Benedict XVI – moved against proponents of Liberation theology by the early 1980s. The new official line of the Church became apparent in 1983 when John Paul II admonished the Nicaraguan priest Ernesto Cardenal for serving as minister of culture in the left wing *Sandinista* government. In 1984, leading Brazilian Liberation theologian Leonardo Boff was ordered to Rome to face the guardians of the doctrine where it was decreed that he be silenced for a year. A year later, the Vatican officially sanctioned the Franciscan Boff for supporting choices which jeopardized the Christian belief. Boff has since left the clergy (Peters, 1988; also see Kraul and Chu, *The Seattle Times*, Apr. 11/05; De Benito, *El País*, March 13/07: 41; Fisher, *The New York Times,* May 4/07; Rohter, *The New York Times*, May 7/07).

In 1985, Brazilian archbishop Helder Camara, also known as the 'Red Bishop', was replaced by a conservative and many of his projects were dismantled. Camara – who passed away in 1999 – was the author of the 1971 book *Spiral of Violence* which discussed the links between structural injustice, rebellion, and repression by the state. The following statement has been attributed to Camara: "When I give food to the poor they call me a saint. When I ask why the poor have no food, they call me a Communist" (Kraul and Chu, *The Seattle Times*, Apr. 11/05; also see Camara, 1971; McGovern, 2001).

In March 2007, another leading Liberation theologian, Spanish-born Jesuit Jon Sobrino, who lived in El Salvador since 1957, became one of the most recent individuals sanctioned. Sobrino had worked with Archbishop Oscar Romero of San Salvador, who was assassinated by a death squad during a church service in 1980. Ironically, deputations from the Vatican had come to see Romero on two occasions prior to his murder requiring the archbishop to justify his criticism of the country's military which had already killed some two dozen clergy members. After the assassination, Pope John Paul II appointed a conservative as Romero's successor. The present Archbishop of San Salvador, Monsignor Fernando Sáenz Lacalle, is a member of Opus Dei. Sobrino has been prohibited from teaching at the Centro-American University in San Salvador, or any other Catholic institution because his theological works are no longer deemed in agreement with Church doctrine (Kraul and Chu, *The Seattle Times*, Apr. 11/05). Gustavo Gutiérrez too lost his post at the Pontifical Catholic University of Peru in Lima and left for France where he entered the Dominican order. Gutiérrez is also frequently in the United States to give seminars and lectures on Liberation theology (*La República*, March 4/01: 38–39; also see Rohter, *The New York Times*, May 8/05).

The Vatican's new line was also applied elsewhere. In the Philippines Pope John Paul II came out against Cardinal Jaime Sin who supported the nonviolent opposition led by Corazon Aquino against the Marcos dictatorship in 1986. However, the pope did not chastise Archbishop Bruno Torpigliano who had publically endorsed the Marcos family. Similarly, in 1987, the Vatican criticised the South African Catholic bishops engaged in the struggle against the apartheid regime telling them to "stay out of politics" (Lernoux, 1990: 48–49).

5. Opus Dei in Peru: Tales from Monsignor Juan Luis Cipriani Thorne, the Good Shepherd

Members of Opus Dei likewise provided crucial support to the Fujimori regime. Peruvian researcher César Arias Quincot observed that the first contacts between the country's entrepreneurs, many of whom belonged to the order, and Fujimori came about following the latter's rebirth as a free market proponent in August 1990. During the elections which he had won in the previous month, Fujimori had campaigned against the very tough economic policies which he subsequently implemented (Arias Quincot, 1994). Furthermore, lawyers linked to "conservative Catholic thinking" were involved in creating many of the laws issued following the April 5, 1992 *autogolpe*. Quincot noted that the links to "Opus Dei lent [Fujimori's] authoritarian project ... ideological coherence and ... [the] ... capacity to transmit its ideas through what we can call 'the common sense of the conservative Peruvian'" (Ibid). As previously noted, he concluded that individuals linked to Conservative Catholic groups not only supported the 1992 autogolpe but "in the [subsequent] constitutional debate ... [they] played a role [that was] little less than decisive" (Ibid). The prominent Peruvian scholar Francisco Durand (2004) claimed likewise that Opus Dei was one of the pillars of the dictatorship (Also see Rochabrun, 1996).

One of the most important as well as controversial figures who provided support to the regime has been the former Bishop of Ayacucho and present Archbishop of Lima and Cardinal of Peru, Monsignor Juan Luis Cipriani Thorne, who is a member of Opus Dei. Peruvian writer and 1990 presidential candidate Mario Vargas Llosa referred to him as "an open and unashamed accomplice of the Fujimori dictatorship" (*Expreso*, Dec. 31/00: 3). Xavier Barrón, a member of the neoliberal *Unidad Nacional* (UN) party asked that "Rome should remove Cipriani from his position" at the head of Peru's Church because of the cardinal's "very controversial personality" and his inability to live up to the "ecclesiastical responsibility" that the office demanded (*Perú 21*, Apr. 17/03: 4). Even if Cipriani was not directly involved in acts of corruption or crime, his support and that of Opus Dei lent legitimacy to an increasingly reprehensible regime.

Cipriani's appointment to cardinal was the first time an OD member was elevated to such a lofty post within the Catholic Church hierarchy. Cipriani is no friend of Liberation theology which he has called "an ideology" that puts "social work" above all else and which politicises priests (Allen, 2005: 289). Shortly after his designation, the new cardinal initiated the removal of Father Jorge García from Peru.

The priest, a practitioner of Liberation theology, had written about human rights abuse in a Church publication (*Liberación*, Sept. 4/00: 12–13; also see Villasís, *Liberación*, Sept. 5/00: 6).

Cipriani was bishop of Ayacucho, the city which is the birthplace of the Shining Path where its leader, Abimael Guzmán, had once taught at the local university of Huamanga. Cipriani had initially supported Peruvian novelist Vargas Llosa in his 1990 presidential bid, and even sent letters to the priests in his diocese asking them to announce to the flock not to vote for a makeshift candidate supported by born-again Christian groups, namely Alberto Fujimori. However, the relationship improved when the eventual election winner Fujimori made a major donation to help with the restoration of Ayacucho churches after which Cipriani became an ardent supporter of the regime which in turn provided for his security. In 1988, as auxiliary bishop of Ayacucho, Cipriani would walk the streets without guards. However, when he moved about the city in 1997 as bishop, Cipriani was "surrounded by ten to fifteen police officers and ... [his residence] was one of the best guarded locations of Ayacucho" (*La República*, Apr. 3/00: n. a; also see *La República*, July 7/00: 16).

After the discovery of the authors of the massacres of *La Cantuta* and *Barrios Altos*, namely the military death squad *Grupo Colina* commanded by Major Santiago Martín Rivas, Cipriani came to the defence of the regime. In April 1994, in reference to the massacres, Cipriani told a local paper:

> In a violent context ... the deaths, disappearances and abuses are part ... of war. The defenders of human rights call it dirty war. I believe that the armed forces had to use these tools to find out how and where things happened. And when they used these instruments, naturally there were deaths (Fraser, *National Catholic Reporter*, March 23/01; also see *Liberación*, Aug. 29/02: 3).

Moreover, the then bishop of Ayacucho defended the 1995 amnesty law which pardoned the perpetrators of the atrocities of La Cantuta and Barrios Altos (*Liberación*, March 5/01: 3). In the following year, Cipriani came to the aid of the regime's No. 2, Vladimiro Montesinos, who had been accused of involvement with drug traffickers, including the previously mentioned *Vaticano*. The bishop blamed the anti-Fujimori media for fabricating facts and argued in favour of censorship (*Gestión*, Aug. 26/96: 7; also see *La República*, Aug. 27/96: 2–3; *El Comercio*, Aug. 28/96; *Expreso*, Aug. 31/96). Today there is little doubt that the now imprisoned Montesinos was deeply involved in the cocaine trade.

In November 1998, Bishop Cipriani told a delegation from the Interamerican Commission of Human Rights – an organism which is associated with the Organization of American States (OAS) – that no rights were being violated in Peru. He accused various NGOs of creating the impression that such breaches took place, while they ignored the deplorable acts committed by Sendero rebels. A day later, the then Archbishop of Lima, Cardinal Augusto Vargas Alzamora, a conservative Jesuit but also a strong critic of the regime's human rights record and Cipriani's superior, dismissed these claims. Alzamora insisted that the delegation was welcome to investigate because doing so represented an important step towards cleansing the justice system. The cardinal also observed that he "constantly received complaints from people" who felt unsafe (*La República*, Nov. 10/98: 2; also see *La República*, Nov. 11/98: 4). In March 1999, Cipriani attacked the US Senate for having produced a study that demonstrated alleged human rights abuse in Peru. By his own admission, the bishop never examined the document claiming that because of his "love" for Peru he had more important things to do (*El Peruano*, March 14/99: A3). According to a poll taken at the time over 60 per cent of Peruvians disagreed and welcomed the US study in the hope it would improve the human rights situation in their country (McClintock and Vallas, 2005).

A year later, during the first round of the 2000 presidential elections, Cipriani assailed critical reports by the National Democratic Centre and the Carter Centre, NGOs which had come to observe the fairness of the electoral process (*El Peruano*, Feb. 13/00: 3). In mid-March of 2000, Cipriani maintained that the ballot in Peru was "fair and transparent" while the reports by local and foreign election observers were flawed because of their "ignorance" of the "electoral system" (*El Peruano*, March 18/00: 5). Conversely, at the end of March

2000, Cardinal Alzamora called on the authorities to ensure the transparency of the electoral process (*El Peruano*, March 31/00: 5).

The first round of the presidential ballot took place on April 5th, 2000, and turned out to be a fraudulent affair of massive proportions (Taylor, 2000). During the political crisis that followed Cipriani attempted to prevent the Church from playing a mediator role between the government and the opposition, although he failed in this (*El Peruano*, Apr. 17/00: 5; also see *El Peruano*, Apr. 23/00: 5; *El Peruano*, Apr. 26/00: 4; *El Peruano*, Apr. 27/00: 4; *La República*, Apr. 28/00: 2). On September 23rd, 2000 – shortly after the showing of the explosive video which depicted spy chief Montesinos bribing an opposition member of Congress – Cipriani still maintained that President Fujimori's continuation in office as leader of an interim government was the best guarantee for a calm transition until new elections could be held (*Expreso*, Sept. 24/00: 6). A few days earlier, Cipriani had defended the president while blaming Montesinos' machinations for all the regime's negative aspects (*Liberación*, Sept. 18/00: 7).

Following the Fujimori government's demise, interim President Valentin Panaguia set up the *Comisión de la Verdad y Reconciliación* or Truth and Reconciliation Commission – composed of Peruvians of known integrity – to study the violence that had gripped the country between 1980 and 2000. It was revealed in the commission's final report, released in August 2003, that the number of killings committed by members of Sendero Luminoso slightly exceeded those by the security forces. Peru thus differs from other Latin American societies that have experienced or still undergo civil conflict. For example, in neighbouring Colombia, the abuses and extralegal killings by the military and its paramilitary allies by far outstrip those of the rebels. Also, in Peru, most of the victims were indigenous peoples. The military was still deemed responsible for almost 50 per cent of all killings estimated to be at 69,000. Yet while Cardinal Cipriani often referred to the outrages committed by the Maoist guerrilla, he consistently downplayed those perpetrated by Peruvian security forces (Sosa, 2000; also see *Gestión*, Aug. 26/96: 7; *Caretas*, March 1/01: 44–45, 52).[7]

In its final report, the commission specifically commented on Cipriani concluding that he not only "never questioned the human rights violations which the ... [security] forces committed" but denied consistently that such abuses even took place (Allen, 2005: 287).[8] The report explicitly identified three Peruvian departments where Church leaders took no position in regards to human rights violations by security forces, and consequently did nothing to prevent them, namely Apurímac, Ayacucho, and Huancavelica. These departments, however, all had bishops associated with Opus Dei. As observed by Carlos Tapia, another member of the commission, the populations of these departments "felt abandoned by the ... Church" (*Gestión*, Sept.13/03;

---

7 Shortly after the successful completion of Operation 'Chavin de Huantar' which put an end to the 1996–1997 MRTA hostage crisis, rumours emerged that Bishop Cipriani, as mediator, had clandestinely introduced microphones hidden in bibles and crucifixes into the residence of the Japanese ambassador. This allowed the security forces to locate the rebels during the operation. These allegations were vehemently denied both by the regime as well as the bishop (*La República*, Apr. 29/97: 3; also see *Tiempos del Mundo*, May 8/97: n. a.). Cipriani's image also suffered after a 1990 video surfaced which showed the then Bishop of Ayacucho addressing army officers where he used a manner of speech best described as "coarse" (Jara, *La República*, Jan. 26/01: n. a.; also see Tamariz, *El Peruano*, Sept. 6/02: n. a.). On another occasion Cipriani had described the concept of human rights with the term "cojudez" which roughly translates as 'bullshit' (Allen, 2005: 288; also see Sosa, 2000; Patriau, *Liberación*, Sept. 13/00: 12–13; *La República*, March 4/01: 38).

8 Salomón Lerner Febres, the ex-President of the Peruvian Truth and Reconciliation Commission, pointed out in an interview: "One cannot understand how the cardinal who was the pastor of Ayacucho wants to deny the violence that took place in this department. One cannot grasp how he, [being involved with] the political and military authorities of the time, did not say anything to condemn the abuses they committed" (Castillo, *La República*, July 29/06: 25). Lerner maintained furthermore that the commandment 'Thou shall not kill' went beyond championing "life at the moment of conception" (Ibid). When Cipriani failed to "defend life ... [as] pastor of Ayacucho, the cardinal ... sinned by omission" (Ibid; also see Sosa, 2000).

also see Castillo, *La República*, July 29/06: 25; *Perú 21*, July 31/06: 6). Youngers (2003) also concluded that "the changes inside the ... Church had negative effects for the human rights" situation in Peru (2003: 188–189). As a result the Church was less of a champion of human rights during the Fujimori era than it could have been.[9] Not surprisingly, Cipriani has been one of the most fervent critics of the Truth and Reconciliation Commission.

The cardinal's name has also come up on various occasions during testimonies given to judicial sub-commissions investigating those involved with the regime. The conservative cleric himself has been called to testify about his knowledge of the criminal activities of the Fujimori government. Among other things, Cipriani was asked about the massacres of Barrios Altos and La Cantuta as well as the alleged assassination of his predecessor, the popular Archbishop of Lima and Cardinal of Peru, Augusto Vargas Alzamora in April 2000 (*Liberación*, Aug. 29/02: 3; also see *La República*, Aug. 29/02: 9; *El Popular*, Aug. 30/02: 3; *El Peruano*, Aug. 31/02: 4; *Perú 21*, Sept. 16/02: 5; *El Comercio*, Apr. 5/04: A10). When Cipriani was requested to appear in front of a sub-commission because his name had come up during the interrogation of former Prime Minister Alberto Bustamante Belaunde, Peru's highest cleric reacted strongly. Not only did the cardinal deny having met Bustamante or possessing any knowledge of the atrocities, Cipriani asserted that such claims were part of a conspiracy against the Church. The allegation that the cardinal's interrogation represented an attack on the Church was refuted by Bishop Luis Bambaren, then President of Peru's Episcopal Commission (*Perú 21*, Aug. 31/02: 3; also see *El Popular*, Aug. 31/02: 3; *La República*, Sept. 7/02: 8).

---

9 OD practices during the Fujimori dictatorship (and similar regimes) are nevertheless in line with the teachings of the order's founder, which can be read in the work *El Camino*. Those who are distressed by oppression and inequity of the world around, Escrivá de Balaguer comforts with maxim 702 which reads: "You are worried. Listen: happen what may in your interior life or in the world that surrounds you, never forget that the importance of events or of people is very relative" (Walsh, 1989: 141; also see Escrivá de Balaguer, 1963).

Cipriani faced strong criticism from APRODEH, Peru's leading human rights NGO whose director general at the time, Eduardo Caceres Valdivia, expressed his surprise that the cardinal, in response to being asked to appear as a witness claimed to be the target of a conspiracy (*Perú 21*, Aug. 31/02: 4; also see *Liberación*, March 5/01: 3). As noted by Caceres, some Church officials, such as the late Cardinal Alzamora, had criticised the government's abuses. Furthermore, "public opinion believes in the version that involves ... [Cipriani] with the crimes of La Cantuta, for one simple reason ... [He] was silent for ten years" (Ibid). Another human rights NGO, IDELE, the Institute for Legal Defence, judged likewise (Ibid). Respected Catholic Church scholar John L. Allen (2005) wrote that Cipriani was commonly seen as a backer of the ex-president "whose ... anti-terrorist campaign broke ... the Shining Path but whose undemocratic and corrupt administration ended in disgrace" (2005: 288).

Indeed, Cipriani has refused to distance himself from Fujimori, instead blaming Montesinos for all the regime's ills while he regularly comes to the support of associates of the former president (Ibid). For example, in late August 2002, the cardinal intervened in the judicial process by proposing the formation of a commission to deal with cases of individuals who had worked for the Fujimori regime but were only accused of minor offences, such as Héctor Chumpitaz, the ex-captain of Peru's national soccer team. A day later, Bishop Bambaren, the President of the Peruvian Episcopal Commission, stated that Cipriani had only expressed a "personal opinion" while he asked the cardinal to refrain from further interventions into judicial matters (*La República*, Aug. 26/02: 3). Those critical of the cardinal felt that given his own involvement with the dictatorship he lacked the "moral authority" to speak up for those wrapped up with the former regime, while others accused him of furthering "impunity" (Ibid; also see *Correo*, Aug. 26/02: n. a.; *Liberación*, Aug. 27/02: 3; *El Comercio*, Aug. 27/02: A2).

While Cipriani, now Archbishop of Lima and Cardinal of Peru, had little to say about the abuses committed by the regime, he pronounced himself on numerous occasions on a variety of topics like abortion, birth control, economic policy, education, or gay marriage.

Indeed, the cardinal has been consistently criticised for overstepping his pastoral boundaries and meddling in politics by his fellow bishops and others alike. In turn, Cipriani has denied charges that he uses the pulpit for political purposes but maintains that "he is the voice of Christ so that the believers can recognize His teaching" while those opposed to the cardinal's views want to "silence the Church" (*Perú 21*, June 26/04: 14; also see *Perú 21*, June 29/04: 14; *Correo*, July 21/04: n. a.; *Expreso*, July 21/04: 7; *El Comercio*, July 25/04: A2; *Correo*, July 25/04: 11; *Expreso*, July 2/05: 3; *Ojo*, May 21/06: 12).

Still, for a cleric who denies being political, the cardinal has made numerous statements on a wide range of topics which are not necessarily related to his position as an official of the Church:

(1) Cipriani has repeatedly called for the inclusion of a religion course in universities as part of the curriculum for those acquiring a bachelor degree (*El Peruano*, Aug. 22/99: 4; also see *El Peruano*, Feb. 23/00: 6).

(2) In early May 2000, Cipriani pronounced himself on the young people as many university students participated in the growing protests against the Fujimori regime. Accordingly, he counselled them to dedicate themselves to study and sports in "an environment of respect for discipline and order because rebellion ... [made] no sense" (*El Peruano*, May 5/00: 6).

(3) Cipriani has regularly attacked the introduction of contraceptive methods like the day-after-pill which is not in accordance with Church doctrine. However, as bishop of Ayacucho he did little when hundreds of thousands of mostly indigenous Peruvian women were illegally sterilized without their knowledge and consent by the regime (Sosa, 2000; also see Vasquez del Aguila, 2006; *La República*, March 4/01: 36–39; *Gestión*, Nov. 20/02: 3; *La República*, Dec. 13/02: n. a.; *El Comercio*, December 19/02: n. a.; *Perú 21*, Oct. 18/04: 14; *La República*, Nov. 2/04: n. a.).

(4) The cardinal has expressed criticism of human rights organizations on countless occasions during the dictatorship and since its fall. Since 2001, he has made numerous unfavourable remarks about the Truth and Reconciliation Commission set up to explore

the years of conflict between 1980 and 2000 (*El Peruano*, March 14/99: 3; also see *El Peruano*, Feb.13/00: 3; *El Peruano*, March 18/00: 5; Allen, 2005).

(5) Cardinal Cipriani described Peruvian society under the democratic government of Alejandro Toledo as corrupt on a number of occasions. In December 2004, he caused a major uproar when he referred to Peru and its government as a "big garbage dump" although he retracted his accusations a few days later (*Perú 21*, July 17/04: 5; also see *Gestión*, Dec. 21/04: 3; *Correo*, Dec. 22/04: 3). While these observations were probably not off the mark, he had little to say about such practices during the Fujimori regime when corruption was far worse.

(6) In July 2002, Cardinal Cipriani decreed that opposition to privatization and the free market was an attitude of "arrogance and ignorance" (*Gestión*, July 1/02: 3; also see *El Peruano*, July 1/02: n. a.).

(7) During the 2006 election campaign the cardinal came out strongly against left wing populist politician Ollanta Humala, the "anti-system candidate" seen by many as Peru's Hugo Chavez (*Expreso*, Apr. 2/06: n. a. ; *El Popular*, Apr. 2/06: n. a.).

6. Conclusion

Opus Dei has made inroads all over Latin America due to nominations made by the late John Paul II. Thus early in the new millennium, in addition to the seven bishops in Peru, there were four in Chile, two in Ecuador and one each in Argentina, Brazil, Colombia and Venezuela, who had been linked to Opus Dei. The Archbishop of San Salvador, El Salvador, Monsignor Fernando Sáenz Lacalle, appointed in 1995, who removed Liberation theologian Jon Sobrino from his university post, has been considered a radical even by Opus Dei standards (Kraul and Chu, *The Seattle Times*, Apr. 11/05). The number of ultraconservatives in the highest offices of the Peruvian Catholic Church has increased as well. According to Straßner (2007), of the forty-nine members of the Peruvian Episcopal Conference, eleven bishops belonged to Opus Dei. In addition, two bishops were members of *Sodalitium Christianae Vitae*, another order often described as Peru's version of Opus Dei. Sodalitium Christianae Vitae was founded in 1974 by the Peruvian priest Luis Fernando Figari to counter the influence of Liberation theology (Peña, 1992).

Following the collapse of the Soviet bloc Opus Dei also established a presence in Eastern Europe, especially Poland.[10] In 2005, the Polish coalition of the Party of Law and Justice, the agrarian Self-Defence Party, and the League of Polish Families, won the election. The President and Prime Minister, the twins Lech and Jaroslav Kaczynsky caused considerable consternation with their views. The coalition government's minister of education was Roman Giertych, the leader of the League of Polish Families and an OD member. He opposed women's rights and openly displayed ultra-nationalist, homophobic and racist views. In March 2007, Giertych proposed a law to the Polish Parliament to persecute those who promote or discuss "homosexuality or any other deviation of a sexual nature" in the universities or any academic institution, which resulted in strong protests by human rights groups (*El País*, March 20/07: 9; also see Galindo, *El País*, March 30/07: 8; Allen, 2005). In Brussels, the 'capital' of the European Union (EU), Giertych proposed a "Charta of Rights of the European Nations" banning abortion and limiting "homosexual propaganda" (*El País*, March 15/07: 3). In Strasbourg, France, the president of the European Parliament admonished a representative from the League of Polish Families party for printing "an anti-Semitic and racist pamphlet" using paper with the institution's logo (Ibid).

Political scientists Paul Rich and Guillermo de los Reyes (1997; 2005) discuss the impact of organizations like Opus Dei on civil society in Latin America and point to the general perception of the order

10 It has been claimed that Opus Dei financed the 1989 Polish election won by *Solidarnosz* against the Polish Communist Party (Bauernfeind, 2006).

as a "dangerous closed" fellowship with "totalitarian" tendencies (1997; 2005: 95). While Rich and de los Reyes concede that even anti-democratic organizations can positively add to the political process, they nevertheless conclude that "groups [such] as Opus Dei are hard to credit with a substantial contribution to democratization" (Ibid; also see Romero, 2001). This observation is significant in light of the fact that many Latin American nations are still recovering from military or authoritarian rule. OD practices are in direct contradiction to the role which private groups are to play in civil society as guardians of the public interest, particularly in a country like Peru where human rights or pro-environment NGOs are harassed and intimidated.

While some observers claim that Liberation theology is disappearing, others point out that it has gone underground and has been subject to change itself. Houtart (2005) describes the present condition of the 'Church of the Poor' as "less visible than in the past ... but no less real" (2005: 39). As noted by Liberation theologist Leonardo Boff, "Latin America's harsh social reality is stronger than Rome's ideology" (Rohter, *The International Herald Tribune*, May 7/07). One of the key achievements of Liberation theology is the creation of base communities which are the grass-roots building blocks of the movement. For example, in Brazil alone some 70–80.000 such communities are in existence, while millions regularly meet in so-called bible circles to talk about the Old and New Testaments as seen from the perspective of Liberation theology. These communities are closely involved with the country's largest grass-roots organization, the Landless Movement. In Colombia, activist priests are in the forefront of the indigenous rights movement, while their Peruvian counterparts help organize against the encroaching mining industry (Drogus, 1999; also see Kraul and Chu, *The Seattle Times*, Apr. 11/05; *La República*, Dec. 3/06: 5; Rohter, *The International Herald Tribune*, May 7/07). Although the Church was not directly involved, the 1994 Chiapas rebellion owed much to the Catholic base communities from which the *Zapatistas* emerged (Norget, 1997; also see Harvey, 1998; Bobrow-Strain, 2007).

In addition, Peru and other countries in Latin America experience a shortage of priests. As a result many parishes, especially those in poor communities, find themselves with foreign-born priests who often still have a Liberation theology background. These members of the clergy, such as the Maryknoll Brothers in the United States, usually belong to orders which are not under the control of local bishops. Liberation theology has grown beyond its roots and influenced the struggles of other excluded in Latin America and elsewhere and has been influenced in turn. Liberation theology was also taken up by non-Catholic Christian denominations such as the Black Churches in the United States. Indeed, its influence has spread to Africa and Asia, while its focus has broadened from the poor to include those shut out because of race, ethnicity, or gender (Cleary, 1992; also see Hennelly, 1995; Gooren, 2002; Powers, 2002).

The policy shifts initiated by the Vatican under the reign of John Paul II caused many priests, nuns, and lay people to depart from the Church in Latin America which is home to almost half of the globe's 1.1 billion Catholics. These changes likewise contributed to the growth of evangelical-protestant denominations to where some 10 percent of the flock in the region defected (Daudelin and Hewitt, 1995; also see Kraul and Chu, *The Seattle Times*, Apr. 11/05; Bauernfeind, 2006; Rohter, *International Herald Tribune*, May 8/07).

While those who identify with Liberation theology have adopted a lower profile, José Comblin from the *National Catholic Reporter* describes the new kind of priest that the Vatican seems to prefer:

> The new clergy appearing on the scene are totally ignorant of what the Church was and did in the 1960s and 1970s. They have been educated far from the real world, protected from all contacts that could be 'dangerous' to their vocations. They live and work in their parishes, ignorant of what is happening in today's world. They are administrators of a parochial Church. They are faithful observers of all canonical rules (Comblin, 2003a).[11]

---

11 Comblin's observations mirror Lernoux's (1990) who wrote: "Opus Dei priests are recruited, usually in their teens and before they have had any sexual experience, for careful grooming in Opus Dei doctrine and practice ... Thus they are shielded from any outside contamination, particularly from liberal Church influence" (1990: 305–306).

Chapter 8

The Military and the Many Uses of Drug Profits

The end cannot justify the means for the simple and obvious reason that the means employed determine the nature of the ends produced.
(Aldous Huxley)

1. Introduction

During the Fujimori era a large number of Peruvian military officials were put on trial and received stiff prison sentences for their involvement with drug traffickers. However, this prosecution of individual cases of corruption served only to conceal the true links that existed between Peruvian military officials and criminals. Among other things, officers who had fallen out with Montesinos were often charged and sentenced. Still, the dramatic increase in the number of military officials who were prosecuted for their involvement in the drug trade even by the inefficient and crooked Peruvian judicial system attested that corruption was systemic rather than individual. Between 1980 and 1985, eight members of Peru's armed forces were put on trial because of links to the drug trade. This number grew to thirty-one for the period between 1985 and 1990, but increased tenfold between 1990 and 1996 to three hundred and nine (*Gestión*, Aug. 25/96: 15).

Dammert (2001) even argued that the 1992 *autogolpe* was in reality a *narcogolpe* [drug coup] that served the purpose of gaining control over the narcotics trade with which Montesinos had been deeply entangled since his days of defending drug traffickers. Dammert also claimed that Fujimori had received US$ 1 million from the Medellín Cartel's Pablo Escobar to help finance the second round of his 1990 election campaign. Thus "Fujimori talked on the phone with ... Escobar to thank him" (Ibid, 283). These allegations were described in detail in a book by the late drug lord's brother (See Escobar, 2000). At any rate, while the Fujimori regime in general and the Peruvian military in particular were involved in the drug trade, it would be misleading to suggest that the April 1992 coup was a narcogolpe comparable to the coup by an alliance of military officers and drug traffickers in Bolivia a decade earlier.

It is certain that Peru's security apparatus and the army in particular underwent a process of narcotisation after the autogolpe of April 5th, 1992, as a result of which numerous military officers personally enriched themselves. More importantly, however, the existing evidence suggests that the central government gave its military commanders a free hand to participate in the drug trade as part of an unofficial strategy to defeat the Shining Path rebels. In a manner that is remindful of the collaboration between the French secret service and the *Binh Xuyen*, a Vietnamese Mafia group, the Peruvian military and organized crime collaborated to deprive *Sendero* of the same resource: the coca grown in the Huallaga valley. Coca provided income to the rebels through 'revolutionary taxes' but the military also needed the proceeds of drug sales to help finance the war effort against the *Sendero Luminoso* insurgency. While some of the available evidence is circumstantial, it is inconceivable that these activities could have transpired without the knowledge and approval of the highest circles of the Peruvian government.

Traditionally, Peruvian traffickers were suppliers of the Colombian cartels. The Peruvian drug trade emerged during the late 1960s and early 1970s in line with Colombia's. So-called Peruvian mini-cartels also engaged in the sale of the final product cocaine in the United States (US) and Canada, but their involvement was rather small compared to their Bolivian and Colombian counterparts (Poole and Rénique, 1992; also see Morales, 1996). Still, at the height of the Sendero conflict in the early 1990s some forty trafficking groups operated in Peru, playing a powerful role in the regions in which they were active. These gangs allegedly controlled 90 percent of the Peruvian drug industry and supplied mostly coca paste and some locally produced cocaine to Colombian cartels (*Oiga*, May 30/94: 14–16; *Oiga*, May 30/94a: 16–19; *Sí*, Nov. 21/94: 26).

2. Drug War or Civil War?

The goal of financing the war against Sendero with funds from the drug trade conflicted with the alternative crop project that was to be implemented by the Fujimori government in the early 1990s to wean peasants off coca. The person assigned to the task was Hernando De Soto, the neoliberal economist and author of the 1986 book *El otro sendero* [The Other Path], a well-known if not controversial work on Peru's informal economy. However, the regime's unofficial policy undermined the crop project as peasants were seemingly encouraged to grow coca to earn funds for the war. At the same time, Peru, like other Andean nations, was – and still is – a participant in the US Drug war. Yet, while Washington strongly leaned on Colombia because of drug corruption, little was done about the Fujimori government although numerous credible allegations had emerged linking Peruvian officials to the narcotics trade. Moreover, military officials who reported these activities were persecuted by the regime.

The origins of the organized crime-military collaboration can be traced to 1989–1990, when General Alberto Arciniega Huby was commander in chief in the Huallaga valley, one of the most important theatres of conflict in the war against Sendero, which at the time was also the largest coca-growing area in the world. Arciniega Huby changed the approach taken by previous commanders. Instead of persecuting coca peasants or *cocaleros*, he allowed them to grow coca and relied on armed peasants to fight Sendero (Arciniega Huby, 1994). This, however, caused a row with the US government because the general was perceived as protecting the drug trade. Arciniega saw the situation as follows:

> What Sendero wants is to win the support of a population who depend on monocrop coca agriculture and who are repressed [by the police] ... which eradicate their crops ... because they consider coca farming to be a crime. We are talking about 80 percent of the population! What we must do, therefore, is to change this situation in order to prevent the ... [coca] peasant – the base on which Sendero thrives – from being harassed (as quoted in Poole and Rénique, 1992: 187-189; also see *Sí*, Oct. 30/89: 17–21; *Caretas*, Oct. 29/90: 13).

Palmer (1996) also described organized crime-military co-operation in the war against Sendero guerrillas. The Peruvian military had suffered greatly due to the country's economic woes. In 1989, the military budget had been slashed by more than half and "the resources to support field operations were severely curtailed ..." (1996: 183-184). Mattos (1989) observed that troops suffered from the "lack of ... equipment, armaments," mattresses and victuals while receiving very low earnings (1989: 34–35).[1] According to one military official, the army did not possess accurate maps and used school atlases when patrolling in jungle regions (Ibid). Thus, Arciniega relied "to a significant extent, on local resources (i.e., drug money) to finance his military operations" (Palmer, 1996: 184).

Although the general succeeded in pushing Sendero out of the Upper Huallaga valley in 1989, he was replaced due to US pressure. The commanders who succeeded Arciniega Huby's on the Huallaga front did therefore not follow his example. The regional military headquarters was relocated and the troops fought rebels from the *Movimiento Revolucionario Tupac Amaru* (MRTA) instead. This left the antidrug police in charge of operations in the Upper Huallaga valley, a move which allowed Sendero to return to the region and

1 Obando (1998: 397) referred to "the incredibly low and compressed" earnings of Peruvian military officials during the early 1990s. For example, the monthly pay of a division general amounted to about US$283 while a second lieutenant received some US$212 (Ibid).

consolidate once again (*Caretas*, Oct. 29/90: 13; also see Gonzáles, 1991; Arciniega Huby, 1994; CVRa, 2003).

Determining all of the factors that contributed to the shift in Peruvian drug policy is difficult. Nevertheless, one significant issue was the difference in threat assessment regarding Sendero and the drug trade by the Fujimori regime and the administrations of US Presidents George Bush senior (1988-1992) and Bill Clinton (1992-2000) respectively. The role of General Arciniega illustrated the fundamental contradiction in perceptions of the conflict as it was seen from Washington and Lima. While the United States focused wholly on fighting the drug war, Peruvians were preoccupied with winning the conflict against Sendero. From the Peruvian perspective, the American demand for coca eradication played directly into rebel hands. Sendero not only received funding through taxing the coca trade in the Upper Huallaga valley, the eradication policies also drove peasants to support the rebels who protected them against the police, the military, and abusive traffickers (Arciniega Huby, 1994).

The timing of the co-operation between military and drug traffickers is also significant. Between the Fujimori autogolpe in April 1992 and 1995, the US government cut military aid which had been slashed by Congress because of Peru's sordid human rights record. The United States released some funding for non-military purposes (Roberts and Peceny, 1997; also see Cotler, 1999). Regardless, given the existing budgetary problems, this development reinforced the Fujimori government's need for funds irrespective of the source to acquire arms, equipment and supplies. From a position that favoured alternative crop projects, the Fujimori government moved to one of collaboration with traffickers for the purpose of defeating Sendero, following the model set by General Arciniega (and the French). Circumstantial evidence suggests that this shift in policy came about in the period between the replacement of General Osvaldo Hanke in the summer 1991 by General Jaime Ríos Araico, as commander in chief in the Upper Huallaga valley, and the autogolpe of April 5, 1992.

The July 1991 assassination of peasant leader Walter Tocas López evidenced the existence of strong resistance to De Soto's alternative crop project within the Peruvian government itself. Tocas represented some 50.000 coca peasants in the Upper Huallaga valley who were willing to sign a deal with the government to obtain aid for alternative development and crop substitution programs. In fact, after receiving death threats the peasant leader had asked General Ríos Araico for protection only days before his assassination which was refused (*La República*, July 7/91: 3; also see *Caretas*, July 8/91: 28-29). Following the murder, the independent researcher Roger Rumrill (1991) claimed that there was great opposition to the alternative crop projects in Peru and that the situation differed little from Colombia's "where the ... forces of public order also ... eliminate the leaders of coca peasant unions" (1991: 16).

The alternative crop program was finally cancelled after the departure of Hernando De Soto on January 28, 1992. Shortly before his resignation, De Soto pointed out that there was "no political will to solve the problem" (*LAWR*, March 28/91: 4). He maintained further that the Peruvian air force was not shooting down the drug dealers' airplanes "because they don't want to" (Ibid). In his letter of resignation he claimed that peasant leader Walter Tocas had been killed by "the state" and that "there are places from where planes loaded with drugs leave regularly" (*La República*, Jan. 29/92: 8). Finally, De Soto asserted that the alternative crop project did not succeed because of opposition from a "criminal-military clique" which he refused to join (Ibid; also see *La República*, March 21/92: 2). Although Montesinos was not named in the letter it should be evident that the informal head of the *Servicio de Inteligencia Nacional* (SIN) was a leading member of the 'criminal-military' clique De Soto was referring to.

The collaboration between traffickers and military continued to develop after the autogolpe. A few days later the coca cultivation areas were declared emergency zones and placed under direct military control in line with Legislative decree 749 (*La República*, Apr. 10/92: 4). The relations between the military and traffickers are best illustrated by the example of one of the country's foremost drug traffickers, Demetrio Chávez Peñaherrera, a.k.a. *Vaticano*, a major supplier for the Cali Cartel. In 1991, Vaticano had been arrested by agents of the US Drug Enforcement Authority (DEA) operating in Peru. However, he was claimed by and handed over to the Peruvian military who let him go although the drug trafficker had various outstanding arrest warrants dating back to 1979 (*Observatoire Géopolitique des Drogues* – OGD, 1993). In fact, Vaticano received a certificate of good conduct from the police (*Gestión*, Aug. 25/96: 15). He was finally caught in Cali, Colombia, and extradited to Peru in 1994, where he was subsequently sentenced to thirty years in prison (*El Tiempo*, Jan. 14/94: 3A; also see *La República*, Aug. 6/96: 10).

Vaticano described his relationship with the military in his official court testimony as follows:

> The military did not interrupt our ... [operations], [but] ... protected us well because we paid them US$5,000 for every airplane of drugs ... It was known that what took place was drug trafficking ... No trafficker could act unless he was on good terms with the army... I was on good terms with the army (*La República*, Aug. 31/96: 16-17).

Similarly, the Colombian trafficker Waldo Simeón Vargas, a.k.a. *El Ministro*, like Vaticano a supplier of the Cali Cartel operating in Peru, acknowledged that he experienced no difficulties because he "knew how to manage the Peruvian police and military" (*La República*, Aug. 12/97: 8; also see Picasso and Martin, 2001).

While the testimony of convicted drug traffickers may not be convincing, other sources have confirmed these claims. The respectable Paris-based *Observatoire Géopolitique des Drogues* received information that several hundred kilos of coca paste were flown daily to Colombia from the military base at Campanilla in the Huallaga valley where Vaticano operated during the early 1990s. In October 1992, the trafficker changed locations and moved to another military post where his organization was again allowed to operate freely (OGD, 1993).

Peruvian journalist Adolfo Isuiza Urquía was the first to report on trafficking at the Campanilla military base, and who made Vaticano's name public when he wrote several articles for the Peruvian daily *La República* between January and March 1992. Isuiza was subsequently murdered in August of that same year (Ibid; also see *La República*, Jan. 27/92: 14–15; *La República*, Aug. 30/96: 16–17; Committee to Protect Journalists (CPJ), July 28/11).

A multiparty commission of the Peruvian Congress investigating military corruption confirmed that Vaticano operated freely with the assistance of high officials (*La República*, Aug. 20/96: 6). Describing the arrangements between the military and Vaticano, Peruvian Congressman Julio Castro Gómez maintained that

> the armed forces are the highest authority in the emergency zones, and the other institutions and powers are practically subordinated under the military command. Consequently, there is no control ... It is evident that ... [Vaticano] operated without problems [at the] Campanilla [army base] ... because of protection offered by the special military commandos of the zone (Ibid).

Other instances of co-operation between the military and drug traffickers include:

Shortly after the 1992 autogolpe, General Eduardo Bellido Mora replaced Ríos Araico on the Upper Huallaga valley (*La República*, June 24/95: 4). In April 1992, Bellido Mora rebuilt a clandestine airfield that had been used by Vaticano during the previous year and which General Ríos Araico claimed to have destroyed (*El Sol*, Sept. 28/96: A6). However, in May 1994, Araico and eleven other officers were charged and subsequently imprisoned because of their dealings with traffickers. The general described himself as the "fall guy" who was being sacrificed to hide the complicity of other officials in the narcotics trade (*Oiga*, May 30/94: 14–16).[2] Meanwhile, his successor, General Bellido Mora, who had also been linked to the drug trade, was never investigated or charged but sent to Israel as a military attaché. Bellido Mora was being protected by the then commander in chief of

2 According to his lawyer, General Ríos Araico became the victim of a political vendetta because he refused to sign a document which denounced another Peruvian military, General Robles, as a traitor. The latter had made public the activities of the *Grupo Colina* (*El Comercio*, Oct. 14/96: A16).

Peru's armed forces, General Hermoza, who described him as a "gentleman" (Ibid).

In 1992, Colonel Alejandro Sime Castillo was appointed the army's official investigator to inquire into military corruption in the Upper Huallaga valley. His report, which linked Bellido Mora to traffickers, was sent to Hermoza who did not act (*La República*, Aug. 23/96: 17). Conversely, an arrest order for Bellido Mora was only issued in January 2003 (*El Peruano*, Jan. 4/03).

While Bellido Mora was being protected, other officers who exposed drug corruption fared less well. In the fall of 1991, Colonel Gustavo Ríos-Pita Yanulaque had been given command of antidrug operations in the Upper Huallaga valley near Vaticano's Campanilla headquarters. Working together with DEA officials, Ríos-Pita ordered the destruction of a secret airfield used by the drug trafficker. The colonel was replaced two days later and his career in the army was finished thereafter (*El Comercio*, Aug. 29/96: A21).

As previously mentioned, Major Evaristo Castillo Aste had reported to both Bellido Mora and Hermoza about military corruption and drug trafficking. He was ultimately removed from the army and had to seek refuge in Spain (*La República*, June 27/94:17–19; also see *La República*, Sept. 22/96: 2; *La República*, Aug. 12/97: 8). In an article written from exile, the major pointed out President Fujimori had named Bellido Mora Peru's military attaché to Israel to prevent him from being investigated (*Oiga*, Feb. 14/94: 35; also see *La República*, Sept. 22/96a: 20–22). Likewise, Captain Gilmar Valdivieso Rejas denounced military corruption and links to drug traffickers on the Huallaga front in November 1994. However, his witnesses all died "strange" deaths that were never investigated (*El Comercio*, Nov. 24/94: A16).

According to a media contact I met in 1997, Peruvian spy chief Vladimiro Montesinos used traffickers to fight Sendero. The army relied on the logistics and intelligence of traffickers and on their money to provide food and supplies to the troops. To facilitate the trafficking activities at a given airport in Peru's coca-growing regions, such as the Upper Huallaga valley, the military would simply shut off their radars for ten to fifteen minutes to allow drug flights to land or take off. Likewise, another of my sources alleged that there existed a list of drug dealers who were not touched by the police. Thus, military officials connected to Vladimiro Montesinos were safe from persecution, although sometimes traffickers were sacrificed to maintain good relations with the United States. The same informant also referred to an alleged 1994 reunion between Fujimori, Montesinos, and several officials from Peru's intelligence services in the *Pentagonito*, or 'Little Pentagon,' as Lima citizens like to call their country's army headquarters. At the meeting, it was decided to sacrifice Vaticano after his 1994 arrest in Colombia and to put him on trial in Peru despite his links to the military. During his trial Vaticano was also accused of dealing with Sendero, a charge which he vehemently denied. He claimed instead that he supported the Peruvian military. Allegedly, Vaticano's men even fought a three-day battle against Sendero in 1991 at Campanilla using weapons they received from the army which itself had withdrawn from the area. The trafficker's mercenary 'troops' succeeded in holding off the rebels who took heavy losses and retreated. Afterwards, during the victory celebrations, Vaticano ordered the hoisting of the Peruvian flag.[3]

General Ríos Araico affirmed in his trial that Vaticano "virtually fed the troops stationed in his region" (*La República*, June 26/96: 3; also see *Oiga*, May 30/94: 14–16; *El Comercio*, Aug. 21/96: A14). The previously mentioned report by *Chanamé* also stated that the "food for troops and officers" was supplied by traffickers (*La República*, Feb. 29/92: 14–15). Relying on the likes of Vaticano the Peruvian military managed by Montesinos netted a considerable portion of annual drug profits. These funds were used to finance the war effort against Sendero. However, as a result the military became a player in the drug trade and grew highly corrupt (OGD, 1993; also see Dammert, 2001; Zapata, 2005). The US government was certainly aware of the Peruvian military's activities. For example, on one occasion in October 1991, US Ambassador Anthony Quainton as well

3 The identity of the sources cannot be revealed to assure their personal safety.

as US Congress representatives visiting the Upper Huallaga valley confronted General Ríos Araico and demanded to know: "Why does the Peruvian army fire with machine guns at DEA helicopters? Why does the army not allow the antidrug police to enter ... [areas] where drugs are loaded onto planes which leave for Colombia?" (*Oiga*, Jan. 24/94: 22; also see *Caretas*, Dec. 28/89: 22; Cotler, 1999).

3. Ronderos and the Drug Trade

The argument that drug trafficking and drug funds were part of an informal strategy adopted by the Peruvian military in its conflict with left wing insurgents is corroborated by the fact that some of the *rondas campesinas* or peasant militias utilized the same approach. These were peasant militias set up independently, or with government assistance, to combat the rebels. The rondas played an important part in the Fujimori regime's defeat of Sendero Luminoso.

One of the regions where Sendero initially emerged was in the river valleys of the Apurímac and Ene in the eastern jungle regions of the country. However, because of brutal Sendero policies, the movement lost its support base. Indeed, the rondas campesinas in the Río Apurímac and Ene region cultivated coca and produced coca paste which they sold to drug traffickers. With their earnings the ronderos acquired arms to fight against Sendero. This approach had become a necessity given the complete absence of the state in the region and the brutal treatment by Sendero rebels. Del Pino (1996) observed that

> between 1985 and 1987 the indifference of the state and of the armed forces concerning the massacres of peasants at the hands of [the Shining Path] ... [induced the ronderos] to establish alliances with the drug trade, in return for arms and resources with which they [not only] defeated the ... [rebels] but also kept the zone clear of police and military... [This is] a very different scenario

than the one in the Upper Huallaga where the drug trade finances the ... [insurgency]" (1996: 119).[4]

These observations mirror those of the Peruvian antidrug police. A 1993 internal police document claimed that 90 percent of the inhabitants of the districts on the Apurímac River engaged in various aspects of the drug economy, and that ronderos "controlled and protected" the airports from where traffickers shipped drugs.[5] Ronderos played a crucial role in defeating the Sendero Luminoso rebels. In 1994–1995, after the great decline in the price of coca leaves, the ronderos in the region demanded assistance programs for alternative products from the government. In an interview, Hugo Huillca Ovalle, the President of the Federation of Coca Growers of the Apurímac and Ene river valleys, even threatened the Peruvian state. He claimed that

> the government seems to have forgotten that we have fought the ... [rebels] with weapons we bought with the proceeds earned from cultivating coca. Now that we defeated the rebels, we do not want to abandon coca cultivation unless we are being offered a possibility of subsistence ... Given our resources, these weapons not only point at the rebels but also at another direction (*La República*, Aug. 13/95: 2).

Indeed, Peru's coca farmers have continued to protest government policies (BBC, Apr. 22/03; also see *La República*, May 14/05: 8). Moreover, representatives of the coca unions have been elected into the Peruvian parliament in recent years. Regardless, the rondas, even those financed through their participation in the cocaine economy, dif-

4 This rather complex situation was misinterpreted in a number of journalistic publications. For example, *The Economist's* Peru correspondent attributed the drug trade in both the Huallaga valley and the Apurímac y Ene region to Sendero Luminoso (*The Economist*, March 4/00: 25).

5 The author of the document cannot be named here to protect his identity. However, a Swiss journalist who researched the drug trade in the Río Apurímac region confirms these findings. Accordingly, the ronderos had defeated Sendero by 1993 with weapons they acquired from the proceeds of drug trafficking. Even when the Peruvian military finally moved in it did not seriously interrupt the trade (Bauer, 1995).

fer greatly from paramilitaries in Colombia funded by the drug trade, although both have engaged leftist rebels. Organizations like Colombia's *Autodefensas Unidas de Colombia* (AUC) were set up by agrarian elites and traffickers to combat rebel movements generated by the struggle over land distribution. Peru's rondas which were initially created to fight local crime were organized – sometimes with government help – by the peasants themselves against an insurgency of which they wanted no part.

4. The FARC Arms Deal

The co-operation between the military and drug traffickers in the first half of the Fujimori years primarily served the purpose of defeating Sendero Luminoso although the officials involved likely also enriched themselves. Conversely, the chief motive behind the links between the military officials and criminals between 1995 and 2000 was profit. Quiroz (2008) observed that Montesinos "ordered the use of military vessels, planes, and helicopters ... to export drugs to Mexico, Spain, Portugal, Italy, Bulgaria, and Russia" (2008: 415). The spy chief's downfall is closely linked to his participation in a major small-arms-for-drugs deal in 1999–2000 with Colombia's most powerful left wing rebel movement, the *Fuerzas Armadas Revolucionarias de Colombia* (FARC). Ilushin-16 cargo jets loaded with small weapons and ammunition began their journey in Russia and Ukraine. The planes landed and refuelled in Jordan, crossed the Atlantic to Colombia where the arms were airdropped and ended up in the hands of FARC (Bagley, 2002). While the complete transaction of 40,000 AK-47s never came about, some 10,000 assault rifles were allegedly parachuted into areas controlled by FARC (McClintock and Vallas, 2005). Dammert (2001) observed in this context that the "Jordanian government ... presented documents" indicating that Washington had approved of the transfer of the weapons which was assumed to be a straightforward shipment from Jordan to Peru (2001: 342). The shipments were stopped once it became apparent that the true recipient of the arms was the FARC (Quiroz, 2008). The rebels financed the acquisition through the sale of cocaine using the services of a Brazilian drug dealer (Bowen and Holligan, 2003).

Peru's military officials under orders from Montesinos had acquired the weapons – which had been produced in the former East Germany – in December of 1998 through the services of a Lebanese arms dealer named Sarkis Soghanalian who had links to the Central Intelligence Agency (CIA) (McClintock and Vallas, 2005). While Colombian journalist Germán Castro Caycedo (2001) corroborated that the delivery of Kalashnikov rifles had indeed taken place he claimed that the operation not only involved the CIA but served the purpose of justifying *Plan Colombia*, the US scheme to fight drugs and FARC concurrently. This claim is supported by the fact that Montesinos' links to this agency dated back to the 1970s (Bagley, 2001; also see Drug Enforcement Agency – DEA, 2001; Loayza, 2003; *La República*, May 1/05: 10). It is certain that the initiative by Colombian President Pastrana to engage in peace talks with FARC rebels was not welcome in Peru where the government had taken a hard line with the insurgents from Sendero and MRTA; a sentiment that it shared with the CIA and the US government which wanted to implement Plan Colombia. Once it became known that the FARC had engaged in weapons trading while officially engaging in peace talks, Pastrana was forced to participate in Plan Colombia (Rojas-Pérez, 2005).

To the US the FARC represented a serious threat to regional stability and economic integration plans. Dammert (2001) argued that the "FARC had acquired such fire power that they had achieved a strategic military equilibrium" (2001: 341). The Colombian chaos was welcomed by Montesinos because it allowed him to present the regime in Lima as a stable partner contributing to regional security. It was his goal to induce Washington to overlook the undemocratic practices and human rights violations in Peru because "the continuation of the regime ... was of vital interest to ... US security" (Rojas-Pérez, 2005: 176). Nevertheless, as a result of his involvement in the arms-for-drugs operation Montesinos achieved the contrary. US policy makers may have been willing to overlook human rights violations and the 2000 electoral fraud as long as the regime contributed to stability in the region. Yet a Montesinos who supplied arms to the FARC coupled with growing public demonstrations against the regime in the streets of Lima and other cities turned Peru into a factor of instability. At first glance it is difficult to explain why Montesinos would even participate in the arms deal. As a savvy operator, it is doubtful that he engaged in such an arrangement unless he believed that his actions were sanctioned. Then again the earnings Montesinos could expect might have been a powerful lure. While the FARC paid for the AK-47s with cocaine, Bowen and Holligan (2003) observed that the rebels gave far more for the weapons in drugs than they would have been worth on the international market. This made it a very lucrative arrangement for Montesinos whose profits were tenfold.

5. Conclusion

Peru's return to democracy in 2000 had little impact on the drug trade. True, the country's coca production saw a considerable reduction from some 300,000 tons in the early 1990s to less than 100,000 tons in 1999–2000. This outcome, however, was the result of overproduction and low coca prices, not government repression. In addition, as noted by Peruvian analyst Carlos Reyna Izaguirre (2001), Plan Colombia, the US operation which aimed at suppressing coca production and FARC rebels alike in neighbouring Colombia reversed this trend. According to UN estimates, the coca-growing areas of Peru increased again by 6.5 percent between 2000 and 2001. The implementation of the plan in Colombia boosted the price of the leaves in Peru which induced farmers there to return to their coca crops which they had abandoned because of low prices. Likewise, the drop in the price of coffee of which Peru is a major producer contributed to the increase in coca cultivation (Ibid; also see BBC, Feb. 17/01; BBC, Sept. 18/02; United Nations Office for Drug Control and Crime Prevention – UNODCCP, 2002: 2).[6]

The other main objective of Plan Colombia, the reduction of the Colombian guerrilla, has also not been accomplished. In early 2005, despite US military aid, the FARC went on a counteroffensive inflicting serious losses on government troops (*La República*, Apr. 28/05: 24; also see *Correo*, Apr. 30/05: 17; *La República*, May 5/05: 27; *El Comercio*, May 29/05: A32). A more recent study by Valencia and Ávila (2011) claimed that FARC attacks had increased from 1,012 during the first half of 2010 to 1,115 actions during the first six months of 2011. During the first half of 2009 FARC rebels went on the attack on 855 occasions. The Colombian military had promised to put an end to the insurgency in 2008. In that year, however, the guerrillas changed strategy by decentralizing operations. The FARC have reorganized into units of between two to three dozen fighters who in turn carry out hit-and-run attacks in even smaller groups. Thus the rebels represent less of a target while they can operate in a theatre of conflict which Colombia's military cannot possibly secure.

Peru's cocaine industry has evolved since the millennium. Having once furnished the criminal networks in Cali and Medellín with coca paste for final refining, since the late 1990s Peruvian mini-cartels often bypass Colombia altogether and directly supply the final product to large Mexican organizations which are responsible for distribution on the North American and even European markets (*The Toronto Star*, March 22/97: A1; also see *El Comercio*, July 13/97: A1; *El Sol*, Aug. 2/97: 8A; BBC, June 11/02). Mexican criminal organizations took advantage of the reduction of the large Colombian trafficking groups in the mid-1990s and now provide the bulk of the cocaine entering the United States. The Mexican cartels have also established direct supply

---

6 Plan Colombia had a similar effect on coca cultivation in Bolivia. After reaching a low of less than fifteen thousand hectares in 2000, the area under cultivation had increased again to 24,400 hectares by 2002 (United Nations Office on Drugs and Crime – UNODC, 2003).

links with Bolivian and Peruvian trafficking groups. Already in the late 1990s, DEA estimates put the annual profits of Mexican drug traffickers at US$ 7 billion (Smith, 1999).

The infiltration of organized crime into the Peruvian state and the economy during the Fujimori era may not have been as deep as in neighbouring Colombia. Still, the corruption of the drug trade had an infectious effect on other sectors of Peruvian society and economy during the 1990s, such as the banking and transportation industries. Economist Lamas Puccio claimed that some US$500 million were being laundered annually in Peru's banking system during the mid-1990s (*El Comercio*, Aug. 25/96: A24). Likewise, various airlines and maritime companies were involved in the transportation of drugs from the coca-growing regions to the coastal cities and for further shipping abroad (*La República,* May 14/97: 7; also see *El Comercio*, May 18/97: A17; *El Sol.* Aug. 2/97: 8A). According to an observer who specialized on the drug trade, Peru was "infected with drug trafficking at all levels" in the early millennium (Gutiérrez, Pers. Comm., Sept. 19/02).

In the year 2004 alone, the area dedicated to coca cultivation increased from 30,000 to 50,000 hectares. More importantly, coca production has risen thanks to the introduction of new agricultural techniques. Peruvian researchers claimed that the acreage of 2004 produced higher yields than the 130,000 hectares under cultivation during the early 1990s. Plan Colombia included the fumigation of poppy plants and increased interception in the Peruvian-Colombian border, the Putumayo. As a consequence, Colombian traffickers moved into Peru where they contributed to the emergence of a growing heroin industry. In 2004, the country's antinarcotics police intercepted four hundred and fifty kilograms of heroin compared to less than three hundred and fifty in 2003. It was estimated that the combined area dedicated to coca and opium poppy cultivation in Colombia, Ecuador, and Peru had grown to 250,000 hectares by 2004. Traffickers also diversified their transportation routes, operating through Ecuador, Brazil as well as Colombia (*La República*, May 14/05: 8; also see *La República*, May 20/05: 8; *La República*, May 21/05: 21; *La República*,

May 23/05: 8). Or as observed by a leading expert on the region, “after five years of Plan Colombia, the price, purity and availability of cocaine in US cities remains unchanged” (Leech, 2005).

Coca production has been on the increase in Peru since the millennium due to the effects of the US Drug war and because of the neglect of the Toledo (2001–2006) and García (2006–2011) administrations. Indeed, cultivation in the Alto Huallaga valley had increased to such an extent that remnant factions of the defeated Sendero Luminoso were fighting over the proceeds of the trade (Romero, *The New York Times*, June 13/10; also see *El Comercio*, May 1/10).

Chapter 9

Geo-economics or Human Rights?

When rich villains have need of poor ones, poor ones may make what price they will.
(William Shakespeare)

1. Introduction

The Fujimori regime was sustained by a number of international actors, although at times these relationships were contradictory and unstable. The most important of these were with the regional hegemonic power, namely the United States (US), as well as the Organization of American States (OAS). The relations with Washington were strongly influenced by the geopolitical transformations of the early 1990s, most notably the collapse of Communism and of the Soviet Union.

In this chapter I will analyse the international geopolitical setting in which the regime functioned. This section will explore how a British concept of geopolitics from the early twentieth century was transformed into the major US foreign policy approach in the late twentieth and early twenty-first century. Also, as previously noted the concepts of soft and hard power developed by US scholar Joseph Nye are useful when analyzing the dark side of international politics. Finally, I will demonstrate how the Fujimori regime used the post-Cold War environment to its own advantage.

Since the late nineteenth century, if not earlier, the United States has considered Latin America as its backyard. Following the end of the Cold War it has been the goal of US foreign policy to preserve/re-establish its hegemony whereby the domination of Latin America plays a key role. Since 1990 Washington's relations with other global powers have been based on their ability to threaten US predominance. After the 1992 Maastricht treaty the European Union (EU) has been perceived as such a threat. The People's Republic of China and Japan were viewed similarly (Dos Santos, 2004). During the 1990s the Fujimori regime found itself in the new global environment of the immediate post-Cold War era (Arias Quincot, 1994).

Petras (2003) observed in the case of Latin America that the United States may be the region's dominant power, but that its "hegemony" is limited to "government circles and ... liberal intellectual elites" (2003: 80). Washington has been challenged by the growing opposition to a US dominated free trade zone of the Americas (FTAA). Latin Americans themselves are engaged in the process of producing their own trade arrangements. Brazil – because of its size and resources already a regional giant – has been a driving force in the integration of the *Mercado Común del Sur* (MERCOSUR) which begun in the early 1990s. The Union of South American Nations or *Unión de Naciones Suramericanas* (UNASUR), officially inaugurated in December 2004, was set up to turn the region south of Panama into a political and economic bloc (Bennet, 2008).

2. Some Observations on Geopolitics

In a very broad sense, geopolitics describes the linkages between power and territorial dominion, or what Kasperson and Minghi (1969) define as the "spatial analysis of political phenomena" (1969: xi). Moreover, the term refers to the relationship between the placement and particulars (e.g., resources) of continents and power. During the Cold War the term was also applied to describe the competition between the United States and the former Union of Soviet Socialist Republics (USSR) (Dalby, 1990). In this chapter, the use for the term will be extended to the post-Cold War era to provide an explanation for the emerging rivalry between Washington and other global power centres. Regardless, according to Agnew and Ó Tuathail (1992), the creation of geopolitical concepts from the early twentieth century to the present

> was never an objective and disinterested activity but an organic part of the political philosophy and ambitions of ... very public intellectuals. While the forms of geopolitical writing have varied ..., the practice of producing geopolitical theory has a common theme: the production of knowledge to aid the practice of statecraft and further the power of the state (1992: 192).

Anglo-American geopolitical thinking rests on the ideas of Halford Mackinder (1861–1947) who laid out his perspectives in a paper titled *The Geographical Pivot of History* to the Royal Geographical Society in London, England, in 1904. Mackinder (1969) was the father of the so-called Heartland theory. The Heartland or the 'geographical pivot of history' refers to the rich interior low lands of Eurasia. The British geographer and politician maintained that the potential for global domination lay with land-based rather than maritime based empires. Mackinder noted that the bulk of the globe's population and resources were located on the Eurasian-African landmass and concluded that the power which achieved dominion over this part of the globe would be in an almost impregnable position to command the world. Control over this expanse would ensure autarchy while its natural barriers provided safety from invasion, except in the west. The key to global control lay therefore with this gateway to the Heartland, namely Eastern Europe. Mackinder assigned extreme importance to the question of who controlled this entryway (Ibid; also see Parker, 1988).[1]

In the United States during the 1930s and 40s the political geographer Nicholas Spykman (1969) was influenced by the Heartland theory, although he redefined some of Mackinder's assumptions. He

1 Mackinder (1969) summed up his perspective as follows: "Who rules East Europe commands the heartland; Who rules the Heartland commands the World Island; Who rules the world island commands the world" (1969: 161-170).

noted that for reasons of climate the amount of arable soil available in the Heartland was quite small when compared to the size of the region. The US scholar agreed with Mackinder that the Heartland likely possessed large amounts of raw materials; however, he expressed uncertainty about the ability to extract and utilize them. Spykman (1969a) played down the importance of Eastern Europe but instead stressed the so-called Rimland, or what Mackinder had styled the inner crescent of states encircling the Heartland, namely, "the European coast land, the Arabian-Middle Eastern desert land, and the Asiatic monsoon land" which referred to the coastal areas stretching north from Southeast Asia to China and beyond (1969a: 40).[2] After the beginning of the Cold War the establishment of a strong US presence in Western Europe through the creation of the North Atlantic Treaty Organization (NATO), and similar military arrangements elsewhere on the globe, aimed at containing the Soviet Union and to prevent its expansion into the Rimland areas. Western Europe, given its economic potential, was the most important Rimland area in the post-World War II era, at least as seen from Washington.

Dalby (1990) observed that from the early 1950s to the 1980s key documents, statements, and writings by politicians, as well as influential scholars, made reference to Mackinder's and Spykman's concepts, most importantly their "concerns with the domination of Eurasia by a single power" (1990: 178). Walt Rostow (1960) warned of the "combined resources of Eurasia" which were "superior to those of the United States" (1960: 543). Another example is Colin Gray (1977) who wrote that Washington could not accept "effective control of Eurasia-Africa by the Soviet Union" (1977: 28). According to Dalby (1990), these concepts also reappeared in the national security documents of the Reagan administration during the 1980s. He concluded that the "key to American geopolitics ... [during the Cold War] has been the prevention of the Soviet domination of Eurasia" (1990: 182). Ó Tuathail (1992) observed likewise that Mackinder's ideas "in-

---

2 Spykman (1969) wrote: "Who controls the Rimland rules Eurasia; who rules Eurasia controls the destinies of the world" (1969: 43).

formed the post-war American policy of containing the USSR" (1992: 101; also see Portillo, 2003).

Finally, these very same geopolitical concepts reappeared in the 1992 Pentagon Paper which espoused the maintenance of US military supremacy by forestalling the ascendency of any potential aggressor in Eurasia, and military intervention anywhere on the globe where Washington's interests were threatened (Krauthammer, 1992). In the early 1990s US policy makers ostensibly determined that the emerging EU had become a potential threat, while the growing ties between Brussels and Moscow were not welcomed by Washington.[3] Indeed, Thurow (1993) pointed out:

> If the sciences of the former Soviet Union and the production technologies of the German-speaking world are combined with the flair of the designs from Italy and France and the London money market which will guide the investments into the most productive regions of Europe, something insuperable will be created (1993: 283).

The growing intra-EU trade combined with access to the huge resource potential of the former Soviet Union would allow the Europeans to acquire a position closely resembling autarchy. As observed by Staab (2008), 68 per cent of the trade done by the EU is commerce between member states. Only 32 per cent is with the rest of the world (Also see Eurostat, 2005). The incorporation of the former USSR into the larger European economic space also decreased the EU's dependency on raw materials from the global South, for example, oil and gas (Thurow, 1993). In addition, European integration, which once served the purpose of preventing conflict, increasingly turned into an enterprise aimed at protecting member states from the impact of US and global economic policies (Sperling, 1990).

---

3 Readers who have observed the recent problems of the EU may be surprised that the integration of the old continent was indeed viewed as a threat in Washington. Conversely, while the EU may be teetering on the brink of breakup, observers have pronounced the demise of European integration on a number of occasions, only to be proven wrong. For example, the Eurosclerosis of the 1970s brought about the major integration processes of the 1980s and 90s.

After the Cold War the United States redefined its understanding of national security; a move that was initiated by President George Bush senior through the so-called Intelligence Reorganization Act of 1992. The act emphasized economic intelligence. Shortly after entering office in 1993 President Bill Clinton established a National Economic Council which demonstrated the perception that national security implied economic security. US spy agencies have since extended their activities beyond the field of traditional security issues to economic ones. In turn, several countries, particularly France, Germany, Britain, Japan and Israel, all of whom are officially US allies, have been subjected to espionage (Todd and Bloch, 2003).[4] In an article published in the *Wall Street Journal* in March 2000 former Central Intelligence Agency (CIA) director James Woolsey admitted that the US engaged in such practices against European companies because the latter used bribery. A 2001 report by a commission of the European Parliament provided a detailed overview of the "surveillance activities by US intelligence agencies" in Europe (Ibid, 54). Thus, US companies secured US$ 145 billion in contracts during the 1990s in this manner which were largely lost by EU countries. French companies, for example, lost some US$ 17 billion during the decade (Ibid). Regardless, while Washington has accused EU companies of using bribery to obtain contracts, it has never supplied any proof. Moreover, Todd and Bloch observe that even if it was demonstrated

4 Little that has changed since in the US soft power approach as revealed by Wikileaks. According to a diplomatic cable from July 2009 US diplomats were encouraged by Secretary of State Hillary Clinton to spy on the United Nations and its top staff. The cable stated that "[r]eporting officers should include as much of the following information as possible when they have information relating to persons linked to: office and organizational titles; names, position titles and other information on business cards; numbers of telephones, cell phones, pagers and faxes; compendia of contact information, such as telephone directories (in compact disc or electronic format if available) and e-mail listings; internet and intranet 'handles', internet email addresses, web site identification-URLs; credit card account numbers; frequent flyer account numbers; work schedules, and other relevant information" (*Der Spiegel* Spezial 1, Dec. 10/10: 32–33).

that the EU companies did use corruption, this does not justify the US spying activities in Europe (Ibid).

3. Latin America after the Cold War

In the summer of 1990 President George Bush senior called for free trade on the American continents in his 'Initiative for the Americas', a move which should be viewed as a response to European integration. Bush's free trade doctrine was based on the so-called Washington Consensus of 1989. The Washington Consensus, in essence, is the blueprint for neoliberal globalization and refers to the privatization of state-owned industries, the elimination of government regulation in most sectors of the economy, the liberalization of trade, capital, service industries, and labour markets. The Washington Consensus also called for the reduction, if not elimination of government subsidies; notably for foodstuffs and agriculture products. Government spending on the economy should serve the interests of corporations, for example, by focusing on infrastructure projects. It is notable that the call for the dismantling of subsidies does not include the United States itself which continues to protect key industries such as agriculture and textile. For example, US cotton growers receive annual subsidies worth over US$ 3.5 billion. The implementation of the Washington Consensus in Latin America did not generate the promised prosperity which in turn implied a decline of public support for neoliberal policies and the election victories of left wing politicians, such as Hugo Rafael Chávez Frías in Venezuela or Luiz Inácio Lula da Silva in Brazil (Rey, 2006; also see Jones, 2007).

The planned free trade zone from Alaska to Patagonia was to have been set up in 2005. A FTAA would provide the US economy with a significant market and the large resources of South America and Canada. US exports to Latin America which in the early 1990s exceeded those to Eastern Europe fiftyfold had suffered greatly because of the economic problems the region suffered (Kennedy, 1993). According to Cadena Montenegro (2009), it is the US objective in Latin America to gain control of a market of more than 800 million people, to acquire access to the region's resources, and to set up a single market of thirty-four countries. This bloc would have a pooled GDP of $US 11.5 billion; or roughly 30 per cent larger than the European Union. With supremacy over Latin America the United States would dominate

> the largest unified market on the planet, with a third of the global GDP and more than a fifth of global trade. This ... geopolitics of postmodernity ... aims at the hearts and markets and not at the territories as in earlier days" (2009: 99; also see Reyno, 2001; Fernández Tabío and Hernández Martínez, 2002).

The US plans for Latin America have two main strands: the control of the strategic resources and military deployments in the region. Accordingly, the US aims to control the three strategic resources available in Latin America: substantial petroleum (and mineral) reserves, biodiversity, and a large labour force. While the oil reserves in the Persian Gulf are superior, those in Latin America are still significant. Saudi Arabia and Iraq have estimated oil reserves of 262 and 112 billion barrel respectively, while Venezuela and Mexico respectively still own 77 and 28 billion barrel of oil (Ornellas, 2003; also see Ceceña, 2002; Salazar Peréz, 2000).

Turning to Peru, the country does most of its trading with Canada, China, the EU, Japan, and the US. Peru mainly exports primary goods such as petroleum, gold, copper, tin, and nonferrous metals as well as agricultural products and textiles. The country's mostly imports secondary and tertiary goods such as machinery, petroleum-based products, motor vehicles, steel, as well as grain. By 2009, Peru was the world's number one producer of silver, number two in zinc, number three in copper and tin, number four in lead, and number six in gold. Mineral exports generally represent the bulk of the country's export earnings which came to 61 per cent of US$ 26.6 billion of the country's export revenues. Peru has also turned into an exporter of oil and natural gas. In 2004, the country began operations at the *Camisea* natural gas project which has lessened energy dependence. The project is worth US$ 3.8 billion and represents the biggest investment in a single business endeavour in Peruvian history (US Department of State. Background Note: Peru, Sept. 30, 2010).

Moreover, the largest concentrations of biodiversity are found in two regions of the globe, namely the Indonesian archipelago and the belt stretching from the Amazon to Mexico. Latin America is home to 68 per cent of the world's tropical forests, and 40 per cent of its animals (not including insects) and plants. Brazil is home to a fifth of all plant and animal life on the planet. These include some 56,000 plants, 417 types of mammals, 1500 and 3000 types of bird and fresh water fish respectively. Colombia is home to 4,800 animal and 51,000 plant species. Peru has over 3500 animal and 23,000 plant species on its territory (Ornellas, 2003).

Population is the third reason that motivates US policies vis-a-vis Latin America. With over 500 million inhabitants of which more than 200 million are people of working age the region is attractive to large corporations as lower wages offer opportunities for decreasing production costs. Moreover, the markets of Latin America offer themselves as alternative outlets for US products to substitute for market losses elsewhere. Finally, population is a factor because of the perceived need to control illegal migration into the United States (Ibid).

Cadena Montenegro (2009: 99) may call it a geopolitics that "aims at the hearts and markets" but the region is also controlled militarily through the US Southern Command, which is one of the five command centres Washington relies on to assert global hegemony. In 2007, the US military was located in seventeen military bases in Latin America and the Caribbean: Aruba, Colombia, Curacao, Ecuador, El Salvador, Cuba (Guantanamo Bay), and Honduras (Kintto, 2007). In 2009, the Ecuadorian government did not renew the contract for the Manta military base and US troops left (*Merco Press*, Sept. 19/09).

It is also important here to recall Gill's (2004) assessment of the role of the School of the Americas in the formation of Latin American military officers. The School therefore is a formidable soft power tool because it "permits [Washington] ... to have the future leaders of the (Latin American) armed forces in its hands" (2004: 111).

4. Economic Integration in Latin America

Recent decades have seen a number of attempts by Latin Americans to bring about regional political and economic integration in South America. Examples include the *Comunidad Andina* (or Andean Pact), MERCOSUR, and the *Alianza Bolivariana para los Pueblos de Nuestra América* [Bolivarian Alliance for the Americas] (ALBA). The latest of these attempts at integration is UNASUR which differs from earlier attempts because it has far-reaching goals and it is truly continental. The plan includes Argentina, Bolivia, Brazil, Chile, Colombia, Ecuador, Guyana, Paraguay, Peru, Suriname, Uruguay, and Venezuela, but excludes the United States. It is UNASUR's goal to create a single South American market. Also, the UNASUR agenda includes a common defence policy to boost military co-operation, support confidence and security-building measures and promote defence industry exchanges, as well as the free movement of visitors and migrant workers among member nations (García, 2008; also see Sepúlveda M., 2010).

Washington's endeavour for a free trade zone in the Americas or FTAA has largely failed, last not least due to Brazilian resistance. The United States has since changed track by establishing bilateral free trade arrangements with key countries in the region, including Peru. Such agreements, as noted by Andrade (2004/05), are preferable to Washington for a number of reasons. Most importantly, negotiations between the United States and a country like Chile are marked by the power differentials between them. In such a setting Washington's interests are likely to prevail. Conversely, negotiations with MERCOSUR or the Andean Pact manifestly provide more negotiation power to the Latin American countries which are part of these blocs.

Indeed, by setting up bilateral arrangements the United States undermines the EU approach of dealing between blocs. Those countries which signed deals with Washington made compromises that make it more difficult to participate in arrangements with the EU. The bilateral free trade agreements thus serve the purpose of forestalling Brazilian designs for a unified Latin American market while simultaneously impeding the competition from Europe (Ibid). The assessment is shared by Jácome (2004) who argues that to the United States

> the free trade agreements with the Andean countries do not only represent a commercial strategy but also a geopolitical one. With these treaties [the United States] seeks access to a market of developing economies which serves the expansion of US transnational corporations who are faced with competition from Europe and Asia (2004: 8).

Although the United States did sign FTAs with a number of countries in the region (Chile, Colombia, Peru), Latin Americans have become more cautious since given that several clauses in these free trade deals were perceived as being harmful to their own economies. These include the provision of full access to US agricultural products which receive large subsidies while Latin Americans were to eliminate any taxation on such imports. Other concerns existed in the areas of intellectual property rights, the privatization of telecommunications and nationalized industries, the production and distribution of generic medications, etc., (Ibid).

Regardless, the above observations provide the background for the following discussion on Peruvian-US relations during the 1990s. The Fujimori regime was in power during a time of great transition after the end of the Cold War, a fact which greatly affected Washington's relations with Lima but which the regime was also able to use to its own advantage.

5. The United States and the Fujimori Regime

According to Palmer (2006), US-Peruvian relations had been strained for much of the twentieth century. During the 1970s Washington was concerned about the policies of the left wing military government which had nationalized US corporations, set up diplomatic links with Cuba, and bought weapons from the Soviet Union. Relations did not greatly improve during the administrations of Belaúnde and García (1980–1990) because of differences over trade and debt payment (Ibid; also see McClintock and Vallas, 2005). In the 1990s the United States was preoccupied with domestic problems such as deficit reduction and economic recovery. If Washington policy makers looked beyond their own borders, they paid attention to events in the Balkans, or the Middle East, not south of the Río Grande. Palmer thus describes US policy toward Latin America as "characterized by improvisation" and interagency rivalry (Ibid, 228). McClintock and Vallas (2005) observed that no high level members of the government were involved in policy-making vis-a-vis Latin America during the Clinton years. Still, Latin America did not completely disappear off the radar. As noted by McSherry (1998), following

> the end of the Cold War, the Clinton government and the Pentagon have aggressively pushed the Latin American militaries to assume an expansive and multidimensional role in confronting drug trafficking, terrorism, insurgency, immigration and refugee flows ... Herein lies the central contradiction of Clinton policy: while espousing democracy, the Administration strengthens the military forces that have been the region's greatest threat to democracy over the past generation (1998: 17).

Palmer (2006) provides two mutually reinforcing accounts to explain US policy vis-a-vis Peru during the Fujimori years. The United States was disposed to overlook the authoritarian tendencies of the regime in return for Peru's collaboration on issues such as "intelligence gathering, counterdrug efforts, and economic liberalization" (2006: 238).

Conversely, Fujimori and Montesinos successfully managed to out-manoeuvre the United States "for their own purposes" (Ibid).

The US administration of George Bush senior was strongly opposed to the 1992 coup and played a key role in forcing the regime to return to democracy. For example, Richard Feinberg, responsible for Latin American Affairs on the US National Security Council, with the backing of the State Department, helped persuade officials at the World Bank, the Interamerican Development Bank (IADB), and the International Monetary Fund (IMF) to delay promised funds to Peru until the country returned to democratic practices (Palmer, 1998). Conversely, Washington did little in response to the increasingly undemocratic practices after the 1995 election (Palmer, 2006). Thus, a number of "US agencies, such as Treasury, Commerce, and the White House Office of Drug Control Policy" ignored the regime's increasingly authoritarian tendencies (Ibid, 233). McClintock and Vallas (2005) observed that the directors of these agencies were generally happy with the performance of Peru's government. Washington therefore played a key role which allowed Peru to return to the international financial community after the 1992 coup. Clinton administration officials were primarily interested in putting relations with Peru on a normal footing to pursue free market reforms and other US policy goals (Ibid). By 1998, Peru was the major recipient of US aid in Latin America (Marcus-Delgado, 2001). Direct foreign investments, primarily in the mining and petroleum sectors, increased from US$ 3 billion to over US$ 8 billion by 1999 (Ibid).

Moreover, Palmer (2006) believed that Washington was reluctant to dispense with "Montesinos, both because of his reputation as a 'fixer' and because of his ... ability to provide the ... CIA with valuable intelligence" (2006: 237; also see Loayza, 1998). The "CIA had the dominant influence on the US embassy in Lima" and was also the agency which most strongly supported Montesinos (McClintock and Vallas, 2005: 89–90). Thus, the spy chief was highly valued and looked after by US intelligence (Ibid). CIA officials had worked with Peruvian police to set up the *Grupo Especial de Inteligencia* (GEIN), which was credited with the 1992 capture of *Sendero* leader Abimael

Guzmán by supplying equipment such as cameras, electronic listening devices, and night vision goggles (Ibid). Given the existing links it is very likely that the CIA co-operated with Peruvian security forces during the takeover of the residence of the Japanese ambassador by the *Movimiento Revolucionario Tupac Amaru* (MRTA) in 1996–1997, although other countries, such as Britain, also sent advisors (BBC, April 22/97).

The *Yanacocha* case is symptomatic of Montesinos' role as a fixer. More importantly, the acquisition of the Yanacocha mine by the US Corporation Newmont, the outcome of corrupt practices, is also an example of the shady side of soft power. The French state-owned company Bureau de Recherches Geologiques et Minieres (BRGM) owned 24.7 per cent of Yanacocha shares. When the French government intended to privatize BRGM, it offered the company's shares to the Australian mining consortium Normandy, although the other partners, Newmont and Buenaventura Minerias, had precedence purchasing BRGM's shares. The case went to Peru's Supreme Court in order to decide whether the French could sell to Normandy or whether Newmont and Buenaventura had priority (*El Peruano*, Dec. 4/03: 4). One of the numerous videos produced by Montesinos, dated May 19th, 1998, shows a meeting between the spy chief and Supreme Court Judge Jaime Beltrán Quiroga. Montesinos asked the judge to vote in favour of Newmont because of the need to maintain good relations with the United States (*La República*, Oct. 26/05: 16–17).

An earlier audio tape, dated February 26, 1998, featured Montesinos in conversation with Larry Kurlander, Newmont's No. 3 executive officer with the spy chief promising his support for Newmont's court case. On the audio tape Montesinos promised to use "some pressure" (*La República*, Aug. 29/02: 10; also see McClintock and Vallas, 2005). Another video dated April 14, 1998, showed Montesinos in conversation with Don Arabian, then the CIA's station chief in Lima where he informed his guest of Peruvian intelligence operations launched against the French. Peru's Supreme Court indeed granted the concession to Newmont in June 1998. In August 2001, during one of his trials, Montesinos also claimed that he had been approached by

Peter Romero, a top official in the US State Department, to help resolve the matter "in favour of Newmont" (Ibid; also see *La República*, Oct. 24/05: 9; *La República*, Oct. 26/05: 16–17; McClintock and Vallas, 2005).

While Kurlander denied any payoffs he charged the French with "inappropriate" behaviour, pointing out among other things that bribery was tax-deductible in France (which was true at the time). According to his own description, Kurlander felt distressed when dealing with Montesinos whom he considered somewhat of a shady personality. However, on the audio tape he appeared quite comfortable with Montesinos even offering his assistance to overcome the regime's Number Two image problems in the United States. The Newmont Mining Corporation officially denied that Kurlander had been sent to influence Montesinos to act on its behalf. This was in turn declared to be untrue by the company's former executive officer who maintained that his superiors forced him to meet Montesinos because the spy chief was the 'guy to talk to' (Ibid; also see *La República*, Oct. 27/05:16–17; PBS Frontline, Oct. 2005; McClintock and Vallas, 2005). The French Ambassador at the time, Antoine Blanca, maintained that Newmont and Buenaventura had "bought" the decision (*La República*, Dec. 4/03: 10). Blanca also insisted that the court's vote was "the result of an accord between the Peruvian government and the US Embassy" which France did not wish to "oppose" (Ibid).

Montesinos was likewise seen as a key ally in the drug war despite the numerous revelations of his involvement with traffickers. Youngers (2003) maintained that US officials consistently ignored trustworthy information which tied Montesinos to the narcotics trade. In Peru such links were common knowledge because he had defended a number of well-known Colombian and Peruvian drug traffickers during the late 1970s and early 1980s. Ugarteche (2002) similarly argued that the US government must have been aware of Montesinos' drug connections because Peruvians knew. Montesinos himself expressed in Vladi-video 1475 that the regime had enjoyed a decade of "optimal relations" with both the Bush and Clinton administrations when it came to combating terrorism and the drug trade (Jochamowitz, 2002a: 92).

In late September 1996, Nicholas Burns from the US State Department issued a statement maintaining that Washington had "no knowledge that any high-ranking Peruvian government official" was involved in drug trafficking or money laundering activities (*La República*, Sept. 22/1996a: 6). According to another interpretation, the US administration was very much aware of Montesinos activities' but did not want to aggravate the Peruvian government (*Gestión*, Sept. 15/96: 7). Dammert (2001) argued that Montesinos' escape in 2000 had been arranged and that the CIA looked out for him for several months thereafter. Still, once in Venezuela Montesinos no longer enjoyed protection. The former "strong man of the dictatorship ... was guarded by people" linked to Venezuelan officials "who were ready to kill him and who [eventually] handed him over for a fistful of dollars" (Ibid, 343).

It is generally agreed upon that the most powerful foreigner in Peru is the US ambassador (McClintock and Vallas, 2006). Nevertheless, the treatment which Washington's ambassadors have received is not always due to their station as envoys of a global hegemonic power. The outspoken Anthony Quainton who began serving as ambassador in 1989 was rather unpopular. As noted earlier, Quainton even visited the Upper Huallaga valley and complained to General Ríos Araico about Peru's noncompliance in the drug war (*Oiga*, Jan. 24/94: 22). US ambassadors Alvin Adams and Dennis Jett had protested the human rights violations of the regime and paid the price by being excluded from "the upper echelons of the Peruvian government" (Palmer, 2006: 236; also see Youngers, 2003). Especially Jett's actions also did not receive support in Washington. The State Department was particularly unhappy when the ambassador publically expressed his misgivings about the regime's human rights abuse, such as in the case of army intelligence agent Leonor La Rosa in 1997 (McClintock and Vallas, 2005). His successor, Ambassador John Hamilton who arrived in Peru in late 1998, believed he could be more successful by operating "behind the scenes" (Palmer, 2006: 237). It was his task to improve relations with the regime which meant working with Fujimori and Montesinos "to get things done" (McClintock and Vallas, 2005: 255).

In Vladi-video 1792 Montesinos expressed his delight about the attitude shown by Hamilton as opposed to his predecessor Jett who had caused "problems ... making declarations" (Jochamowitz, 2002a: 91). Montesinos himself believed that Peru was not important enough for the United States to care about (Ibid). Montesinos also thought that because of his good relations with US 'drug tsar' Barry McCaffrey Washington was willing to overlook the regime's defects because of the "close co-operation on the counterdrug front" (Palmer, 2006: 236–237). Finally, Fujimori and Montesinos deemed that the United States needed a stable Peru as a regional partner because of the escalating situation in Colombia.

Washington's influence was strongly evident in the activities of the Organization of American States. Created in 1948 the OAS had largely served the purpose of preserving US interests in the hemisphere during the Cold War, while most of its members ignored the organization's articles which specified that democracy was a "condition of membership" (Levitt, 2006: 94). Still, in 1991, the OAS implemented the so-called Resolution 1080 which exhorted governments to adhere to democratic practices but which also required them to react if democracy in a member state was threatened. It was thus the OAS which played a major role in forcing President Fujimori to return to democracy after the April 1992 coup. Fujimori's initial proposal to have the "autogolpe ratified by referendum" was rejected by the organization (Ibid, 103). The OAS did accept the president's offer to hold "elections for a Democratic Constituent Congress [to] draft a new constitution" which would have to be approved via national referendum (Ibid).

Conversely, the OAS had been perceived as a vehicle that furthered Fujimori's and Washington's interests. The observers sent by the OAS to the 1995 election witnessed many electoral irregularities which were subsequently played down in their report. The opposition candidate in 1995, Javier Peréz de Cuellar, complained that his campaign had been interfered with in various ways. For example, phone calls were intercepted by the *Servicio de Inteligencia Nacional* (SIN). However, these claims were ignored by both the OAS and Washington (McClintock and Vallas, 2005). The OAS delegation's head, Santiago Murray, did express concern about the unlawful "participation of public officials in the Fujimori campaign" (*Oiga*, Apr. 3/1995: 8; also see *Sí*, Jan. 23/95: 10–19; *Oiga*, March 20/95: 17–20). Nevertheless, he absolved Fujimori of any wrongdoing stating that those involved had acted "without having received any directive from the government" (Ibid). After the election Murray insisted no fraud had been committed despite numerous verifiable claims by the opposition, most importantly the fact that some 40 per cent of the congressional votes had been declared void by the *Jurado Nacional de Elecciones* (JNE) (*Caretas*, Apr. 20/95; also see *Oiga*, Apr. 24/95: 10; McClintock, 1999). Thus, the Fujimori government strongly backed an OAS delegation for the 2000 election in the hope "that the low electoral standards of earlier ... missions would continue ..." (McClintock and Vallas, 2005: 260). In turn, the OAS mission was greeted with scepticism by Peru's opposition (Ibid).

The head of the 2000 OAS mission, Eduardo Stein, was confronted with numerous infractions of the electoral process which have been described elsewhere in this book. Still, one of the most pronounced irregularities was the fact that during the first round of elections some 1.4 million more votes had been cast than there were eligible voters (Taylor, 2000). Stein reported "serious concerns for the overall quality of elections" and requested that the second round be postponed until an improved voting system could be set up; a proposal that was rejected by Fujimori (Levitt, 2006: 109). This left Stein no alternative but to conclude that the regime "would not permit a victory" of an opposition candidate (McClintock and Vallas, 2005: 264). Still, even though Washington policy makers viewed the electoral process as flawed, the State Department was unhappy about the withdrawal of presidential candidate Alejandro Toledo from the second round. Fujimori thus won the runoff vote unopposed (Ibid).

Moreover, Washington and the OAS believed that it would be possible to get rid of Montesinos while keeping Fujimori in power. The United States continued to support Fujimori himself even after Montesinos' downfall and US Ambassador Hamilton worked hard to keep the president in office despite growing protests in the streets (Ibid; also see Palmer, 2006). Thus, Fujimori teamed up with Hamilton to arrange for Montesinos' escape to Panama in September 2000 (Ibid). Both the US and the OAS pressured the country to give asylum to Montesinos but Panama refused (Youngers, 2003). Hamilton later explained his own participation with the need to move quickly because of an alleged coup plan by Montesinos. Conversely, it is difficult to believe that a coup would have been possible at this point. Indeed, Hamilton himself contacted Washington maintaining "that there was no threat of a coup" (Ibid). As noted by McClintock and Vallas (2005), between the 2000 election and the collapse of the regime the United States "did not take any action against the Peruvian government" (2005: 266–267). Indeed, the US ambassador attended Fujimori's inauguration in July 2000. However, Washington seriously underestimated the explosive domestic situation. According to Youngers (2003), Peru's president and his advisor had similarly miscalculated. Thus, even if the duo had succeeded "one more time to appease neighbouring governments and Washington, they overestimated their capacity to calm down the Peruvians" (Ibid, 373).

6. Conclusion

It is true that Washington and the OAS condemned the fraud that resulted in Fujimori's re-election in 2000 (Burt, 2009). At the same time, the roles played by both were ambiguous which led Levitt (2006) to conclude that "Fujimori's fall was in no sense caused by ... OAS activities" (2006: 110). The head of the OAS mission in Peru in 2000, Eduardo Stein, pointed out shortly after the collapse of the regime that national and international human rights organizations played a fundamental role "in the transition to democracy" (Youngers, 2003: 416). Levitsky and Cameron (2003) also pointed to the domestic front which triggered the regime's collapse. Palmer (2006) noted likewise that Fujimori's demise in late 2000 resulted from "growing internal pressures," not US foreign policy (2006: 240).

Conversely, Tanaka (2001) maintained that the collapse of the regime was caused by "external factors ... which precipitated the internal contradictions of the regime" (2001: 101). The drug war in Latin America presented Washington with the justification for increasing its military presence in Colombia to counter the growing threat posed by the capacities of the rebels from the *Fuerzas Armadas Revolucionarias de Colombia* (FARC). Also, the creators of *Plan Colombia* were less interested in fighting the drug trade but in "protecting US political and economic interests in the region" (Leech, 2005). US backing for Montesinos ended when it became evident that the spy chief had participated in an illegal arms-for-drugs deal with the FARC. As noted by Tanaka (2001), the arms scandal positioned "the regime in open opposition to the strategic interests of the United States" (2001: 101). This fact brought about "strong US pressures" to get rid of the spy chief which in turn "produced the divorce between Fujimori and Montesinos" that cracked "the nucleus ... of the regime" (Ibid; also see Palmer, 2006; Burt, 2009). Still, without the popular protests Washington and the OAS may have succeeded to stabilize the Fujimori government – sans Montesinos – for another five years.

In sum, the growing antidemocratic tendencies of the regime were not seriously questioned by Washington. US policy makers never publically stated that Peru was not a democracy or that another presidential re-election was indeed unconstitutional. This despite the fact that the State Department's own reports consistently commented negatively on Peru's human rights situation in general and the 2000 electoral fraud in particular (McClintock and Vallas, 2005). Former Ambassador Hamilton's description of US relations with Montesinos is also revealing. Thus, Washington "dealt with him in a way consistent with our commitment to democracy and human rights through-out the ten years" (Todd and Bloch, 2003: 93).

Chapter 10

Pecunia ... Olet (And Not All that Shines is Gold)

Corrupt, stupid grasping functionaries will make at least as big a muddle of Socialism as stupid, selfish and acquisitive employers can make of Capitalism.
(Walter Lippmann)

1. Introduction

The *Río Tinto* basin in Andalucía, Spain, is one of the oldest mining sites in the world dating back some 5,000 years. It has been exploited by Iberians, Phoenicians, Carthaginians, Romans, Visigoths, Arabs, Spanish, and British. In the 1880s the British Rio Tinto Mining Corporation was involved in the exploitation of gold, silver, and copper. The company not only provided extremely poor conditions and pitiful wages to its workers, mining activities also released highly toxic fumes of sulphur dioxide which destroyed the pastures, decimated the farm animals, polluted the air, and wrecked people's health. Company officials had told locals that the poisonous substances had positive health effects because they killed off viruses. When some 11,000 miners, farmers, and inhabitants of the nearby town of Río Tinto gathered to protest these abuses and demand improvements, the company called on its friends in high places who sent in the military. Upon their arrival the soldiers fired several salvoes into the crowd that included women, children, and old people. Thereafter, the troopers charged and bayoneted those on the ground. The number of dead was never determined because the bodies vanished, but according to estimates several dozen protesters perished. Subsequently, the slaughter was deleted from the official history of Río Tinto. In 1954, the Río Tinto mines were returned to the Spanish state, then the Franco dictatorship, which continued the cover-up of the slaughter although locals referred to 1888 as the 'year of the shootings'. Today the mines of Río Tinto are a tourist attraction. What gives these events a special significance is the fact that the slaughter occurred in response to the first recorded ecological protest in Europe. The Río Tinto massacre, which occurred on February 4th, 1888, forms the background to the 2007 film titled *El Corazon de la Tierra* [The Heart of the Earth] by Spanish director Antonio Cuadri. Moreover, as noted by the director,

> Andalucía was then the Third World and [the story] ... the film tells we can see today in many Latin American and African countries ... The purchase of political will [i.e., corruption], slavery, and the exploitation of foreign resources ... [are] present today in many countries of Africa, Asia, or Latin America ... (*El País*, Apr. 13/07: 60; also see *El Mundo*, Apr. 11/07: 62; *El País* – Supplement La Tierra, Apr. 21/07: 39).[1]

Multinational corporations (MNCs) from the developed world not only produce the medications we take or the food we eat, they also effectively control the natural resources in many parts of the globe. A good number of countries in the global South own an abundance of resources, but they do not possess the technological knowledge and the means to extract and market them. Investments by multinationals are therefore commonsense and essential, and it would be unreasonable that such companies would not expect to make profits. However, upon inspection it becomes evident that only in a very few instances are the accords reached between multinational corporations and developing nations just. Under pressure from international financial institutions, such as the World Bank, debt-ridden countries impose taxes which are

1 The company is today called the Rio Tinto Western Holding. It is one of the largest mining companies in the world producing aluminium, copper, gold, iron, diamonds, coal and titanium dioxide in some forty countries, including Peru. In 2005, Rio Tinto gained the concession to exploit copper at the La Granja mine in the Department of Cajamarca (*El Peruano*, Dec. 17/05: 8).

extremely low compared to the incredible earnings made by corporations who extract and export these resources. Large sections of the populations of these countries live in abject poverty, while their nations' wealth is effectively being stolen (Werner and Weiss, 2006; also see McMullan, 1993; Green and Ward, 2004). These outcomes are the result of

> bribes obtained by local elites in return for advantageous conditions for multinationals. Due to the lack of transparent controls there is more money which disappears into channels of corruption than remains in the country in form of taxes (Ibid, 45; also see Robbins, 2000).

In addition, the exploitation of mining resources often takes place under conditions "inconceivable" in developed nations (Ibid). These include, for example, habitat destruction or the poisoning of people and livestock as toxic substances are carelessly released into the environment. The damage is also due to the changes in technology which have transpired since the 1950s. Until that time, the extraction of gold or other precious mineral ores took place mostly in subterranean mines whereby one would simply follow the veins of the metals which generally appeared in high concentrations. By now most of these locations have been exploited. However, modern technologies make possible the extraction of every gram through open pit mining even when the concentration of the desired metal is low. The practice, however, is far more destructive than earlier methods. Open pit mining involves the daily use of explosives which results in large clouds of dust that spread over rivers and agricultural land. The explosives contain arsenic and other toxic substances that spread by rain fall. Open pit mining results in the removal of top soil which not only creates large scars in the landscape. The top soil can be compared to a sponge that absorbs the rain water which then seeps into rivers and subterranean water systems. Once the soil has been removed, not only will the subterranean lagoons go dry but so does the land that is used for agricultural purposes (*La República*, Aug. 27/06a: 4–6; also see US Bureau of Mines, 1996; *La República*, Dec. 10/06: 4–5).

In addition, the process of extracting precious metals involves the use of toxic substances. According to Roopnarine (2002), Canadian companies revolutionized the industry with the introduction of heap leaching, a method adopted worldwide since. Heap leaching requires that hundreds of thousands of tons of ore are piled on a small hill onto prepared beds of supposedly impermeable materials. At large mining operations up to 600.000 tons of ore are removed daily as one ton only contains small amounts of the desired metals. These mounts of ore, which are up to 150 meters high and are referred to as lixiviation or leaching piles, are subsequently treated with a cyanide solution to extract the gold, silver, or other metals. The construction is "supported by dams lined with plastic and clay" (2002: 88). However, levees can leak, break, or overflow and release toxins into the local environment, especially after heavy precipitation. Moreover, the plastic liners used to prevent leakage into the soil below can tear, particularly if they are set up and maintained haphazardly.

The above should be considered in light of the unique ecosystems encountered in the Andes where most of the mining in Peru takes place. These ecosystems made possible the emergence of entire agricultural societies at 4,000 metres above sea level thousands of years ago, while little to no farming at all occurs in Europe or North America above 1,500 metres (Ibid; also see US Bureau of Mining, 1996; *La República*, Aug. 27/06: 4–6; *La República*, Dec. 10/06: 2).

This chapter will provide an overview of mining in Peru followed by a discussion of corrupt practices in the country's extractive industries. Particularly in the case of the mining sector the harmful consequences carry over from the 1990s into the present as practices established by the Fujimori regime have continued to this day. I will focus on three corporations whose activities are descriptive of other national or multinational mining companies operating in Peru. The corporations selected are engaged in similar activities in mining properties owned around the world:

(1) The mining giant Newmont from the United States (US) which owns the *Yanacocha* mine, the largest gold mine in Latin America;

(2) The Doe Run Company, also from the US, extracts copper and so-called poly-metals at its mine at *La Oroya*;
(3) The Canadian Barrick Gold Corporation, the world's largest gold mining company, which owns the *La Pierina* mine.

As elsewhere corporate crime in Peru is difficult to verify, the more so as unethical or illegal practices were authorized under the Fujimori regime. Under these circumstances, the proof relied upon has to be in line with the previously noted observation of a fictitious detective namely that "once one eliminated the impossible, whatever is left, no matter how improbable, must be the truth" (Doyle, 1987: 185). The argument is that the activities discussed in this chapter transpire because of corporate corruption and crime even though it may not be possible to assign responsibility to a specific company. Still, the practices described, such as massive environmental contamination, leave the reader no other possible conclusion. While it is hopeless to demonstrate unscrupulous activities in every detail, I believe it is reasonable to conclude that the existing conditions of extraction which permit these abuses to occur could only have come about through a form of corruption. Finally, the activities described here have continued to negatively impact Peru after 2000 even though the dictator is gone and imprisoned, because the contracts signed by the regime with various MNCs have expiry dates of between fifteen and twenty years.

2. A Short History of Mining in Peru

Mining has been in evidence among the pre-Columbian societies of Peru from the *Chavín* civilization which existed between 800 and 1000 BC. Indeed, Andean metallurgy was highly developed in the Inca Empire of the early fifteenth century. After the *Conquista* the Spanish began the exploration and exploitation of gold, silver, mercury, and lead. During the colonial period the labour was done by natives who were drafted into the work force through the *mita*, a practice introduced by the Spanish that obliged the Indians to work for their overlords for a given period during the year (*Sociedad Nacional de Minería, Petroleo, y Energía* – SNMPE, 2005; also see Brown, 2001; Mann, 2006).

It is noteworthy that miners in Peru during the Inca as well as the colonial period used coca leaves while working. Indeed, as mining activities intensified coca took on an important role in the colonial economy. The Indian labourers in the gold and silver mines received coca as part of their wages because it made them work harder (Naranjo, 1981; also see Unanue, 1794; Del Olmo, 1992).[2] In Potosí, Spain's silver-mining capital in South America, located in today's Bolivia, the coca trade alone was worth half a million pesos annually during the second half of the sixteenth century (Keen, 1974). Henman (1981) observed that a trader bringing 60,000 pounds of coca leaves to the Potosí mines could expect to make 7,500 pesos, the equivalent of over 34 kilos in gold, enough to retire in comfort in sixteenth century Spanish America. More importantly, the precious metals looted from the Americas played a key role in the growth of the European economies as Spanish commerce distributed gold and silver over much of the continent (Galeano, 1982).

Following independence, the mining sector – and by the late nineteenth century – the exploitation of petroleum remained key factors in the Peruvian economy. After Peru lost the War of the Pacific (1879–1883) against Chile mineral mining was fundamental to economic recovery. By the turn of the twentieth century various foreign companies, such as the US owned Cerro de Pasco Mining Corporation, had entered Peru. Between 1898 and 1918, exports grew eightfold

2 The Quechua and Aymara people have used coca for thousands of years. The plant and its derivatives are still employed as medicines against altitude sickness, colds, stomach pains, colic, diarrhoea, cramps, nausea, toothache, stomach ulcers, rheumatism, and asthma. Those who use it in the traditional manner, by chewing the leaves, claim that it is a stimulant which gives them stamina and strength and also relieves "feelings of hunger, thirst, cold, and fatigue" (Grinspoon and Bakalar, 1981: 150–151).

because of mineral exploitation by foreign companies. Until the discovery of large petroleum reserves in Venezuela in the mid-1920s, Peru was also the primary exporter of crude in South America. Like most of the world Peru was negatively affected by the crash of the stock market in 1929, leading to the collapse of the country's exports. The global economic crisis caused a shortage of foreign investment which was replaced by local capital, particularly in the petroleum sector. During the 1930s public air transport became available resulting in a boost to exploration and exploitation. By the 1950s mining and petroleum exports as well as foreign investments into these sectors were on the increase, encouraged by government legislation. The 1968 leftist military coup brought fundamental changes and resulted in the nationalization of much of the Peruvian mining industry which was organized into state conglomerates, such as the Empresa Minera del Centro del Perú (Centromin Perú). However, not all mining companies were nationalized. For example, the US owned Southern Peru Copper Corporation (SPCC) was exempted (Carhuarica and Velásquez, 2005; also see SNMPE, 2005).

After the end of military rule and the return of democracy in 1980, the country's economy was negatively affected by the disruptions caused by *Sendero* attacks against mining installations. The Shining Path relied strongly on local resources, such as dynamite from mining camps, for its war. After the election of the Fujimori government in 1990 and the defeat of the rebels after 1993–1994, the mining, gas and petroleum sectors experienced once again great changes. The policies introduced by the earlier military government were reversed, and companies were once again privatized (Ibid; also see Naylor, 1993; SNMPE, 2005).

Following the liberation of investment policies, and due to the extremely generous conditions offered by the Fujimori regime and thereafter, some US$ 9 billion of foreign private investments entered the mining sector between 1992 and 2007 (Barrantes, Zárate, and Durand, 2005). In 1992, mining activities in Peru took place on 4 million hectares; however, by 2004 the total area that was being mined had doubled to about 8 million hectares affecting 55 per cent of rural and indigenous communities in Peru. By 1999, mining concessions given away by the government covered some 22 million hectares (De Echave, 2003). By 2005, the Peruvian state had handed out concessions for an area totalling 60 million hectares. In those departments where mining is concentrated the landscape is covered with exploitation concessions granted by the Lima government. By 1999, the year before the demise of the Fujimori regime, over 50 per cent of the territory of the Department of Cajamarca had been given away to mining companies. For the Departments of Cuzco, Huancavelica and Lima, the figures were 42, 40 and 38 per cent respectively. Even in Apurímac which is not considered to be a mining department 28 per cent of the territory had been handed to mining companies. By 2006, Peru had become the world's fifth largest producer of gold, second of silver, third of copper and fourth of zinc. In the same year, the mining industry contributed 45 per cent to the country's exports, but paid only 4 per cent of taxes into state coffers and provided a mere 1 per cent in direct employment (Ibid; also see Cuadros, Consiglieri F., and de Echave, 2005; Portocarrero, Márquez, and Cárdenas, 2006; *La República*, Aug. 12/06: 11; *La República*, Dec. 10/06: 4–5).

According to Bebbington et al (2008), the increasing investment made into Peru's extractive industries has gone hand in hand with rising social polarization. For the year 2005, Peru's Office of the Ombudsman, the *Defensoría del Pueblo*, registered "thirty-three separate conflicts related to mining" (2008: 3). In his study of the causes behind the protests in Peruvian mining communities Bury (2002) refers to four factors: the reduction in the quality and quantity of the local water supply for agriculture; the decrease in available land to local farmers for their crops and livestock; the increase in social problems such as prostitution and crime; and the lack of economic development in the regions where mining takes place.

The mining boom which began in the 1990s was not limited to Peru. Rather, it is international in scope and has resulted in a geographic restructuring of global mining activities. Until the early 1990s, the principal mining countries were Australia, Canada, the United States, and some Pacific island nations. In 1990, Latin America only received 12 per cent of mining investments, compared to 36 per cent in North America. By 1995, the figure for Latin America had risen to 28 per cent, while investments into mining in North America had declined to 23 per cent. By the year 2000 Latin America had become the primary region for new mining investments, followed by Africa and Asia (De Echave, 2003).

3. Unethical Practices during the Process of Privatization

In early September 2006, Canada's Ambassador to Lima, Genèvieve des Rivières, discussed her country's economic relations with her host nation in an interview given to *El Comercio*, one of Peru's leading dailies. For several years Peruvians had been debating whether or not to impose royalties and higher taxes on the earnings of international mining companies, some of which are Canadian-owned. These companies' profits had skyrocketed since 2002–2003 due to high metal prices. Ambassador De Rivières was asked "whether the present debate" on increased taxes had "generated any unfavourable reaction" in Canada? (*El Comercio*, Sept. 2/06: B2). In response, De Rivières maintained that "existing treaties" should be honoured (Ibid). "If Peru was to begin revising contracts ..., it sends a negative message to the international community" (Ibid). Also, the ambassador claimed that the Lima government had been unable to come up with suggestions for projects already funded with the existing contributions by mining companies. Hence, what possible purpose would any additional funds derived from taxes serve? (Ibid).

Various commissions were formed during the interim government of President Valentin Paniagua (November 2000–July 2001) to investigate the economic crimes of the Fujimori regime. These revealed that various illegalities were committed during the process of privatization. The most important of these commissions were the ones presided over by Javier Diez Canseco (2001–2002) as well as Ernesto Herréra (2003–2004). Between 1991 and 2000 over two-hundred public companies were privatized generating "an estimated income of US$ 9.221 billion" although only US$ 6.993 billion entered the public treasury (Ugarteche, 2002: 25; also see Diez Canseco, 2002; Diez Canseco, 2002a). The commission identified the following crimes as specified in Peru's penal code which were committed during the period of privatization:

(1) Illicit Association for the purpose of breaking the law (art. 317);
(2) Embezzling public funds (art. 389);
(3) Illegal Collusion (art. 348);
(4) Fraud (art. 387);
(5) Incompatible negotiation (art. 397);
(6) Falsification of public documents (art. 427);
(7) Suppression, destruction, concealment of evidence (of wrong doing), failure to charge those responsible (art. 407);
(8) Treason (art. 332) (Alejos Calderon, 2002).

The contracts which Canada's top envoy to Peru referred to were established with representatives of an unsavoury regime. The agreements made with mostly foreign MNCs generally imposed very low taxes but asked for voluntary contributions to the mining communities and promises to invest in the companies bought. Unfortunately, many foreign corporations did not comply with these minimal requests made. Moreover, while earning record profits due to high prices, the same companies are often guilty of contaminating flora and fauna, endangering the health of people and farm animals, as well as repressing dissent to mining activities.

Already the acquisition of the mining properties was often marred by unethical practices. Kamphuis (2010) observed that Newmont Mining initially paid very little for the farming properties near its Yanacocha mine taking advantage of the locals' ignorance of land prices, or the fact that most people did not know how to read or write. One of the first farmers to sell his property to Newmont in the 1990s, Nicolás Cruzado, received a mere 100 Soles (less than 30 US$) per hectare for his property (*La República*, Dec. 10/06: 8). According to Bury (2002), property prices had increased to over US$ 1000 after the millennium. Kamphuis (2010) also noted in the case of the community Los Negritos that persons claiming to represent the district signed deals handing over land to the company in return for compensation. Kamphuis comments further that

> no evidence [exists] that the compensation funds were ever distributed to the Negritos Community in accordance with communal laws or decision-making processes. There is no evidence that the Negritos Community received information regarding the legal meaning of the land transfers, the right to fair compensation, the estimated value of the land at issue, the benefits that Yanacocha stood to acquire, or the possible environmental impacts of the planned mining activities. Rather, the documentary evidence reveals, not only that the signatories to the expropriation and easement agreements were not legitimately elected, but that they later became implicated in systematic acts of fraud, falsification of documents and intimidation in order to affect the transfer and sale of the community's land to Yanacocha (Ibid, 12–13).

4. A Digression on Profits, Royalties, and Windfall Taxes

Durand (2004: 128) noted that the ministry of economics and finance introduced numerous rules for the benefit of the investing corporations. "The pearl" among these was the previously mentioned "Supreme Decree 120–94–EF" (Ibid). The decree implied the following: "If you buy something which has one value, it can be re-evaluated at the price of the market (knowing that what was paid was not the real market price) and afterwards you can depreciate it as if it was a new product" (Ugarteche, 2002: 28). Fujimori himself – in conjunction with the ministry of economics and finance – actively participated in the talks resulting in the privatization of many companies in the Peruvian public sector, where he "secretly" put the presidential approval on hundreds of contracts providing the buying companies with tax-free status (Durand, 2004: 124). In turn, a number of multinationals, including the Canadian mining company Barrick, included the norm into their agreements with the government. Durand commented further that "given the climate of ... corruption it is difficult to imagine that these were favours freely given" (Ibid, 128).

The case went to court during the Toledo government where these companies successfully argued that they had "acquired rights" (Ibid). It should be noted, however, that Supreme Decree 120–94–EF had been "declared unconstitutional" by Peru's Congress in July 2002 (Campodónico, *La República*, July 5/05: 11; also see *Gestión*, March 8/05: 18). Moreover, former President Alberto Fujimori and the former Minister of Economics and Finance, Jorge Camet, had been charged with breaking the constitution for issuing the decree. In May 2003, Peru's Congress had banned Camet from participating in political life for the period of five years because of said decree. Campodónico adds that Rosario Alemenara, a former Vice-Minister of Economics in 1994, testified "before the Herrera Commission" that the decree "neither had the approval of the [*Superintendencia Nacional de Administración Tributaria*] SUNAT [Peru's official tax agency] nor of the Directorate of Fiscal Policies of the ... [the ministry of economics and finance]" but had been given out directly by Camet (Ibid). The 'existing treaties' Canada's ambassador insists are valid have also been declared unconstitutional by Peru's Congress. Indeed, Campodónico referred to the contracts as a form of "state capture" (Ibid; also see Campodónico, *La República*, March 6/05: n. a.; *El Comercio*, Sept. 2/06: B2).

The tax exemptions given to large corporations served the purpose of attracting investments at a time when the country was still considered unstable during the last days of the Sendero rebellion. It is difficult to change the arrangements, however, because they have been enshrined in the constitution introduced by the regime in 1993. For example, article 62 reads that "through contracts ... the state can establish guarantees and other securities. They cannot be modified legislatively ..." but in exceptional cases (*La República*, Sept. 3/06: 13; also see Arias Quincot, 1994).

The accords awarding these exemptions to companies called *Convenios de Estabilidad Juridica* [Contracts of Judicial Stability] have been granted for a minimum of ten years. However, the majority of contracts will only expire between 2018 and 2020. In other words, only a few can be renegotiated. In turn companies like Newmont or Barrick pay no royalties and contribute very little to the development of the communities despite the great riches generated (*La República*, Apr. 24/06: 11; also see *La República*, May 4/06: 10).

As observed by Peruvian constitutional expert Francisco Eguiguren, eighteen mining projects run by foreign MNCs paid no royalties in 2006 although such exemptions were no longer necessary to attract investment (*La República*, Sept. 3/06: 13). As a result of rising prices, the average profits of mining companies in Peru had risen 300 per cent between 2002 and 2006. For example, the earnings at the Yanacocha gold mine increased by 225 per cent between 2002 and 2005. Yet, the mining departments Ancash, Cajamarca, Cuzco, Huancavelica, and Pasco which produced these riches had a poverty rate of 70 per cent. Eguiguren also observed that the 1979 Constitution abolished by Fujimori contained "instruments ... to satisfy social goals" (Ibid).

Peru's Congress did indeed approve a law on royalties that went into effect in 2005. However, some international mining companies, such as Barrick, refused to pay because of the agreements reached with the Fujimori government when the contracts were signed. The Toledo government returned with the argument that the law did not create a tax, but a royalty which the owners of mining concessions had to pay to the state in return for the rights to exploit non-renewable resources. In fact, the case went to the Peru's highest tax court. Although the companies lost, they did not pay (*La República*, Aug. 24/06: 4). Carlos de Solar, the President of the *Sociedad Nacional de Minería*, *Petróleo* y *Energía* (SNMPE) or the National Society of Mining, Petroleum and Energy – the roof organization of the national and multinational companies in the business of exploiting Peru's mineral, petroleum and gas resources – claimed that the tax discussion was over and existing accords needed to expire. Moreover, the agreements made with the Fujimori government should be respected in order not to interrupt the flow of investment into the mining and energy sectors. These expected investments over the next five years (2006–2011) for the mining industry alone were US$ 10 billion and twice that amount for the mining and energy sectors combined (*La República*, Aug. 12/06: 11; also see *El Comercio*, Aug. 26/06: A2; *Gestión*, Sept.19/06: 10).

Furthermore, the mining lobbies managed to influence the legislation on royalties. Thus it is the norm to apply the payment of the royalty to gross earnings before deductions, as is the case in a number of countries with mining industries, such as Australia, Bolivia, Brazil, Chile and South Africa. However, the law introduced in Peru applies the royalty only to the earnings after the income tax as well as labour and production costs have been deducted. The difference is considerable. For example, the 2003 gross earnings of the Southern Peru Copper Company or SPCC amounted to US$ 798 million. A 3 per cent royalty on US$ 798 million generates US$ 24 million. However, SPCC deducted 59 per cent or US$ 470 million in income tax, labour and production costs which reduced earnings to US$ 328 million. A 3 per cent royalty on that amount comes to about US$ 10 million (*La República*, May 23/04: 27).

Another major issue is the question of windfall taxes which are generally imposed by governments if the earnings of a given industry skyrocket. Between 2002 and mid-2006, the price of copper increased by 402 per cent, zinc by 420 per cent, and silver by 185 per cent (*El Comercio* (Día_1), Aug. 7/06: 12). By January 2007, the price of an ounce of gold had reached US$ 620; a 23 per cent increase over the previous year (*Gestión*, Jan. 3/07: 19).[3]

Mining production in Peru is far cheaper than in other countries. For example, according to Newmont Mining, the average production costs of an ounce of gold for all its subsidiaries in 2004 was US$ 231, while the average price for the ounce of gold stood at US$ 412. Most profitable among its properties was the *Batu Hijau* mine in Indonesia where costs amounted to US$ 128, allowing for earnings of US$ 284 per ounce. Production costs at Yanacocha – which generates four times more gold than Batu Hijau – stood at US$ 132, and providing

3 On April 20, 2011 the price of an ounce of gold reached US$ 1,500 (*News Just Now*, Apr. 20/11).

for profits of US$ 280 per ounce (Campodónico, 2006a; also see *New Internationalist*, Dec. 06: 14). Peruvian economist Dennis Falvy already commented in late January 2003 that the rise of the price of gold only resulted in more earnings for companies but brought few benefits to the regions where the precious metal was being exploited. Mining companies made profits in Peru when the gold price was at US$ 250 because of the revenue arrangements made with the Fujimori regime. However, as observed by Falvy, the gold price had risen to US$ 364 while companies neither paid increased taxes to the central government nor substantially contributed to the development of the mining regions (*Liberación*, Jan. 26/03: n. a.).

Alan García had loudly demanded a law on windfall taxes during the 2006 presidential election campaign and maintained his anti-mining rhetoric until the very day he was inaugurated in office as president (*La República*, Aug. 12/06: 11). In early July 2006 then President-elect García postulated that the *Alianza Popular Revolucionaria Americana* (APRA), which claims to have social democratic roots, was not "the party of investors or managers" and that the state would not be the "night watchman of these gentlemen [in the mining industry] defending them against social protests" (*La República*, July 13/06: 3). APRA party leader Mauricio Mulder echoed his boss. Mining companies should make investments in social development projects and improve the working conditions of their employees. Moreover, he noted that "Father State" would not come to the defence of the mining companies unless they paid more taxes (Ibid).

Indeed, the previously mentioned law on royalties introduced and approved by Congress in 2005 had been a project designed largely by APRA, then in opposition. However, in his inauguration speech on July 28, 2006, García made no mention of any additional taxes or royalties for the mining industry to gain more income for state coffers. Instead, out of fear to scare away investors, the newly elected president opted to set up a roundtable with industry representatives to discuss a 'special voluntary contribution' (*La República*, July 30/06: 16; also see *La República*, July 13/06: 3). Critics of the plan expressed that the voluntary payment would not result in additional funds because companies would simply deduct it from the little income tax they paid (Ibid). The García plan was even viewed as counter-productive by the neoliberal opposition party *Unión Nacional* (UN). Party leader Lourdes Flores referred to the idea as "passing around the hat" (*La República*, Aug. 27/06: 3).

Similarly, a law on windfall taxes, proposed by Congresswoman Gloria Ramos from the *Unión por el Perú* (UPP), and prepared by a congressional commission, was archived in December 2006 after being rejected by the representatives of APRA, the neoliberal UN, and the *Grupo Parlamentario Fujimorista* (GFP) which consisted of former supporters of Fujimori regime. The law would have established taxes of fifty, forty or thirty per cent respectively on excessive earnings depending on the size of the company. According to the director of the non-governmental organization (NGO) *Grupo Andes*, Juan Aste, one of Peru's leading experts on mining issues, the law would have resulted in additional revenues of about 5.2 billion Soles (approx. US$ 1.6 billion) over three years. Meanwhile, the García government's voluntary contribution received from the industry amounted to an estimated 2.5 billion Soles (approx. US$ 774 million) over a period of five years. Santiago Fujimori, the commission's president and brother of the former president, noted that the proposed law to tax excessive earnings "had the opposition of the ministry of energy and mining and the National Society of Mining, Petroleum and Energy" which represents national and international mining interests (*El Comercio*, Aug. 3/06: B3; also see *La República*, Aug. 10/06: 11; *La República*, Aug. 12/06: 11; *Gestión*, Aug. 25/06: 10; *El Comercio*, Aug. 26/06: A2; *La República*, Aug. 28/06: 12; *Gestión*, Dec. 22/06: 13).

Garcia's flip-flop had gone full circle by mid-August 2006. Following an outbreak of violence at the Yanacocha mine the government introduced law 28878 which modified the criminal code to "penalize and repress social discontent ... and the legitimate protests ... of the denizens of mining zones" (*La República*, Aug. 20/06: 13). In addition, the government introduced a new law aimed to control the activities of foreign and domestic NGOs whose activities, it was claimed, contributed to unrest in the mining regions (Crabtree, Nov.

22/06; also see Toche, 2003). Despite rising metal prices the government of Alan García did not bring in a windfall tax. It did introduce a new royalty law in 2008 which asked for payments between 1 to 3 per cent which is very low.[4] In neighbouring Chile the government requests 35 per cent. Meanwhile, the five largest mining MNCs in Peru, including Newmont and Barrick, had net earnings of US$ 20 billion between 2005 and June 2010 (Salazar, 2010; also see *247wallst.com.*, June 6/11). Lora Cam (2005) summarized as follows:

> [B]etween 1992 and 2002, Peru exported US$ 29 billion and the regions of this country which lost their resources, soil, water and lives, received 0.7 per cent of the amount obtained. Nevertheless, Peruvian President Alberto Fujimori ... gave great benefits to these transnational [corporations] (2005: 318).

5. Tales from Three Multinational Corporations

A) The Newmont Mining Corporation

In 1994, the US mining company Newmont became the owner of the largest gold mine in Latin America at Yanacocha. Newmont is one of the world's main producers of gold with subsidiaries in a number of countries, including Australia, Ghana, Indonesia, Peru, and the United States (Newmont Gold, 2011; also see *New Internationalist*, Dec. 06: 15). Initially the Yanacocha mine, located at 3.500 metres above sea level, was only expected to yield 80.000 ounces of gold a year when it began operating in 1993; however, growth was far higher than expected reaching 250.000 ounces in the first year. By 2004, production at Yanacocha had increased to 2.4 million ounces, reaching 3.3 million ounces in 2005. This represented 45 per cent of the gold

4 A windfall tax on mining profits was finally signed into law by García's successor, Ollanta Humala in September 2011 (Emery, *Business Week*, Sept. 28/11).

mined in Peru that year (*El Comercio* (Dia_1), Aug. 21/06: 14–15; also see *La República*, Dec. 3/06: 8; *La República*, Dec.10/06: 4–5).

The minority shareholders of Yanacocha are the Peruvian mining company Minas Buenaventura which owns 43.65 per cent of shares, and the World Bank which holds 5 per cent, compared to 51.35 per cent for Newmont Mining. Conversely, Newmont is minority shareholder with 46.94 per cent of shares of the *La Zanja* mine while Minas Buenaventura owns 53.06 per cent. However, production at La Zanja with about 100,000 ounces of gold a year is much lower than at Yanacocha, the mother lode (*Gestión*, Apr. 12/02; also see *Peru 21*, Nov. 18/04; *La Razón*, May 21/05: 10–11).

The Newmont Mining Company and the Environment

According to the majority of local residents Newmont's mining activities at the Yanacocha mine have created a "contamination problem" which can be demonstrated, for example, by the death of fish and live stock (Barrantes et al, 2005: 119). In addition, it is the opinion of locals that the authorities as well as the company have done "little or nothing to undo the damage" (Ibid). The ecological harm caused by Newmont's practices has been considerable and directly affects more than 150.000 people according to anti-mining NGOs. As previously noted, changes in technology introduced since the 1950s make possible the extraction of every gram through open pit mining and heap leaching. However, these methods are more destructive to the environment than earlier practices. Those in charge of the Yanacocha mine claim that no cyanide escapes from the site. However, anti-mining activists maintain that some 25 per cent of the cyanide used evaporates during the extraction process, which is subsequently spread by wind and rain. An additional 25 per cent remain in the lixiviation fields whereby it is feared that the poison filters into the subsoil and the ground water through damaged plastic lining. Since 1996, the public service company in charge of supplying water to Cajamarca citizens has been increasing controls to detect contaminants. Studies done in 1996 and 1999 demonstrated that the water contained large quantities of the highly carcinogenic substance chromium VI+. According to World Health Organization (WHO) standards the maximum permissible level of chromium VI+ is 0.05 parts per million, while the levels encountered in the water supply near the Yanacocha mine were 375 parts per million or 7000 times higher. A 1999 study by Peru's national water quality agency SUNASS found poisonous heavy metals and other pollutants deriving from Yanacocha. In 2002, an expert from Montana State University, Steve Boldgett (MSc), confirmed that cyanide was indeed seeping into the watershed below the mine.[5] A commission studying water quality between January 2001 and December 2002 found the presence of heavy metals, sulphurs, phenols, and nitrates. A study undertaken in 2002 by Stratus Consulting concluded that mining had reduced the quality as well as quantity of the water. Aside from contaminating water, the Newmont Mining Corporation uses some 18 million cubic metres annually at Yanacocha for which it does not pay (Stratus Consulting, 2003; also see Ramírez and León, 2004; *Perú 21*, June 10/04: 19; *Liberación*, June 11/04: n. a.; *La República*, Dec. 10/06: 2–3).

According to its former executive officer, Larry Kurlander, the Newmont Mining Corporation was certainly aware of the environmental problems it caused. Kurlander maintained that he initiated a study which identified some "twenty problems of high priority" (*La República*, Oct. 27/05: 16–17). Apparently, he became so concerned he informed the company's highest executive officer, Wayne Murdy, pointing out that those responsible could end up in prison due to criminal negligence. Kurlander also argued that Newmont Mining did little to earn the trust of locals. He believed that it was not sufficient to get the government's permission to open up a mine but also to maintain good relations with the communities where mining took place. However, none of his recommendations were implemented (Ibid).[6]

---

5 Blodgett and Kuipers (2002) maintain that mining can cause movements at geological fault lines, negatively impact agricultural production, and result in ground water contamination.

6 The suggestions by Kurlander in fact mirror the publicity used by Newmont to show itself as a good corporate citizen as presented in one of the mining

Newmont has also been accused of bearing responsibility for the killings of individuals opposed to mining. In November 2006, Edmundo Becerra Cotrina, a leading figure in the anti-mining movement, was murdered by unknown gun men. While it is unlikely that Yanacocha officials were directly involved, Becerra had been identified as a threat by the private security company Forza which is in charge of protecting the Yanacocha site. According to local sources, at least six people had been murdered for their opposition to mining. Also, in 2006, during protests at the mine, the local farmer Isidro Llanos was shot and killed, likely by a member of Forza. It was revealed in January of 2009 that police and Forza officials had participated in the torture of several dozen individuals who were protesting the activities at the Majaz Mine in a neighbouring region (*La República*, Dec. 10/06: 6–7; also see Kamphuis, 2010).

In 2004, Newmont Mining Peruvian partner, Minas Buenaventura, became embroiled in violent protests when it began mining explorations at La Zanja in the province of Santa Cruz, Department of Cajamarca, where the US company was the minority shareholder. Locals worried about the ecological damages that mining would cause demanded the company's withdrawal in May 2004. After six months, approximately a thousand members of the local militia or *ronda campesina*, some of whom were armed, accompanied by the representatives of nine local farming communities, staged a protest in front

---

industry's mouth pieces, such as *Minería*. For example, an article published in May 2001, written by two mining consultants working for Newmont, contains the following observations: "If the relations with the neighbours are not cooperative ones, mining operations can come to a quick hold. Many of us are aware of some frictions and unfortunate incidents between miners and their neighbours. These problems can, at any moment, cause mine closures and, in extreme cases result in deaths caused by conflicts between the mine and the rural communities ... To involve the people of the community, the [business] partners of the company, its contractors, local and national governments as well as the providers of goods and services is a key factor. The [company's social, health and work] programs should ... promote a friendly relationship with the neighbors of the mine without resulting in paternalism and an excessive dependency (Harris and Harris, *Minería*, May 2001: 28, 33).

of the mining camp on the morning of November 16th, 2004, and attempted to bring about the company's withdrawal. After several hours the initially peaceful protest turned violent causing one death and numerous injuries. According to witnesses, the *rondero* Juan Montenegro Lingán was shot and killed by a member of the private security company guarding the site. During the violent encounter, the members of the ronda campesina stormed the mining camp and destroyed most of the equipment. A regional politician blamed the bloodshed on Sendero agitators and anti-mining NGOs. However, the takeover and subsequent destruction of the mining camp was initiated by the local militia, an organization created to fight crime and Sendero rebels. The decision of locals not to allow the project to go ahead was caused by the fear that mining activities would destroy their way of life. This they had observed in the case of the Hualgayoc mine run by a different company in the neighbouring province of San Pablo. In addition, as noted, Newmont was a minority shareholder in the project and the US company's practices were not a secret to people in Santa Cruz province which is also located in the Department of Cajamarca (*La República*, Nov. 18/04: 4; also see *Perú 21*, Nov. 18/04: n. a.; *La República*, Nov. 23/04: 20; *La Razón*, May 21/05: 10–11).

In Peru today those opposed to mining are often denounced and even persecuted, including members of the Church. Former left wing congressional representative Javier Diez Canseco, for example, described a "campaign of demonization" against "environmental NGOs" which are allegedly supported by "red priests" and other "political" radicals (*La República*, Aug. 31/06: 13). Carlos de Solar, the then President of the SNMPE, the National Society of Mining, Petroleum and Energy, even put activist priests into the same category with drug traffickers (*El Comercio*, Oct. 2/06: A8). The following excerpt from the editorial section of one of the mouth pieces of the country's mining industry is telling. Accordingly, the anti-mining movement even "had the audacity to infiltrate the bosom of the Catholic Church ... compromising some Church authorities ... and this we say with considerable sorrow as Catholics ... turning them into useful idiots ... " (*Mundo Minero*, July 2006: 42). This perspective is very similar to the views expressed by Vladimiro Montesinos during the 1990s. Accordingly, "NGOs and human rights organizations" represent "a new threat" because of their intent to "destabilize democracy and the state of law" (Jochamowitz, 2002a: 182–182).

The following incidents demonstrate the power of large corporations to corrupt the police and justice systems in Peru: Shortly before the end of the Fujimori regime, on June 2nd, 2000, a truck which was en route to the Yanacocha mine spilled a hundred and fifty kilos of mercury on the road; much of it near the village of Choropampa. Not only were the locals not told of the danger posed by this highly toxic substance, Newmont officials Peter Orams and Marcos Valdéz urged villagers to recover the mercury with their bare hands offering small financial rewards for every kilo returned. Unaware of the danger many villagers even brought the substance into their homes. In consequence, over a thousand individuals in Choropampa suffered mercury poisoning.[7] Malavé and Carrero (2003) write that

> among the heavy metals mercury is considered to be the most dangerous environmental contaminant, not only because of the seriousness of the illnesses it causes in human beings but also because of its accumulative effect in natural food chains. It has been demonstrated that this metal is absorbed and accumulated through the food chain affecting human beings ... [In recent years mercury has increasingly been used in industry] ... above all its irrational utilization in the gold mining [industry] in Asia, Africa and Latin American countries like Bolivia, Peru, Colombia, Venezuela and Brazil (2003: 60).

Choropampa Mayor Lot Saavedra led the efforts of locals to sue Newmont Mining for compensation in a US court. In August 2001, the US law firm Engstrom, Lipscomb & Lack presented the case in the Federal Court in Denver, Colorado, where it dragged on for several years. The case has been settled privately through arbitration, and Newmont has

---

7 It is difficult to argue that these individuals were unaware of the consequences of their actions. While it is true that only modern medicine can explain the negative consequences of mercury exposure to the human body, observations on the negative health risks posed by this substance date back to the sixteenth century physician Paracelsus (Brown, 2001).

paid money for cleanup and for compensation to those afflicted, however, villagers continue to suffer serious health problems. The lawyers representing the residents of Choropampa and two other villages moved the case to a US court because of the corrupt justice system in Peru that Newmont could easily have manipulated. Indeed, the Newmont officials who had encouraged locals to pick up the mercury with their bare hands were cleared of any wrongdoing. Meanwhile, Choropampa mayor Lot Saavedra was charged by police with causing public disorder which can result in a prison sentence of up to three years. The case went to trial and he received a three-year sentence that was suspended. Still, the case demonstrates Newmont's influence over the local justice system and law enforcement (*La República*, Sept. 3/04: 35; also see Bury, 2002; *La Razón*, Apr. 29/05: 10–11; Barretto et al, 2007; *Andean Airmail & Peruvian Times*, Jan. 8/09).

The adversities endured by the Catholic priest, Father Marco Arana, offer a more recent example. As investigated by the Peruvian daily *La República*, Arana, the cofounder of the pro-environment NGO GRUFIDES had been the target of an illegal spying operation launched by a Lima private security company which in turn was on the payroll of Forza which is responsible for security at Yanacocha. The spying had the purpose of finding evidence of sexual misconduct in the private lives of Arana and his closest associates, Father Francisco Centurion Abend, and Father Segundo Alarcón Coveñas, to destroy their reputations. It was claimed that Centurion and Alarcón were paedophiles and/or maintained incestuous sexual relations with female members of their families, while Arana had supposedly fathered his brother's child. The photo, which was supplied as 'proof' of Father Arana's indiscretions showed him entering his brother's house using his own key at a time when his sister-in-law was home alone. It was later determined that the house was that of the priest's mother. Another photo submitted as 'evidence' depicts Father Segundo Alarcón leaving a residence together with an adult female who carries an infant child. The woman in question turned out to be Alarcón's sister, a mother of three. According to representatives of the private detective firm said photo 'established' that the priest had sexual relations, not only with his sister but also her children. Indeed, these alleged incestuous and paedophile acts occurred while Alarcón and his family members would regularly take a bath together. No credible evidence has been produced to substantiate any of these claims. It was also determined that another private security company planted listening devices in the offices of GRUFIDES. When the spying was brought to the attention of the local police, various persons were indeed arrested and their material confiscated. However, the individuals in question were subsequently freed and the 'documentation' of the above described offences was returned to the perpetrators (Kamphuis, 2010; also see *La Republica* (Dossier), Dec. 3/06: 1–8; *La República*, Dec. 3, 2006a: 3; *La República*, Dec. 7/06: 2–3; *La Republica*, Dec. 9/06: 4).

It is also telling that the only newspaper which extensively investigated the Arana case was the moderate left wing daily *La República*. Peru's main daily *El Comercio*, a pro-business publication comparable to Canada's *The Globe and Mail* or Germany's *Frankfurter Allgemeine Zeitung*, often documents negative events involving the mining industry, even on environmental issues. However, *El Comercio* was silent in this case. It is also a commonly known fact that *El Comercio* is the main recipient of advertising funds in the country. In truth, most other national dailies do not even have an advertising section, or a very modest one. Regardless, while *La República* investigated the case, the only other national newspaper which mentioned it at all was the economic daily *Gestión* (See, for example, *Gestión*, Dec. 6/06: 6; *Gestión*, Dec. 15/06: 6).

The Cajamarca press, which is largely controlled by Newmont Mining, ignored the issue altogether, except for one local daily. In fact, the scandal was – at least initially – largely unknown in the city of Cajamarca. All editions of *La República* mysteriously vanished from the newspaper kiosks because they had been bought up to prevent the information from spreading. Most television and radio stations also did not report the case (*La República*, Dec. 9/06: 4). Only on December 11, 2006, the Cajamarca daily *Panorama Cajamarquino* lashed out at *La República* in an attempt to "play down accusations against Yanacocha" (*La República*, Dec. 14/06: 5). The owner of *Panorama Cajamarquino* is Armando Loli. Loli not only runs Yanacocha ads in his paper, he is also the president of the Cajamarca sports club which receives US$ 147.000 in annual subsidies from Yanacocha. Meanwhile, Loli's brother Hugo owns a company that provides contract labour to the mine (Ibid). Regardless, the above described practices, particularly the persecution experienced by Father Marco Arana, do not differ greatly from activities perpetrated by Montesinos and the SIN.

B) The Doe Run Company

Mining exploitation at La Oroya began in 1922 by the US owned Cerro de Pasco Copper Corporation. Following the 1968 left wing military coup, the mine was nationalized and merged with the state-owned Centromin Perú. In 1997, the La Oroya mine was acquired by the Doe Run Company, a US corporation which in turn is owned by the Renco Group, "a conglomerate of more than twenty companies" (Carhuarica and Velásquez, 2005: 90; also see *La Razón*, Apr. 30/05: 10–11, *El Peruano*, Oct. 20/06: 16; BBC, Nov. 15/07). Doe Run also owns a subsidiary in Herculaneum, Missouri in the United States (*Perú 21*, Apr. 7/04: n. a.). Doe Run Peru is of great importance to the regional economy. In January 2005, it employed over 3,000 workers in the country. The majority of these, about 2,500 people, work at the mine and metallurgical complex near the city of La Oroya in the Department of Junin in central Peru. Some 24,000 people or 40 per cent of the population of La Oroya are economically dependent on the company. It is estimated that 70 per cent of the city's commercial activities – or about US$ 50 million – are generated by the mining operation (Carhuarica and Velásquez, 2005).

Doe Run Peru is highly indebted. By 2004, the company was about US$ 300 million in arrears, owed an additional US$ 38 million to a Peruvian bank, while it had failed to pay US$ 50 million in outstanding taxes. Doe Run therefore repeatedly postponed the implementation of its environmental programme which meant that a rather deplorable situation was allowed to persist until 2009 when the company operation was temporarily shut down (Ibid; also see *Third World Network* – TWN, Jan. 19/11).

The Doe Run Company, the Environment, and Public Health

The metallurgical complex at La Oroya processes 600.000 tons of concentrated metals daily. Of these 450,000 tons are so-called poly-metals containing a number of different minerals, while 150,000 tons are zinc concentrates (*La Razón*, Apr. 30/05: 10–11). According to the Blacksmith Institute, as a result of the ore processing at the mine's smelter located right in La Oroya, the city was among the ten worst polluted places on earth; a distinction shared with environmental disaster zones like Chernobyl in Ukraine which took first place. The health consequences caused by the pollution at the smelter affect particularly the young. Based on a 2005 study undertaken by Peru's ministry of health, 82 per cent of 788 children tested at the location showed between 20 and 44.9 micrograms of lead per decilitre in their blood, while 8.4 per cent had levels between 45 and 69 micrograms. Indeed, these children had to be hospitalized and removed from the city.[8] Meanwhile, the maximum limit permissible according to WHO standards is 10 micrograms per decilitre of blood. In addition, 23 per cent of children tested had growth problems. Other symptoms included damage to nervous system and loss of intelligence, behavioural problems, autism, hyperactivity, hearing disabilities as well as Alzheimer's Syndrome and diabetes. A similar investigation by experts

8 Large amounts of lead may harm the brain, kidney, liver, nervous system and abdomen, notably among children because they absorb the poisonous substance more easily. This in turn may lead to loss of intelligence and autism, while it may bring on other illnesses later on in life such as Alzheimer's Syndrome, diabetes, and neural problems (*La República*, May 31/05: 18; also see *El Peruano*, Oct. 20/06: 16). According to Espinoza et al (2003), the "growing evidence for a direct link between low-level lead exposure and deficits in the neurobehavioural-cognitive performance evidenced in childhood through adolescence has led to a worldwide initiative to reduce the lead content of gasoline" (2003: 210). The lead levels found in the blood of children at La Oroya were far higher than what could be absorbed through exposure to street traffic (Yucra et al, 2008).

from the University of St. Louis, Missouri, which had been requested by the Peruvian Catholic Church, examined three hundred and sixty people in the households of La Oroya. The study demonstrated that aside from lead the blood of test subjects contained a potpourri of substances such as cadmium, antimony and arsenic. Regarding cadmium, the study concluded that children aged between 0 and 6 years exhibited especially high levels. Also, the amount of cadmium found in the blood and urine of all age groups examined by far exceeded the level permitted in the United States. In addition, until being shut down in 2009, Doe Run operations spewed 750 tons of sulphuric acid into the atmosphere every day, while even the very generous Peruvian legislation only permitted 195 tons (Ibid; also see *Perú 21*, May 30/05: n. a.; *La República*, May 31/05: 18; *El Comercio*, Dec. 7/05: B2; *El Peruano*, Oct. 20/06: 16; BBC, Nov. 15/07; BBC, June 5/09).

As noted, Doe Run owes a large debt which caused the company to renegotiate and postpone the fulfilment of its environmental obligations, most importantly the construction of a sulphur acid plant to cut emissions into the air, soil, and water, the cost of which is over US$ 100 million (Carhuarica and Velásquez, 2005). The installation would have greatly reduced the emissions of toxic gases from Doe Run's chimneys, however, the demand for sulphuric acid as well as its price on the world market have been low – which has reduced the company's incentive to build such a plant. Conversely, Doe Run sent over US$ 260 million annually in remissions and transfers to its US parent instead of giving precedence to the environment and public health at La Oroya (Ibid; also see *La Razón*, April 30/05: 10–11; *Gestión*, Feb. 21/06: 9).

The Doe Run Company had made a commitment to reduce the lead level found in children less than six years of age to one viewed as acceptable by the WHO. By mid-2009, Doe Run had evidently failed to implement the environmental obligations required under Peruvian law. In June of that year the company was temporarily shut down after filing for bankruptcy, although metal prices were going through the roof. Since then Doe Run and the Peruvian government have been engaging in unsuccessful negotiations (*Third World Network* – TWN, Jan. 19/11).

C) *The Barrick Gold Corporation*

The Canadian-owned Barrick Gold Corporation has been present in Peru since 1994, while it also owns mining projects in Argentina, Australia, Canada, Chile, Tanzania, and the United States. In 2001, Barrick was responsible for 20.5 per cent of the gold production in Peru which made it the No. 2 company in the country (*La República*, July 24/03: 29; also see *El Peruano*, July 24/03: n. a.). In December 2005, Barrick acquired Placer Dome and turned into the largest gold mining company on the globe surpassing Newmont Mining and South Africa's Anglo-Gold Ashanti (*El Comercio*, Dec. 23/05: n. a.; also see *Canadian Broadcasting Corporation* – CBC, Dec. 22/05). In May 2011, the company made headlines when half a dozen villagers were killed by police at a Barrick-owned mine in Tanzania. The shooting was only the most recent "in a series of deadly incidents over the past several years" at the site (*The Globe and Mail*, June 8/11: A11). While largely unreported in Canada, Barrick's mining projects in Peru have also seen large-scale protests resulting in deaths and injuries (*Expreso*, March 6/05: 3; also see *La República*, March 8/05: 10; *La República*, May 7/06: 24).

A Barrick Tax Sham?

The Barrick Gold Corporation has been accused of tax evasion after having initiated a fake merger of the companies running its La Pierina mine. The merger was based on decree 120–94–EF which allowed the company to avoid paying taxes worth US$ 141 million owed to the Peruvian treasury. According to Peruvian tax law, 50 per cent of this amount would have been used for local development (*Gestión*, May 8/03: V; also see *Expreso*, May 14/03: A7). Barrick was the major share holder in the companies running the La Pierina mine, Minera

Barrick Misquichilca and Acuarios Minera y Exploradora, owning over 90 per cent of each. In December 1996, the two companies merged into one which took the name Minera Barrick Misquichilca. The Peruvian tax agency SUNAT claimed that the merger was on paper only. Minera Barrick Misquichilca did not engage in any financial activity prior to the 1996 merger although it had been formally registered in 1994. Decree 120–94–EF permitted merging corporations to deduct from their income tax parts of the costs which were caused by the absorption of the other business enterprise. However, in this case not only did the two companies have the same owner, the Barrick Gold Corporation, but the absorbed company was re-evaluated a day before the operation from about US$ 2.5 million to over US$ 468 million, going up in value 188 times. In other words, not only did Barrick merge with itself but it subsequently inflated the value of the company with which it had allegedly incorporated and deducted the arbitrarily enlarged amount from the income tax owed to the Peruvian state (*La República*, May 17/03: 16–17).

Such practices are commonplace. According to Rey (2006), Latin American scholar Osvaldo Sunkel had already observed in 1967 that multinational corporations do not determine their activities based on market mechanisms. Rather, these are decided depending on the specific taxation policies of individual host countries. Also, such corporations engage in the so-called internal transfer of resources with their affiliates which technically speaking has no value that can be taxed. Rey provides examples from Argentina, Uruguay, and Mexico where mostly US corporations transferred goods internally whose value was artificially reduced to decrease import taxes. These same goods, however, were then sold at far higher prices in the host nations (Ibid, 104).

Regardless, when the congressional commission investigating financial crimes during the Fujimori presented a preliminary report on the Barrick tax issue in 2003 to the authorities in Huaraz, the city which is located near the mine, the company charged that the "confidentiality of the tax secret" had been violated (*Gestión*, May 8/03: V; also see *Expreso*, May 20/03: A 12). The commission members pointed out in turn that the material released had been publically available information that could be found on Barrick's own website. Barrick defended itself claiming that the merger and re-evaluation had been in accordance with Peruvian law at the time (Ibid; also see *El Comercio*, May 8/03: A6). Moreover, the commission's final report, which was supported by four of the five members, determined that the operation aimed to "recover the US$ 760 million paid in the stock market of Canada for the company Arequipa Resources" which in turned owned Acuarios Minería y Exploradora with whom the allegedly fraudulent merger had taken place (*La República*, Aug. 2/03: n. a.).[9] The report also noted that the actual documents with which the merger was registered did not contain any reasons behind the move. In addition, company officials who testified before the commission could not supply satisfactory explanations as to why the merger had taken place (Ibid).

According to Humberto Campodónico, one of the most respected Peruvian economists, the merger between Barrick Misquichilca and Acuarios Minería y Exploradora would not have been fictitious and the re-evaluation as well as the subsequent tax reduction justified if Barrick Gold had indeed invested the amount of US$ 468 million into the newly created company. However, there is no record that Barrick made any investment prior to the merger. Thus, Barrick claimed and received a tax reduction based on an investment it never made (Campodónico, *La República*, March 6/05: n. a.; also see Campodónico, 2006). Elsewhere the Peruvian economist points out that Barrick's tax free status was the result of "Law 26283 and Supreme Decree 120–94–EF" (Campodónico, *La República*, July 5/05: 11). Yet while the Supreme Decree 120–94–EF was indeed the law of the land, it was formally revoked in 1998 by the Peruvian Congress. Indeed, the contract signed in 1998 between Barrick and the ministry of energy and mining made no mention of the decree. Still, the company benefited from the tax reduction in 1999 although the decree had officially expired (*La República*, Aug. 2/03: n. a.).

---

9 The commission's fifth member was Rafael Rey, formerly a strong supporter of the Fujimori regime.

Furthermore, as noted earlier, Supreme Decree 120–94–EF had been "declared unconstitutional" by Peru's Congress in July 2002 while former President Fujimori and the former Minister of Economics and Finance Jorge Camet had been indicted with breaking the constitution for issuing it (Ibid; also see *Gestión*, March 8/05: 18). Nevertheless, after Barrick had refused in December 2002 to honour the request by SUNAT, Peru's national tax agency, to hand over the US$ 141 million it owed, the case went into arbitration, and the company lost in the first instance. Barrick subsequently appealed to the Fiscal Tribunal, the country's highest court in tax matters, where it won the case. Indeed, the SUNAT then wanted to pursue the matter further. To do so, the tax agency needed the authority given by the ministry of economics and finance which, however, was not granted (*Expreso*, Feb. 10/05: n. a.; also see *Gestión*, Feb. 10/05: 10). It is worthwhile knowing that the three members of the Fiscal Tribunal were indeed appointed by the very same ministry. It was later revealed that María Eugenía Caller, the president of the tribunal which made the decision in favour of the mining corporation had previously worked with the same law office whose associates defended Barrick (*La República*, March 16/05: n. a.).

To protest the rejection of SUNAT's request, regional organizations in the Department of Ancash – where the mine is located – prepared a strike for early March 2005 to impede company activities (*Gestión*, Feb. 11/05: 9). Indeed, Huaraz became the scene of violent protests by local villagers on March 7th and several days thereafter. Marchers set up a road block at the mine and clashed with police resulting in twenty wounded. Even the local military was called in. Subsequently, organizers declared a department-wide strike against Barrick in Ancash (*La República*, March 8/05: 10; also see *Perú 21*, March 8/05: n. a.; *El Comercio*, March 8/05: A12). Carlos Del Solar, the SNMPE President, blamed left-over elements of the defeated rebel movements "as well as non-governmental organizations" with "large financial resources" for the violence. Conversely, according to Huaraz mayor, Lombardo Mautino Ángeles, the strike actions organized in March 2005 were to remind Barrick "to invest in works of development of the province and the region" and to "pay ... royalties" (Ibid; also see *La República*, March 5/05: 8; *La República*, March 9/05: 8). Indeed, the mayor noted that the contribution received by the mine in 2003 came to 140.000 Nuevos Soles (about US$ 45.000) which climbed to 250.000 Nuevos Soles (about US$ 76.000) in 2004. Meanwhile, Barrick's annual earnings were in the hundreds of millions of dollars (*Expreso*, March 6/05: 3).

Barrick and Contamination

In Information Bulletin Nr. 21, published in October 2001 by the public relations office at Barrick's La Pierina mine in Ancash province, the company boasted of its environmentally clean practices. The company's director of public relations specifically denied claims that Barrick was contaminating a nearby river, the Río Santa. Huaraz mayor Rommel Ríos Alcántara pointed to the progress achieved since the arrival of the Canadian multinational, while various locals, including company employees, praised the environmental practices of the mining giant (*Gente de Pierina*, Oct. 2001: 2–6). Then Canadian Ambassador Hugues R. Rousseau called Barrick a "model company" in the "conservation of the environment" and lauded its contributions to "social and community development" (Ibid, 7).

Conversely, a local political leader asked health authorities in 2003 to examine the residents in villages living near the mine after the discovery of several cases of cyanide poisoning in the city of Huaraz (*Liberación*, Apr. 3/02: 16). While the former mayor Ríos Alcántara may have favoured Barrick's presence in the community, his successor Lombardo Mautino Ángeles accused the company of contaminating pastures and causing the death of "numerous animals" (*La República*, March 8/05: 10). The mayor also expressed fears that the extension of mining activities had indeed resulted in the contamination of the Río Santa (Ibid). Barrick also acquired a concession and had its environmental impact study approved for the mine *La Libertad* in Alto Chicama in the Department of Trujillo in northern Peru, although the local population had rejected the company's environmental impact study. However, according to Peruvian law no concession can be granted unless approved by the local community (*El Comercio*, Apr. 24/02: n. a.; also see *Síntesis*, Oct. 30/03: 10).

Barrick Gold is not only present in Peru, but the company also operates a mining project in Pascua-Lama, San Juan, Argentina. In 2005, various local NGOs provided a report on the environmental damages and problems caused by mining activities. These included deforestation; loss of water; melting glaciers to obtain water; contamination of water with toxic substances such as cyanide, mercury, or lead; as well as soil erosion and noise pollution (La Red Provincial de ONGs de San Juan, 2005). One may assume that the company's activities have a comparable impact in neighboring Peru.

6. Conclusion

The practices described would qualify as forms of corporate crime as defined by Ross (2003) or Michalowski and Kramer (2006) (See Chapter 2 in this book). The companies described were and still are able to engage in such activities because of the contracts signed with the Fujimori government. Also, the contamination levels at Yanacocha or La Oroya are so scandalously high that any description which does not include factors such as corporate corruption and crime would hardly be explanatory. This chapter has focussed on the practices of three companies, but the problems extend to others.[10]

---

10 Other examples could have been discussed instead of those selected. These include the Southern Peru Copper Corporation (SPCC) which operates the mines *Toquepala* and *Cuajone* as well as a foundry and a refining plant in the south of the country since 1956. SPCC was never nationalized by the military government in power during the 1970s. In the late 1990s, SPCC installations emitted 480 million tons of sulphur dioxide annually. This is more than the combined discharge by Austria, the Netherlands and Sweden. According to Lora Cam (2005) SPCC had earnings worth US$ 650 million in 2001 while it paid a

The following comparisons are insightful. After numerous protests by "diverse NGOs, communities and [local] mayors," Peru's Congress decided to study the environmental practices by mining companies to determine whether they were in fulfilment of their obligations, a step which caused some consternation among industry representatives. The move was challenged by Barrick officials who claimed that Peru's Congress "tried to usurp functions of the executive" (*Peru 21*, May 22/03: n. a.). Barrick protested that the laws of the country did not indicate that a congressional "sub-commission should study these matters" (Ibid). However, a survey on the compliance of mining companies with the country's environmental laws was indeed ordered by the ministry of health and supervised by a multi-party commission of Congress. The final report of May 2005 which referred to several large companies, including Newmont and Barrick, concluded that they had failed to provide the necessary information about the investment done into environmental protection at their respective mining sites. Consequently, the commission was unable to make a satisfactory appraisal of these corporations' environmental practices. It should be noted that according to Peruvian law companies have to provide detailed information such as environmental impact studies as well as contingency plans before mining operations are

mere US$ 4.5 million in taxes. Another example would be the Camisea natural gas project in the Peruvian jungle. The endeavour – which includes a pipeline bringing the gas from the jungle regions of southern Peru to the port of Callao – was developed by a consortium that includes Hunt Oil from the US as well as a Spanish and South Korean company. Camisea went on line in August 2004 but production was marred by problems. Between December 2004 and September 2005 the pipeline ruptured four times spilling tens of thousands of litres of natural gas. In March 2006, it came apart again discharging "enough gas onto the rain forest floor to fill the tanks of 30,000 cars" (Hearn, 2007: 12–13). The subsequent investigation revealed that the consortium building the pipeline had done a rush job, used material left over from earlier projects, while workers lacked the necessary qualifications. Most importantly, the consortium had never undertaken a geotechnical study of the conditions in the Peruvian jungle (Ibid).

allowed to commence (*La Razón*, May 8/05: 10–11; also see *El Comercio*, Nov. 18/06: B12).[11]

Moreover, Doe Run confronted contamination problems in its US subsidiary in Herculaneum, Missouri. The lead levels encountered in the children there came to 15 micrograms per decilitre of blood, while the maximum permissible limit in the United States is 0.4 micrograms. Local residents sued the company and following a three-year court battle, Doe Run had to compensate the population, clean up people's living environments, and implement further security measures (*Perú 21*, April 7/04: n. a.; also see *El Comercio*, Dec. 7/05: B2). In 2010, several dozen La Oroya citizens also sued Doe Run in a Missouri court. In response, Doe Run took legal action against the Peruvian government claiming that it had acted in violation of the US-Peru free trade deal and that Peru was responsible for any damages that the company would incur as a result of the court case. It is noteworthy that even the SNMPE, which usually defends the interests of mining corporations, has expressed strong criticism of Doe Run's actions (Dube, *Business News Americas*, Nov. 8/10; also see *Third World Network* – TWN, Jan. 19/11).

In conclusion, one has to agree with the assessment of *The Economist's* Latin America editor, Michael Reid, who maintained that Peru was "paying the price for [having] offered very advantageous tax conditions which the government of Alberto Fujimori deemed necessary to attract foreign investments" (as quoted in *La República*, Apr. 24/06: 11).

---

11 Peru only created a ministry of the environment in 2008 (BBC, May 14, 2008).

Chapter 11
Conclusion

The Earth is degenerating today. Bribery and corruption abound. Children no longer obey their parents; every man wants to write a book, and it is evident that the end of the world is fast approaching.
(Assyrian Tablet)

1. Introduction

At the end of a work that informs about a topic such as corruption the author is expected to provide uplifting thoughts. Indeed, it would not be difficult to point to some successful reform project or other and the advances made in the fight against corruption. It is my argument, however, that corruption is an expression of power and of power relations. And the corruption of the powerful cannot be defeated by introducing a few reforms. Lascoumes (2000) argues that this question harks back to US criminologist Edwin Sutherland (1949) who asked whether white-collar crime – including the delinquent economic and financial practices of those in charge of large corporations – represented criminal wrongdoing in the eyes of society? Unfortunately, despite the manifest consequences of corruption the weakness of the social response to the practice often amounts to systematic impunity.

2. Sentencing and Impunity in Post-Fujimori Peru

While the main actors of the regime received stiff prison terms for their crimes, many middle and lower ranking officials were given relatively light sentences, despite the enormity of the offences they had committed. Vladimiro Illich Montesinos Torres, General Juan de Bari Hermoza Ríos as well as Major Santiago Martín Rivas were sentenced to twenty-five years in jail for their roles in the murders of the *Grupo Colina*, notably the *Barrios Altos* and *La Cantuta* massacres in 1991 and 1992. General Julio Salazar Monroe, the formal director of the *Servicio de Inteligencia Nacional* (SIN), received thirty-five years for his part in the activities of the Grupo Colina. Twenty other members of the organization received prison terms of between fifteen to twenty-five years. Montesinos was also given twenty years for his involvement in the drugs-for-arms deal with the FARC. In 2009, Fujimori was sentenced to twenty-five years in prison for sanctioning the Grupo Colina murders. In the same year, the former president received an additional fifteen years for shelling out millions of dollars in bribes to Montesinos. In 2007, Fujimori had already received six years for ordering an illegal search of the residence of Montesinos' wife in 2000. At the time, Fujimori prepared his departure for exile and he was looking for evidence that would have incriminated him. Under Peruvian law an individual who receives various sentences does not have to serve these consecutively but has to spend the longest one behind bars. Both Montesinos and Fujimori therefore are to remain twenty-five years in prison (*zeenews*, Oct. 2/10; also see *La Primera*, May 6/11).

According to Dargent (2005), over 1300 persons were charged and sentenced in 126 trials for offences committed during the Fujimori era. Of these, 106 individuals received prison long sentences like Montesinos or Hermoza. However, a large number of individuals were sentenced to prison terms between eighteen and thirty-six months. These persons did not go to prison because under Peruvian law anybody who receives less than four years spends his or her time under house arrest (Salas Lopéz, 2005). Accordingly, seventy-three persons sentenced received house arrest. Among these were individuals who committed grave offences. They included Alex and Moisés Wolfenson who accepted bribes from Montesinos for smearing opposition politicians in *prensa chicha* publications they owned. Samuel and Mendel Winter, the minority owners of *Frecuencia Latina*, who took money from Montesinos and put their channel at the service of Fujimori's second re-election, ended up with house arrest. Talk show host Laura Bozzo also received a suspended sentence of house arrest which she spent in her refurnished production studio to be able to continue taping her show. The former Minister of Economics and Finances Jorge Camet, responsible for serious economic crimes during the privatization of Peruvian state-owned industries, likewise had house arrest (*El Mercurio*, Dec. 23/03; also see *Justicia Viva*, July 2005). High ranking members of the regime whose prison sentences were converted to house arrest included former Prime Minister Federico Salas Guevara, the former Minister of Economics and Finance Carlos Boloña Behr (who preceded Camet), the former Minister of Agriculture Absalón Vásquez, and the ex-Minister of Defence César Saucedo Sánchez; all of whom had been sentenced on corruption charges (*La Primera*, May 6/11). Not surprisingly, a 2005 poll by Peru's anti-corruption non-governmental organization (NGO) *Proética* revealed that 79 per cent of respondents felt that corruption was not being penalized (Rotta Castilla and Navarte Olivares, 2006).

Various members of the Grupo Colina who in 2000–2001 received lengthy prison terms of between fifteen to twenty years for serious crimes also had them converted to house arrest after they spent a few years behind bars. These include the former chief of the *Servicio de Inteligencia del Ejército* (SIE), Colonel (ret.) Víctor Silva Mendoza. He was sentenced to a lengthy prison term for committing murder but has lived under house arrest since 2003. Retired Colonel Fernando Rodríguez Zabalbeascoa, who worked in the *Dirección de Inteligencia del Ejército* (DINTE) and the Grupo Colina, received fifteen years for committing murder but has been living at home since October 2005. Former SIE official Pedro Santillán Galdós has been under house arrest since early 2004. He had been condemned to a long prison term for crimes committed during his membership in the Grupo Colina. Santillán Galdós participated in the 1991 Altos Barrios massacre and the disappearance of radio journalist Pedro Yauri Bustamante. Another member of the Grupo Colina who received a long prison sentence for murder, César Alvarado Salinas, left prison for house arrest in early 2005 (*La República*, March 14/09).

In many respects the Fujimori era has never ended. The 1993 Constitution is still in force. The victims of his policies, such as the indigenous women who were forcibly sterilized, are still seeking justice. In fact, this issue was not even addressed by Peru's Truth and Reconciliation Commission. Mining companies still have rights acquired illegally during the Fujimori era and commit serious violations but have no fear of prosecution (Gertgen, 2009; also see *La República*, Aug. 3, 2005; *La República*, Aug. 7/10: 10). The former president still enjoys lots of support despite having received long prison sentences for his crimes. On June 5, 2011, Peruvians attended the second round of the presidential election and narrowly elected left wing populist Ollanta Humala with 51.5 percent over Fujimori's daughter Keiko who received 48.5 percent of the vote. During the first round Humala had gained 31.7 percent while Keiko Fujimori finished second with 23.5 percent. It can be assumed that the votes she received in the first round represent the block of support her father, the former president, can still rely on. Burt and Youngers (2011) noted that supporters at Keiko Fujimori's election rallies would cheer her imprisoned father. It seems out of the ordinary that Peruvians would come close to electing the daughter despite her father's record. Conversely, observers expressed surprise when Alan García was re-elected in 2006 despite his disastrous first term as president between 1985 and 1990 (See, for example, McClintock, 2006). Many Peruvians with whom I discussed the 2006 presidential poll merely shrugged and explained that Peru was *el país de las maravillas*, the country of marvels, where the unusual is the norm.

To conclude with the words of Hugo Neira (2001):

> Fujimorism has demonstrated the ease with which a government that supplants democracy can link 'masses' and 'elites' without falling into the rhetoric of either the Caudillos, or of historical Fascism. The components ... [of the phenomenon] have not disappeared from Peruvian society: Presidentialism without institutional bounds, the necessity for a leader, the indifference of the governed ... [vis-a-vis] power and the struggle for ... power (2001: 168).

Selected Bibliography

Abad Yupanqui, Samuel B. La reforma del servicio de inteligencia nacional: Aportes para un diseño y control democráticos. In: *Las fuerzas armadas en la transición democrática en el Perú.* Edited by Daniel Mora, Fernando Rospigliosi, Samuel Abad B. Yupanqui, and Carlos Basombrío, Lima, Peru: IEP, 2001: 53–71.

Abrahamsen, Rita. *Disciplining Democracy: Development Discourse and Good Governance in Africa.* London, UK: Zed Books, 2000.

Acevedo Rojas, Jorge. Los talk shows: Fascinación o rechazo. In: *Revista latino-americana de comunicación CHASQUI*, 75, 2001: 1–6.

Adamek, Sascha and Kim Otto. *Der gekaufte Staat: Wie Konzernvertreter in deutschen Ministerien sich ihre Gesetze selbst schreiben.* Cologne, Germany: Kiepenheuer and Witsch, 2008.

Adamson, Walter L. Modernism and Fascism: The Politics of Culture in Italy, 1903–1922. In: *The American Historical Review*, 95, 2, 1990: 359–390.

Adams, Francis. *Deepening Democracy: Global Governance and Political Reform in Latin America.* Westport, CT: Praeger, 2003.

Adorno, Theodor. Some Aspects of Religious Ideology as Revealed in the Interview Material. In: Adorno, Theodor, Else Frenkel-Brunswik, Daniel J. Levinson, and R. Nevitt Sanford. *The Authoritarian Personality*, Vol. 1. New York: Wiley and Sons, 1964: 727–743.

Adorno, Theodor W. Reflexionen zur Klassentheorie. In: *Gesammelte Schriften*, Vol. 8. Frankfurt a. M., Germany: Suhrkamp, 1990: 373–391.

Agnew, John, and Gearóid Ó Tuathail. Geopolitical Discourse: Practical Geopolitical Reasoning in American Foreign Policy. In: *Political Geography*, 11, 2, 1992: 190–204.

Albert, Michael, Leslie Cagan, Noam Chomsky, Robin Hahnel, Mel King, Lydia Sargent, Holly Sklar. *Liberating Theory.* Boston, MA: South End, 1986.

Alejos Calderon, Walter. Disposición de fondos públicos con normas secretas, nuestra experiencia reciente. Balance de la inversion privada y privatización 1990–2001. Comisión investigadora de los delitos económicos y financieros cometidos entre 1990–2001. Edited by Javier Diez Canseco. Lima: Fondo Editorial del Congreso del Perú, 2002: 53–58.

Allen, John L. *Opus Dei.* New York: Doubleday, 2005.

Alvarez Pedroza, Alejandro. *Normas del sistema de defensa nacional.* Lima: Edición Particular, 1996.

Ames, Rolando, and Samuel Rotta Castilla. Corrupción, sociedad y crisis del estado en el Perú. In: *Vicios públicos*. Edited by Óscar Ugarteche. Lima: Fondo de Cultura Económica, 2005: 275–306.

Amundsen, Inge. Political Corruption. In: *U4*, 6, 2006: 1–33. <http://www.cmi.no/publications/file/2565-political-corruption.pdf>

Anderson, Perry. The Antimonies of Antonio Gramsci. <http//www.workersliberty.org/files/anderson.pdf> (Originally published in *New Left Review*, 100, 1976/1977: 5–78).

Andrade A., Pablo. La politica exterior de Estados Unidos: Una vision desde la periferia. In: *Oasis*, 10, 2004/05: 129–140.

Arciniega Huby, Alberto. Civil-Military Relations and a Democratic Peru. In: *Orbis*, 38, 1, 1994: 116–120.

Arias Quincot, César. *La modernización autoritaria*. Lima: Fundación Friedrich Ebert, 1994.

Arias Martinez, Luis M., Los usos de las pantallas en un contexto cambiante: Losmedios electrónicos en la revolución Peruana. In: *Nómadas: Revista crítica de ciencias sociales y jurídicas*, 4, 2001. <http://www.ucm.es/info/nomadas/4/lamartz.htm>.

Aroche, Fidel. Apuntes desde de la perplejidad. La teoría económica y el análisis económico de la corrupción. In: *Vicios públicos*. Edited by Óscar Ugarteche. Lima: Fondo de Cultura Económica, 2005: 229–244.

Arrighi, Giovanni. The Three Hegemonies of Historical Capitalism. In: *Gramsci, Historical Materialism and International Relations*. Edited by Stephen Gill. Cambridge University Press, 1993: 148–185.

Arrighi, Giovanni. Forum on Hegemony and Social Change with Christopher Chase-Dunn, Peter Taylor, Giovanni Arrighi, Robert Cox, Henk Overbeek, Barry Gills, Andre Gunder Frank, George Modelski, David Wilkinson. In: *Mershon International Studies Review*, 38, 2, 1994: 361–376.

Ávila Molero, Javier. Nuevos discursos y actores del desarollo social en el Perú. In: *Política y cultura*, 20, 2003: 101–116.

Avirgan, Tony, and Martha Honey. *John Hull: El finquero de la CIA*. San José, Costa Rica: Varitec, 1989.

Bagley, Bruce M. Drug Trafficking, Political Violence and US Policy in Colombia in the 1990s. In: *Mama Coca*, 1, 2001. <http://www.mamacoca.org/junio2001/bagley_drugs_and_violence_en.htm>.

Bagley, Bruce M. Globalization and Transnational Organized Crime: The Russian Mafia in Latin America and the Caribbean. In: *Mama Coca*, 3, 2002. <http://www.mamacoca.org/feb2002/art_bagley_globalization_organized_crime_en.html>.

Bakan, Joel. *The Corporation: The Pathological Pursuit of Power and Profit*. Toronto, Canada: Penguin, 2004.

Bannenberg, Britta. Korruption in Deutschland. Ergebnisse einer kriminologisch-strafrechtlichen Untersuchung. In: *Korruption: Netzwerke in Politik, Ämtern und Wirtschaft*. Edited by Hans H. von Arnim. Munich: Knaur, 2003: 204–238.

Bannenberg, Britta, and Wolfgang Schaupensteiner. *Korruption in Deutschland: Portrait einer Wachstumsbranche*. Munich: C.H. Beck, 2004.

Barak, Gregg. Crime, Criminology and Human Rights: Towards an Understanding of State Criminality. In: *Journal of Human Justice*, 2, 1, 1990: 11–28.

Bardhan, Pranab. Corruption and Development: A Review of Issues. In: *Journal of Economic Literature*, 35, 1997: 1320–1346.

Barrantes, Roxana, Patricia Zárate, and Anahí Durand. *Te quiero pero no*. Lima, Peru: Instituto de Estudios Peruanos, 2005.

Barretto, Robert, and Amanda Heyman, Lauren Schrero, and David Weiss. Harmonizing Growth & Environmentalism in the Peruvian Mining Sector: Lessons from Yanacocha. University of Michigan. Gerald Ford School of Public Policy.Policy Paper 4, 2007: 1–47. <http://www.umich.edu/~ipolicy/IEDP/2007peru/4%29%20Harmonizing%20Growth%20&%20Environmentalism%20in%20the%20Peruvian%20Min.pdf>.

Bauer, Richard. Alle sprechen von Koka, niemand von Kokain. In: *Neue Zürcher Zeitung, NZZ–Folio*, June 1995: 28.

Bauernfeind, Kurt C. *Schwarze Tauben des Vatikans*. Linz, Austria: Denkmayr, 2006.

Bebbington, Anthony, Jeffrey Bury, Denise Humphreys Bebbington, Jeannet Lingan, Juan Pablo Muñoz, and Martin Scurrah. Mining and Social Movements: Struggles over Livelihood and Rural Territorial Development in the Andes. In: *Brooks World Poverty Institute Working Paper 33*. April 2008: 1–36. <http://papers.ssrn.com/sol3/papers.cfm?abstract_id=1265582>.

Bedoya, Jairo. *La protección violenta en Colombia: El caso de Medellín desde los años noventa*. Medellín, Colombia: Instituto Popular de Capacitación, 2010.

Bellamy, Richard, and Darrow Schecter. *Gramsci and the Italian State*. Manchester, UK: Manchester United Press, 1993.

Bennet, Jackson. The Union of South American Nations: The New(est) Regionalism in Latin America. In: *Suffolk Transnational Law Review*, 32, 1, 2008: 1–34.

Bernales Ballesteros, Enrique. Del parlamento constitucional a la ficción parlamentaria. In: *El poder en el Perú*. Edited by Augusto Alvarez Rodrich. Lima: Editorial APOYO, 1993: 55–71.

Birkbeck, Christopher. Conceptos criminológicos derivados de la experiencia latinoamericana. In: *Revista CENIPEC*, 15, 1994: 1–14.

Blodgett, Steve, and James A. Kuipers. Underground Hard Rock Mining: Subsidence and Hydrological Environmental Impacts. In: Centre for Science in Public Participation. Bozeman, MT, 2002: 1–50.

Bøås, Morten. Governance as Multilateral Bank Policy: The Cases of the African Development Bank and the Asian Development Bank. In: *European Journal of Development* Research, 10, 2, 1998: 117–134.
Boas, Taylor C. Television and Neopopulism in Latin America. In: *Latin American Research Review*. 40, 2, 2005: 27–49.
Boberski, Heiner, Josef Bruckmoser, and Andreas Pfeifer. *Geheimnis Vatikan*. Hamburg, Germany: Rowohlt, 2008.
Bobrow-Strain, Aaron. *Intimate Enemies: Landowners, Power and Violence in Chiapas*. Durham, NC: Duke University Press, 2007.
Boff, Leonardo, and Clodovis Boff. *Introducing Liberation Theology*. Maryknoll, NY: Orbis, 1986.
Boff, Clodovis. Methodology of the Theology of Liberation. In: *Systematic Theology*. Edited by Jon Sobrino and I. Ellacuría. Maryknoll, NY: Orbis, 1998: 1–21.
Bonpane, Blase. *Guerillas of Peace*. Boston, MA: South End Press, 1985.
Bou, Marc. El sistema de justicia en América Latina: Entre las reformas y la inercia institucional. In: *Documentos de Trabajo*, 4, Institut Internacional de Governabilitat de Catalunya, 2004: 1–26.
Bowen, Sally, and Jane Holligan. *El espia imperfecto*. Lima: Ediciones Peisa, 2003.
Box, Steven. *Power, Crime and Mystification*. New York: Tavistock Publications, 1983.
Braithwaite, John. Transnational Corporations and Corruption: Toward some International Solutions. In: *International Journal of Sociology and Law*, 7, 1979: 125–142.
Briscoe, Ivan. The Proliferation of the Parallel State. *Fundación para las Relaciones Internacionales y el Diálogo Exterior* (FRIDE), Working Paper 71, 2008: 1–28. <www.fride.org/descarga/WP71_Paralell_state_ENG_oct08.pdf>.
Broszat, Martin. *The Hitler State*. New York: Longman, 1981.
Browder, George C. *Foundations of the Nazi Police State*. Lexington: The University of Kentucky Press, 1990.
Brown, Kendall W. Workers'Health and Colonial Mercury Mining at Huancavelica, Peru. In: *The Americas*, 57, 4, 2001: 467–496.
Buci-Glucksmann, Christine. *Gramsci and the State*. London: Lawrence and Wishart, 1980.
Burgos, Hernando. El gobierno y la prensa: La libertad condicionada. In: *QUEHACER*, 109, 1997: 14–22.
Burkholder, Mark and Mark D.S. Chandler. *From Impotence to Authority: The Spanish Crown and the American Audiencias 1687–1808*. Columbia: University of Missouri Press, 1978.
Burt, Jo-Marie. Facade of Democracy Crumbles. In: *NACLA Report on the Americas*, 26, 1, 1992: 3–6.
Burt, Jo-Marie. Unsettled Accounts: Militarization and Memory in Post-war Peru. In: *NACLA Report on the Americas*, XXXII, 2, 1998: 35–40.
Burt, Jo-Marie. "Quien habla es terrorista": The Political Use of Fear in Fujimori's Peru. In: *Latin American Research Review*, 41, 3, 2006: 32–62.

Burt, Jo-Marie. *Political Violence and the Authoritarian State in Peru: Silencing Civil Society*. New York, NY: Palgrave MacMillan, 2007.
Burt, Jo-Marie. Guilty as Charged: The Trial of Former Peruvian President Alberto Fujimori for Human Rights Violations. In: *The International Journal of Transitional Justice*, 3, 2009: 384–405.
Burt, Jo-Marie, and Coletta Youngers. Peru: What's Next for Humala? In: *Foreign Policy in Focus* (FPIF), June 17, 2011. <http://www.fpif.org/articles/peru_whats_next_for_humala>.
Bury, Jeffrey. Livelihoods, Mining and Peasant Protests in the Peruvian Andes. In: *Journal of Latin American Geography*, 1, 1, 2002: 1–19.
Buttigieg, Joseph A. Gramsci on Civil Society. In: *boundary*, 2, 22, 3, 1995: 1–32.
Cadena Montenegro, José Luis. 200 Años de independencia de Latinoamerica y su evolución geopolítica. Una vision de Sudamérica. In: *Revista de Relaciones Internacionales, Estrategia y Seguridad*, 4, 2009: 91–111.
Camara, Helder. *Spiral of Violence*. London: Sheed and Ward, 1971.
Cameron, Max. *Democracy and Authoritarianism in Peru: Political Condition and Social Change*. New York: St. Martin's, 1994.
Cameron, Max. Political and Economic Origins of Regime Change in Peru: The Eighteenth Brumaire of Alberto Fujimori, In: *The Peruvian Labyrinth.* Edited by Max Cameron and Phillip Mauceri. Pennsylvania State University Press, 1997: 37–69.
Cameron, Max. A. Self-Coups: Peru, Guatemala, and Russia. In: *Journal of Democracy*, 9, 1, 1998: 125–139.
Cameron, Max. Latin American Autogolpes: Dangerous Undertones in the Third Wave of Democratization. In: *Third World Quarterly*, 19, 2, 1998a: 219–239.
Cameron, Max. Endogenous Regime Breakdown: The Vladivideo and the Fall of Peru's Fujimori. In: *The Fujimori Legacy: The Rise of Electoral Authoritarianism.* Edited by J.F. Carrión, University Park: The Pennsylvania State University Press, 2006: 268–293.
Campbell, David and Michael Dillon. The End of Philosophy and the End of International Relations. In: *The Political Subject of Violence*. Edited by David Campbell and Michael Dillon, Manchester: Manchester University Press, 1993.
Campbell, Bruce, and Arthur D. Brenner (Eds). *Death Squads in Global Perspective: Murder with Deniability*. New York: St. Martin's Press, 2000.
Campodónico, Humberto. Barrick, SUNAT, el defensor y la captura del estado. In: *La República* (Lima), March 6, 2005: n. a.
Campodónico, Humberto. El escándalo de la minera Barrick y sus defensores en el estado. In: *Cristal de Mira 2002–2006: La economía peruana bajo la lupa.* Lima: Universidad Major de San Marcos, 2006: 351–352.
Campodónico, Humberto. Newmont, Cerro Quilish y un yacimiento de 'clase mundial'. In: *Cristal de Mira*, 2006a: 353–354.
Campodónico, Humberto. Respuesta a minera Barrick. In: *La República*, July 5, 2005: 11.

Cappellini, Mónica S., La prensa chicha en Perú. In: *Revista Latinoamericana de Comunicación CHASQUI*, 88, 2004: 32–37.
Cardenal, Rodolfo. Radical Conservatism and the Challenge of the Gospel in Guatemala. In: *Church and Politics in Latin America*, Edited by Dermot Keogh. London: MacMillan, 1990: 205–224.
Caretas-Dossier. Montesinos: Toda la historia. Lima, Caretas: 2000.
Carhuaricra Meza, Eduardo y Jaime Velásquez Rodríguez. *Flor de tajo abierto: Impacto ambiental de la minería en la salud pública de los Andes centrales del Perú*. Informe final del grupo de trabajo. Lima: Fondo Editorial del Congreso del Perú, 2005.
Carrión, Julio F. Las elecciones peruanos de 2001: Desmontelando la herencia autoritaría. In: *Reflexión Política*, 3, 6, 2001: 1–12.
Carrión, Julio F. (Ed). *The Fujimori Legacy: The Rise of Electoral Authoritarianism in Peru*. University Park: The Pennsylvania State University Press, 2006.
Castillo Aste, Evaristo. *La conjura de los corruptos*. Lima: Editorial Brasa, 2001.
Castillo, María Elena. Lerner: Cipriani pecó por omisión en Ayacucho. In: *La República*, July 29, 2006: 25.
Castro Caycedo, Germán. *Con las manos en alto.* Bogotá: Planeta, 2001.
Cavero-G. Juan A. Fermento revolucionario del catolicismo latinoamericano. In: *Nueva Sociedad*, 13, 1973: 3–27.
Ceceña, Ana Esther. América latina en la geopolítica estadounidense. In: *Revista Theomai*, 6, 2002: 1–13.
Chambliss, William J. *On The Take: From Petty Crooks to Presidents.* Bloomington: Indiana University Press, 1988.
Chambliss, William J. State-Organized Crime – The American Society of Criminology, 1988 Presidential Address. In: *Criminology*, 27, 2, 1989: 183–208.
Chanamé. Drugs, Soldiers, and Guerrillas. In: *The Peru Reader: History, Culture, Politics.* Edited by Orin Starn. Durham: Duke University Press, 1998: 415–417.
Charap, Joshua, and Christian Harml. Institutionalized Corruption and the Kleptocratic State. In: *Working Paper of the International Monetary Fund* (IMF), 1999: 1–24. <http://ssrn.com/abstract=880618>.
Cisneros Hamann, Luis Jaime. El poder de la prensa. In: *El poder en el Perú.* Edited by Augusto Alvarez Rodrich, Lima: Editorial Apoyo, 1993: 119–125.
Cleary, Edward L. Conclusion: Politics and Religion – Crisis, Constraints, and Restructuring. In: *Conflict and Competition: The Latin American Church in a Changing Environment*. Edited by Edward L. Cleary and H. Stewart-Gambino. Boulder, CO: Lynne Rienner Publishers, 1992: 197–221.
Cleaves, Peter S., and Henry Pease García. State Autonomy and Military Policy Making. In: *The Peruvian Experiment Reconsidered.* Edited by Cynthia Mc Clintock and Abraham F. Lowenthal. Princeton: Princeton University Press, 1983: 209–244.
Cockroft, James D. *America Latina y Estados Unidos*. Mexico City: Siglo Veintiuno, 2001.

Comblin, José. Changes in the Latin American Church during the Pontificate of John Paul II, Part 1. In: *National Catholic Reporter – The Independent Newsweekly*, 1, 14, 2003. <http://www.nationalcatholicreporter.org/globalpers/gp070203.htm>.

Comblin, José. Changes in the Latin American Church during the Pontificate of John Paul II, Part 2. In: *National Catholic Reporter – The Independent Newsweekly*, 1, 15, 2003a. <http://www.nationalcatholicreporter.org/globalpers/gp070903.htm>.

Comisión Interamericana de Derechos Humanos (CIDH). *Demanda en el caso de Pedro Huilca Tecse (Caso 11.768) contra la República de Perú,* Organización de los Estados Americanos; Washington, D.C., March 12, 2004. <http://www.cidh.oas.org/demandas/11.768%20Pedro%20Huilca%20Tecse%20Peru%2012mar04.pdf>.

Comisión de la Verdad y Reconciliación (CVR). *La Universidad Nacional de Educación Enrique Guzmán y Valle, La Cantuta.* Informe Final, Tomo V, 2.19. Lima, 2003: 605–636. <http://www.cverdad.org.pe/ifinal/pdf/TOMO%20V/SECCION%20TERCERA-Los%20Escenarios%20de%20la%20violencia%20(continuacion)/2.%20HISTORIAS%20REPRESENTATIVAS%20DE%20LA%20VIOLENCIA/2.19%20LA%20CANTUTA.pdf>

Comisión de la Verdad y Reconciliación (CVRa). *Narcotráfico, conflicto armado interno y corrupción.* Informe Final, Tomo V, 2.23. Lima, 2003: 739–773. <http://www.cverdad.org.pe/ifinal/pdf/TOMO%20V/SECCION%20TERCERA-Los%20Escenarios%20de%20la%20violencia%20(continuacion)/2.%20HISTORIAS%20REPRESENTATIVAS%20DE%20LA%20VIOLENCIA/2.23.%20NARCOTRAFICO.pdf>.

Comisión de la Verdad y Reconciliación (CVRb). *Las desapariciones de los estudiantes de la Universidad Nacional del Centro* (1990–1992) Informe Final, Tomo VII, 2.44. Lima, 2003: 455–473. <http://www.cverdad.org.pe/ifinal/pdf/TOMO%20VII/Casos%20Ilustrativos-UIE/2.44.%20UNIVERSIDAD%20DEL%20CENTRO.pdf>.

Comisión de la Verdad y Reconciliación (CVRc). *Las ejecuciones extrajudiciales en Barrios Altos* (1991). Informe Final, Tomo VII, 2.45. Lima, 2003: 475–493. <http://www.cverdad.org.pe/ifinal/pdf/TOMO%20VII/Casos%20Ilustrativos-UIE/2.45.%20BARRIOS%20ALTOS.pdf>.

Comisión de la Verdad y Reconciliación (CVRd), *La desaparición de campesinos del Santa* (1992). Informe Final, Tomo VII, 2.53. Lima, 2003: 561–577. <http://www.cverdad.org.pe/ifinal/pdf/TOMO%20VII/Casos%20Ilustrativos-UIE/2.53.%20CAMPESINOS%20DEL%20SANTA.pdf>.

Comisión de la Verdad y Reconciliación (CVRe). *El asesinato de Pedro Huillca Tecse* (1992). Informe Final, Tomo VII, 2.58. Lima, 2003: 629–647. <http://www.cverdad.org.pe/ifinal/pdf/TOMO%20VII/Casos%20Ilustrativos-UIE/2.58.%20PEDRO%20HUILCA.pdf>.

Comisión de la Verdad y Reconciliación (CVRf). *La desaparición de Pedro Yauri* (1992). Informe Final, Tomo VII, 2.59. Lima, 2003: 649–658. <http://

www.cverdad.org.pe/ifinal/pdf/TOMO%20VII/Casos%20Ilustrativos-UIE/2.59.%20PEDRO%20YAURI.pdf>.

Comisión de la Verdad y Reconciliación (CVRg). *Los asesinatos y lesions graves producidos en el atentado de Tarata* (1992); Informe Final, Tomo VII, 2.60. Lima, 2003: 661–668. <http://www.cverdad.org.pe/ifinal/pdf/TOMO%20VII/Casos%20Ilustrativos-UIE/2.60.%20TARATA.pdf>.

Committee to Protect Journalists (CPJ), Adolfo Isuiza Urquia, July 28, 2011. <http://www.cpj.org/killed/1992/adolfo-isuiza-urquia.php>.

Conaghan, Catherine. Entre las amenazas y la complicidad: El estado y la prensa en el Perú de Alberto Fujimori. In: *El juego político: Fujimori, la oposición y las reglas*. Edited by Fernando Tuesta Soldevilla. Lima, Peru: Fundación Friedrich Ebert, 1999: 65–95.

Conaghan, Catherine. *Fujimori's Peru: Deception in the Public Sphere*. Pittsburgh, KS: University of Pittsburgh Press, 2005.

Congreso del Peru. Comisión investigadora de la gestión presidencial de Alberto Fujimori. *Informe Final*. Lima, June 15, 2002. <http://www.congreso.gob.pe/historico/ciccor/excomi/infomulder.pdf>.

Congreso de la República, Aprueba la ley del sistema de inteligencia nacional November 12, 1991. <http://www.congreso.gob.pe/ntley/Imagenes/Decretos/Legislativos/00746.pdf>.

Coordinadora Nacional de Derechos Humanos. *Informe sobre la situación de los derechos humanos en el Perú en 1994*. Lima: Coordinadora Nacional de Derechos Humanos, 1994.

Corbière, Emilio J. *Opus Dei: El totalitarismo catolico*. Buenos Aires: DE BOLS!LLO, 2007.

Cordero, Jaime. 25 años de prisión para Montesinos por las matanzas del Grupo Colina. In: *El País* (Spain), October 2, 2010. <http://elpais.com/diario/2010/10/02/internacional/1285970413_850215.html>.

Costa Ferrero, Eduardo. Peru's Presidential Coup. In: *Journal of Democracy*, 4, 1, 1993: 28–40.

Cotler, Julio. *Drogas y política en el Perú*. Lima: Instituto de Estudios Peruanos, 1999.

Cotler, Julio. La gobernabilidad en el Perú: entre el autoritarismo y la democracia. In: *El Fujimorismo: Ascenso y caída de un regimen autoritario*. Edited by Julio Cotler and Romeo Grompone. Lima: IEP, 2001: 13–75.

Cox, Robert W. Forces, States and World Orders: Beyond International Relations Theory. In: *Millennium*. 10, 2, 1981: 126–155.

Crabtree, John. Peru: Outing the NGOs. In: *Open Democracy*, November 22, 2006. <http://www.opendemocracy.net/democracy-protest/peru_ngos_4117.jsp>.

Cribb, Robert. Introduction: Para-politics, Shadow Governance and Criminal Sovereignty. In: *Government of the Shadows: Para-politics and Criminal Sovereignty*. Edited by Eric Wilson. London: Pluto Press, 2009: 1–9.

Cuadros F., Julia, Jaime Consiglieri F. and José de Echave C., *Mapeo de la situación del proyecto Las Bambas*. Lima: CooperAcción, 2005.

Cuellar, Francisco Ramírez. *The Profits of Extermination: How US Corporate Power is Destroying Colombia.* Monroe, Maine: Common Courage Press, 2005.

Daeschner, Jeff. *La guerra del fin de la democracia: Mario Vargas Llosa versus Alberto Fujimori*. Lima: Peru Reporting, 1993.

Dalby, Simon. 1990. American Security Discourse. In: *Political Geography Quarterly*, 9, 2: 171–188.

Dammert Ego Aguirre, Manuel. *Fujimori-Montesinos: El estado mafioso.* Lima: Ediciones El Virrey, 2001.

Daraul, Arkon. *A History of Secret Societies*. New York: Pocket, 1969.

Dargent, Eduardo. Juzagando a los Senores. Reflexiones sobre los procesos anticorrupción en el Perú. In: *El pacto infame: Estudios sobre la corrupción en el Perú*. Edited by Felipe Portocarrero. Lima: Red para el Desarrollo de las Ciencias Sociales en el Perú, 2005: 377–402.

Davis, James R. *Fortune's Warriors: Private Armies and the New World Order.* Vancouver: Douglas & McIntyre, 2002.

Daudelin, Jean, and W. E. Hewitt. Churches and Politics in Latin America: Catholicism at the Crossroads. In: *Third World Quarterly*, 16, 2, 1995: 221–236.

De Althaus, Jaime. Las denuncias y los motives del general Robles. In: *Expreso* (Lima), May 9, 1993: 30.

De Bari Hermoza, Nicolás. *Fuerzas armadas del Peru: Lecciones de este siglo*. Lima: Editores & Impresores, 1996.

De Benito, Emilio. El Vaticano sanciona a Jon Sobrino, el principal teólogo de la liberación. In: *El País*, March 13, 2007: 41.

De Blaye, Eduard. *Franco and the Politics of Spain.* London: Pelican Books, 1976.

De Echave, José. Transnacionales mineras, evolución y tendencias. In: Asociación Pro Derechos Humanos (APRODEH). *Transnacionales, estados nación y derechos humanos de los pueblos*. Lima, 2003: 141–149.

De Eiden, T. L. *Environmental Policy under Political Transition: The Peruvian Mining Sector and the Yanacocha Goldmine*. Doctoral Dissertation, University of Bonn, Germany, 2006. <http://hss.ulb.uni-bonn.de/2006/0743/0743.pdf>

Degregori, Carlos Iván (Ed). *Las rondas campesinas y la derrota de Sendero Luminoso.* Lima: IEP, 1996. Degregori, Carlos Iván. The Maturation of a Cosmocrat and the Building of a Discourse Community: The Case of Shining Path. In: The Legitimation of Violence. Edited by David Apter. London: MacMillan, 1997: 33–82.

Degregori, Carlos Iván. *La década de la antipolítica*. Lima: IEP, 2001.

Dehan, Nicolas. Opus Dei: A Strange Pastoral Phenomenon. In: *Le Sel de la Terre*, 11, 1994. <http://www.sspx.org/miscellaneous/opus_dei.htm>.

Della Cava, Ralph.Thinking about Current Vatican Policy in Central and East Europe and the Utility of the 'Brazilian Paradigm'. In: *Journal of Latin American Studies*, 19, 2, 1993: 257–281.

Del Olmo, Rosa. Limitations for the Prevention of Violence: The Latin American Reality and Its Criminological Theory. In: *Crime and Social Justice*, 3, 1975: 21–29.

Del Olmo, Rosa. *¿Prohibir o domesticar?* Caracas: Editorial Nueva Sociedad, 1992.

Del Pino, Ponciano. Tiempos de guerra y de dioses: Ronderos, evangélicos y senderistas en el valle del río Apurímac. In: *Las rondas campesinas y la derrota de Sendero Luminoso.* Edited by Carlos Iván Degregori, José Coronel, Ponciano del Pino, and Orin Starn. Lima: Instituto de Estudios Peruanos, 1996: 117–188.

De Soto, Hernando. *The Other Path: The Invisible Revolution in the Third World.* New York: Harper & Row, 1989.

Diez Canseco, Javier. Introducción. Balance de la inversion privada y privatización 1990–2001. Comisión investigadora de los delitos económicos y financieros cometidos entre 1990–2001. Edited by Javier Diez Canseco. Lima: Fondo Editorial del Congreso del Perú, 2002: 25–61.

Diez Canseco, Javier. Promoción de la inversion privada y privatización: Balances y perspectivas del proceso para el desarollo nacional. In: *Balance de la inversión privada y privatización 1990–2001.* Comisión investigadora de los delitos económicos y financieros cometidos entre 1990–2001. Edited by Javier Diez Canseco. Lima: Fondo Editorial del Congreso del Perú, 2002a: 91–109.

Diez Canseco, Javier. Recursos naturales: ¿soberanía o súplica? In: *La República*, August 3, 2006: 17.

Diez Canseco, Javier. Yanacocha: Legitimidad y defensa popular. In: *La República*, August 31, 2006: 13.

Diez Canseco, P. P. Análisis: La experiencia de las rondas campesinas en el Perú. In: *Ciudad politíca – portal de ciencia política.* 2003. <http://www.ciudadpolitica.com/modules/news/article.php?storyid=245>.

Domenach, Jean-Marie, *La propaganda política*. Buenos Aires: Eudeba, 2005.

Dos Santos, Theotônio. *Economía mundial: La integración latinoamericana.* Mexico, D.F.: Random House Mondadori, 2004.

Doyle, Sir Arthur C. The Sign of Four. In: *Sherlock Holmes: The Long Stories.* Leicester: Galley, 1987: 143–271.

Drogus, Carol Ann. No Land of Milk and Honey: Women CEB Activists in Post-Transition Brazil. In: *Journal of Interamerican Studies and World Affairs*, 41, 4, 1999: 1–20.

Drug Enforcement Agency (DEA). Congressional Testimony by Donnie R. Marshall, Administrator, DEA, before the Senate Caucus on International Narcotics Control. February 28, 2001. <http://www.usembassy.it/file2001_02/alia/a1022807.htm>

Dube, Ryan. US lawsuit could affect restructuring of Doe Run Peru. In: *Business News Americas*, November 8, 2010. <http://www.minesandcommunities.org/article.php?a=10530>.

Durand, Francisco. El fenómeno Fujimori y la crisis de los partidos politicos. In: *Revista mexicana de la sociología*, 58, 1, 1996: 97–120.

Durand, Francisco. The Growth and the Limitations of the Peruvian Right. In: *The Peruvian Labyrinth.* Edited by Max Cameron and Philip Mauceri, 1997: 152–175.

Durand, Francisco. Cleptocracia y empresariado en el Perú. In: *Nueva sociedad*, 194, 2004: 119–132.

Durand, Francisco. Dinámica política de la corrupción y participación empresarial. In: *El pacto infame: Estudios sobre la corrupción en el Perú.* Edited by Felipe Portocarrero. Lima: Red para el Desarrollo de las Ciencias Sociales en el Perú, 2005: 287–330.

Elbert, Carlos. Rebuilding Utopia? Critical Criminology and the Difficult Road of Reconstruction in Latin America. In: *Crime, Law and Social Change*, 41, 4, 2004: 385–395.

Elias, Robert. Drug Wars as Victimization and Social Control. In: *New Political Science*, 20, 1991: 41–61.

Emery, Alex. Peru President Humala Signs Law Establishing Mining Windfall Tax, In: *Business Week*, September 28, 2011. <http://www.businessweek.com/news/2011-09-28/peru-president-humala-signs-law-establishing-mining-windfall- tax.html>.

Encinoza Riera, Argenis, and Rosa del Olmo. The View from Latin America against Transnational Criminology: A Call for Democratic International Cooperation. In: *Crime and Social Justice*, 15, 1981: 61–67.

Escobar Gaviria, Roberto. *Mi hermano Pablo: Los secretos de Pablo Escobar.* Bogotá: Quintero Editores, 2000.

Escrivá de Balaguer, José María. *The Way*. New York: All Saints Press, 1963.

Espinoza, Rocio, Mauricio Hernández-Avila, Juan Narciso, Carmen Castañaga, Shirley Moscoso, Georgina Ortiz, Luz Carbajal, Steve Wegner, and Gary Noonan. Determinants of Blood-Lead Levels in Children in Callao and Lima Metropolitan Area. In: *Salud pública de México*, 45, 2, 2003: 208–219.

Etzioni-Halevy, Eva. Exchanging Material Benefits for Political Support: A Comparative Analysis. In: *Political Corruption: A Handbook.* Edited by Arnold J. Heidenheimer, Michael Johnston, and Victor T. LeVine. New Brunswick: Transaction Publishers, 1989: 287–304.

Eurostat. *External and intra-European Union trade*. Data 1999–2004. Luxembourg: Office for Official Publications of the European Communities, 2005. <http://gesd.free.fr/kscv00501.pdf>.

Femia, Joseph. *Gramsci's Political Thought: Hegemony, Consciousness and the Revolutionary Process.* London: Clarendon, 1981.

Fernández Segado, Francisco. El nuevo ordenamiento constitucional del Perú: Aproximación a la constitución de 1993. In: Comisión Andina de Juristas. *La constitución de 1993: Analisis y comentarios I.* Lima: CAJ, 1994: 11–65.

Fernández Tabío, Luis R., and Jorge Hernández Martínez. Estados Unidos y el ALCA: La institucionalización de la hegemonía hemisférica en el siglo XXI. In: *Del TLC al Mercosur*. Edited by Víctor López Villafañe and Jorge Rafael Di Masi, Mexico, D.F.: Siglo XXI Editores, 2002: 299–324.

Ferrero Costa, Eduardo. Peru's Presidential Coup. In: *Journal of Democracy*, 4, 1, 1993: 28–40.

Feyerabend, Paul. *Against Method.* London: Verso, 1993.

Fisher, Ian. Benedict to Face Challenges in Latin America. *The New York Times,* May 4, 2007. <http://www.nytimes.com/2007/05/04/world/americas/04web-fisher.html?ref =popes2007latinamericatrip>.

Fleet, Michael. The Church and Revolutionary Struggle in Central America. In: *Social Text*, 7, 1983: 106–114.

Fonseca, Francisco C. P. Media and Democracy: False Convergences. In: *Revista de sociologia e política*, 22, 2004: 13–24.

Fontana, Benedeto. *Hegemony and Power.* Minneapolis: University of Minnesota Press, 1993.

Fowks, Jacqueline. *Suma y resta de la realidad: Medios de comunicación y elecciones generales 2000 en el Perú.* Lima: Fundación Friedrich Ebert, 2000.

Fraser, Barbara, J. Peru's New Cardinal Known for Standing with the Powerful (Special to the *National Catholic Reporter*), March 23, 2001. <http://natcath.org/NCR_Online/archives2/2001a/032301/032301g.htm>.

Friedmann, Jan, John Goetz, Ralf Neukirch, Marcel Rosenbach, and Holger Stark. How America views the Germans. In: *Der Spiegel*, November 30, 2010. Wikileak Diplomatic Cables. <http://www.spiegel.de/international/germany/0,1518,731645,00.html>.

Friedrich, Carl. Political Pathology. In: *Political Quarterly*, 37, 1966: 70–85.

Friedrich, Carl. Corruption Concepts in Historical Perspective. In: *Political Corruption: A Handbook.* Edited by Arnold J. Heidenheimer, Michael Johnston, and Victor T. LeVine. New Brunswick: Transaction Publishers, 1989: 15–24.

Fuhr, Harald and Marion Hörmann. Peru. In: *Handbuch der Dritten Welt: Südamerika.*Edited by Dieter Nohlen and Franz Nuscheler. Bonn, Germany: Dietz, 1992: 437–476.

Fusi, Juan Pablo. *Franco: Autoritarismo y poder personal.* Madrid: Grupo Santillana de Ediciones, 2001.

Galeano, Eduardo. *Las venas abiertas de América Latina.* Mexico City: Siglo Veintiuno, 1982.

Galindo, Cristina. Polacos contra el mundo, el demonio y la carne. In: *El País*, March 30, 2007: 8.

Gamarra, Rodolfo. *Terrorismo: tratamiento juridico.* Lima: Instituto de Defensa Legal, 1995.

García Calderon, Ernesto. Peru's Decade of Living Dangerously. In: *Journal of Democracy*, 12, 2, April 2001: 46–58.

García, Jonás. El consejo de defensa sudamericano: ¿Instrumento de integración regional o mecanismo para la hegemonía del Brazil? In: *UNISCI Discussion Papers,* 18, 2008: 159–176.
Gargurevich R., Juan. *La prensa sensacionalista en el Peru.* Lima: Fondo Editorial de la Pontifica Universidad Católica de Peru, 2000.
Gente de Pierina. Boletín informativo No. 21, Huaraz, Barrick Pierina, October 2001: 1–15.
Gerassi, John. *The Great Fear in Latin America.* New York: Collier Books, 1973.
Gerth, H. H., and Mills, C. Wright. *From Max Weber: Essays in Sociology.* New York: Oxford University Press, 1958.
Gertgen, Jocelyn E., Untold Truths: The Exclusion of Enforced Sterilizations from the Peruvian Truth Commission's Final Report. In: *Cornell Law School Berger International Speaker Papers.* Paper 8, 2009. <http://scholarship.law.cornell.edu/biss_papers/8>.
Gibbons, Kenneth. Introduction. In: *Political Corruption in Canada.* Edited by Kenneth M. Gibbons and Donald C. Rowat. Toronto: McClelland and Stewart Limited, 1976.
Gibbons, Kenneth. Toward an Attitudinal Definition of Corruption. In: *Political Corruption: A Handbook.* Edited by Arnold J. Heidenheimer, Michael Johnston, and Victor T. LeVine. New Brunswick: Transaction Publishers, 1989: 165–172.
Giddens, Anthony. *The Nation-State and Violence.* Cambridge: Polity Press, 1985.
Gill, Lesley. *The School of the Americas.* Durham: Duke University Press, 2004.
Gill, Lesley. 'Right There With You': Coca-Cola, Labor Restructuring and Political Violence in Colombia. In: *Critique of Anthropology*, 27, 2007: 235–260.
Girling, John. *Corruption, Capitalism and Democracy.* London: Routledge, 1997.
González, José E. Guerrillas and Coca in the Upper Huallaga Valley. In: *Shining Path of Peru.* Edited by David Scott Palmer. New York: St. Martin's, 1994: 123–144.
González, Osmar. La crisis de los partidos peruanos. Apuntes para una lectura socio-histórica. In: *Espacio abierto*, 8, 3, 1999: 305–324.
Gonzáles, Raúl. El Huallaga: Todos los conflictos. In: *Quehacer*, 71, 1991: 46–52.
Goodman, Margaret. Preserving Privilege in Yucatan. In: *Political Corruption: A Handbook.* Edited by Arnold Heidenheimer, Michael Johnston, and Victor Levine, New Jersey: Transaction Publishers, 1989: 639–658.
Goodspeed, D. J. *The Conspirators: A Study of the Coup d'Etat.* Toronto: Macmillan, 1967.
Gooren, Henri. 'Catholic and Non-Catholic Theologies of Liberation: Poverty, Self-Improvement, and Ethics Among Small-Scale Entrepreneurs in Guatemala City. In: *Journal for the Scientific Study of Religion*, 41, 1, 2002: 29–45.
Gosch, Martin A., and Richard Hammer. *The Last Testament of Lucky Luciano.* New York: Dell, 1976.
Gott, Richard. *Guerrilla Movements in Latin America.* Bungay, Suffolk: Chaucer, 1970.
Gramsci, Antonio. Quotation from *Ordine Nuovo* by Eugenio Garin in Studi Gramsciani, 407. As quoted in Williams, Gwyn A., The Concept of 'Egemonia'in the

Thought of Antonio Gramsci: Some Notes on Interpretation. In: *Journal of the History of Ideas*, 21, 4, 1960: 586–599.

Gramsci, Antonio. *Selections From the Prison Notebooks*. Edited by Quentin Hoare and Geoffrey N. Smith. New York: International Publishers, 1971.

Gratius, Susanne. The "Third Wave of Populism" in Latin America. In: Working Paper 45, *Fundación para las Relaciones Internacionales y el Diálogo Exterior* (FRIDE), 2007. <http://www.fride.org/download/WP45.english.pdf>.

Gray, Colin. *Geopolitics of the Nuclear Era*. New York: Crane, 1977.

Graziano, L. Patron-Client Relationship in Southern Italy. In: *Friends, Followers and Factions*. Edited by L. G. Schmidt, C. Lande, and J. Scott. Berkeley: University of California Press, 1977: 360–378.

Green, Penny and Tony Ward. *State Crime: Governments, Violence and Corruption*. London, UK: Pluto Press, 2004.

Grindle, Merilee S. and Edward S. Mason, *Good Enough Governance: Poverty Reduction and Reform in Developing Countries*. Harvard University. Prepared for the Poverty Reduction Group of the World Bank, 2002. <http://docs.google.com/viewer?a=v&q=cache:7KCleI5zkwUJ:ocw.library.nenu.edu.cn/pluginfile.php/25741/mod_resource/content/1/HD32.pdf+Grindle,+Merilee+S.+and+Edward+S.+Mason,+Good+Enough+Governance:+Poverty+Reduction+and+Reform+in+Developing+Countries.+Harvard+University&hl=en&gl=ca&pid=bl&srcid=ADGEESimVEfL24OrlWoLS5UBlWRw44dBvwSepacY5RwYCzvS7GC0SDi7h9I7-uTPi4fp89ODGv2PaB4df2LIO-QDP6LG1zgMOZRtWDxv8EJvsNZujMdhkp9OODhOS69TrrdDcYeMm5E&sig=AHIEtbSC2B0939KohYGGV0H_M5yN-xfmwQ>.

Grinspoon, Lester and James B. Bakalar. Coca and Cocaine as Medicines: An Historical Review. In: *Journal of Ethnopharmacology*, 3, 3, 1981: 149–160.

Grompone, Romeo. Al día siguente: El Fujimorismo como proyecto inconcluso de transformación política y social. In: *El Fujimorismo: Ascenso y caída de un regimen autoritario*. Edited by Julio Cotler and Romeo Grompone. Lima: IEP, 2001: 77–174.

Gutiérrez, Gustavo. *A Theology of Liberation*. Maryknoll, N.Y.: Orbis Books, 1973.

Gutiérrez, Miguel. Ex narcotraficante relata a Comisión Townsend cómo el ex asesor se convirtió en socio de cárteles. In: *La República*, July 2, 2002. <http://www.larepublica.com.pe/node/135238>.

Gutiérrez, Miguel. Personal Communication Electronic Mail. September 19, 2002a.

Han Chen, Pablo L. Los linchamientos en el estado de derecho Venezolano (1995–1996). In: *Capítulo criminológico*, 26, 1, 1998: 67–87.

Hansen, Guillermo. When Parallel Lines Converge: Roman Catholic Integrism and Evangelical Fundamentalism – Some Reflections from Latin America. In: *Journal of Lutheran Ethics*, 6, 11, 2006. <http://archive.elca.org/jle/print.asp?k=674>.

Harris, Robert. *Political Corruption: In and Beyond the Nation State*. New York: Routledge, 2003.

Harris, Leonard and Rosa H. Harris, Importancia del apoyo comunitario en la industria minera. In: *Minería*, 48, 284, May 2001: 26–33.

Haynes, Jeffrey. Introduction. In: *Democracy and Political Change in the 'Third World'*. Edited by Jeffrey Haynes, London: Routledge, 2001: 1–21.

Harvey, Neil. *The Chiapas Rebellion: The Struggle for Land and Democracy*. Durham, NC: Duke University Press, 1998.

Hearn, Kelly. The Camisea Cover-up. In: *NACLA Report on the Americas*, 40, 1, 2007: 12–17.

Heckethorn, Charles William. *The Secret Societies*, Vol. I. New York: University Books, 1966.

Heidenheimer, Arnold. Introduction. In: *Political Corruption: Readings in Comparative Analysis*. New York: Holt Rinehart and Winston, 1970: 3–8.

Heidenheimer, Arnold, Michael Johnston and Victor Levine. Terms, Concepts, and Definitions: An Introduction. In: *Political Corruption: A Handbook.* Edited by Heidenheimer, Arnold, Michael Johnston, and Victor Levine. New Brunswick, NJ: Transaction Publishers, 1989: 3–14.

Hein, Wolfgang, and Georg Simonis. Theoretische und methodische Probleme einer kritischen Theorie internationaler Politik. In: *Politische Vierteljahresschrift*, Wiesbaden, Germany. XIV, 1, 1973: 85–106.

Hellman, Joel S., Geraint Jones, and Daniel Kaufmann. Seize the State, Seize the Day State Capture, Corruption, and Influence in Transition. In: *World Bank Policy Research Working Paper No. 2444*. World Bank Institute, September 2000: 1–45.

Henman, Anthony. *Mama Koka.* Bremen, Germany: Verlag Roter Funke, 1981.

Hennelly, Alfred T. S. J. (Ed). *Liberation Theologies: The Global Pursuit of Justice*. Mystic, CT: Twenty-Third Publications, 1995.

Horkheimer, Max. Traditionelle und kritische Theory. In: *Zeitschrift für Sozialforschung*. VI, 1937: 245–292.

Horkheimer, Max. The End of Reason. In: *The Essential Frankfurt School Reader*. Edited by Andrew Arato and Eike Gebhardt. New York: Continuum, 1982: 26–48.

Horkheimer, Max. Zur Soziologie der Klassenverhältnisse. In: *Gesammelte Werke*, Vol.12. Edited by Gudrun Schmid Noerr. Frankfurt a. M., Germany: Fischer, 1985: 75–104.

Horkheimer, Max. Die Rackets und der Geist. In: *Gesammelte Werke*, Vol.12, 1985a: 287–291.

Horkheimer, Max. Die Utopie vom Reich der Freiheit (I). In: *Gesammelte Werke*, Vol. 14, 1988: 132.

Horkheimer, Max. Herrschende Klasse, die von Rackets beherrschte Klasse und die Rolle der Fachleute. In: *Gesammelte Werke*, Vol.14, 1988a: 334–335.

Horkheimer, Max. Theorie der Rackets. In: Gesammelte Werke, Vol. 14, 1988b: 340.

Horkheimer, Max. Aus einer Theorie des Verbrechers. In: *Gesammelte Werke*, Vol. 5, 1997: 257–260.

Horkheimer, Max. Vernunft und Selbsterhaltung. In: *Gesammelte, Schriften*, Vol. 5, 1997a: 321–350.

Houtart, Francois, Los pontificados de Juan Pablo II y de Benedicto XVI frente a América Latina. In: *Nueva sociedad*, 198, 2005: 32–41.

Howson, Richard. *Hegemony: Studies in Consensus and Coercion*. New York: Routledge, 2008.

Hülst, Dirk. Kritische Theorie und Ideologiekritik. In: *Handbuch Politischer Theorien und Ideologien*. Edited by Franz Neumann, Hamburg: Rowohlt, 1989: 529–546.

Huggins, Martha (Ed). *Vigilantism and the State in Modern Latin America*. New York: Praeger, 1991.

Human Rights Watch (HRW). Torture and Political Persecution in Peru. *Human Rights Watch*, December 1, 1997. <http://www.unhcr.org/refworld/docid/ 3ae6a84b8.html>.

Human Rights Watch. Peru: Human Rights after Fujimori. March 20, 2002. <http://www.hrw.org/node/82663>.

Huntington, Samuel. *Political Order in Changing Societies*. New Haven, CT: Yale University Press, 1968.

Isbell, Billie Jean. Shining Path and Peasant Responses in Rural Ayacucho. In: *Shining Path of Peru*. Edited by David S. Palmer, New York: St. Martin's Press, 1992: 127–53.

Jácome E., Hugo. A las puertas del abismo. Las implicaciones del TLC para Ecuador. In: *Iconos: Revista de ciencias sociales*, 20, 2004: 6–13.

Jamieson, Ruth, and Kieran McEvoy. State Crime by Proxy and Juridical Othering. In: *British Journal of Criminology*, 45, 4, 2005: 504–527.

Jara, Edgar. Cardenal Cipriani es un mal ejemplo para los católicos. In: *La República*, January 26, 2001: n. a.

Jara, Umberto. *Ojo por ojo. La verdadera historia del Grupo Colina*. Lima: Página Uno Editores, 2007.

Jiménez de Parga, Manuel. *La corrupcíon en la democracía*. In: *La corrupcíon política*. Edited by Francisco J. Laporta and Silvina Álvarez. Madrid: Alianza Editorial, 1997: 135–155.

Jochamowitz, Luis. *Ciudano Fujimori: La construcción de un politíco*. Lima: Peisa, 1994.

Jochamowitz, Luis.*Vladimiro: Vida y tiempo de un corruptor*. Lima: Empresa Editora El Comercio, 2002.

Jochamowitz, Luis. *Vladimiro: Conversando con el doctor*. Lima: Empresa Editora El Comercio, 2002a.

Jones, Adam. Parainstitutional Violence in Latin America. In: *Latin American Politics and Society*, 46, 4, 2004: 127–148.

Jones, Bart. ¡Hugo! *The Hugo Chavez Story from Mud Hut to Perpetual Revolution*. Hanover, NH: Steerforth Press, 2007.

Kamphuis, Charis. The Convergence of Public and Corporate Power in Peru: Yanacocha Mine, Campesino Dispossession, Privatized Coercion. In: *Comparative Research in Law & Political Economy* (CLPE), Research Paper No. 11, 2010: 1–34.
Kahn, Joel S. and Francesco Formosa. The Problem of 'Crony Capitalism': Modernity and the Encounter with the Perverse. In: *Thesis Eleven*, 69, 2002: 47–66.
Kasperson, Roger E., and Julian V. Minghi (Eds). *The Structure of Political Geography*. Chicago, IL: Aldine Publishing Company, 1969: xi–xii.
Kauzlarich, David, Rick Matthews and William Miller. Toward a Victimology of State Crime. In: *Critical Criminology*, 10, 3, 2001: 173–194.
Kauzlarich, David, Christoher W. Mullins, and Rick Matthews. A Complicity Continuum of State Crime. In: *Contemporary Justice Review*, 6, 3, 2003: 241–254.
Kay, Bruce H. Fujipopulism and the Liberal State in Peru, 1990–1995. In: *Journal of Interamerican Studies and World Affairs*, 38, 4, 1996: 55–98.
Keen, Benjamin. *Latin American Civilization: The Colonial Origins*. Boston, MA: Houghton, 1974.
Kennedy, Paul. *In Vorbereitung auf das 21. Jahrhundert*. Frankfurt a. M.: Fischer, 1993.
Kintto, Lucas. A World without Foreign Military Bases. In: *IPS Newsnet*, March 7, 2007. <http://ipsnewsnet/news.asp?idnews=36825>.
Klaiber, Jeffrey. The Church in Peru: Between Terrorism and Conservative Restraints. In: *Conflict and Competition: The Latin American Church in a Changing Environment*. Edited by E. L. Cleary and H. Stewart-Gambino. Boulder, CO: Lynne Rienner Publishers, 1992: 87–103.
Klitgaard, Robert. *Controlling Corruption*. University of California Press, 1988.
Klitgaard, Robert. Combatiendo la corrupción. Información e incentivos. In: *Nueva Sociedad*, 145, 1996: 56–65.
Kramer, Ronald C, Raymond J. Michalowski, and David Kauzlarich. The Origins and Development of the Concept and Theory of State-Corporate Crime. In: *Crime & Delinquency*, 48, 2, 2002: 263–282.
Kraul, Chris, and Henry Chu, Latin American Catholics: Problem with Pope John Paul II. In: *The Seattle Times*, April 11, 2005. <http://community.seattletimes.nwsource.com/archive/?date=20050411&slug=popelatam11>.
Krauthammer, Charles. A New 'Pentagon Paper' Charts America's Direction in Post-Cold War World. In: *philly.com*. March 17, 1992. <http:// articles.philly.com/1992-03-17/news/26017687_1_superpower-multipolarity-pentagon-paper>.
Laclau, Ernesto. *On Populist Reason*. New York: Verso, 2005.
Lamo de Espinosa, Emilio. Corrupción política y ética económica. In: *La corrupción politíca*, Edited by Francisco J. Laporta and Silviana Álvarez, Madrid Alianza Editorial, 1997: 271–292.
Landa Arroyo, Cesar. Notas sobre el transfuguismo parlamentario peruano. In: *Derecho y sociedad*, 16, 2001: 217–229.
LaPalombara, Joseph. *Politics within Nations*. Englewood Cliffs, NJ: Prentice-Hall, 1978.

Laporta, Francisco. La *corrupción política*: Introducción general. In: *La corrupción política*. Edited by Francisco Laporta and Silviana Álvarez. Madrid: Alianza Editorial, 1997: 13–36.

La Red Provincial de ONGs de San Juan. Sobre el informe de impacto ambiental presentado por La Barrick Gold Corporation del proyecto Pascua-Lama a realizarse en la provincial de San Juan. In: *Revista Theomai*, 11, 2005. <http://revista-theomai.unq.edu.ar/numero11/sobreeiabarrickgold11.htm>.

Lascoumes, Pierre. *Corrupciones: El poder frente a la ética*. Barcelona: Ediciones Bellaterra, 2000.

Leech, Gary. Armed Blockade Illustrates Failure of Plan Colombia. In: *Colombia Journal*, August 1, 2005. <http://colombiajournal.org/armed-blockade-illustrates-failure-of-plan-colombia.htm>.

Leff, Nathaniel H., Economic Development through Bureaucratic Corruption. In: *Political Corruption: A Handbook*. Edited by Arnold Heidenheimer, Michael Johnston, and Victor T. Levine. New Brunswick, NJ: Transaction Publishers, 1989: 389–403.

Leftwich, Adrian. Governance, Democracy and Development in the Third World. In: *Third World Quarterly*, 14, 3, 1993: 605–624.

Lernoux, Penny. *People of God: The Struggle for World Catholicism*. New York: Penguin, 1990.

Levenson, Deborah. The Life That Makes Us Die/The Death That Makes Us Live: Facing Terrorism in Guatemala. In: *Radical History Review*, 85, 2003: 94–104.

Levitsky, Steven. Fujimori and Post-Party Politics in Peru. In: *Journal of Democracy*, 10, 3, 1999: 78–92.

Levitsky, Steven and Maxwell Cameron, Democracy without Parties? Political Parties and Regime Change in Fujimori's Peru. In: *Latin American Politics and Society*, 45, 3, 2003: 1B33.

Levitt, Barry S. A Desultory Defense of Democracy: OAS Resolution 1080 and the Interamerican Democratic Charter. In: *Latin American Politics and Society*, 48, 3, 2006: 93–123.

Lewy, Guenther. *The Catholic Church and Nazi Germany*. Cambridge, MA: Da Capo Press, 2000.

Linz, Juan. Autoritäre Regime. In: *Wörterbuch Staat und Politik*. Edited by Dieter Nohlen. Munich: Piper, 1991: 40-43.

Linz, Juan. *Totalitarian and Authoritarian Regimes*. Boulder, CO: Lynne Rienner Publishers, 2000.

Loayza Galván, Franciso. *El rostro oscuro del poder*. Lima: San Borja Ediciones, 1998.

Loayza Galván, Francisco. *Fujimori y Montesinos en el trafico de armas a las FARC*. Lima: Ediciones Peru Diario Punto Final, 2003.

Long, William R. Peru: Amnesty Law for Rights Abuses Doesn't Get Military Off the Hook. In: *Los Angeles Times*, June 30, 1995. <http://articles.latimes. com/1995-06-30/news/mn-18901_1_human-rights>.

López, Jaime. Periodismo Latinoamericano: Los casos más comunes de corrupción. In: *Revista latinoamericana de comunicación CHASQUI*, 76, 2001. <http://chasqui.comunica.org/76/lopez76.htm>.
Lora Cam, Jorge. Trasnacionales mineras y ecocidio en el Perú: El Grupo México y su política neocolonial. In: *Quivera*, 7, 1, 2005: 316–337.
Lyman, Michael D., and Gary W. Potter. *Organized Crime*. Upper Saddle River, NJ: Prentice Hall, 2000.
Lynch, Nicolás. Los usos de los medios en el Perú de Fujimori. In: *Controlando la politica*. Edited by Enrique Peruzotti and Catalina Smulovitz. Buenos Aires: Temas Grupo Editorial, 2002: 263–287.
Macassi Lavander, Sandro. La prensa amarilla en América Latina. In: *Revista latino americana de comunicación CHASQUI*, 77, 2002: 14–19.
MacKenzie, Norman. *Secret Societies*. New York: Collier, 1971.
Mackinnon, María M. and Mario Alberto Petrone (Eds). *Populismo y neopopulismo en América Latina*. Editorial Universitaria de Buenos Aires, 1999.
Mackinder, Halford J. The Geographical Pivot of History. In: *The Structure of Political Geography*. Edited by Roger E. Kasperson and Julian V. Minghi. Chicago, IL: Aldine Publishing, 1969: 161–169 (Originally published in *The Geographical Review*, 23, 4, 1904: 421–444).
Maingot, Anthony. Confronting Corruption in the Hemisphere: A Sociological Perspective. In: *Journal of Interamerican and World Affairs*, 37, 2, 1994: 49– 74.
Maingot, Anthony. Offshore Secrecy Centers and the Necessary Role of States: Bucking the Trend. In: *Journal of Interamerican and World Affairs*, 37, 4, 1995: 1–24.
Mainwaring, Scott. The Crisis of Representation in the Andes. In: *Journal of Democracy*, 17, 3, 2006: 13–27.
Malavé A., Auristela, and Pablo Carrero M. Un método sencillo para monitoreo de mercurio en humanos. In: *Saber*, 15, 1–2, 2003: 60–65.
Mallimaci, Fortunato. El catolicismo latinoamericano a fines del milenio: Incertidumbres desde el cono sur. In: *Nueva sociedad*, 136, 1995: 164–176.
Mann, Charles C. *1491: New Revelations of the Americas before Columbus*. New York: Vintage Books, 2006.
Mann, Michael, *The Sources of Social Power*, vol.1. Cambridge, UK: Cambridge University Press, 1986.
Marcus-Delgado, Jane. El fin de Alberto Fujimori: Un estudio de legitimidad presidencial. In: *Lecciones del final del Fujimorismo*. Edited by Jane Marcus-Delgado and Martin Tanaka. Lima: IEP, 2001: 9–55.
Marcuse, Herbert. *One-Dimensional Man: Studies in the Ideology of Advanced Industrial Society*. Boston: Beacon Press, 1964.
Martin, Brian G. *The Shanghai Green Gang*. Berkeley: University of California Press,1996.
Martín de Pozuelo, Eduardo. *Los secretos del Franquismo*. Barcelona: La Vanguardia Ediciones, 2007.

Marx, Karl. Corruption at Elections. In: *The New York Daily Tribune* (September 4, 1852). <http://www.marxists.org/archive/marx/works/1852/08/20.htm>.
Marx, Carlos. *El Dieciocho Brumario de Luis Bonaparte*. Barcelona: Ariel, 1971. (Originally published as *Der Achtzehnte Brumaire des Louis Bonaparte* in Germany in 1869).
Matthews, Rick A. and Kauzlarich, D. The Crash of ValuJet Flight 592: A Case Study in State-Corporate Crime. In: *Sociological Focus*, 3, 3, 2000: 281–298.
Mattos, Francisco. ¿Economía de guerra para el ejército? In: *Debate*, 11, 57, 1989: 34–35.
Mauceri, Phillip. Military Politics and Counter-Insurgency in Peru. In: *Journal of Interamerican Studies and World Affairs*, 33, 4, 1991–1992: 83–109.
Mauceri, Phillip. State Reforms, Coalitions, and the Neoliberal golpe in Peru. In: *Latin American Perspectives*, 30, 1, 1995: 7–38.
Mauceri, Phillip. Return of the Caudillo: Autocratic Democracy in Peru. In: *Third World Quarterly*, 18, 5, 1997: 899–911.
Mauceri, Phillip. An Authoritarian Presidency: How and Why Did Presidential Power Run Amok in Fujimori's Peru? In: *The Fujimori Legacy: The Rise of Electoral Authoritarianism in Peru*. Edited by Julio F. Carrión. The Pennsylvania State University Press, 2006: 39–60.
Mauro, Paolo. Corruption and Growth. In: *Quarterly Journal of Economics*, 110, 3, 1995: 681–711.
Mayer, Robert. Marx, Lenin, and the Corruption of the Working Class. In: *Political Studies*, XLI, 1993: 636–649.
McCamant, John F. Governance without Blood: Social Science's Antiseptic View of Rule; or the Neglect of Political Repression. In: *The State as Terrorist*. Edited by Michael Stohl and George A. Lopez. Westport, CT: Greenwood, 1984: 11–42.
McClintock, Cynthia. ¿Es autoritario el gobierno de Fujimori? In: *El juego politico: Fujimori, la oposición y las reglas*. Edited by Fernando Tuesta Soldevilla. Lima: Fundación Friedrich Ebert, 1999: 65–95.
McClintock, Cynthia, and Fabian Vallas T. *La democracia negociada: Las relaciones Peru-Estados Unidos (1980–2000)*. Lima: IEP, 2005.
McClintock, Cynthia. An Unlikely Comeback in Peru. In: *Journal of Democracy*, 17, 4, 2006: 95–109.
McCoy, Alfred W. *The Politics of Heroin*. New York: Lawrence Hill, 1991.
McCoy, Alfred W. *A Question of Torture*. New York: Owl Books, 2006.
McGovern, Arthur F. *Liberation Theology and its Critics*. Maryknoll, NY: Orbis Books, 1993.
McGovern, George. The Real Cost of Hunger. In: *United Nations Chronicle*, 38, 3, 2001: 24.
McMillan, John and Pablo Zoido. How to Subvert Democracy: Montesinos in Peru. In: *Journal of Economic Perspectives,* 18, 4, 2004: 69–92.
McMullan, John. *Beyond the Limits of the Law: Corporate Crime and Law and Order*. Halifax, Canada: Fernwood, 1993.
McMullan, M. A Theory of Corruption. In: *The Sociological Review*, 9, 2, 1961: 18–201.

McSherry, Patrice J. The Emergence of 'Guardian Democracy'. In: *NACLA Report on the Americas*, 32, 3, 1998: 16–26.
Means, Philip A. The Rebellion of Tupac-Amaru II, 1780–1781. In: *The Hispanic American Review*, 2, 1, 1919: 1–25.
Merrington, John. Theory and Practice in Gramsci's Marxism. In: *The Socialist Register*, 5, 1968: 145–176.
Meschkat, Klaus, Petra Rohde, and Barbara Töpper. *Kolumbien: Geschichte und Gegenwart eines Landes im Ausnahmezustand*. Berlin: Wagenbach, 1983.
Messori, Vittorio. *Opus Dei: Leadership and Vision in today's Catholic Church*. Washington, D.C., Regnery Publishing, 1997.
Michalowski, Raymond, and Ronald Kramer. The Original Formulation. In: *State Corporate Crime: Wrong-doing at the Intersection of Business & Government*. Edited by Raymond Michalowski and Ronald Kramer. Piscataway, NJ: Rutgers University Press, 2006: 18–26.
Midlarsky, Manus, and Kenneth Roberts. Class, State and Revolution in Central America. In: *Journal of Conflict Resolution*, 29, 2, 1985: 163–194.
Mires, Fernando. Los diez peligros de la democracia en America Latina. In: *Cuadernos del CENDES*, 23, 61, 2006: 1–38.
Molina Sanhueza, Jorge. *Crimen imperfecto: Historia del quimico DINA Eugenio Berrios y la muerte de Eduardo Frei Montalvo*; Santiago, Chile: Colección Nuevo Periodismo, 2002.
MoLoney, Anastasia. Vigilante Heaven. In: *New Internationalist, 376*, March 1, 2005. <http://www.newint.org/issue376/vigilante-heaven.htm>.
Morton, James. *Gangland International*. London: Warner, 1999.
Moyano, Antonio L. *Sectas: la amenaza en la sombra*. Madrid: Ediciones Nowtilus, 2002.
Morales, Edmundo. The Andean Cocaine Dilemma. In: *Drug Trafficking in the Americas*. Edited by Bruce M. Bagley and William O. Walker III. Miami, FL: North-South Center Press, 1996: 161–178.
Mujica, María Eugenia. Crimen versus 'mal gobierno': Textos regionales en la lucha contra la corrupción. In: *El pacto infame: Estudios sobre la corrupción en el Perú*. Edited by Felipe Portocarrero. Lima: Red para el Desarrollo de las Ciencias Sociales en el Perú, 2005: 403–418.
Myrdal, Gunnar. *Asian Drama: An Enquiry into the Poverty of Nations*. New York: 20th Century, 1968.
Naranjo, Plutarco. Social Function of Coca in Pre-Columbian America. In: *Journal of Ethnopharmacology*, 3, 1981: 161–172.
Nash, Nathaniel C., Fugitive General Accuses Peruvian Army, Saying Officers Run Hit Squad. In: *The New York Times*, May 12, 1993: A10.
National Democratic Institute. NDI/Carter Centre; Peru Elections 2000; Final Report of the National Democratic Institute/Carter Centre Joint Election Monitoring Project,

2000. <http://aceproject.org/regions-en/countries-and-territories/PE/reports/Final%20Report%20on%20Peru%202000.pdf>.

Navarro, Vincente. Opus Dei and John Paul II. In: *Counterpunch*, April 8, 2005. <http://www.counterpunch.org/navarro04082005.html>.

Naylor, R.T. The Insurgent Economy: Black Market Operations of Guerrilla Organizations. In: *Crime, Law and Social Change*, 20, 1, 1993: 13–53.

Needler, Martin C. Political Development in Latin America. New York: Random House, 1968.

Nef, Jorge. The Politics of Repression: The Social Pathology of the Chilean Military. In: *Latin American Perspectives*, 1, 2, 1974: 58–77.

Nef, Jorge. Government Corruption in Latin America. In: *Where Corruption Lives*. Edited Gerald E. Caiden, O. P. Dwivedi, and Joseph Jabbra. Bloomfield, CT: Kumarian Press, 2001.

Neira, Hugo. Peru. In: *Guide to the Political Parties of South America*. Edited by Richard Gott. Middlesex, UK: Penguin, 1973: 393–468.

Neira, Hugo. *El mal peruano*. Lima: Sidea, 2001.

Neuwirth, Robert. Rio Drug Gangs Forge a Fragile Security. In: *NACLA Reporton the Americas*, 36, 2, 2002: 32–37.

Newmont Gold Corporation. Our Operations. 2011. <http://www.newmont.com/our-operations>.

Newnham, Randall. Coalition of the Bribed and Bullied? US Economic Linkage and the Iraq War Coalition. In: *International Studies Perspectives*, 9, 2, 2008: 183–200.

Nieto, Franscisco. Desmitificando la corrupción en América Latina. In: *Nueva Sociedad*, 194, 2004: 54–68.

Njaim, Humberto. Clientelismo, mercado y liderazgo partidista en América Latina. In: *Nueva sociedad*, 145, 1996: 138–147.

Nohlen, Dieter. *Lexikon Dritte Welt*. Hamburg: Rowohlt, 1989.

Nohlen, Dieter, and Bernhard Thibaut. Struktur- und Entwicklungsprobleme Lateinamerikas. In: *Handbuch der Dritten Welt: Südamerika*. Edited by Dieter Nohlen and Franz Nuscheler, Bonn: Verlag J. H. W. Dietz, 1992: 13–90.

Noonan, John T. *Bribes*. New York: Macmillan, 1984.

Norget, Kristin. The Politics of Liberation: The Popular Church, Indigenous Theology, and Grassroots Mobilization in Oaxaca, Mexico. In: *Latin American Perspectives*, 24, 5, 1997: 96–127.

North, Douglas C. *Structrure and Change in Economic History*. New York: Norton, 1981.

Nye, Joseph S. Corruption and Political Development: A Cost-Benefit Analysis. In: *Polltical Corruption: A Handbook*. Edited by Arnold Heidenheimer, Michael Johnston, and Victor T. Levine. New Brunswick, NJ: Transaction Publishers, 1989: 963–983.

Nye, Joseph S. Soft Power and American Foreign Policy. In: *Political Science Quarterly*, 119, 2, 2004: 255–270.

Nye, Joseph S. *Soft Power: The Means to Success in World Politics*. New York: Public Affairs, 2004a.

Nye, Joseph S. America Must Learn the Hard Facts of Soft Power. In: *The South China Morning Post*, March 18, 2008. <http://belfercenter.ksg.harvard.edu/publication/18173/america_must_learn_the_hard_facts_of_soft_power.html?breadcrumb=%2Fpublication%2F21193%2Fwhat_next_on_climate>.

Obando, Enrique. El poder de los militares. In: *El poder en el Perú*. Edited by Augusto Alvarez Rodrich. Lima: Editorial Apoyo, 1993: 75–85.

Obando, Enrique. Fujimori and the Military: A Marriage of Convenience. In: *NACLA Report on the Americas*, 30, 1, 1996: 31–36.

Obando, Enrique. Civil-Military Relations in Peru, 1980-1996: How to Control and Coopt the Military (and the consequences of doing so). In: *Shining and Other Paths*. Edited by Steve Stern. Durham, NC: Duke University Press, 1998: 385–410.

Observatoire Géopolitique des Drogues (OGD). *Der Welt-Drogen-Bericht*. Munich: DTV, 1993.

O'Donnell, Guillermo A. *Modernization and Bureaucratic-Authoritarianism*. Berkeley, CA: University of California Press, 1979.

O'Donnell, Guillermo A. Polyarchies and the (Un)Rule of Law in Latin America: A Partial Conclusion. In: *The (Un)Rule of Law and the Underprivileged in Latin America*. Edited by J. E. Mendéz, G. A. O'Donnell, and P. S. Pinheiro, Notre Dame, IN: University of Notre Dame Press, 1999: 303–337.

Olano Alor, Aldo. Reforma política y autoritarismo en el Perú. In: *Reflexíon política*, 2, 4, 2000: 1–10.

Olano Alor, Aldo. El renacer de la democracia en el Perú. In: *Reflexión política*, 3, 6, 2001: 1–9.

Oldenburg, Philip. Middlemen in Third-World Corruption: Implications of an Indian Case. In: *World Politics*, 39, 4, 1987: 508–535.

Oliart, Patricia. A President like You. In: *NACLA Report on the Americas*, 30, 1, 1996: 16–24.

O'Phelan, Scarlett. Orden y control en el siglo XVIII. La política borbónica frente a la corupción fiscal, comercial, y administrativa. In: *El pacto infame: Estudios sobre la corrupción en el Perú*. Edited by Felipe Portocarrero. Lima: Red para el Desarrollo de las Ciencias Sociales en el Perú. 2005: 13–33.

Opus Dei Awareness Network (ODAN). What is Opus Dei? 2002; <http://www.odan.org/what_is_opus_dei.htm>.

Organization for Economic Co-operation and Development (OECD), 2003; Glossary of Statistical Terms. <http://www.oecd.org/dataoecd/8/61/2376087.pdf>.

Ornellas, Raul. America Latina: territorio de construccion de la hegemonia. In: *Revista venezolana de economia y ciencias sociales*, 9, 2, 2003: 117–135.

Ortega y Gasset, José. *The Revolt of the Masses*. New York: Norton and Co, 1960 (Originally published in Spain as *La rebelión de las masas* in 1930).

Ortiz de Zevallos, Gabriel and Carlos Calderón, Un enfoque neoinstitucional sobre la corrupción en el Perú. In: *El pacto infame: Estudios sobre la corrupción en el Perú*. Edited by Felipe Portocarrero. Lima: Red para el Desarrollo de las Ciencias Sociales en el Perú. 2005: 129–146.

Orwell, George. *Nineteen Eighty-Four*. New York: Signet, 1960.

Ó Tuathail, Gearóid. 1992. Putting Mackinder in his Place: Material Transformations and Myth. In: *Political Geography*, 11, 1: 100–118.

Painter, Joe. *Politics, Geography and 'Political Geography': A Critical Perspective*. London: Arnold, 1995.

Palacio Castañeda, Germán Alfonso. A. Institutional Crisis, Para-institutionality, and Regime Flexibility in Colombia: The Place of Narcotraffic and Counter-insurgency. In: *Vigilantism and the State in Modern Latin America: Essays on Exralegal Violence*. Edited by Martha K. Huggins. New York: Praeger, 1991: 105–123.

Palmer, David Scott. Peru, Drugs, and Shining Path. In: *Drug Trafficking in the Americas*. Edited by Bruce M. Bagley and William O. Walker III, Miami, FL: North-South Center Press, 1996: 179–200.

Palmer, David Scott. Relaciones entre Estados Unidos y el Perú en la década de los noventa: Dinámicas, antecedentes y proyecciones. In: *América latina hoy*, 19, 1998: 111–123.

Palmer, David Scott. The Often Surprising Outcomes of Asymmetry in International Affairs: United States – Peru Relations in the 1990s. In: *The Fujimori Legacy: The Rise of Electoral Authoritarianism in Peru*. Edited by Julio F. Carrión. The Pennsylvania State University Press, 2006: 227–241.

Palomino, Fernando. Perú: Marketing and Vladivideos. In: *Revista latinoamericana de comunicación CHASQUI*, 75, 2001. <http://chasqui.comunica.org/palomino75.htm>.

Patriau, Mariella. Cipriani será el Cardenal que el Opus Dei y Fujimori deseaban. In: *Liberación* (Lima), September 13, 2000: 13.

Parker, William H. *The Geopolitics of Domination*. London: Routledge, 1988.

Payne, Stanley G. *The Franco Regime 1936–1975*. Madison: University of Wisconsin Press, 1987.

Pearce, Frank, and Steve Tombs. *Toxic Capitalism*. Toronto: Canadian Scholarly Press, 1999.

Pearce, Jennifer. The Dirty War. In: *NACLA Report on the Americas*, 23, 6, 1990: 22–28.

Peñaflor, Giovanna. Los retos de la re-eleción. In: Quehacer, 117, 1999. <http://w3.desco.org.pe/publicaciones/QH/QH/qh117gp.htm>.

Peña, Milagros. The Sodalitium Vitae Movement in Peru: A Rewriting of Liberation Theology. In: *Sociological Analysis*, 53, 2, 1992: 159–173.

Peña Kolkenkautsky, Saúl. *Psicoanálisis de la corrupción*. Lima: Peisa, 2003.

Perry, P.J. Political Corruption: The Last Geographical Taboo? In: *Political Geography*, 16, 3, 1997: 187–188.

Peters, Edward. *Inquisition*, New York: Free Press, 1988.

Petras, James. *El nuevo orden criminal*. Buenos Aires: Libros del Zorzal, 2003.
Petrella, Ivan. *The Future of Liberation Theology*. Aldershot, Hampshire: Ashgate Publishing Ltd., 2004.
Philip, George. *The Rise and Fall of the Peruvian Military Radicals 1968-1976*. London: Athlone, 1978.
Philip, George.The Dilemmas of Good Governance: A Latin American Perspective. In: *Government and Opposition*, 34, 2, 1999: 226–242.
Philp, Mark. Defining Political Corruption. In: *Political Corruption*. Edited by Paul Heywood. Oxford, Blackwell: 1997: 20–46.
Picasso, Connie and Gonzalo Martin. *Itinerario de mil desactciertos politicos, 1990-2001*. Lima: Editorial Don Augustin, 2001.
Pizarro, Eduardo. Revolutionary Guerrilla Groups in Colombia. In: *Violence in Colombia*. Edited by Charles Bergquist, Ricardo Peñaranda, and Gonzalo Sánchez. Wilmington, DE: SR Books, 1992: 169–193.
Planas, Pedro. ¿Que es la partido-cracia? In: *Oiga* (Lima), March 4, 1991: 39–41.
Planas, Pedro. *El Fujimorato: estudio politico constitucional*. Lima: NP, 1999.
Planas, Pedro. *La democracia volátil*. Lima: Fundación Friedrich Ebert, 2000.
Poole, Deborah, and Gerardo Rénique. *Peru: Time of Fear*. London: Latin America Bureau, 1992.
Poole, Deborah, and Gerardo Rénique. Terror and the Privatized State. In: *Radical History Review*, 85, 2003: 150–163.
Porch, Douglas. *The French Secret Services*. New York: Farrar, Straus and Giroux, 1995.
Portillo, Alfredo. Misión y vision geopolítica global de Estados Unidos y Gran Bretaña. In: *Aldea mundo*, 7, 14, 2003: 59–61.
Portocarrero, Gonzalo. *Rostros criollos del mal*. Lima: Red para el Desarrollo de las Ciencias Sociales en el Perú, 2004.
Portocarrero, Gonzalo. La 'sociedad de los cómplices' como causa del (desorden) social en el Perú. In: *Vicios públicos*. Edited by Óscar Ugarteche. Lima: Fondo de Cultura Económica, 2005: 103–131.
Portocarrero, Juan C. H., Renzo Chiri Márquez, and Jans Cavero Cárdenas. *Gestión de conflictos sociales: Perú, Bolivia y Ecuador*. Lima: Comisión Andina de Juristas, 2006.
Postman, Neil. *Amusing Ourselves to Death: Public Discourse in the Age of Show Business*. New York: Penguin, 1985.
Pottenger, John R. *The Political Theory of Liberation Theology*. State University of New York Press, 1989.
Powers, Tom. S. J. *The Call of God: Women Doing Theology in Peru*. State University of New York Press, 2003.
Protzel, Javier. Mediática política y política mediática. El autoritarismo era una fiesta. In: *Quehacer*, 121, 1999. <http://w3.desco.org.pe/publicaciones/QH/QH/qh121jp. htm>.
Protzel, Javier. Televisión: La legitimidad perdida. In: *Quehacer*, 130, 2001. <http:// w3.desco.org.pe/publicaciones/QH/QH/qh130jp.htm>.

Qualter, Terence H., *Propaganda and Psychological Warfare*. New York: Random House, 1962.

Quincot, César Arias. *La Modernización autoritaria*. Lima: Fundación Friedrich Ebert, 1994.

Quiroz, Alfonso W. Costos históricos de la corrupción en el Perú Republicano. In: *El pacto infame: Estudios sobre la corrupción en el Perú.* Edited by Felipe Portocarrero S. Lima: Red para el Desarrollo de las Ciencias Sociales en el Perú, 2005: 75–95.

Quiroz, Alfonso W. Redes de alta corrupción en el Perú: poder y venalidad desde el virrey Amat a Montesinos. In: *Revista de Indias*, 66, 236, 2006: 237–248.

Quiroz, Alfonso W. Corrupt Circles: A History of Unbound Graft in Peru. Washington, D.C.: Woodrow Wilson Center Press, 2008.

Rapley, John. Jamaica: Negotiating Law and Order with the Dons. In: *NACLA Report on the Americas*. 37, 2, 2003: 25–29.

Ramírez, Augusto and Teresita León. Impacto del crecimiento industrial en la salud de los habitants de una ciudad minera del Perú. In: *Anuales de la facultad de medicina*, 65, 2, 2004: 111–118.

Ramirez Cuellar, Francisco. *The Profits of Extermination: How US Corporate Power is Destroying Colombia.* Monroe, ME: Common Courage Press, 2005.

Ravenhill, John. 1990. The North-South Balance of Power. In: *International Affairs*, 66, 4, 1990: 731–748.

Revesc, Bruno. El ocaso del sistema de partidos en la escena electoral peruana. In: *Revista Mexicana de Sociología,* 58, 1, 1996: 77–95.

Rey, Romeo. *Geschichte Lateinamerikas vom 20. Jahrhundert bis zur Gegenwart.* Munich: C.H. Beck, 2006.

Reyna Izaguirre, Carlos. Hard-Learned Lessons: Plan Colombia and Democracy in Peru. In: *Foreign Policy in Focus*, May 1, 2001. <http://www.foreignpolicy-infocus.org/commentary/2001/0105peru.html>.

Reyno, Jaime Estay. El acuerdo de libre comercio de las Américas (ALCA), la integración latinoamericana, y los retos para una inserción internacional alternativa. In: *Aportes*, 6, 17, 2001: 75–88.

Rich, Paul, and Guillermo de los Reyes. Opus Dei as a Political Force in Latin America: Civil Society, Associationalism, and Democracy. Presented at the Annual Meeting of the American Political Science Association (APSA), Washington, D.C., 1997. <http://www.paulrich.net/papers/opusdei.html>.

Rich, Paul, and Guillermo de los Reyes, Opus Dei and Mexico: Civil but Sinister? In: *Review of Policy Research*, 22, 1, 2005: 93–102.

Rico, José M. *Crimen y justicia en América Latina.* Mexico City: Siglo Veintiuno, 1998.

Rico, José M., and Chinchilla, Laura. *Seguridad ciudadania en América Latina.* Mexico City: Siglo Veintiuno, 2002.

Rigakos, George S. *The New Parapolice: Risk Markets and Commodified Social Control.* Toronto: University of Toronto Press, 2002.

Robbins, Paul. The Rotten Institution: Corruption in Natural Resource Management. In: *Political Geography*, 19, 4, 2000: 423–443.

Roberts, John M. *The Mythology of Secret Societies*. London: Secker and Warburg, 1972.

Roberts, Kenneth M. Economic Crisis and the Demise of the Legal Left in Peru. In: *Comparative Politics*, 29, 1, 1996: 69–92.

Roberts, Kenneth M. Neoliberalism and the Transformation of Populism in Latin America: The Peruvian Case. In: *World Politics*, 48, 1, 1996a: 82–116.

Roberts, Kenneth, and Mark Peceny. Human Rights and United States Policy toward Peru. In: *The Peruvian Labyrinth.* Edited by Max Cameron and Phillip Mauceri. Pennsylvania State University Press, 1997: 192–222.

Robinson, William I. Gramsci and Globalisation: From Nation-State to Transnational Hegemony. In: *Critical Review of International Social and Political Philosophy*, 8, 4, 2005: 1–16.

Robles, Rodolfo. General (ret). Peruvian Armed Forces. Interview. Lima, August 1996.

Rochabrun, Guillermo. The de facto powers behind Fujimori's regime. In: *NACLA Report on the Americas*, 30, 1, 1996: 31–36.

Rodrich, Augusto Alvarez (Ed). *El poder en el Perú*. Lima: Editorial Apoyo, 1993.

Rodríguez Beruff, Jorge. *Los militares y el poder: Un ensayo sobre la doctrina militar en el Perú (1948–1968)*, Lima: Editorial Mosca Azul, 1983.

Rogow, Arnold, and Harold D. Lasswell. The Definition of Corruption. In: *Political Corruption: Readings in Comparative Analysis*. Edited by Arnold Heidenheimer. New Brunswick, NJ: Transaction Books, 1970: 54–55.

Rohter, Larry. Peru's Catholics Brace for Fissures in their Church. In: *The New York Times*, May 8, 2005. <http://www.nytimes.com/2005/05/08/international/americas/08peru.html>.

Rohter, Larry. As Pope Heads to Brazil, Rival Theology Persists. In: *The New York Times,* May 7, 2007. <http://www.nytimes.com/2007/05/07/world/americas/07theology.html?ref=popes2007latinamericatrip>.

Rojas-Perez, Isaías. 'Ahorita lo solucionamos': Guerra, intimidad y corrupción en Perú. In: *Vicios públicos*, Edited by Óscar Ugarteche. Lima: Fondo de Cultural Económica, 2005: 161–195.

Romero, Catalina. Globalization, Civil Society and Religion from a Latin American Standpoint. In: *Sociology of Religion*, 64, 2, 2001: 475–490.

Romero, Simon. Coca production makes a comeback. In: *The New York Times*, June 13, 2010. <http://www.nytimes.com/2010/06/14/world/americas/14peru.html>.

Roopnarine, Lomarsh. Wounding Guyana: Gold Mining and Environmental Degradation. In: *European Review of Latin American and Caribbean Studies*, 73, 2002: 83–92.

Roslycky, Lada. Organized Transnational Crime in the Black Sea Region: A Geopolitical Dilemma. In: *Trends in Organized Crime*, 12, 2009: 21–29.

Roslycky, Lada. *The Soft Side of Dark Power. A Study in Soft Power, National Security and the Political-Criminal Nexus*. PhD Dissertation, Faculty of Arts, University of Groningen, Netherlands, 2011.

Rospigliosi, Fernando. El poder del narcotráfico. In: *El poder en el Perú*. Edited by Augusto Alvarez Rodrich. Lima: Editorial Apoyo, 1993: 161–168.

Rospiglioso, Fernando. *Montesinos y las fuerzas armadas*. Lima: IEP, 2001.

Ross, Jeffrey Ian. *Controlling State Crime*. New Brunswick, NJ: Transaction Publishers, 2000.

Ross, Jeffrey Ian. *Varieties of State Crime and its Control*. Monsey, NY: Criminal Justice Press, 2000a.

Ross, Jeffrey Ian. *The Dynamics of Political Crime*. Thousand Oaks, CA: Sage, 2003.

Ross, Robert J. and Kent C. Trachte. *Global Capitalism: The New Leviathan*. State University of New York Press, 1990.

Rostow, Walt W. *The Stages of Economic Growth: A Non-Communist Manifesto*. Cambridge, UK: Cambridge University Press, 1960.

Rotta Castillo, Samuel. Peru. In: *Global Corruption Report 2005*. Transparency International. London: Pluto Press, 2005: 189–193.

Rotta Castillo, Samuel, and Leonardo Narvarte Olivares. Peru. In: *Global Corruption Report 2006*. Transparency International. London: Pluto Press, 2005: 223–226.

Rumrill, Roger. Piden ampliar diálogo con todos los gremios cocaleros. In: *La República*, July 8, 1991: 16.

Rydell, C. Peter, and Susan S. Everingham. *Controlling Cocaine: Supply versus Demand Programs*. Rand Drug Policy Research Center. Santa Monica, CA: 1994.

Salas Lopéz, Carlos. *El sistema de la corrupción al descubierto*. Lima: n. a., 2005.

Salazar, Milagros. Peru: Resistance to Increasing Mining Royalties. In: *Global Issues*, December 10, 2010. <http://www.globalissues.org/news/2010/12/10/7907>.

Salazar Peréz, Robinson. Los avatares del Plan Colombia, Plan Dignidad y el Plan Pueblo Panamá. In: *Convergencia*, 30, 2002: 97–120.

Salvatteci, Jose F. *Los militares en el Peru: De libertadores a genocidas*. Lima: Edición Anonima, 1995.

Salvemini, Gaetano. *Under the Axe of Fascism*. New York: Citadel Press, 1971.

Sánchez Jiménez, José. *La España contemporánea*, Vol. 3. Madrid: Ediciones Istmo, 1991.

Sandoval, Clara. The Challenge of Impunity in Peru: The Significance of the Inter-American Court of Human Rights. In: *Essex Human Rights Review*, 5, 1: 2008: 1–20.

Sartori, Giovanni. *Homo videns. La sociedad teledirigida*. Madrid: Taurus, 1998.

Schieder, Wolfgang. Thesenpapier zur Tagung bei der Katholischen Akademie in Schwerte. April 29, 1972. As cited in: *Texte zur Faschismusdiskussion*, Vol. II. Edited by Reinhard Kühnl, Hamburg: Rowohlt, 1979.

Schmidt, Gregory D. Fujimori's Upset Victory in Peru. In: *Comparative Politics*, 28, 3, 1996: 321–354.

Schmidt, Gregory D. Crónica de una reelección. In: *El juego politico: Fujimori, la oposición y las reglas.* Edited by Fernando Tuesta Soldevilla, Lima: Fundación Friedrich Ebert, 1999: 97–130.
Schmidt, Gregory D. Delegative Democracy in Peru? Fujimori's 1995 Landslide and the Prospects for 2000. In: *Journal of Interamerican Studies and World Affairs,* 42, 1, 2000: 99–132.
Scholl-Latour, Peter. *Der Tod im Reisfeld: Dreißig Jahre Krieg in Indochina.* Stuttgart, Germany: Deutsche Verlags-Anstalt, 1979.
Schulte-Bockholt, Alfredo. *The Politics of Organized Crime and the Organized Crime of Politics.* Lanham, MD: Lexington Books, 2006.
Scott, Peter Dale, and Jonathan Marshall. *Cocaine Politics.* Berkeley: University of California Press, 1991.
Sepúlveda M., Isidro. Las relaciones internacionales en Suramérica: Liderazgo y geopolítica. In: *La creacción de UNASUR en el marcode la seguridad y defensa.* Ministry of Defense (Spain). Documentos de Seguridad y Defensa, 29, 2010: 9–17.
Skidmore, Thomas, and Peter H. Smith. *Modern Latin America.* New York: Oxford University Press, 1984.
Silvert, Kalman H. *The Conflict Society.* New York: American Universities Field Staff, 1966.
Simmel, Georg. The Sociology of Secrecy and of Secret Societies. In: *The American Journal of Sociology,* 11, 4, 1906: 441–498.
Smith, Brian. *The Church and Politics in Chile.* Princeton, NJ: PUP, 1982.
Smith, Brian C. *Good Governance and Development.* New York: Palgrave Mac Millan, 2007.
Smith, Daniel J. *A Culture of Corruption: Everyday Deception and Popular Discontent in Nigeria.* Princeton University Press, 2007.
Smith, Peter H. Semi-organized International Crime: Drug Trafficking in Mexico. In: *Transnational Crime in the Americas.* Edited by Tom Farrer. New York: Routledge, 1999: 193–216.
Sociedad Nacional de Minería, Petroleo, y Energía (SNMPE). *Perú mineroengético:110 años de desarollo descentralizado.* Lima: SNMPE, 2005: 1–60.
Sosa, Magno. *Cipriani, el Teólogo de Fujimori.* Lima: n. a., 2000.
Speck, Mary. Swift Military-Court Trial Seen as Cover-Up in Peru. In: *The Miami Herald,* March 18, 1994: 18A.
Sperling, J. C. West German Foreign Economic Policy during the Reagan Administration. In: *German Studies Review,* 13, 1, 1990: 85–110.
Spykman, Nicholas, Heartland and Rimland. In: The Structure of Political Geography.Edited by Roger E. Kasperson and Julian V. Minghi. Chicago, IL: Aldine Publishing Company, 1969: 170–177.
Spykman, Nicholas J. *The Geography of the Peace.* Hamden, CT: Archon Books, 1969a (Published originally in 1944 by Harcourt and Brace).

Staab, Andreas. *The European Union Explained: Institutions, Actors, Global Impact.* Bloomington: Indiana University Press, 2008.

Stanley, William. *The Protection Racket State: Elite Politics, Military Extortion, and Civil War in El Salvador.* Philadelphia, PA: Temple University Press, 1996.

Stepan, Alfred. *The State and Society: Peru in Comparative Perspective.* Princeton University Press, 1978.

Stokes, Susan C,. Democratic Accountability and Policy Change: Economic Policy in Fujimori's Peru. In: *Comparative Politics*, 29, 2, 1997: 209–226.

Stirk, Peter M. R. *Max Horkheimer: A New Interpretation.* Hempel Hempstead Hertfordshire: Harvester Wheatsheaf, 1992.

Straßner, Veit. Die Nerven liegen blank. In: *Herder Korresporrenz*, 61, 5, 2007: 256–261. <http://www.herder-korrespondenz.de/service/overview/inhalt/index_html?onlstrnr=1323542>.

Stratus Consulting Inc., Water and Soil Quality Study of Cajamarca, 2003: 1–9. <http://intranet2.minem.gob.pe/web/archivos/dgm/publicaciones/expedientes/yanacocha/justificacion/2.8.1-R5%20Informe%20Stratus%20Consulting%20Inc%20(Comit%C3%A9%20de%20Mesa%20de%20Di%C3%A1logo%20CAO-Cajamarca).pdf>.

Strong, Simon. *Shining Path: The World's Deadliest Revolutionary Force.* London: Harper Collins, 1992.

Strong, Simon. *Whitewash: Pablo Escobar and the Cocaine Wars.* London: Pan,1996.

Sumner, Colin. Crime, Justice, and Underdevelopment. Beyond Modernization Theory. In: *Crime, Justice, and Underdevelopment.* Edited by Colin Sumner. London: Heinemann, 1982: 1–39.

Sutherland, Edwin. *White Collar Crime.* New York: Holt, Rinehart & Winston, 1949.

Talwar, Prakash. *Corporate Crime.* Delhi, India: Gyan Books, 2006.

Tamariz L., Domingo. Más allá de una prédica. In: *El Peruano*, September 6, 2002: n. a.

Tamayo, Giulia. Planificación familiar: Metas que matan. In: *Quehacer*, 111, 1998: 29–35.

Tamayo, Giulia. *Nada personal: Reporte de derechos humanos sobre la aplicacion de la anticoncepción quirurgica en el Peru 1996–1998.* Lima: CLADEM, 1999.

Tanaka, Martin. Los partidos póliticos y el Fujimorismo (1992–1998), y las elecciones del 2000. Hacia un cambio de régimen. In: *Perfiles latino-americanos*, 16, 2000: 101–126.

Tanaka, Martin. ¿Crónica de una muerte anunciada? Determinismo, voluntarismo, actores y poderes estructurales en el Perú, 1980–2000. In: *Lecciones del final del Fujimorismo.* Edited by Jane Marcus-Delgado and Martin Tanaka. Lima: IEP, 2001: 9–55.

Tanaka, Martin. *La situación de la democracia en Colombia, Perú y Venezuela a inicios del siglo.* Lima: Comisión Andina de Juristas, 2002.

Taylor, Lewis. Patterns of Electoral Corruption in Peru: The April 2000 General Election. In: *Crime, Law and Social Change*, 34, 2000: 391–415.

Taylor, Lewis. Politicians without Parties and Parties without Politicians: The Foibles of the Peruvian Political Class, 2000–2006. In: *Bulletin of Latin American Research*, 26, 1, 2007: 1–23.
Tefft, Stanton K. *The Dialectics of Secret Society Power*. New Jersey: Humanitie Press, 1992.
Teivainen, Teivo. The World Social Forum and Global Democratisation: Learning from Porto Alegre. In: *Third World Quarterly*, 23, 4, 2002: 621–632.
Teivainen, Teivo. *Enter Economism, Exit Politics: Experts, Economic Policy and the Damage to Democracy*. London, Zed, 2002.
The Oedipus Plays of Sophocles. *Antigone*. Translated by Paul Roche. New York: Mentor, 1958.
Theidon, Kimberley. How We Learned to Kill our Brother?: Memory, Morality, and Reconciliation in Peru. In: *Bulletin de l'Institut Françaìs d'Ètudes Andines*, 29, 3, 2000: 539–554.
Theobald, Robin. *Corruption, Development, and Underdevelopment*. London: MacMillan, 1990.
Thoumi, Francisco E. *Political Economy and Illegal Drugs in Colombia*. Boulder, CO: Lynne Rienner, 1995.
Thoumi, Francisco E. From Drug Lords to Warlords: Illegal Drugs and the Unintended' Consequences of Drug Policies in Colombia. In: *Government of the Shadows: Para-politics and Criminal Sovereignty*. Edited by Eric Wilson. London: Pluto Press, 2009: 205–225.
Thurow, Lester. *Kopf an Kopf: Wer siegt im Wirtschaftskrieg zwischen Europa, Japan und den USA?* Düsseldorf, Germany: ECON Verlag, 1993 (Originally published in 1992 by Morrow, New York, under the title *Head to Head: The Coming Battle among Japan, Europe and America*).
Tilly, Charles. War Making and State Making as Organized Crime. In: *Bringing the State Back In*. Edited by P.B. Evans, D. Rueschemeyer, and T. Skocpol, Cambridge, UK: Cambridge University Press, 1993: 169–190.
Timofeyev, Lev. *Russia's Secret Rulers*. New York: Alfred Knopf, 1992.
Toche, Eduardo. *ONG: Enemigos imaginados*. Lima: DESCO, 2003.
Toche, Eduardo. Los servicios de inteligencia: la historia que se resiste a morir. In: *Quehacer*, 155, 2005: 23–31.
Toche, Eduardo. *Guerra y democracia: Los militares peruanos y la construcción nacional*. Lima: DESCO, 2008.
Todd, Paul and Jonathan Bloch. *Global Intelligence: The World's Secret Services Today*. Halifax: Fernwood Publishing, 2003.
Transparency International (TI). *Global Corruption Report 2006*. London: Pluto Press, 2006.
Ugarteche, Óscar. Introducción. In: *Decretos secretos y mal use de fondos públicos: El Perú bajo el Fujimorismo*. Comisión investigadora de los delitos económicos y financieros cometidos entre 1990–2001. Edited by Javier Diez Canseco. Lima: Fondo Editorial del Congreso del Perú, 2002: 19–33.

Ugarteche, Óscar. Cleaning up after Fujimori. In: *NACLA Report on the Americas*, 35, 4, 2002: 42–43.

Ugarteche, Óscar. Notas sobre la nueva corrupción económica en el Perú finisecular: Desde la fafia, el mercantilismo y la teoría económica. In: *El pacto infame: Estudios sobre la corrupción en el Perú.* Edited by Felipe Portocarrero S. Lima: Red para el Desarrollo de las Ciencias Sociales en el Perú, 2005: 99–127.

Unanue, Hipolitó. *Sobre el aspecto, cultivo, comercio y virtudes de la famosa planta de Perú nombrada coca.* Dissertation. Lima: Mercurio Peruano, 1794 (I purchased a direct copy of the 1794 original. The copy itself has no date).

United Nations Declaration of Basic Principles of Justice for Victims of Crime and Abuse of Power (UN, 1985). <http://www.unhchr.ch/html/menu3/b/h_comp49.htm>.

United Nations Economics and Social Commission for Asia and the Pacific (UNESCAP, 2006). What is Good Governance? <http://www.unescap.org/huset/gg/governance.htm>.

United Nations Office for Drug Control and Crime Prevention (UNODCCP, 2002). *Annual Coca Cultivation Survey 2001.* <http://www.undcp.org/pdf/peru/peru_cocasurvey_2001.pdf>.

United Nations Office on Drugs and Crime (UNODC, 2003). *Bolivia: Coca Survey in the Yungas of La Paz in 2002.* <http://www.undcp.org/pdf/bolivia/bolivia_coca-survey_2002.pdf>.

United States (US) Bureau of Mines. *Dictionary of Mining, Mineral, and Related Terms*. 1996. <http://www.maden.hacettepe.edu.tr/dmmrt/textintro.html>.

United States (US) Department of State. Bureau of Western Hemisphere Affairs. Background Note: Peru. September 30, 2010. <http://www.state.gov/r/pa/ei/bgn/35762.htm>.

United States (US) Embassy (Lima) Cable. Cantuta/Cieneguilla Investigations, September 22, 1993, Confidential, 7pp. The Search for Truth: The Declassified Record on Human Rights Abuses in Peru. Edited by Tamara Feinstein, Director; Peru Documentation Project, August 28, 2003. <http://www.gwu.edu/~nsarchiv/NSAEBB/NSAEBB96/930922.pdf>.

United States (US) Embassy (Lima) Cable, Claimed Member of 'Colina' Describes Barrios Altos Executions, March 15, 1994, Secret. 7pp. The Search for Truth: The Declassified Record on Human Rights Abuses in Peru. Edited by Tamara Feinstein, Director, Peru Documentation Project; August 28, 2003. <http://www.gwu.edu/~nsarchiv/NSAEBB/NSAEBB96/940315.pdf>.

United States (US) Senate Committee on Foreign Relations, Drugs, Law Enforcement and Foreign Policy. A Report Prepared by the Subcommittee on Terrorism, Narcotics and International Operations, Washington, DC: US Government Printing Office, 1989.

Valencia, León, and Ariel Ávila. *La nueva realidad de las FARC*. Bogotá: Corporación Nuevo Arco Iris, 2011.

Van Engeland, Anisseh. Failed Attempts: The Fuerzas Armadas de Colombia (FARC) and the Union Patriotica (UP). In: From Terrorism to Politics. Edited by Anisseh van Engeland and Rachel M. Rudolph, Hampshire, UK: Ashgate, 2008: 135–150.
Van Klaveren, Jacob. The Concept of Corruption. In: *Political Corruption: Concepts and Contexts*. Edited by Arnold Heidenheimer, Michael Johnston, and Victor T. Levine. New Brunswick, NJ: Transaction Publishers, 1989: 25–28.
Van Klaveren, Jacob. Corruption as a Historical Phenomenon. In: *Political Corruption: Concepts and Contexts*. Edited by Arnold Heidenheimer and Michael Johnston. New Brunswick, NJ: Transaction Publishers, 2002: 83–94.
Vargas Haya, Héctor. *184 Años de corrupcion e impunidad*. Lima, Editorial Rocio, 2005.
Vargas Gutiérrez, José Luis. Full talk show. In: *Quehacer*, 112, March–April 1998. <http://w3.desco.org.pe/publicaciones/QH/QH/qh112jlv.htm>.
Vasquez del Aguila, Ernesto. Invisible Women: Forced Sterilization, Reproductive Rights, and Structural Inequalities in Peru of Fujimori and Toledo. In: *Estudos e Pesquisas em Psicologia*, 6, 1, 2006: 109–124.
Vibert, Frank. Soft Power and International Rule-Making. In: *Occasional Paper 43*. Berlin: Friedrich-Naumann-Stiftung, 2008. <http://www.fnfkorea.org/uploads/document/OC43_Vibert.pdf>.
Villasís, Graciella. Sacerdote perseguido por Cipriani abandona el país pero insta a enfrentarse con valentía a la dictadura. In: *Liberación*, September 5, 2000: 6.
Von Arnim, Hans H. *Das System: Machenschaften der Macht*. Munich: Knaur, 2001.
Walsh, Michael. *The Secret World of Opus Dei*. London: Grafton Books, 1989.
Ward, Peter M. *Corruption, Development and Inequality*, London, Routledge, 1989.
Warren, Mark. Political Corruption as Duplicitous Exclusion. In: *Political Science and Politics*, 37, 4, 2006: 803–807.
Weiland, Severin. Mole in Germany's FDP Party Comes Forward. In: *Der Spiegel*, December 2, 2010. Wikileak Diplomatic Cables. <http://www.spiegel.de/international/germany/0,1518,732579,00.html>.
Weir, Carol. Costa Rica and the Drug Trade. In: *Drug Trafficking in the Americas*. Edited by Bruce M. Bagley and William O. Walker. Miami, FL: North-South Center Press, 1996: 455–466.
Weiss, Thomas G. Governance, Good Governance and Global Governance: Conceptual and Actual Challenges. In: *Third World Quarterly*, 21, 5, 2000: 795–814.
Welling, Bruce. *Corporate Law in Canada*. Toronto, Butterworths, 1991.
Werner, Klaus, and Hans Weiss. *El libro negro de las marcas: El lado oscuro de las empresas globales*. Madrid: DEBOLS!LLO, 2006. (Originally published by Franz Deuticke Verlagsgesellschaft, Frankfurt a. M., Germany, 2001, under the title *Das Neue Schwarzbuch Markenfirmen: Die Machenschaften der Weltkonzerne*).
Wiener, Rául A. Bandido *Fujimori: El releectionista*. Lima: WWW Editores, 2001.

Williams, Gwyn A., The Concept of 'Egemonia' in the Thought of Antonio Gramsci: Some Notes on Interpretation. In: *Journal of the History of Ideas*, 21, 4, 1960: 586–599.
Wilson, Eric. Deconstructing the Shadows. In: *Government of the Shadows*. Edited by Eric Wilson. London: Pluto Press, 2009: 13–55.
Wisotsky, Steven. *Breaking the Impasse in the War on Drugs*. New York: Greenwood Press, 1986.
Wisotsky, Steven. *Beyond the War on Drugs*. Buffalo, NY: Prometheus, 1990.
Young, T. R. Paradigm Theory: Foundations of Postmodern Science, 1994. <http://critcrim.org/redfeather/chaos/004paradigm.html>.
Youngers, Coletta. *Violencia política y sociedad civil en el Perú*. Lima: IEP, 2003.
Yucra, Sandra, and Manuel Gasco, Julio Rubio, Gustavo F. Gonzales. Exposición pacional a plomo y pesticidas órganofosforadas: Efecto sobre la salud reproductiva masculina. In: *Revista peruana de medicina experimental y salud publica*, 25, 4, 2008: 394–402.
Zakaria, Fareed. The Rise of Illiberal Democracy. In: *Foreign Affairs*, 76, 6, 1997: 22–43.
Zapata, Antonio. La corrupción bajo el Fujimorismo. In: *El pacto infame: Estudios sobre la corrupción en el Perú*. Edited by Felipe Portocarrero S. Lima: Red Para el Desarrollo de las Ciencias Sociales en el Perú, 2005: 247–285.
Zegarra, Luis Felipe. *Causas y consecuencias económicas de la corrupción: Un Análisis teórico y empírico*. Lima: Universidad del Pacífico, 2002.
Zimmermann, Augusto. *El espia de Fujimori: descubiertos sus secretos*. Lima: Imprepsa, 1997.

Dailies, Weeklies, and Internet Sources

British Broadcasting Corporation (BBC)
"1997: Troops storm Embassy in Peru", April 22, 1997. <http://news.bbc.co.uk/onthisday/hi/dates/stories/april/22/newsid4297000/4297347.stm>.
"Peru set to be drug leader", February 17, 2001. <http://news.bbc.co.uk/2/hi/world/americas/1176452.stm>.
"Peru makes huge drugs haul", June 11, 2002. <http://news.bbc.co.uk/2/hi/world/americas/2039043.stm>.
"Coffee slump fuels Peru's coca bonanza", September 18, 2002. <http://news.bbc.co.uk/2/hi/americas/2266657.stm>.
"Peru's coca farmers stage protest", April 22, 2003. <http://news.bbc.co.uk/2/hi/business/2965423.stm>.
"Life in Peru's most polluted town", November 15, 2007. <http://news.bbc.co.uk/2/hi/americas/7057749.stm>.

"Peru sets up Environment ministry", May 14, 2008. <http://news.bbc.co.uk/2/hi/7400588.stm>.
"Peru smelter pollution at crisis point, June 5, 2009. <http://news.bbc.co.uk/2/hi/business/8081907.stm>.

Caretas (Lima, Peru)
"El embajador Quainton", December 28, 1989: 22.
"Hablando a calzón quitado", October 29, 1990: 13.
"Señal de guerra", July 8, 1991: 28-29.
"Réquiem por un cómputo parlamentario", April 20, 1995. <http://www.caretas.com.pe/1359/requiem/requiem.html>.
"Acusacion: La denuncia de Vaticano", August 22, 1996: 16–19.
"El dedo en la llaga", November 28, 1996: 12–16.
"Suplicios de Inteligencia", April 10, 1997: 10–16.
"Firmeza a Prueba de Golpes", June 19, 1997: 18–21.
"La Promoción '66", April 8, 1998: 36–43.
"¡Llegaron!" January 14, 1999: 19.
"¿Inocentes pagan por Marky? March 4, 1999. <http://www.caretas.com.pe/1999/1557/marky/marky.htm>.
"Crimen electoral", May 26, 2000: 12–13.
"La Memoria de La Rosa", June 2, 2000. <http://www.caretas.com.pe/2000/1621/articulos/leonor.phtml>.
"Las confesiones de 'Vaticano'", November 9, 2000: 18–20.
"Crimen y archivos", November 21, 2002: 12–14.
"Lo que dijo Hermoza", July 10, 2003: 12–14.
"El huarique de Matilde", April 28, 2005: 28–31.
"Plegarias no atendidas", April 19, 2007: 56–59.

Correo (Lima, Peru)
"Cipriani plantea creación de comisión que revise casos de corrupción", August 26, 2002: n. a.
"Bambarén le pide al Cardenal no utilizar la iglesia como tribuna", July 21, 2004: n. a.
"Cardenal Cipriani: Quieren silenciar a la Igleasia", July 25, 2004: 11.
"Cipriani: No quise ofender a nadie", December 22, 2004: 3.
"Las FARC y ejército colombiano usan civilies como escudos humanos", April 30, 2005: 17.

Diario La Primera (Lima, Peru)
"Crónica de una masacre anunciada", July 18, 2010. <http://www.diariolaprimeraperu.com/online/especial/cronica-de-una-masacre-anunciada_66436.html>.

"Fujimorismo pretende liberar a los corruptos", May 6, 2011. <http://www.diariolaprimeraperu.com/online/noticia.php?IDnoticia=85492>.

El Chino (Lima, Peru)
"Mujeres darán la vida por Comedores Populares", March 27, 2000: Cover.
"Laura desnudo a abortero y mentiroso Toledo", March 29/00: Cover.

El Comercio (Lima, Peru)
"Muy extraños muertes . . .", November 24, 1994: A16.
"Narco afirma que puede ubicar la casa de San Borja", August 21, 1996: A14.
"Lavado de dinero se extiende a toda la economía peruana", August 25, 1996: A24.
"Se require conducta ética para informar debidamente", August 28, 1996: n. a.
"Hasta ahora no me explicó las razones de mi cambio", August 29, 1996: A21.
"Aislado en el Real Felipe", October 14, 1996: A16.
"Testigo dice que entregó dos toneladas de droga a Zevallos", May 18, 1997: A17.
"Narcos de Perú operan en México desde 1980", July 13, 1997: A1.
"Cipriani: Monseñor problema", March 1, 2001: 44–45, 52.
"Descubren yacimiento aurífero en el norte del país", April 24, 2002: n. a.
"Bambarén afirma que la posición de Cipriani no es la de la Iglesia", August 27, 2002: A2.
"Cipriani sí se opuso a las esterilizaciones", December 19, 2002: n. a.
"Denuncian a Herrero por azuzar a población ancashina contra minera", May 8, 2003: A6.
"Cipriani dijo que investigación maltrata memoria de su antecesor", April 5, 2004: A10.
"Cipriani cree que hay complejo en interpretación de mensajes", July 25, 2004: A2.
"Atacaron a pedradas locales de la SUNAT y el Ministerio Público", March 8, 2005: A12.
"Las Farc siguen atacando con violencia a los poblados indígenas", May 29, 2005: A32.
"Estudio revelaque La Oroya atraviesa grave crisis ambiental", December 7, 2005: B2.
"Barrick compra Placer y pasa a ser la mayor minera de oro del mundo", December 23, 2005: n. a.
"Impuesto a sobreganancias sigue en pie", August 3, 2006: B3.
"El reto de la próxima gestión edilicia es la profesionalización del serenazgo." August 6, 2006: A16.
"Caja dorada", (Día_1), August 21, 2006: 14–16.
"Aporte voluntario o impuesto forzoso", (Día_1), August 7, 2006: 12.
"Próxima semana definirán destino del aporte voluntario minero", August 26, 2006: A2.
"El Perú es como Canadá: los fondos deben llegar de afuera", September 2, 2006: B2.
"No se puede vivir negociando los conflictos, debe haber canales locales", October 2, 2006: A8.
"Identifican 300 ecosistemas fragile y areas para conservación", November 18, 2006: B12.
"Entre el celo y el desvelo", September 3, 2006: A11.
"Negocio seguro", (Dia_1), December 11, 2006: 16–17.

"Cabecillas de Sendero Luminoso se disputarían el control del Alto Huallaga", May 1, 2010. <http://elcomercio.pe/peru/470289/noticia-cabecillas-sendero-luminoso-se-disputarian-control-alto-huallaga>.

El País (Spain)
"La milicia indígena de Morales", February 19, 2007. <http://elpais.com/diario/2007/02/19/internacional/1171839616_850215.html>.
"Los vetos de Polonia se convierten en una pesadilla para la UE", March 15, 2007: 3.
"El Gobierno polaco prepara una ley para perseguir a los gays", March 20, 2007: 9.
"Romanticismo contra las minas asesinas", April 13, 2007: 60.
"Tiros en el corazón de la tierra", (Supplement Tierra), April 21, 2007: 39.

El Peruano (Lima, Peru)
"Monseñor Cipriani: No necesito que EEUU me cuente la realidad peruana", March 14, 1999: 3.
"Monseñor Cipriani: Se tiene que incluir el curso de religión en el bachillerato", August 22, 1999: 4.

"Monseñor Cipriani demanda respeto para nuestro país", February 13, 2000: 3.
"Arzobispo destaca inclusión del curso de religión en bachillerato", February 23, 2000: 6.
"Monseñor Cipriani reclama debate de planes de gobierno", March 18, 2000: 5.
"Cardenal Vargas Alzamora invoca que comicios sean transparentes", March 31, 2000: 5.
"Monseñor Cipriani: no involcren a la Iglesia en temas electorales", April 17, 2000: 5.
"Cipriani: Obispos aún no se reúnen para dicidir si serán mediadores", April 23, 2000: 5.
"Conferencia Episcopal se definirá este viernes para el rol de mediador", April 26, 2000: 4.
"Perú 2000: Es poco prudente involcrar a Iglesia en política", April 27, 2000: 4.
"No utilicen a la Iglesia", May 5, 2000: 6.
"Iglesia critica a los que rechazan privatización", July 1, 2002: n. a.
"Sí, acudiré", August 31, 2002: 4.
"Confirman orden de captura a ex general Eduardo Bellido Mora", January 4, 2003. <http://www.editoraperu.com.pe/edc/03/01/04/soc6.asp>.
"Geólogo muere en asalto a campamento de Barrick", July 24, 2003: n. a.
"FBI investiga venta de acciones de Yanacocha", December 4, 2003: 4.
"Río Tinto ganó subasta de yacimiento La Granja", December 17, 2005: 8.
"La más contaminada", October 20, 2006: 16.

El Popular (Lima, Peru)
"Fuijministro echó a Cipriani", August 30, 2002: 3.
Estaré presente ante los poderes que me atacan", August 31, 2002: 3.
"¡Chanca a Humala!" April 2, 2006: n. a.

El Sol (Lima, Peru)
"Ríos Araico dice que lo accusan por venganza politíca", September 28, 1996: A6.
"En barcos mercantes iba la droga hacia Europa", August 2, 1997: 8A.

Expreso (Lima, Peru)
"Cipriani vuelve a criticar a los medios de communicación", August 31, 1996: n. a.
"Toledo pactó cronograma de pagos con Manrique", March 13, 2000: 5.
"Continuad de Fujimori es fundamental para la transición", September 24, 2000: 6.
"Cipriani dice que acusaciones de Vargas Llosa son mentiras", December 31, 2000: 3.
"Peligrosamente politizan el caso Barrick", May 14, 2003: A7.
"Barrick exige que se respete debido proceso", May 20, 2003: A12.
"Pretenden apagar la voz que reclama moralización", July 21, 2004: 7.
"MEF se opone a que la SUNAT apele fallo en favour de Barrick", February 10, 2005: n.a.
"Huaraz puede ser un polvorín", March 6, 2005: 3.
"Sin hombre y mujer no hay matrimonio", July 2, 2005: 3.
"Candidato antisistema no debe gobernar", April 2, 2006: n. a.

Gestión (Lima, Peru)
"Los galones del narcotráfico", August 25, 1996: 15.
"Monseñor Cipriani: violencia se basa ahora en la sospecha, la calumnia y la mentira", August 26, 1996: 7.
"Estados Unidos estaría cauteloso ante denuncias de vinculaciones del narcotráfico en Perú", September 15, 1996: 7.
"Yanacocha en jucio por yacimiento aurífero en Cajamarca", April 12, 2002: n. a.
"Cardenal considera que oponerse a privatizaciones es una posición ignorante y soberbia", July 1, 2002: 3.
"Esterilizaciones", November 20, 2002: 3.
"Barrick acusa a congresistas de violar confidencialidad en proceso tributario", May 8, 2003: V.
"Cipriani: No soy fujimorista ni le di la espalda a ayacucho", September 13, 2003: n.a.
"Cipriani rompe silencio y califica de basural a situación política", December 21, 2004: 3.
"En el Congreso se pretende desconocer fallo del tribunal fiscal sobre caso Barrick", February 10, 2005: 10.
"Ancash realizará paro contra Barrick por pago de impuestos", February 11, 2005: 9.
"APRA cuestiona a SUNAT por caso Barrick", March 8, 2005: 18.
"Comisión de ambiente: Doe Run no quiere firmar carta fianza para cumplir con PAMA", February 21, 2006: 9.
"Aporte voluntario de companies mineras ascendeá a S/. 2,500 mlls. en cinco años", August 25, 2006: 10.
"Convenios para concreter aportes voluntarias estarían listos en dos semanas", September 19, 2006: 10.

"Premier preocupado por 'reglaje'a padre Marco Arana", December 6, 2006: 6.
"Nuevo presidente de la region Cajamarca pone en la mira a Yanacocha", December 15, 2006: 6.
"43 mineras participarán en aporte voluntario", December 22, 2006: 13.
"Se incrementa participación del cobre y zinc en exportaciones mineras", January 3, 2007: 19.

La Razón (Lima, Peru)
"Choropampa: 18000 pobladores rurales intoxicados por letal derrame de mercurio", April 29, 2005: 10–11.
"Refinería La Oroya causa envenenamiento grave por plomo a 788 niños menores de 7 años", April 30, 2005: 10–11.
"El 92 por ciento de 354 empresas mineras no tienen autorización de vertimientos tóxicos", May 8, 2005: 10–11.
"Pueblo de Santa Cruz desalojó de la Zanja a dúo Buenaventura-Newmont", May 21, 2005: 10–11.
"La inseguridad ciudadana preocupa cada vez más", December 29, 2006: 10–11.

La República (Lima, Peru)
"Matan a dirigente de cocaleros que respaldó a convenio antidroga, July 7, 1991: 3.
'Vaticano' y 'Colocho Juan' se reparten la selva", January 27, 1992: 14–15.
"Hernando De Soto renuncia como asesor del Presidente Fujimori", January 29, 1992: 8.
"Droga corrompe a soldados y subversivos", January 31, 1992: 13–14.
"Identifican a militares corrompidos por narcos", February 29, 1992: 14–15.
"Hernando De Soto asegura que la subversión puede triunfar", March 21, 1992: 2.
"Declararon en emergencia los aeropuertos de zona cocalera", April 10, 1992: 4.
"Sí, hay militares en caso de Vaticano", June 27, 1994: 17–19.
"Amenazaron asesinar a la esposa de General Robles", July 27, 1994: 2.
"Hubiera preferidos que criminales continúen presos", June 17, 1995: 9.
"Ley encubre a criminals", June 18, 1995: 15.
"87% de población rechaza ley de la impunidad", June 19, 1995: 3.
"Piden 15 años de carcel para 10 oficiales y dos subalternos del ejército", June 24, 1995: 4.
"25 mil ronderos armados defienden cocales en valles de Apurímac y Ene", August 13, 1995: 2.
"Vaticano niega todo y dice que combatió a terroristas", June 26, 1996: 3.
"Suzy Díaz defiende a narco Vaticano y plantea que revisan su sentencia", August 6, 1996: 10.
"Oposición pide al congreso se investigue a Montesinos", August 20, 1996: 6.
"Colaboradores del SIN ligados al narcotráfico", August 23, 1996: 17.
"Hermoza para siempre", (Sunday Supplement) August 25, 1996: 5.

"Atentar contra la libertad de prensa de defender la corrupción en el poder", August 27, 1996: 2–3.
"Vaticano y militares mataron a periodista por revelar a mafia", August 30, 1996: 16-17.
"Todo traficante debía negociar con el Ejército", August 31, 1996: 16-17.
"Los lazos de la conexión", September 22, 1996: 2.
"Informe del departamento de estado no exculpa a Montesinos", September 22, 1996a: 6.
"El juicio del descaro", September 22, 1996b: 20-22.
"Monseñor Cipriani no introdujo micrófonos a residencia nipona", April 29, 1997: 3.
"Solicitan a la Interpol búsqueda de empresario Zevallo", May 14, 1997: 7.
"Autoridades corruptas liberaron dos veces a 'El Ministro' en Peru", August 12, 1997: 8.
"Violenta advertencia de monseñor Luis Cipriani a mission de la OEA", November 10, 1998: 2.
"Cardenal Vargas Alzamora descalifica opiniones de Cipriani", November 11, 1998: 4.
"Publican libro polémico sobre monseñsor Cipriani", April 3, 2000: n. a.
"Cipriani busca frustrar mediación de la Iglesia en segunda vuelta", April 28, 2000: 2.
"Cipriani debería colgarla sotana y dedicarse de lleno a la política", July 7, 2000: 16.
"Juan Luis Cipriani", March 4, 2001: 36–38.
"Cardenal Cipriani pide a Toledo que perdone a procesados por corrupción", August 26, 2002: 3.
"Citan a Cipriani por matanza de Barrios Altos", August 29, 2002: 9.
"Newmont negoció con Montesinos", August 29, 2002: 10.
"Cipriani y el aborto", December 13, 2002: n. a.
"Cipriani declaró ante la justicia", September 7, 2002: 8.
"Matanza del Santa fue un 'trabajo particular' del grupo Colina", January 5, 2003. <http://www.larepublica.pe/05-01-2003/matanza-del-santa-fue-un-trabajo-particular-del-grupo-colina>.
"Minera Barrick intentó eludir pago de US$ 141 millones en impuestos", May 17, 2003: 16–17.
"Balean a 5 geólogos en minera Barrick Gold", July 24, 2003: 29.
"Barrick quiso recuperar US$760 millones con elusión tributaria", August 2, 2003: n. a.
"Ex embajador de Francia afirma que Newmont pagó soborno a jueces", December 4, 2003: 10.
"Regalías o mendrugos", May 23, 2004: 27.
"Los abogados de Erin Brockovich defienden a pueblo de Choropampa", September 3, 2004: 35.
"Cipriani reitera rechazo al aborto durante última misa procesional", November 2, 2004: n. a.
"Ronderos de Santa Cruz exigen retiro de minera Buenaventura", November 18, 2004: 4.
"Paro total en Santa Cruz en rechazo a la exploración minera de Buenaventura", November 23, 2004: 20.
"El caso Barrick y las facultades del defensor del contribuyente", March 5, 2005: 8.
"Veinte heridos déjà movilización en Huaraz contra mineras", March 8, 2005: 10.

"Segundo día de huelga en Huaraz déjà 22 heridos y 40 detenidos", March 9, 2005: 8.
"Congreso investigará acotación a Barrick", March 16, 2005: n. a.
"Visita de Rice a Colombia coincide con 'razzia' militar", April 28, 2005: 24.
"Alemania no entrega al piloto que descargó las armas para las FARC", May 1, 2005: 10.
"Marinos proveían de armas a paramilitares", May 5, 2005: 27.
"Cocaleros y paperos se unirían en paro nacional", May 14, 2005: 8.
"Se disparan los cultivos de amapola a 2 mil hectáreas", May 20, 2005: 8.
"Mafia colombiana distribuye semillas de amapola en Perú", May 21, 2005: 21.
"El repunte de la coca en el Monzón", May 23, 2005: 8.
"La Oroya: donde la población vive con plomo en la sangre", May 31, 2005: 18.
"Enfrentamiento en Majaz deja un comunero muerto y 19 heridos", August 3, 2005. <http://www.larepublica.pe/archive/all/larepublica/20050803/pasadas/15/97721>.
"Ventilarán vínculos Newmont-Montesinos", October 24, 2005: 9.
"The New York Times revive el caso de Yanacocha", October 26, 2005: 16–17.
"Newmont guardó en secreto contaminación en Yanacocha", October 27, 2005: 16–17.
"SUNAT debe acotar a las grandes mineras que no pagan regalías", April 24, 2006: 11.
"MEM determine que más de 10 mineras no paguen regalías", May 4, 2006: 10.
"Disputa en mina déjà dos víctimas", May 7, 2006: 24.
"Comunidades piden suspensión de operaciones de minera Majaz", July 12, 2006: 9.
"García advierte que el Estado no sera el 'guachimán'de empresas mineras", July 13, 2006: 3.
"Lerner: Cipriani pecó por omisión en Ayacucho", July 29, 2006: 25.
"García olvidó cobro de las regalías", July 30, 2006: 16.
"Cardenal Cipriani insiste en satanizar a la Comisión de la Verdad", August 6, 2006: n. a.
"El Congreso debatirá sobreganacias", August 10, 2006: 11.
"Mineras tienen elevadas ganancias", August 12, 2006: 11.
"Gobierno utilizará código penal para bloquear protestas", August 20, 2006: 13.
"Estado dejará de recibir US$ 140 millones por no cobrar regalías", August 24, 2006: 4.
"Gobierno saca dinero como en tómbola", August 27, 2006: 3.
"Mineros ven a los campesinos como manada de borregos", August 27, 2006a: 4–6.
"Aporte de mineras carece de seguridad legal", August 28, 2006: 12.
"Constitución del 93 es neoliberal y protégé convenios de estabilidad", September 3, 2006: 13.
"Espionaje: Operación El Diablo", (Sunday Supplement), December 3, 2006: 1–8.
"Destapamos la operación El Diablo", December 3, 2006a: 3.
"Las intrigas de César Cáceres", December 7, 2006: 2–3.
"La desigual información del caso Arana", December 9, 2006: 4.
"No todo que brilla . . .", (Dossier), December 10, 2006: 2–3.
"Yanacocha, la verdad a tajo abierto", (Dossier), December 10, 2006: 4–5.
"Una mina de conflictos", (Dossier), December 10, 2006: 6–7.
"Los nuevos dueños de la tierra", (Dossier), December 10, 2006: 8.
"Diario vinculado a Yanacocha ataca a La República", December 14, 2006: 5.

"Agentes de 'Colina' y masacrador de Accomarca con arresto domiciliario", March 14, 2009. <http://www.larepublica.pe/14-03-2009/agentes-de-colina-y-masacrador-de-accomarca-con-arresto-domiciliario-0>.
"Fiscalía archiva investigación sobre esterilizaciones forzadas", May 29, 2009: 11.
"Minera ordenó torturar a campesinos", August 7, 2010: 10.
"A mí me esterilizaron a la fuerza y hasta hoy sufro las consecuencias", April 26, 2011: 10.
"No se puede negar que fue política de Estado", June 3, 2011: 11.

Latin American Weekly Report (LAWR)
"Fujimori gives way on agreements", March 28, 1991: 4.
"Fujimori to 'privatize' war by arming urban self-defense groups", March 5, 1992: 1.
"Army on the Spot", May 27, 1993: 236.
"General denounces army 'hit squad'", May 30, 1993: 22.
"Debate begins on new constitution", July 15, 1993: 322.
"More secret graves found near Lima", August 26, 1993: 395.
"Sendero Luminoso back on offensive", September 23, 1993: 436–437.
"Changes in Army Command", January 20, 1994: 23.
"Meeting between Sendero factions", June 16, 1994: 257.

La Yuca (Lima, Peru)
"Toledo se cree Ricky Martin", March 8/00: Cover.
"Fuji da a madres y Toledo les quita", March 27, 2000: Cover.
"Toledo niega a su propia hija", March 29, 2000: Cover, 7.
"Toledo mentiroso ... Estas divorciado", April 5, 2000: Cover.
"Con Terrucos y Mafiosos", May 3, 2000: 4.
"Toledo quire Guerra, Fuji paz y desarollo", May 4, 2000: 4.
"Rechazo diálogo y busca violencia, Toledo juega sucio al Perú", May 5, 2000: Cover, 1.
"Fuji quiere diálogo y Toledo violencia", May 7, 2000: Cover.
"Apuestan los Terrucos", May 7, 2000: 4.
"A Fuji lo apoya el pueblo, a Toledo los Terrucos", May 12, 2000: 4.
"Choledo se orina de miedo", May 17, 2000: 4.

Liberación (Lima, Peru)
"Laura Bozzo hizo lo que pudo pero nadie creyó su lacrimógena hístoria", March 29, 2000: 5.
"La dictadura ultraderechaista de Cipriani", September 4, 2000: 12–13.
"Cipriani culpa al SIN de originar retiro de Fujimori y lo califica de valiente", September 18, 2000: 7.
"Manifestantes repudian a Cipriani y sus lagrimas de cocodrillo", March 5, 2001: 3.
"Campesinos de Atupa exigen a minera Barrick Misquichilca que los reubique", April 3, 2002: 16.

"Cardenal debe invocar a colaborar con la justicia", August 27, 2002: 3.
"Cardenal Cipriani es citado como testigo de las matanzas de Barrios Altos y La Cantuta", August 29, 2002: 3.
"Precio del oro sube y mineras ganan más sin pagar impuestos", January 26, 2003: n. a. "Yanacocha atenta contra la vida de cajamarquinos", June 11, 2004: n. a.

Oiga (Lima, Peru)
"En manos de los indecisos", April 2, 1990: 32–35.
"Mascaras ¡afuera!" April 16, 1990: 13–18.
"La historia los condena", April 23, 1990: 18–20.
"Los fouls de Fuji", May 14, 1990: 13–16.
"El samurai mentiroso", May 14, 1990a: 16.
"Las mentiras de Fujinocho", May 28, 1990: 15–16.
"El secuestro de Fujimori", July 16, 1990: 16–17.
"El Fujishock sin maquillaje", Sept. 17, 1990: 18–20.
"El comercio no tiene salida", Sept. 17, 1990a: 20–21.
"Hablamos con la CIA", November 25, 1990: 8–13.
"Me rompieron la denuncia en la cara", April 8, 1991: 20–25.
"Democracía, desarollo, y seguridad", August 26, 1991: 8–10.
"Es puro parche", November 11, 1991: 12–17.
"Con guerra sucia nos vamos al carajo", November 11, 1991a: 18–22.
"El estado no puede hacer la guerra solo", November 18, 1991: 30–36.
"La F.A. ahora delibera", January 6, 1992: 8–12.
"El show de Vaticano", January 24, 1994: 18–22.
"En el país de la inmoralidad", February 14, 1994: 35.
"Las asambleas del gral. Hermoza", March 21, 1994: 23.
"Carnival de gastos", March 21, 1994a: 43–50.
"Narcotráfico en salsa 'china'", May 30, 1994: 14-16.
"Por que somos narcoestado", May 30, 1994a: 16–19.
"Creciente malestar en el ejécito", May 30, 1994b: 22–23.
"Escándalo en el Palacio de Justicia", February 6, 1995: 20–21.
"Cronología de un fraude anunciado", February 6, 1995a: 29–35.
"Solo el fraude salvara a Fuji", March 20, 1995: 17–20.
"Voto escondido tiene la palabra", April 3, 1995: 5–10.
"Perú: 'Paraiso' de la libertad de prensa", April 3, 1995a: 27–30.
"OEA consagra gabinete de minoria nacional", April 24, 1995: 10–12.
"Fiscal acusa a jefe del SIN", April 24, 1995: 13.
"Murio otro inocente", May 1, 1995: 24–27.
"Reagrupamiento senderista", May 29, 1995: 6–7.
"Los Municipios del 'nuevo Perú'", May 29, 1995a: 11.
"¡No haga polladas! El Grupo Colina anda suelto", June 19, 1995: 4–11.

"La ola de la indignación", June 26, 1995: 6–8.
"Balance y liquidación del CCD", July 10, 1995: 21–25.
"Yoshima: el hombre nuclear del regimen", July 17, 1995: 5–9.
"Aciertos a trompicones", July 17, 1995a: 8–9.
"Una mujer se consume", July 17, 1995b: 10–14.
"El mundo repudia leyes de impunidad", July 24, 1995: 16–19.
"Gran avance a costa de muchos inocentes", July 24, 1995a: 27.
"Próximo objetivo: la iglesia", August 4, 1995: 10–12.
"El asalto a los municipios", August 4, 1995a: 16–17.

Perú 21 (Lima, Peru)
"Cipriani dice que se está pisoteando a la Iglesia", August 31, 2002: 4.
"El Cardenal nunca defendió la vida, la verdad ni la justicia", August 31, 2002: 4.
"Jóvenes exigen enjuciar al Cardenal Cipriani", September 16, 2002: 5.
"El Congreso investiga programas ambientales", May 22, 2003: n. a.
"Martín Rivas admite existencia de Colina", December 10, 2002: 6.
"Roma debe separar a Cipriani de su cargo", April 17, 2003: 4.
"Población de Oroya respira aire envenenado", April 7, 2004: n. a.
"Denuncian a minera Yanacocha", June 10, 2004: 19.
"Homosexuales otra vez en la mira de Cipriani", June 26, 2004: 14.
"Acusan a Cipriani de promover la homofobia", June 29, 2004: 14.
"El Perú está corrompido", July 17, 2004: 5.
"Cipriani arremete contra el aborto en Nueva York", October 18, 2004:14.
"Ataque de comuneros a minera déjà un muerto", November 18, 2004: n. a.
"Violencia durante paro contra Barrick", March 8, 2005: n. a.
"Niños de La Oroya deben soportar exceso de plomo", May 30, 2005: n. a.
"Rechazan que Cipriani haga política en púlpito", July 31, 2006: 6.
"El crimen de La Cantuta fue respuesta de Fujimori al atentado de Tarata", January 26, 2009. <http://peru21.pe/noticia/237256/afirman-que-crimen-cantuta-fue-respuesta-fujimori-al-atentado-tarata>.

Referéndum (Lima, Peru)
"Pinocho Toledo obedece órdenes de Alan García", March 7, 2000: Cover.
"No digas que fui tu asesor", March 8, 2000: Cover.
"Manrique pagó viajes de Toledo", March 16, 2000: Cover, 2.
"Oposición no debe ensuciar elecciones", March 18, 2000: 3.
"Monseñor Cipriani insiste informes de observadores tienen sesgo politíco", March 19, 2000: 4.
"Equipo de Alan detrás Toledo", March 16, 2000: Cover.
"Toledo insiste en quitar Comedores Populares a madres de PRONAA", March 27, 2000: Cover.

"Crece el rechazo de Comedores Populares hacia Alejandro Toledo", March 27, 2000: Cover.
"Prueba de sangre demuestra que Toledo es el padre", March 30/00: Cover.
"Toledo no da cara", April 1, 2000: Cover.
"¿Porque me niegas?" April 2, 2000: Cover.
"Toledo optó por la violencia", May 6, 2000: Cover.

Sí (Lima, Peru)
"Así es el juego", October 30, 1989: 17–21.
"¿Su pasado lo condena?" April 10, 1990: 23–25.
"Retrato de familia", April 10, 1990: 28–29, 80–B.
"¿Fujishock inevitable?" April 16, 1990a: 13–15.
"Paquete verde", August 5, 1990: 16–19.
"Desembarco", August 5, 1990a: 20–23.
"Aqui se preparaba el golpe", November 19, 1990: 8–12.
"Pacificación en conflict", January 20, 1992: 8–9.
"Vuelve con fuerza", April 20, 1992: 10–16, 88.
"El no de la OEA", April 27, 1992: 20–23, 88.
"Relaciones congeladas", May 11, 1992: 19.
"Susana a su casa", May 11, 1992a: 34.
"Manos arriba", May 18, 1992: 32, 83.
"Informe polémico", May 25, 1992: 20.
"Derechos torcidos", June 1, 1992: 38–40.
"El golpe y su bandera", November 16, 1992: 5–11.
"FF.AA.: ya vienen los cambios", November 30, 1992: 22–23.
"Estos son los capos", November 21, 1994: 26.
"Fábrica no tradicional", January 23, 1995: 10–19.
"Reinventando 'pintas'", July 17, 1995: 11–15.

Other
"Environmentalist priest appeals to premier and health minister for "just and humanitarian" solutions to Choropampa's health crisis", *Andean Airmail &Peruvian Times* (Peru), January 8, 2009. <http://www.peruviantimes.com/08/ environmental-priest-appeals-to-premier-and-health-minister-for-%e2%80%9cjust-and-humanitarian%e2%80%9d-solutions-for-choropampa%e2%80%99s-health-crisis/1268/>.
"Future of 'Fujimorismo' challenged by Referendum Results", *Americas Update*, 15, 3, January–February 1994:4–5.
"Die Spione vom East River, " *Der Spiegel* Spezial 1 (Germany), December 10, 2010: 32–33.
"Placer Dome accepts Barrick's sweetened $10.4B US takeover bid", *Canadian Broadcasting Corporation* (CBC), December 22, 2005. <http://www.cbc.ca/news/business/story/2005/12/22/barrick-051222.html>.

"Laura Bozzo", In: *El Mercurio* (Santiago, Chile), December 23, 2003. <http://diario.elmercurio.com/detalle/index.asp?id={b113795b-8884-416f-b29b-dc2e25d3fb84}>.

"Capturado en Cali el Pablo Escobar de Perú", *El Tiempo* (Colombia), January 14, 1994: 3A.

"Toledo es un fraude que no reconoce a su hija", *El Tío* (Lima, Peru) April 3, 2000: Cover.

"Fujimori sobrevive a intento de golpe", *El Mundo* (Colombia), November 14, 1992: 9.

"El director Antonio Cuadri presenta la mayor producción de cine rodada en Andalucía", *El Mundo* (Spain), April 11, 2007: 62.

"Quien fue, cómo y porqué fue desaparecido Pedro Yauri", *Huacho.info* (Peru), October 3, 2010. <http://huacho.info/2010/10/03/quien-fue-como-y-porque-fue--desaparecido-pedro-yauri/>.

"Comentarios a la ley 28568 que modificó el artículo 47 del código penal sobre el arresto domiciliario", *Justicia Viva* (Peru), July 2005: 1–22.

"Last US forces abandon Manta military base in Ecuador", *Merco Press*, September 19, 2009. <http://en.mercopress.com/2009/0919/last-us-forces-abandon-manata-military-base-in-ecuador>.

"Editorial", *Mundo Minero* (Peru), XXVI, 244, July 2006: 42.

"Perú: 25 años de cárcel a Montesinos", *Observadorglobal.com.*, October 2, 2010. <http://observadorglobal.com/peru-25-anos-de-carcel-a-montesinos-n10994.html>.

"Cipriani versus Bambarén", *Ojo* (Peru), May 21, 2006: 12.

"Peru – The Curse of the Inca Gold", *PBS Frontline/World.* Interviews. Larry Kurlander. October 2005. <http://www.pbs.org/frontlineworld/stories/peru404/pkurlander.html>.

"Gold Price Hits New Record", *News Just Now*, April 20, 2011. <http://newsjustnow.com/today-gold-price-per-ounce-1500/>.

"Barrick aprobó studio de factibilidad de projecto Alto Chicama", *Síntesis*, (Lima), October 30, 2003: 10.

"A crop that refuses to die", The *Economist* (UK), March 4, 2000: 25.

"Colombian rebels impose law of the gun", *The Globe and Mail* (Toronto, Canada). July 19, 1999: A11.

"In an African mine, gold fever sparks a deadly clash", *The Globe and Mail*, June 8, 2011: A10–11.

"Coca-Cola sued over bottling plant 'terror campaign,'" *The Guardian* (UK), July 21, 2001. <http://www.guardian.co.uk/Archive/Article/0,4273,4225809,00.htm>.

"$37-Billion-a-year cash crop brings killings, corruption", *The Toronto Star* (Toronto, Canada), March 22, 1997: A1.

"Humpty Dumpty, the Scriptwriter and the Little Bean", *The New Internationalist*, July 1989: 24-25.

"Corruption's Big Funder – or how to 'lose' $100 billion without really trying", *New Internationalist*, December 2006: 15.

"Monseñor Cipriani: ¿mediador o espía?" *Tiempos del Mundo* (Latin America), May 8, 1997: n. a.
"Opus Dei", *Time Magazine*, March 18, 1957. <http://www.time.com/time/magazine/article/0,9171,809216,00.html>.
"Peru: Doe Run's Latest Move", *Third World Network* (TWN), January 19, 2011. <http://www.twnside.org.sg/title2/FTAs/info.service/2011/fta.info.173.htm>.
"Commodities Focus as Nationalist Win in Peru Sends Chills to Miners", *247wallst.com*. June 6, 2011. <http://247wallst.com/2011/06/06/commodities-focus-as-nationalist-win-in-peru-sends-chills-to-miners-bhp-nem-paas-tck-abx-gg-xsray-aauky-fcx>.
"How do you define corruption?" In: *Transparency International* (TI), August 3, 2011. <http://www.transparency.org/news_room/faq/corruption_faq#faqcorr1>.
"Fujimori ex-aide sentenced for 1990s Peru massacres" *Zeenews* (India), October 2, 2010. <http://zeenews.india.com/news/world/fujimori-ex-aide-sentenced-for-1990s -peru-massacres_659136.html>.
"Indemnities, Salaries and Allowances Members of the House of Commons", Ottawa, Canada, 2010. <http://www2.parl.gc.ca/Parlinfo/lists/Salaries.aspx?Menu=HOC-Politic&Section=03d93c58-f843-49b3-9653-84275c23f3fb&Year=2010>.

Index

www.ingramcontent.com/pod-product-compliance
Ingram Content Group UK Ltd.
Pitfield, Milton Keynes, MK11 3LW, UK
UKHW020153290926
15471UKWH00005B/854

9 783034 306164